OCT – 2003

Israel Horovitz
Collected Works: Volume II

Israel Horovitz
Collected Works: Volume II

New England Blue:
Plays of Working-Class Life

Contemporary Playwrights Series

SK
A Smith and Kraus Book

A Smith and Kraus Book
Published by Smith and Kraus, Inc.

Copyright © 1995 by Israel Horovitz
All rights reserved

Manufactured in the United States of America

Cover and Text Design by Julia Hill

First Edition: October 1995
10 9 8 7 6 5 4 3 2

Library of Congress Cataloguing-in-Publication Data
Catalogue Card Number 93-46378

Contents

Introduction

During the past 15 years, I have written a group of plays that I call my "blue-collar" plays. This work serves to create, among other things, a record of what working-class life was like during my time on my little dot on the planet Earth. It seemed to me that working-class life in small-town America was rapidly disappearing. I won't burden you here with my particular analysis of the whys and wherefores. My job is to dramatize, make theatrical. So, let me try to make my point, quickly and cleverly, by posing two questions…and then, I'll move on to introducing my plays: How would you feel if your daughter/son became a truck-driver? How would you feel if your daughter/son married a plumber?

Hopefully, the people of my blue-collar plays will explain themselves through their actions. Like their author, they won't attempt to offer a tidy polemic, a smug or simple reason why the world is changing as it is…but, hopefully, the characters of these plays will be quick to show you how they have responded, to let you know how they feel about a world that has begun to exclude them.

My impulse in limiting my plays to small-town New England was this: I thought that if I could focus my particular telescope/microscope, and get it right, really right, for one small New England town, I might possibly have it right for the world. Let me be quick to cite my influences. I had, for one, an excellent mentor in Thornton Wilder and a nearly perfect model in his beautiful play *Our Town*.

Several years ago, in the 1970s, I wrote another cycle of plays, "The Wakefield Plays." I was recently out of a Ph.D. program in English Lit, and "The Wakefield Plays" were brim-full of complex, arcane literary allusion. Martin Esslin called the work "an American Orestia." Thornton Wilder had something else to say.

I had dinner with Mr. Wilder, from time to time. He was 86 years old and not able to get around, easily. When we came together, we talked about playwriting, and about life. He read my "Wakefield Plays" and was extremely flattering in his praise...But, at the end of it all, Thornton Wilder spoke one sentence that would alter the course of my playwriting for years and years to come. He ended his praise of "The Wakefield Plays" with "...Of course, there isn't very much Wakefield in those plays."

Spoken by Thornton Wilder, who had created Grovers Corners, New England's best-known, best-loved small-town, that ten-word sentence, had, for me, great meaning, and great impact. If my New England-based plays would be nothing else, they would be brim-full of New England.

Mr. Wilder often talked about a notion that "all knowledge flows through the trunk of the tree..." That was to say, if one thing could be learned to its fullest, then, all things could be at the same time learned. Consider a carpenter who is truly a master, an ultimate genius-level joiner. Couldn't this carpenter easily do skillful brain surgery? After all, the fundamental elements of great carpentry and of great brain-surgery are the same: cutting and joining.

In the end, of course, Wilder had *invented* Grovers Corners, and my goal was to somehow use real people, real places, real events, in a mix with dramatic fiction. I began with *Hopscotch,* a one-act play in my "Wakefield Plays" cycle. Unlike the longer, more literary plays of the cycle (*Alfred the Great, Our Father's Failing, Alfred Dies, Spared*), *Hopscotch* used Andrew Wyeth-like detail...something I've come to call "super-realism"...an overabundance of real-life detail mixed with imagined detailed...observed dialogue that concerns itself with accent...real time, real place, local reference, local idiom, musicality of local language, etc., etc. Ten pages into the writing of *Hopscotch*, I knew I would be, like a hungry fish, hooked. I had stumbled into a style...a method of writing, a method of digging into real life...psycho-archaeology...And, not incidentally, a way of making certain inalterable facts of my own particular real life much more stage-worthy, much more special. And the result would be more than a decade of work...a dozen full-length plays about blue-collar New Englanders in a time of crisis...

By way of introduction to six of those plays, collected herein, I have allowed myself (and written down) a series of memories of the whens and whys (I think) I wrote each of these particular plays...in hope that the reader (actor, director, designer, critic...) will gain some special insight into my work that no doubt eluded me as author: unqualified judge.

THE WIDOW'S BLIND DATE

My father was a truck-driver, until age 50, when he went to law school, nights, and made a lawyer of himself. Some fifteen years ago, I began *The Widow's Blind Date*, a play that drew heavily on easily-remembered detail...and, as it turned out, much to my shock, detail not so easily recalled.

When I was a young boy, I worked on Saturdays for my father's eldest brother, Max, in Uncle Max's junk-shop in Stoneham, Massachusetts, a few miles from my birth-place, Wakefield. My uncle's shop's main function was the creation of bales of old books, bales of old and new (unread) newspapers, and bales of old and new magazines, which my uncle sold to my father, who, in turn, trucked and sold them to paper mills, where old paper was recycled into new paper. One of my frequent tasks was the tearing of bindings and covers from the old books, preparing them for the crush of the book-baling press. I would, single-handedly, rip bindings and covers from some two thousand books, each Saturday. (I say 'single-handedly', but, I did, of course, use both hands.) From time to time, some book or another would catch my eye, my attention, and I would stop awhile and read. And, thus, I had my earliest introduction to English literature.

Years later, when I was teenaged, a friend—a fine, upstanding lad from a fine, upstanding family—pointed to a young woman and excitedly blurted out a story of a gang-rape he'd been part of the night before. I turned and looked at the young girl who had been the object of my friend's lust. And his friends' lust. Her frightened, defeated eyes are still etched in my memory.

And some fifteen years after that, through the magic that is writing, I brought the same young woman back to "life" to enter my Uncle Max's shop, and to confront two of her unwanted lovers. And *The Widow's Blind Date* was born. To my amazement, when my mother saw *The Widow's Blind Date* in its premiere production in my own little the-

atre in Massachusetts, she said to me: "I didn't think you knew!"…
"Knew *what?*" I asked. And she told me a story of a gang-rape that had
taken place in my uncle's junk-shop, some twenty-five years earlier. A
young woman working in the laundry next door to the shop was somehow enticed into the shop, where she was raped by several of the men,
many of them "winoes" who worked for 50-cents a day. As a boy, I
must have overheard these men talking, bragging, and buried their sor-
did story somewhere in my deepest, darkest sub-conscious. Thus, *The
Widow's Blind Date* is partly true, and partly invented. But, it is also
coherent, organized, and conclusive. And, in the end, these are not
qualities of Life. This is Writing.

The *Widow's Blind Date* was first produced at The Actors Studio in
NYC, and then in Los Angeles, at The Los Angeles Actors Theatre, and
then in my own theatre, Gloucester Stage, in Gloucester,
Massachusetts. The production I directed at Gloucester Stage trans-
ferred to the Circle-in-the-Square in NYC for its commercial premiere.
Since then, *Widow* has found audiences around the globe. The play is
particularly popular in France, where it was in fact seen prior to its
NYC premiere.

Widow has just had a fourth major revival in Paris, at Nouveau
Théâtre de Mouffetard, and Le Figaro's drama critic has just today written of my play as "du grand art" Yuh, well, perhaps. I have just now
completed a screenplay, based upon *The Widow's Blind Date*, for a film
that I will be (hopefully) directing in the USA in late Fall, 1995.

In any event, with *The Widow's Blind Date*, I found a new voice,
again…as I had a decade earlier with *The Indian Wants the Bronx*…
but, this new voice was miles more personal, more satisfying. Sitting in
a theatre in France, recently, watching *Widow*…watching the audience
watching *Widow*, I thought to myself, "I am a lucky man."

A number of my working class plays (ten, at last count) are set in Gloucester, Massachusetts, my adopted home-town. Gloucester is 38 miles north of Boston, and precisely marathon distance from my birth-place, Wakefield, Massachusetts. Gloucester was where my parents took my sister and me on special days.

My first play, ever (with a devilishly ironic title: *The Comeback*), opened in Boston, about 100 years ago, when I was 19. Some years and several plays later, after I'd found the courage to actually leave New York City, summers, without fear that my "New York Playwright" logo would be passed to a younger, fresher out-of-towner, I thought to myself, "Why not put my life down where special days are spent?"...I bought my first (and last) Gloucester house, a tiny wood-framed Victorian with slightly Gothic pretensions.

I thought that I'd bought a house for summers, and for the odd warm weekend. And then I noticed that I'd stayed in Gloucester for sixteen consecutive months. In 1985, my (twin) children, Hannah and Oliver, were born at the Addison-Gilbert Hospital, in Gloucester. They are Gloucester kids.

Gloucester is a place of great natural beauty. Majestic cliffs over-look a Kodak-perfect coastline. Every Gloucester kid knows a half-dozen secret sandy beaches. Every Gloucester kid knows a dozen secret swimmable granite quarries. Tourists in search of cheap lobsters and/or early Americana usually bypass Gloucester, opting for the calendar-cute village of Rockport, five miles up the road. And as Brackish says in *Park Your Car In Harvard Yard*, come Labor Day... "the summ'ah people pack up their greasy hot-dog colored bodies and their grotesque char-coal sketches of Motif #1"...and we locals smile, because we locals know that September and October are, simply, the best months...

When I first began spending time in Gloucester as an adult, I remember, quite vividly, observing "Gloucester's heroes are carpenters and fishermen, not playwrights." Quite clearly, Gloucester, located on an island (Cape Ann), land's end, was to be one of America's final bas-tions of blue-collar life. The more time I spent in Gloucester, the more I felt the need to have a theatre in town, a place to see plays ...a place to try my new work, first. In 1980, with two friends, I co-founded The Gloucester Stage Company. We started out as a summer theatre, pro-ducing one-act plays in the back room at the Blackburn Tavern. From Day #1, we had an audience.

Although Gloucester had also boasted a tradition of High Art (Winslow Homer, Edward Hopper, Milton Avery, T.S. Eliot, Charles Olson, etc, all lived and worked in Gloucester), Gloucester is and was and always will be, essentially, a working-person's town, blue collar, a place for "fish people"…fishermen, lobstermen, lumpers (stevedores), fish-cutters. Once a bustling, world-class seaport, Gloucester's best days are either past, or deeply-buried in secret days ahead. At the moment, Gloucester is in trouble. The fish business has all but gone away. The economy is floating belly-up. Drug traffic is unthinkably high. Gloucester people are, in a word, worried.

My first Gloucester-based play, *Mackerel*, was whimsical…a sort of Nixon/Bush parable about a Gloucester man, Ed Lemon, who watches a 250,000-lb. mackerel crash through the wall of his house. *Mackerel* was written in the 1970's, just after *The Primary English Class*, just before *Hopscotch*…As I settled into actually living life in Gloucester, my notion to write blue-collar plays that were actually set in Gloucester became more serious. As did the plays themselves.

Park Your Car In Harvard Yard is probably the most famous of my Gloucester-based plays. Like *Widow*, *Park Your Car In Harvard Yard* was first done at the Los Angeles Actors Theatre in collaboration with Gloucester Stage. Bill Bushnell, L.A.A.T.'s artistic director, came to Gloucester to work with me on the developing script of *Park Your Car In Harvard Yard*, while at the same time working for me at Gloucester Stage, directing *The Widow's Blind Date*. *Park Your Car In Harvard Yard* had been a success at Bushnell's theatre in Los Angeles, but, it was a *triumph* in Gloucester. Local people made quick identification with the people of my play…led easily into this not-quite-make-believe world by the play's abundance of detail…the new style …super-realism…with people talking like Gloucester people about real-life Gloucester events, people and places…and with the play's real-life politics. The Gloucester audience was deeply moved by my play. And I was deeply moved by my play's audience. There is no better support-system for a playwright than an appreciative audience. A clap on the back from a teary-eyed playgoer is, for me, so much more satisfying than a rave in the *Times*, Gloucester or otherwise. I mean this. The praise I remember most from my three decades of being a produced playwright are moments of direct contact with audience. A pick-up truck screeches to a stop along Gloucester's back shore. I'm out there, running my daily six. A burly man blocks my path, shakes my hand: "The play was great!" In the subway in New York City, a skinny lady asks me if I'm me, tells me the woman in *Park Your Car...* was so much like her mother!... And she begins to weep. And I begin to weep, because I have touched somebody. And in France, even though it's called *Quelque Part Dans Cette Vie*, it still works...an impeccably-dressed older couple seek me out and find me, at the back of the theatre, and they embrace me. They are weeping. And I am so pleased to be a playwright, in spite of all.

Park Your Car In Harvard Yard centers on Gloucester High School's toughest teacher, ever, and the housekeeper he hires to tend to him at the end of his life. But for his education, Jacob Brackish (the teacher) would be the same person as Kathleen Hogan (his housekeeper and former student). In the way that *Park Your Car In Harvard Yard* contrasts an educated life with a non-educated life, this play became a kind of paradigm for me in my writing a dozen plays that, among other things, dramatize a changing attitude toward working-class life.

HENRY LUMPER

Henry Lumper was by the far most sensational of my Gloucester-based blue-collar plays to premiere at Gloucester Stage. *Henry Lumper* retells Shakespeare's *Henry IV — Parts One and Two*, sort of. The play is set on the Gloucester waterfront. Among other things, I used this particular play to dramatize/chronicle Gloucester's terrible drug problem. Heroin was being run through Gloucester, much of it arriving by boat, hidden in the bellies of frozen fish. Local people were dealing drugs. Local boats were "running heavy." A lobsterman could make more money carrying one cigar-box filled with cocaine than he could in a month of hauling traps. But, worst of all, local people, in great number, were using drugs, themselves. Such was the frustration of a community that hadn't just lost its jobs, but had also lost its primary industry, its primary way of life...its essential dignity.

Henry Lumper shocked Gloucester. Because of this play, I made many new friends in town, but I made an even greater number of new enemies, many of whom who thought the "dirty laundry" I'd aired in this particular play was, simply, "private stuff."After seeing a performance of *Henry Lumper*, the then-Mayor of Gloucester told me he learned of his city's drug problem from my play. Ultimately, so did the *Boston Globe* and the *New York Times*. Gloucester's drug problem was out in the open, ready, finally, for a cure. It was a thrilling time in my life. To be a playwright and to actually have some small impact on a community! To be...timely!

NORTH SHORE FISH

For a time, I was fearful of becoming known as a regional playwright. It occurred to me that many of our theatre's Greats and Near-Greats had fled blue-collar, small-town backgrounds and were not showing a great deal of interest in returning to their roots through my particular body of working-class plays. Matters of Career clouded matters of The Heart. *North Shore Fish* was the play that brought me back to my senses, and brought me back to completing this large body of plays of working-class New England life.

A local woman, Gail Randazza, helped me research *North Shore Fish*, a play specifically about the quantum relationship of loss-of-work to loss-of-hope. Gail was a stage-mother, Gloucester variety. Her 7-year-old son, Louis, was acting in *Henry Lumper* at Gloucester Stage. Gail was at the theatre, every night.

Gail was "fish people." She was a fish-packer, as had been several generations of women in her family before her. While Gail and I were visiting fish plants, together, Gail reacted to *Henry Lumper*, and told me a great deal about the inner workings of Gloucester's drug scene. She knew a lot. I asked her why she knew a lot. She said she had "a junkie in the family." Less then a year later, I was stunned to learn of Gail's death...from an overdose of heroin. Gail turned out to be her family's junkie. I modeled Florence, one of the central characters of *North Shore Fish*, on Gail, sort of. After losing her job, Florence ends the play, in tears, with a simple, plaintive "I've got nothing left to teach my children!"

I dedicated *North Shore Fish* to Gail's memory, and returned to writing plays set in Gloucester with renewed purpose and renewed enthusiasm.

North Shore Fish was the first production in Gloucester Stage's present performance space. We'd been forced out of our old home in the Blackburn Tavern by a new owner/landlord. Gorton's of Gloucester came to our rescue with an 175'x175' abandoned warehouse space overlooking the harbor at Rocky Neck. The warehouse was filled with obsolete fish-processing equipment...exactly what we needed for the set of *North Shore Fish*. To open the theatre and the play, we "arranged" the equipment, cleaned the space of its twenty years of accumulation (wharf rats included!), brought in 100+ seats. And *North Shore Fish* opened to a world. The play ran for six consecutive months, only closing at Gloucester Stage in order to re-open at the WPA Theatre in New York. *North Shore Fish* was nominated for that season's Drama Desk Award as Best New American Play. Neil Simon won it, of course, but Gloucester Stage and still another of my Gloucester-based blue-collar plays had had a great outing in New York City...and had begun its life on stages around the world.

STRONG-MAN'S WEAK CHILD

Strong-Man's Weak Child was born of a single image. One summer Sunday, after finishing a long run, I was at a local gym, lifting weights. A local body-builder, well-known to Gloucester women as "Todd the God," arrived for his daily weights-workout. Todd's wife was evidently ill and he had charge of his year-old daughter for the day. Todd the God carried his tiny child in his massive arms, oh so delicately, cuddling and cradling her fragility...This odd Madonna-image captivated and haunted me. I began to sketch a play...a local body-builder in a garage gym...a weak and dying daughter...complicated issues of paternity that had haunted my own real life...With terrifying ease, the play began to take on a life of its own.

I directed the world premiere of *Strong-Man's Weak Child* in still another joyous co-production between Bill Bushnell's Los Angeles Theatre Center and my own beloved Gloucester Stage. I have never enjoyed directing more than I did with this particular play. Both productions, in L.A. and in Gloucester, were triumphant. Silly boy that I am, I sold the movie-rights to *Strong-Man's Weak Child* during the Gloucester production, and never brought the play to NYC. I got sidetracked writing countless drafts of a screenplay that never got produced. I have gotten back the stage-rights, and will see the play produced at Penguin Rep, just outside NYC, this coming Fall. And begin again.

UNEXPECTED TENDERNESS

Unexpected Tenderness is the most recent of my plays in this collection. *Unexpected Tenderness* seems to me to be the sort of play a writer should write as his/her first play. It is a rite-of-passage... extremely personal, dark, funny and sad. However bizarre, *Unexpected Tenderness* is, more than anything else, a family play. It is also that thing that audiences seem to love and critics seem to loathe: a *memory* play. In fact, *Unexpected Tenderness* is a play I avoided writing for some thirty years. It is a story I never particularly wanted to tell.

Unexpected Tenderness is not, strictly speaking, the blow-by-blow story of my childhood, exactly as I lived it. By no stretch of imagination, even mine, is my particular childhood stage-worthy. Many lies had to be told to make *Unexpected Tenderness* work for an audience, not only to cover the truth, but, to cover the boring patches. We tend to look back at life and say "My, how it's flown by!"...But, we tend to live life, as we watch plays, at a snail's pace, moment by moment. People constantly ask me if *Unexpected Tenderness* is really my life's story..."Was that the way it was?" Mike Geller, my friend/my rabbi, walked past me, as he exited the Gloucester Stage production, with a whispered "I didn't know you grew up in my house!" So, let me say it, now, once and for all time, simply and clearly: while *Unexpected Tenderness* contains some of the most dramatic moments of my particular childhood, at the very same time, it is filled to the brim with some of my very best adult lies. In the end, *Unexpected Tenderness*, like my other blue-collar plays, is partly true, partly invented. It is, also, coherent, organized, and conclusive. Again, this is not Life. This is Writing.

For many years, I have written two kinds of plays...One group, I call "Plays of My Mother." The other group, I call "Plays of My Father." The Mother-plays tend to be softer, gentler plays, such as *Today, I Am A Fountain Pen* and *Park Your Car In Harvard Yard*... while the Father-plays tend to be stronger, more frightening plays, such as *The Indian Wants The Bronx* and *The Widow's Blind Date*. *Unexpected Tenderness* represents my first play to combine both styles ...and, not surprisingly, it is the first time in my 50+ years and 50+ produced plays that I have ever written directly about my mother and my father.

Like *The Widow's Blind Date* and *Strong-Man's Weak Child*, *Unexpected Tenderness* was written within the context of the New York Playwrights Lab, a secret society I founded back in the 1970s. Lab members are all fairly well-known, working playwrights. We start our new plays on approximately the same day, and meet, frequently, throughout the year, to read and criticize each other's developing new plays. The first draft of *Unexpected Tenderness* was started in September 1992 , and evolved quite quickly (for me), being completed by late Summer 1993, in time for the Lab's annual "retreat." Subsequently, with minor revisions, the play had readings at The Joseph Papp Public Theatre in NYC, and, a few months later, at the John Harms Theatre in New Jersey. Audiences and actors were instantly enthusiastic about *Unexpected Tenderness*. I got production-offers from both regional and NYC-based theatres. For my own part, I found the play to be painful, too painful, very nearly unwatchable. Nonetheless, I set August 1994, at Gloucester Stage, for the world premiere production of *Unexpected Tenderness*. At the same time, I accepted a production-offer from the WPA Theatre in NYC. I wanted things to move quickly. *Unexpected Tenderness* was not a play with which I wanted to linger for years and years, as I had with plays like *Park Your Car...*and *Widow*.

Prior to the Gloucester Stage premiere of *Unexpected Tenderness*, the only real stumbling block I could foresee was my 84-year-old mother. At the end of the day, *Unexpected Tenderness* was my mother's play, not mine. I felt that I could not possibly allow *Unexpected Tenderness* to be staged without her first reading the play and giving it her blessing. If, in fact, she'd read the play and wanted it burned, I was prepared to light the match.

My mother came to stay with Gill and me for a few days at our house in Gloucester. I gave her a newly-revised draft of *Unexpected Tenderness* to read, mid-morning, as soon as the children were out of earshot, outside, playing. I explained to my mother why she was being asked to read the play, and why she was being asked to make her decision about the play being staged. She said "Don't worry about me. I'm a tough cookie. Just go ahead and do the play. I don't have to read it." To which I replied, "I love you and I want to make you happy, not unhappy. Making this play public might upset you. Please, read it and decide what you want me to do."

Gill and I left my mother alone, script spread out in front of her on the dining table. Mama read *Unexpected Tenderness* for the first time, ever, while Gill and I went for a long, long, long run by the sea. Two-and-a-half hours later, when we returned to the house, my mother wasn't quite as tough a cookie as she'd been at the time we'd left. The play had shaken her, and forced her to remember some of the worst moments of her life. In the end, obviously, she wanted the play to be staged and witnessed…and indeed it was. But, for the next two hours, my mother shared with my wife and me some of her deepest thoughts about life and marriage and family. Much of what she said to us was being said aloud for the first time in her 84-year-long life. Within those particular two hours, my mother allowed herself to have many revelations…and proved herself to be a woman of great strength, profound dignity…and of amazing grace. She is the primary reason I love and respect women as I do.

Unexpected Tenderness marked the thirteenth new play of mine to have its world premiere at Gloucester Stage; and the third new play of mine to have its New York premiere at the WPA. Clive Barnes, writing in the New York Post, championed the play, calling it "among Horovitz's very best." (Mr Barnes had an indisputable right to make that particular statement, as he had previously reviewed some twenty-five of my plays.) I watched very nearly every performance of *Unexpected Tenderness* during its 5-week run at the WPA. Not only did I love the show, I also wanted the play out of my system. I wanted to rid myself of the demons, as quickly as possible, and move on.

There are already several productions of *Unexpected Tenderness* planned in the USA, next season, and translations are already underway for productions in France, Germany and Italy. So, happily, it looks at though *Unexpected Tenderness*, like its lucky author, will have a worldly life.

Nine months have passed since *Unexpected Tenderness* first opened in New York, and I have just recently completed a first draft of a new play, *The Barking Sharks*. This new play is set in Gloucester, Massachusetts…three children of fishermen have a garage band. One boy leaves Gloucester, goes to college, has a high-powered career in NYC, and returns to Gloucester…to be a fisherman, like his father and grandfather before him. I tell myself that *The Barking Sharks* will be the last of my New England blue-collar plays, for a while, at least, if not forever. I'm back living in NYC much more than I am in Gloucester (and spending almost as much time, these days, in Paris, as I am in NYC)…It's time to print and collect these plays…to give them over to a world…and to move on to something new, something more frightening. It's always been important to me to be writing scared…to be reaching, stretching toward something I don't quite understand. I want my writing to take me somewhere. I want to be astonished…I've started to sketch out a new play that's set in France …about people out of their familiar places, off their friendly old spots…half in French, half in English…

La lutte commence…encore.

Israel Horovitz,
NYC-Gloucester-Paris,
May-June, 1995.

The Widow's Blind Date

For Agnès
Al
Anke
Barbara
Biff
Bob
Bush
Catherine
Charles
Chris
Christian
Christine
David
Diane
Dossy
Ebbe
Fabrice
Frank
Frank
Gill
Götz
Grey
Hawk
Heidi
Jacques
Jérôme
Jill
Kim
Niels
Olivier
Patricia
Paul
Peter
Philippe
Pop
René
Tom
Uncle Max
Xavier

PRODUCTION HISTORY

The Widow's Blind Date was first produced in a staged reading by the New York Playwrights Lab under the auspices of The Actors Studio, featuring Jill Eikenberry, Robert Field and Ebbe Roe Smith, directed by Sheldon Larry. The play then had its World Premiere at the Los Angeles Theatre Center, featuring Frank McCarthy, Charlie Parks and Patricia Wettig, directed by Bill Bushnell. Subsequent major productions, prior to the play's NYC opening included: three separate productions at The Gloucester Stage Company, featuring Kim Armeen, Tom Bloom, Al Mohrmann, Paul O'Brien and Dossy Peabody, directed by Bill Bushnell, Grey Cattell Johnson and Israel Horovitz; the French premiere, featuring Catherine Gandois, Olivier Granier and Christian Rauth, directed by Philippe Lefebvre, and the German premiere, featuring Sebastian Koch, Frank Schroder and Anke Schulbert, directed by Götz Burger.

The Widow's Blind Date was first produced at Los Angeles Actors Theatre, Los Angeles, California on September 24, 1980 with the following cast:

Archie Crisp . . . . Frank McCarthy
George Ferguson . . . . Charles Parks
Margie Burke. . . . . Patricia Mattick

The play was directed by Bill Bushnell and produced by Diane White. The sets, light and costumes were done by Barbara Ling. The LAAT production of the play later toured under the auspices of the California Arts Council Theatre Touring Program.

The Widow's Blind Date opened on November 7, 1989 in New York City at Circle in the Square Downtown. It was produced by David Bulasky, Barbara Darwall and Peter von Mayrhauser. It was directed by Mr. Horovitz. The set was designed by Edward T. Gianfrancesco; lighting was designed by Craig Evans; costumes were designed by Janet Irving. The Production Stage Manager was Crystal Huntington. The cast was as follows:

Archie Crisp. . . . . Paul O'Brien
George Ferguson . . . . Tom Bloom
Margy Burke . . . . Christine Estabrook

CHARACTERS
Archie Crisp, age thirty, a goat.
George Ferguson, age thirty, a weasel.
Margie Burke, age thirty, a goshawk.

PLACE
Baling-press room, wastepaper company, Wakefield, Massachusetts.

TIME
Saturday afternoon, October.

NOTE ON PRONUNCIATION
Massachusetts accents are essential to the playing of this text. "Margie" is pronounced "Mahh-ghee." "Sure" is pronounced "shoo-ah." Etc.

THE WIDOW'S BLIND DATE

ACT ONE

*5 p.m., Saturday afternoon, late fall, yellow light, slight chill in air.
A tinny-speakered radio plays "easy-listenin'" tunes.*

Interior of baling press room. Large, high-ceilinged space with sky-lights and hanging, caged-in bare bulbs as light source.

Eight bales of newspaper stretch across the front edge of the stage, sep-arating the audience from the stage. The bales will be removed in the opening minutes of the play by the actors, who, in a sense, "set the stage"...start the play.

A huge baling press is set upstage-center of room: the main object. Stage-right of the baler is a dune-like mound of loose newspapers from which armfuls of newspapers are carried to the press, into which they are loaded. Opposite side of baler, upstage, a small mountain of newspaper-bundles, tied with twine; stacked. A smaller mound of bundled newspa-per is in evidence downstage right of baler. Loading doors are placed mid-stage right. 800-lbs. bales of newspaper are in evidence all around perimeter of stage. Each bale is 4' wide by 3' thick by 4' high.

It is possible that a large hook and chain is suspended from ceiling, on a track. Also, a roller-track may be constructed in front of the baler to be used for propelling completed bales from baler to bale-stack.

A sharp-toothed hand truck is in evidence, also used for transporting bales from place to place in shop; and for loading doors on to truck for shipment to mills. N.B. If the stage is large enough, it is suggested that a gasoline or electricity powered "Towmotor" [forklift] be included among the scenery/props. Also, an enormous floor-scale should be insinuated into the scenic plan, upstage-right wall, so that completed bales can be shuttled by hand truck (or driven by Towmotor) across the scale, and weighed.

Upstage, there is a locker—probably housing the radio. Archie's "dress-up" clothes (suit, shirt, tie, good shoes, etc.) are in evidence, inside locker, as is George's jacket and scarf. There is an old easy chair, probably a vintage leatherette "Barca-lounger," set downstage of the locker.

The baling press should be large and ominous. A version of an old-fashioned wooden baler is wanted [c.1940], with removable walls, a weighted, permanent base, and adjustable top. Such a baler functions as follows: the press walls form an empty "box", which is filled with over-issue newspapers or magazines. The top of the baler is fitted in place, steel oblong into side grooves more distant from top, causing top to squash overissues of magazines into a bale. When the proper size is achieved, men negotiate the tying of the bale with long black wire. When bale is tied, the steel oblongs are carefully removed from the baler's side-teeth and all sides and top are removed, causing the bale to stand alone. A roller-track is stored under the baler, slides out and is slotted into position at the baler's front door for bale-removal. A hand truck is brought to the end of the roller-track, and the bale is removed. The baler's front door and sides are replaced, the press is refilled, the process is repeated.

The lights come up on switch on Archie Crisp and George Ferguson. Archie is in the midst of performing a story for George, who is enthralled. As Archie tells his story, he moves the bales upstage, clearing the audience's view of the front edge of the stage.

ARCHIE: So, this jamoca thinks he can take me real fast, throws a left, and I roll under and come up from down like a fuckin' toad, George... and I throw my two arms out wicked straight and yell "Whoooooo-eeee!"...and he looks left and right...and I butt this jamoca with the top of my head, and he is out! O.U.T.!
(Archie continues to move the remainder of the eight bales, upstage, lining them up, neatly, like soldiers, ready to be tagged, weighed and loaded on to an imagined truck, presumably out-side the loading doors, off-stage. George sweeps, cleans. Note: Archie's work must be substantial, authori-

tative: the boss's work. George's labor, by constrast, is menial, unimportant: the helper's work.

They both swig beer from cans as they work and chat.)

GEORGE: So, what do I do next?

ARCHIE: Sweep up under there, okay? And then separate the overissues from the loose shit in the pit, like I showed you before.

GEORGE: How many bales we got now?

ARCHIE: Counting this, five, plus the two corrugated…seven…so's we need one more after this. Then we still got to sort 'em and run 'em over the scale and weigh 'em before we load. *(pauses)* I might hav'ta go away and come back.

GEORGE: We loadin' tonight?

ARCHIE: Use your head, will ya? You can't leave a load out there, all night. It's an open truck. The night air gets into these bales, they'll weigh twice as much in the morning.

GEORGE: I don't mind stickin', now, for the sortin' and weighin' part…I mean, I ain't got too much goin' in the plans-for-tonight department…

ARCHIE: Oh, yuh, well, I got kind of a supper thing I got ta do…I'm on for supper with Margie…

GEORGE: Margie? Swede's sistah, Margie?

(George runs to radio, shuts it off.)

ARCHIE: Oh, yuh, yuh. I bumped into her down Mal's Jewel Craft a while back. She called me up…to have supper with her.

GEORGE: She called you up?

ARCHIE: Oh, yuh, well, yuh, she did, yuh…

GEORGE: Jees! Still the aggressive one, Margie, huh?

ARCHIE: Oh, well, yuh, I guess…

GEORGE: I read in the paper she was comin' ta town. Swede's finally dyin', huh?

ARCHIE: She said that, yuh. Bad shape, yuh.

GEORGE: She's up and done som'pin' famous, I guess, huh? You read it in the *Item*?

ARCHIE: Me? Naw. Never touch a paper after I leave here. I get my fill, sorta, I guess…this line of work 'n' all…

GEORGE: *(Laughs.)* I even clipped the article…to show you. I can't goddam believe it, Arch! It's unbelievable! You got supper going with Swede's sistah?

ARCHIE: Hey, listen, huh, ya know? Sure…Sure! Swede Palumbo's sister Margie. She finds me…attractive.

GEORGE: Oh, yuh? Maybe she can find you a *job! (Laughs.)* Where're you pickin' her up? 33 Elm?

ARCHIE: Uh uh. She's pickin' *me* up, here, 6 sharp.

GEORGE: *Here?*

ARCHIE: Yuh, here. Somethin' the matter with here?

GEORGE: It's a junk shop, for Christ's sake...*(Laughs.)* Boy, you really got 'em hoppin' for you, Arch...I gotta hand it to ya...Pickin' him up at his goddam junk shop...What a guy...*(Laughs.)* Hey, maybe you could send her over ta' my place, later, huh? For old time's sake...

ARCHIE: *(Twists George's arm, forcing him to the ground.)* Take it back! Take it back! Ya *derr!*

GEORGE: Lemme up, ya jerk!

ARCHIE: Take it back, take it back!

GEORGE: *Archie...God damn it...GOD DAMN IT, Archie!*

ARCHIE: You take it back?

GEORGE: Okay, yuh, okay, yuh, I take it back. *(Pauses.)* Now lemme up, huh?

ARCHIE: You're free. *(Releasing George.)* Let's finish this bale, okay?

GEORGE: *(Stands, rubs arms.)* Top of your head, huh?

ARCHIE: I split his jaw.

GEORGE: Any bleeding?

ARCHIE: Why? You thirsty, or som'pin'?

(There is a pause in the chat. The men work, wordlessly. George re-starts the conversation.)

GEORGE: Blind-Peter-Holier-Than-Fucking-Thou-Palumbo...Never liked the peckah...

ARCHIE: Which one of us did?

GEORGE: You gonna try to get anything off her?

ARCHIE: Who?

GEORGE: Swede's sister.

ARCHIE: Margie? Nothin' ta get. She's flatter'n a pancake...two raisins on a bread-board.

GEORGE: Carpenter's Delight: flat as a board and easy to screw!

ARCHIE: *Pirate's* Delight:

GEORGE: What's that?...

ARCHIE: Sunken chest!

(They share a laugh.)

GEORGE: Margy ain't so bad, actually.

ARCHIE: *(Grabs George from behind, tickles him.)* You were lookin'? You were peekin'? You were snoopin' in between the buttons when she stretches? You were watchin' her take off her coat...on the arms-be-hind-the-back part...when the two of them were shoved right out there...on view for all? That what you were doin', George?

GEORGE: Who? *Me?*

ARCHIE: Just us balin' here, right? I mean, I ain't seen nobody else pressin' these bales, right? Just you and me...

GEORGE: Yuh, I've thought about it now and again. But I haven't seen her in twenty years, Arch.

ARCHIE: How come you never moved on her?

GEORGE: On Swede's sistah?

ARCHIE: You sufferin' from a sho't memory problem, or what?

GEORGE: I never moved on Swede's sister on account of she was married. Also counta Swede. Also on account of I haven't actually seen her since high school.

ARCHIE: She ain't been married in years and years!

GEORGE: Even worse. Widows give me the creeps, ya know. I look at her and her kids, and alls I think about is what's-his-name dyin' an' all...What's his name?

ARCHIE: You know...what's'his'name.

GEORGE: What's his name?

ARCHIE: What's his name?...Uh, uh, uh, *don't tell me!* Uh, uh, uh...*(Suddenly.)* I got it! Cootie!

GEORGE: Cootie Webber?

ARCHIE: Wasn't that him?

GEORGE: Are you nuts? Cootie Webber never married Swede's sister. Sides...ain't Cootie Webber still alive?

ARCHIE: You crazy? Cootie Webber got hit by lightning...head of the lake.

GEORGE: You out of your mind? Cootie Webber ate bad clams.

ARCHIE: You off your gourd? *(Turns and faces George.)* A woman's got a right to take off her coat, same as a man, when she comes in. The world's changed, in case ya haven't noticed! You got no right to be starin' at her like she's public property, anymore, 'cause she ain't. You get me? *Get me?*

GEORGE: *(After a long pause.)* You're really gone on her, huh?

ARCHIE: I like her.

GEORGE: It doesn't give you the willies...that she's got one husband in the grave...and kids? That doesn't give you the willies, Arch?

ARCHIE: Death is a part of life, the way I see it.

GEORGE: No doubt about it.

ARCHIE: A widow's got a right to go out with me...same as a non-widow.

GEORGE: I can see that.

ARCHIE: I like her.

GEORGE: I never stared.

ARCHIE: I never said you did.

GEORGE: I mean, I noticed she was good lookin' and all...

ARCHIE: Kinda flat-chested, though...

GEORGE: It's a gland, that's all. For feeding babies. I mean, how excited can a person get over a gland, right? You know what I mean? You follow me?

ARCHIE: I like 'em, myself.

GEORGE: Margie's, or in general?

ARCHIE: In general, I like 'em to be more ample than Margie's...I like them in general...to be more ample than...what Margie has to offer.

GEORGE: I was thinkin': If Swede heard us going on about his sister this way, we'd be goners, right.

ARCHIE: What are you? Nuts or something?

GEORGE: He's got a temper, Swede...

ARCHIE: The man's dyin', George. What have you got goin' upstairs? Mashed potatoes? 'Cause there sure ain't no gray matter up there!

GEORGE: All's I'm sayin' here is "ya never know!"...Dyin' or not, Swede Palumbo wouldn't've shed a tear if the school bus run us down...and that's a fact... *(Smiles.)* Course, it's *you* he really hates, ain't it?

ARCHIE: What's this?

GEORGE: Senior Class Beach Party...what was Swede yellin', poor blind son-of-a-bitch? "I'm gonna kill you, Billy-Goat Crisp! I'm gonna kill you dead! Billy-Goat's gonna die!" Ain't that right?

ARCHIE: What am I hearin' here?

GEORGE: Still makes me laugh ta' think about it...

ARCHIE: If you spill one word about this in front of Margie, I'll kill you, George!

GEORGE: What are you? Kidding? You don't think it's gonna' come up?

ARCHIE: I'll be the judge of what stays down and what comes up. You get me?

(George giggles.)

I don't hear an answer here, George.

(George laughs.)

I wanna' hear an answer, you!

(George tries to stop his laugh, but a fresh laugh explodes from him. Archie is enraged.)

I'm gonna' butt your jaw with the top of my head...

GEORGE: C'mon, Arch, it just stands ta' reason…

ARCHIE: Nothin' stands ta' reason, you get me? You open your mouth one time on that subject, and you won't be standin' to piss, let alone standin' to reason! You follow me, George? Huh?

GEORGE: Okay, okay!

ARCHIE: I'll hav'ta kill ya, otherwise…

GEORGE: I just said "okay," okay?

ARCHIE: *(After a pause.)* Okay.

GEORGE: *(An involuntary giggle.)* Heee…*(Shows palms to Archie.)* Just a laugh.

ARCHIE: And you keep your eyes to yourself, you hear me?

GEORGE: Honest to Christ, Arch, I never once looked. Cross my heart.

ARCHIE: Cross your ass, George! I don't like what I'm hearing from you, George, ya know that? There must be ten thousand different women around, ya know, if you add up Wakefield, Reading, Stoneham, Melrose and Woburn. You got no right to be movin' in where I'm having supper tonight.

GEORGE: God strike me dead if I'm movin' in, Arch.

ARCHIE: You better mean what you say.

GEORGE: I mean what I say. God strike me dead, and that's a fact. *(Pause.)* Don't you worry. *(Smiles.)* I wouldn't add in Woburn women, if I were you, though.

ARCHIE: *(Smiles.)* True enough.

GEORGE: Woburn women are dogs.

ARCHIE: The worst.

GEORGE: Pigs.

ARCHIE: The lowest.

GEORGE: I wouldn't touch 'em on a bet.

ARCHIE: Rot your hand.

GEORGE: Remember Ax Landry?

ARCHIE: The skinny one?

GEORGE: Went with Rufus What's'it's Woburn cousin…

ARCHIE: The fat one with the wigs?

GEORGE: Remember?

ARCHIE: *(Hoots with laughter.)* Who could forget?

GEORGE: Ax. Dumb fuck.

ARCHIE: Wicked dumb.

GEORGE: His sister, Dixie Cups…she had a mouth like a toilet, huh?

ARCHIE: Wicked awful.

GEORGE: She says to me one night, up by the bandstand, lookin' out at

Lake Quannapowitt…summer…peaceful…sittin' on the grass…me with my arm around her…thinkin', peaceful…she says to me… *(Changes his posture, now in imitation of Dixie-Cups Landry.)* "A lot of people wonder why I wear cotton underpants."

ARCHIE: What?

GEORGE: I swear ta Christ, Arch! Out'ta nowhere this broad is tellin' me a lot of people wonder why she wears cotton underpants.

ARCHIE: You're makin' this up.

GEORGE: On my mother's grave…

ARCHIE: Ax Landry's sister?

(George nods affirmatively.)

I'll be dipped…*(Looks up.)* What happened after?

GEORGE: After she said that? *(Smiles.)* Well…*(Pauses.)* The good part. I says, "How come?" And she says, "How come a lot of people wonder? Or how come I wear them?" *(Pauses, confidentially.)* "How come you wear 'em?" I ask…quietlike…serious. *(Pauses.)* "Ask me nicely," she says. So I do. "How come you wear cotton underpants, Mary Ellen?" I ask. She looks up, pokerface…*(Imitates her.)* "So *it* can breathe," she says. "So *it* can breathe." *(Pauses, laughing, mock disgust.)* Imagine, huh? Straight out, no shame, thinks this is funny. Ax Landry: his sister.

ARCHIE: Dumb fuck. *(Standing, shaking leg.)* C'mon, George, let's shake a leg. Grab the roller, will ya?

GEORGE: *(He moves to baler; works.)* I, personally, would never take out a Woburn girl, even if she was the Pope's niece.

ARCHIE: There isn't a one of them that washes herself properly.

GEORGE: They never learned properly…

ARCHIE: It's all in the bringing up.

GEORGE: You said a mouthful.

ARCHIE: The manners. The washing and the scrubbing…

GEORGE: The don't talk back to your parents…

ARCHIE: The mind your manners…

GEORGE: The go to bed early and get up early.

ARCHIE: The you mind your tongue around your mother and your sisters…

GEORGE: The honor thy father…

ARCHIE: The honor thy father…*(Pauses.)* I do agree with you there, George. The honor they father's the thing. *(Pauses; lost in memory. Then, quietly.)* Jesus…I never figured when I was twelve and doin' this, that twenty/twenty-five years later I'd still be here, you know…doing this.

GEORGE: You could be doin' worse.

ARCHIE: Oh, yuh? What? *(Laughs. He rolls hand truck to base of roller-track.)* Let's shake a leg here, huh? *(He shakes his leg, doing the "shake a leg" joke a second time. He goes behind baler to shove bale forward and out of baler.)*

GEORGE: *(Calls out to Archie.)* You always had the sense of humor, Arch. Even when you weren't funny…*(George "shoulders" bale; waits for Archie's help.)*

ARCHIE: *(Archie runs to George. Together, they guide bale down roller-track to hand truck. As they unload the bale, they chatter.)* Careful…

GEORGE: Careful…

ARCHIE: Got it?

GEORGE: Yuh, yuh…let her go…Careful!

ARCHIE: Careful!

GEORGE: Right. I got her!

(Archie rolls hand truck to line-up of bales; hurls bale forward and off hand truck, into stack. Then Archie gets two beers from locker.)

ARCHIE: Bury the roller.

(George does, wordlessly. Archie continues.)

Seven down, one to go…After this one, we got the overissue bale, then we just got'ta make the crap clean-up bale, George. Nothin' loose can be left in sight lyin' around. My Uncle Max goes apeshit if it ain't tidy when he gets in here, mornin's…So's anything here that isn't part of the building and don't have the strength to run away, up and in the baler! Like this…and *this…Ooopp…*

(Archie moves to George, pretending he's going to throw him up and into the baler. George rolls backwards into baler, giggling nervously. Archie has carried two beers with him. He shakes George's can.)

ARCHIE: Little reward for you, George.

GEORGE: Yo, thanks, Arch. Little wet for the whistle…

(George flips can open, it explodes; spraying George with beer. George is delighted.)

GEORGE: Heyyy!

ARCHIE: Early shower for you, kiddo! Lower the gate, Georgie.

(George lowers gate. They drink beer awhile, tired, but pleased to be with one another.)

GEORGE: Where's this load goin'?

ARCHIE: Fitchburg. Felulah's Mill.

GEORGE: Wicked lot'ta drivin', huh?

ARCHIE: Oh, yuh, wicked. My uncle's out'ta here by 4:00 in the mornin'…He hits Fitchburg by 6:00 or 7:00, gets unloaded by maybe 8:00, back here by 10:00, maybe 10:30. It's no fuckin' life for humans, I can tell ya that.

GEORGE: I never liked Fitchburg.

ARCHIE: Fitchburg never liked you, George.

GEORGE: Bunch of boozers.

ARCHIE: The worst.

GEORGE: Can't be trusted.

ARCHIE: All cons and ex-cons.

GEORGE: They'd steal yo'r eyeteeth.

ARCHIE: Fillings and all.

GEORGE: That's the truth.

ARCHIE: When's the last time we seen each other, George? Before the funeral? Three years ago?

GEORGE: Nearly, at the reunion.

ARCHIE: At the Fifteenth?

GEORGE: Yup.

ARCHIE: Shit, time flies.

GEORGE: So, Arch, where're ya takin' the widow for supper? Hazelwood?

ARCHIE: That's for me to know and you to find out!

GEORGE: Whoa!

ARCHIE: I'd love ta' bullshit with you all night, but I've got to get this overissue bale done and get out of here…Okay?

GEORGE: *(George sips his beer, slowly, happily. He sits back in the reclining chair, reclining…certainly not working.)* I'm enjoyin' this workin' with ya, Arch. I kid you not! This is enjoyable…

ARCHIE: Oh, yuh? Well, get to work! *(They load paper into the baler awhile.)*

ARCHIE: Well, ya know, George, sometimes, it's life's tragedies that bring people closer than life's joys…

GEORGE: Well said, Arch…

ARCHIE: I ain't finished.

GEORGE: Sorry.

ARCHIE: Sometimes, George, it's the tragedy more than the joys of life that brings two guys like you and me back into close contact…

GEORGE: Yup, you were sayin' that…

ARCHIE: I mean, we've had our differences over the years, haven't we?

GEORGE: Oh, sure…Many differences, Arch…

(They pass each other carrying bundles to baler. Neither seems to take notice of what the other is saying.)

ARCHIE: I mean, I've really *hated* you, George…and with due cause…but when guys like us share the tragedy that we just have…

GEORGE: Oh, *I* see! You mean losin' Spike the Loon as we did…

ARCHIE: I never like hearin' people say "losin'" when they mean somebody died. It always seemed dumb ta me. Like when Pa died, and people'd say, "Jees, Archie, you lost your Pa…" and I'd think ta myself: Do they mean I lost him like in Filene's Bargain Basement kinda thing?

GEORGE: Yuh, I guess. Just sayin' d-e-a-t-h out loud is kinda morbid, though…

ARCHIE: You gotta be able ta take the bad with the very bad…that's life…

GEORGE: I s'pose. There's the morbid with the very morbid…

ARCHIE: Right. The way Spike the Loon died was very morbid…

GEORGE: Gives me the willies…

ARCHIE: Spike the Loon worked for me and my Uncle Max, right here in this shop, ever since he flunked out'ta Salem State…

GEORGE: No great brain there…

ARCHIE: Why? You got the cancer cure figured out?

GEORGE: I was just sayin' Spike the Loon wasn't any genius…

ARCHIE: He was a friend.

GEORGE: I thought you couldn't stand him?

ARCHIE: That's only recent years…

GEORGE: Oh…

ARCHIE: See, George, you gotta live each day like it was your last…

GEORGE: I dunno…

ARCHIE: I know. That is an ancient Oriental philosophy. I heard it on WBZ, Sunday night…call-in show…

GEORGE: Japs called in?

ARCHIE: *(Glares at George, angrily.)* Jesus, you can be one aggravating son-of-a-bitch, George. What I'm tryin' ta do here is ta give you a compliment, but you're makin' it damn near impossible…

GEORGE: Sorry, Arch…

ARCHIE: *("Toasts" him with beer can raised.)* Look, I woulda be'n in real trouble gettin' this load out for my Uncle for tomorrow, what with Spike the Loon dead and all…but…who's here ta help, no questions asked? Not a stranger, but a former best buddy, 'cause that is life. Georgie K. Ferguson, townie and friend from his toes to his limp pecker to the top of his Boston Bruins stocking cap, right?…This former best buddy looks across to Archie Crisp at the funeral of their mutual lifelong friend and co-worker, Spike the Loon, and asks if there is anything he can do ta help out at the shop. And I says "yes" and here he is…helpin'…Now that is worth more ta me than any rich bitch from Wakefield's Park section or Stoneham's Spot Pond district, and that is the God's-honest!

GEORGE: *(Sips and tips his beer.)* I'm drinkin' ta that, Archie.

ARCHIE: Hop in, George.

(George hops into the baler.)

GEORGE: I personally ain't be'n that close ta death before…I said the "D" word. *(Crosses himself.)* 'Course there was a time I did stay too long under water…

ARCHIE: Takin' a swim in the lake?

GEORGE: Takin' a bath, in the tub…*(Pauses.)* I was little. *(Pauses.)* Trying to beat my brother's record. *(Pauses.)* We were quite competitive…with one another. *(Pauses.)* Takin' a bath. *(Pauses.)* That was about as close as I've come to it, I suppose…I watched my dog die… Vergil…my cocker…I watched him die. That was something to see…four hours it took…Four hours and twenty-two minutes… *(Pauses.)* He died by the clock…in the pantry…*(Pauses.)* I watched *that*…*(Pauses.)* God damn. God damn…

ARCHIE: I remember Vergil. Nice. Nice…

GEORGE: Hit by a '51 Studebaker. Squashed.

ARCHIE: I remember…

GEORGE: '51 Studies looked the same front and back…You couldn't tell whether they were coming or going. Vergil probably got confused.

ARCHIE: No doubt.

GEORGE: God damn.

ARCHIE: Nice little mutt.

GEORGE: They went bankrupt, too, those cars. They don't make 'em anymore. Gone! Off the face of the fucking Earth!

ARCHIE: Not much of an idea, even then.

GEORGE: It would've be'n one thing, ya know, if he'd died right off the bat. But four hours and twenty-two minutes of painful excruciation? And for *what*, I ask you? For God damn *what*? Studebaker cars go totally fucking bankrupt and that is *it*, right? I mean Vergil is gone and so is the entire *brand!* This is beyond fucking ironic and tragic! This is definitely Robert Frost-your-balls/seek out and find Studebaker himself and *run him down!* Am I right on this?

ARCHIE: The good with the bad, George. Only natural. But you've gotta' move on from it. You can't dwell in it. It's all a part of life. Part of life. *(Margie Palumbo enters at the loading platform, behind the baler, far upstage, looking about nervously, confused.)*

MARGY: *(Softly.)* Archie Crisp?

GEORGE: *(Stays in baler, looks, taunts Archie in grade-school way.)* Hey, Archie, *somebody's* here! *(Sees Margy.)* Hey, Arch, look who's here...

ARCHIE: I see her! I see her! *(Archie runs grabs a towel; wipes ink smears and dirt from his skin. He pulls his suit-jacket on over sleeveless undershit. He is in a panic, trying to look presentable. He grabs his watch from locker shelf.)* Christ, it's five-pah'st-Six! We pissed away an hour!

(Archie calls out to Margy.) Just a minute!

GEORGE: *(George hides in baler, peering out at Margy.)* Jesus, Arch, she got old!

ARCHIE: *(Upstage.)* Shhh. C'mon, huh, George...Shut it, huh. She can hear and all...

(Calls out to Margy.) Hey, Margy, down here...

(Worried; to George.) Mind your language, okay?

GEORGE: Sure, Arch, sure...no sweat...*no fuckin' sweat!*

(Margy enters baling-press area; stands facing Archie and George. She wears a full black skirt, long, black coat-seater, full peasant-cut blouse, overbelted. She wears driving [eye]glasses, which she will soon remove. She carries a purse. Her car-keys are still clutched in her hand.)

ARCHIE: Hey, Marg.

MARGY: Hello, Archie.

ARCHIE: How's it goin'? Long time, huh? How long since we saw each other—before Mal's the other day?

MARGY: Fifteen years, maybe, huh?

ARCHIE: Not that long. I saw you in Santuro's, buyin' subs...Maybe ten/twelve years ago, after you, uh, lost your husband...You came back up here for the funeral and all. You remember seein' me?

MARGY: Did we talk?

ARCHIE: To each other? No...You remember George Ferguson?

MARGY: *(Sees George; freezes. She stares blankly for a moment; doesn't seem to recognize George.)* No, I'm sorry, I don't. Nice to meet you.

GEORGE: We went to school together.

MARGY: We did?

GEORGE: Sure. All twelve years. Georgie Ferguson? Gould Street? Up near the Stoneham line?

MARGY: *(Smiles at George, blankly.)* No. Sorry.

(To Archie.) Nice to see you again, Archie. Nice to see you.

ARCHIE: Nice yourself, Marg.

(There is a short silence, which George will break.)

GEORGE: *(Still in baler.)* There was a squirt-gun fight in second grade and you got hit in the face and you cried and told Mrs. Linder…you remember?

MARGY: I…I think so.

GEORGE: That was me. I squirted you.

MARGY: On purpose?

GEORGE: Accident.

MARGY: I remember.

GEORGE: George Ferguson. Second row, third seat in from the left… nearly in the middle…

MARGY: Yes, I think so…Georgie Ferguson…I think so…*(She smiles at George.)*

GEORGE: Great ta see ya again, Margie. How's it goin'?
(There is another short silence.)
How's Swede doin'?

ARCHIE: Hey, George! C'mon, huh?

MARGY: Swede's dying. They don't think he'll make it through the night, tonight. He's dying…That's why I'm here, right now…

GEORGE: In town?

MARGY: Hmmm?

GEORGE: Why you're here in Wakefield, or why you're here at Archie's Uncle Max's junk-shop?

ARCHIE: Don't mind him…

MARGY: I've been over at Melrose-Wakefield Hospital since 8, this morning…*(Pauses.)* They've got him on a respirator…*(Pauses.)* I told the doctor I'd get back there by 8:30 or so. He's sleeping now…

GEORGE: Swede?

MARGY: Mmm. Swede.

ARCHIE: Well, now…that's a tragedy…
(Margie and George both look at Archie waiting for his move.)
Well…his age, huh? Death: That's the worst…*(Archie looks at his shoes, silently.)*

GEORGE: *(Confidently; smiling.)* I remember Swede when he could see…
(There is another short silence.)

ARCHIE: *(Stares George down. Sits by Margie on bale.)* So, Margy…how're the kids doin'?

MARGY: Fine.

ARCHIE: How many you got now?

MARGY: Same as ever.

ARCHIE: Five?

MARGY: Two. *(Pauses.)* Rosie and Raymond.

ARCHIE: Little Cootie?

MARGY: I beg your pardon?...

ARCHIE: Your son?

MARGY: *(Smiles quizzically.)* I don't understand.

GEORGE: *(Moves a bale Down Center and sits.)* Your boy. Your son. Archie thinks you were married to Cootie Webber...

ARCHIE: Wasn't that him?

MARGY: My husband?

ARCHIE: Yuh.

MARGY: Who is Cootie Webber?

ARCHIE: He wasn't your ex?

MARGY: Edgar Burke...

ARCHIE: ...Your husband?

MARGY: Passed away twelve years ago...

ARCHIE: Sorry to hear that.

MARGY: The children were still babies...Raymond was only three months old; Rosie was two and a half...

GEORGE: You didn't waste much time, did you?

MARGY: Hmmm?

GEORGE: Havin' the kiddoes: You didn't waste your time.

ARCHIE: What are you sayin', George?

GEORGE: I was just telling Margie here, that I could see she didn't waste any of her valuable time...waiting to get right down to have the little ones. She got right down to it...
(To Margie)...didn't cha?

MARGY: We waited two years.

GEORGE: How old are you now?

MARGY: Nearly thirty-seven...soon.

GEORGE: *(Walks around space while calculating.)* Twelve years since he died...add two for the kid is fourteen...plus nine months for the being pregnant and all...that's fifteen...plus the two you waited...is seventeen...that makes you about twenty when you hooked up with him...

ARCHIE: You didn't go to college?

GEORGE: I thought you were in the college course?

ARCHIE: You didn't get accepted?

GEORGE: You change your plans or what?

MARGY: I went to college.

GEORGE: For just a year?

ARCHIE: Junior college or a regular full college?

MARGY: Boston State...
GEORGE: Boston Teachers?
MARGY: Well...yes.
ARCHIE: You a teacher?
MARGY: No...
ARCHIE: You had to quit teaching when you were having your baby, huh?
MARGY: No, I finished. We waited...
GEORGE: Oh. Right.
ARCHIE: Right.
GEORGE: I couldn't figure how you could've done both, ya know what I mean. Teachers can't have babies...
MARGY: Now they can...
GEORGE: Uh uh.
MARGY: They can. The rule changed. They changed the rule.
ARCHIE: Is that a fact?
MARGY: It is.
ARCHIE: I wouldn't want my teacher to be having her own children...
GEORGE: Me, neither... *(Sits on bale.)*
ARCHIE: They've got no need... *(Margie looks at Archie; quizzically.)*
ARCHIE: They've got all us kids, anyway: you, me, George...
GEORGE: Swede, Cootie, Delbert... *(Pauses.)* What did you say his name was?
(Margy looks at George, blankly.)
Your husband's.
MARGY: Edgar's?
GEORGE: Yuh.
MARGY: Edgar's name?
GEORGE: Yuh.
MARGY: You want to know what Edgar's *name* was?
GEORGE: Yuh.
MARGY: Edgar's name was Edgar.
GEORGE: *(Annoyed; a childish tone.)* His *lah'st* name!
MARGY: Oh. I see. You mean Edgar's *sur*name. Your question was unclear. *(Pauses.)* Burke.
ARCHIE: Related to Doctor Burke?
MARGY: Oh, yes, Doctor Burke...top of Prospect Street...Nope, uh uh. Edgar came from different Burkes.
ARCHIE: Greenwood?
MARGY: Uh uh. Edgar's family's from Woodville District...
GEORGE: Oh, yuh? *Burke?*

MARGY: Why do you *doubt* me, George? The name was Burke.

GEORGE: What did the father do?

MARGY: Edgar's? Oh, well, he worked...head of the lake.

ARCHIE: Filling station?

MARGY: Uh, no...

GEORGE: Lakeside Furniture?

MARGY: Cemetery.

ARCHIE: Oh, yuh? Doin' what?

MARGY: Well, uh, lawn care.

ARCHIE: Oh, yuh? Lawn care, huh?

GEORGE: You mean graves and all?

MARGY: Well, yuh, that, too...

GEORGE: Lawn care and digging kind of thing?

MARGY: I guess.

ARCHIE: Oh, yuh?

GEORGE: Willies: That's what this gives me. I swear to Christ!

MARGY: Hmmm?

ARCHIE: What are you driving these days, Marg?

MARGY: Me?

ARCHIE: A Chrysler LeBaron?

MARGY: No.

GEORGE: A Ford Mustang?

ARCHIE: Somethin' big?

GEORGE: A Pontiac Monte Carlo?

MARGY: No...

GEORGE: Maybe one of those Jap jobs! A Toyota? A Nissan?

ARCHIE: Mitsubishi?

GEORGE: Suburu!

ARCHIE: Mazda!

GEORGE: Isuzu!

MARGY: My husband's father's car...That's what I'm driving: my husband's
    father's car.

ARCHIE: No kidding?

MARGY: Ancient.

GEORGE: Model-T sort of thing?

ARCHIE: Something classic?

MARGY: '51 Studebaker...two door...*(Smile.)* Powder blue...I...You can't
    tell the front from the back...*(Pauses.)* I can't, anyway...I'm always
    opening the trunk to check the oil. That sort of thing. Wicked
    funny...odd...unique, though, if you like that sort of thing...

GEORGE: Do you?

MARGY: Hmmm?

GEORGE: Like that sort of thing?

MARGY: The Studie? Sure. I love it. Makes me feel…nice. *(She giggles.)* I'm always opening the trunk to check the oil…

ARCHIE: Was he kinda skinny?

MARGY: The antecedent to the pronoun "he" is not precisely clear, Archie. Do you mean my father-in-law? Was my father-in-law skinny?

ARCHIE: Well, no. Your *husbin'*…Is your husbin' skinny?

MARGY: Is my husband skinny? My husband has been dead and in his grave for twelve years, Archie! Don't you find the question "Is he skinny?" rather *grim!*

ARCHIE: I didn't mean "is." I meant "was"…

MARGY: Oh, was…

ARCHIE:…In high school…

MARGY: Was my husband skinny in high school. *(Pauses.)* Oh, I see…*(Considers this.)* I suppose. He was more tall than skinny…

GEORGE: He play ball?

ARCHIE: Naw, I woulda known him…

GEORGE: Basketball, I mean…

ARCHIE: I woulda known him, George. I knew everybody.

GEORGE: Was he definitely our year, Marg?

MARGY: Definitely.

GEORGE: I'll hav'ta look it up…In the yearbook.

ARCHIE: How come you never came to any of our reunions?

MARGY: Our what?

ARCHIE: Our reunions.

GEORGE: Our reunions.

MARGY: Oh, well…I just didn't.

GEORGE: Didn't want to.

MARGY: Yes. I didn't want to.

ARCHIE: How come? They were pretty rich…

MARGY: I'll just bet they were!

GEORGE: They were good…

ARCHIE: They were fun…

GEORGE: Good to see the old gang sort of thing…*(Gets up to play with Archie at Center.)*

ARCHIE: Makes you laugh.

GEORGE: Shadow Flint, with his weird hats…

ARCHIE: "Longest Hair?" Fred who's'its…*(He moves toward George.)*

GEORGE: "Longest Distance Traveled?"…Arthur, the Jew…

ARCHIE: "Most Kids?"…Remember who?

GEORGE: Maureen…

ARCHIE: And Whopp'ah…Every reunion…

GEORGE: Started right away…

ARCHIE: Spike the Loon used ta always say Whopp'ah nailed Maureen first time while they were still in their caps and gowns…

GEORGE: "Most Kids" by a mile…Every reunion…

ARCHIE: Wicked devout Catholics…

GEORGE: Makes you laugh…

ARCHIE: *(Laughing.)* You missed a couple of great ones, Marg…The Fifth…

GEORGE: The Tenth was better…

ARCHIE: The Tenth was good, too…The Fifteenth was great!…*(Laughs.)* The Twentieth comin' up soon, too…

MARGY: Maybe I'll peek in…

ARCHIE: You gotta see it ta believe it…

GEORGE: Unbelievable…

ARCHIE: Everybody lookin' awful…

GEORGE: Beer bellies…

ARCHIE: Bald…

GEORGE: Some dead, even…

> *(Archie stares at George; a pause.)*

Sorry, Marg, huh?

ARCHIE: He didn't mean anything. Did you, Georgie?

MARGY: It's okay…

GEORGE: I'm really sorry…

MARGY: It's *okay*…*(Pauses.)* Ree*ally*…*(Pauses.)* I'll need a date.

ARCHIE: For the Twentieth?

> *(She smiles.)*

Should be no sweat for you, Marg…*(He smiles.)* Good-lookin' girl…

GEORGE: Got her own car and all…

ARCHIE: No sweat at all. Not at all…

GEORGE: I wouldn't mind takin' ya myself, Marg…

MARGY: *(Darkly.)* Oh, okay, George. It's a date…

GEORGE: Hey! Well! Great!

ARCHIE: That s'posed ta be funny?

GEORGE: Naw…Just kidding, Arch…

ARCHIE: I don't find that kind of kiddin' too ho-ho-that's-rich funny, George…

GEORGE: Meant no harm, Arch…

ARCHIE: *Not funny now, not funny then*…

GEORGE: C'mon, Arch…

ARCHIE: *(Goes to George to confront him.)* What is it? In your blood? Or *what?* You out of control or som'pin'? Or *what?*

GEORGE: You startin' in again, Arnold?

ARCHIE: *(To Margy.)* I go back a ways with this one, Marg…*(Pauses.)* We got a history. *(Pauses.)* All the ways back to West Ward School…I shoulda known then, I swear ta Christ! *(Pauses.)* A history. George Ferguson messing with Archie Crisp's girls…Can't find none of his own. He's got to move in on his buddy like…you follow me, Marg? *(Pauses. Looks at Margie, at bales.)* I mean, don't be flattered none if this one makes a move on you, 'cause it's not that he's likin' you any…*(Pauses.)* The fact is, he made some wicked awful remarks just before you came in through the doors, didn't ya, Georgie?

GEORGE: *C'mon*, Arch!

ARCHIE: *Bullllshit*, buddy! *Bullllshit!*

GEORGE: *(To Margy.)* Here we go.

ARCHIE: First grade. I'm seeing Esther what's'it. Walking her home from school every day. What do you think I find out? This one here: he's sending her notes. Notes. He's slipping them to her behind my back…Six to eight of 'em fell out ta her reader…"Dick and Jane" and six to eight goddamned love letters from old George K. Ferguson…*(Pauses; then angrily.)* God damn it, Georgie. *God damn it!*

GEORGE: This was a resolved matter. This was an incident that was put to bed.

ARCHIE: *(At George.)* I'm wakin' it up, George. I'm callin' it right down for breakfast…

MARGY: *(Calls out.)* Excuse meee!

(Archie and George turn to her; their altercation postponed.)

MARGY: Listen, you guys…you two should be alone. You two seem…busy. I should…well…*go.*

ARCHIE: What's this?

(Margy goes to locker, gets her coat, pocketbook; moves toward door, pausing only to say her goodbye. Archie stands stunned.)

MARGY: It was lovely to see you both, again, really, but I do think enough in one lifetime is actually *enough*…so, I'll just be moseying along… *(Archie rushes to loading doors, stands and blocks Margy's exit. He talks to her, plaintively, sincerely.)*

ARCHIE: Oh, God, please, don't go, Margy. Please. Stay…

(To George.) I'll kill you, George.

(Leans against door, blocking Margy's intended exit. He forces her forward, downstage.) Please stay, Marg. Please, don't go. I was so happy to be seein' you like this…to be goin' out with you and all. Please…don't go. He's not my friend, Marg. Georgie K. Ferguson is no friend of Archie Crisp's. Honest ta' God. I'm not like that at all. Don't you worry none.

(To George.) I'll kill you, George. I swear to God, I'll kill you!

(To Margy). Please, stay with me. Don't go. *Please?*

MARGY: I don't think so, Archie, really…I mean, well, *why?*

ARCHIE: Because it's *us!* Because we haven't *talked*…we haven't, I dunno', *be'n together yet!* Jesus, Margy, I think about you all the time. I mean, gawd!, I've be'n *waitin' and waitin' and waitin'* for tonight, and here it is, and, oh, God, please…don't go. Stay. You got nothin' to worry about here…with us…*(Flashes a look at George.)* It's okay. I swear to you. Please? Stay?

MARGY: *(Looks at Archie. Pauses. Looks at George. Pauses. Speaks to Archie, softly.)* Okay, Archie. I'll stay. I'll do that for you…

ARCHIE: That's good. That's great.

(To George.) She's staying.

(To Margy.) That's really *so incredibly great!*

(Margy hands Archie her coat. He is puzzled for a moment, but then realizes that the coat is to be replaced on the hanger/hook. He does this. Turns, smiles at Margy, awkwardly. Archie is delighted.

Margy looks about the room, silently. She looks at George; smiles. She looks at Archie; smiles; speaks.)

MARGY: What's his "K" for?

ARCHIE: Huh?

MARGY: His "K"…you mentioned a "K." I have a vague memory of an extremely nasty little guy with a "K" in the middle. What's it for?

(George moans.)

ARCHIE: *(Giggles.)* Tell her.

GEORGE: C'mon, huh, Arch?

ARCHIE: You tell her, or I'll tell her. You got a choice.

GEORGE: Kermit.

MARGY: No kidding?

ARCHIE: *(To George, teasing.)* Kermie, Kermie…

GEORGE: C'mon, Archie…

ARCHIE: Kermie, Kermie, Kermie…

GEORGE: God damn it, Archie, c'mon…

ARCHIE: Kermie, Kermie, Kermie, Kermie…

GEORGE: *(Throws a punch, while Archie sidesteps, laughing.)* I said COME OFF IT, Archie! *(Work at baler.)*

ARCHIE: *(Laughing, moves across the room away from George to Margy.)* I love a laugh.

MARGY: *(A sudden memory.)* Esther *Larkin*: that was the name of your first grade girlfriend. She lived on the corner of Prospect and Elm. Pigtails.

ARCHIE: Yup. That's her.

MARGY: Edgar went with Esther Larkin.

ARCHIE: Who's Edgar?

GEORGE: Her *husband. (Throws paper into baler.)*

ARCHIE: Oh. *(Smiles.)* Too much alcohol. Rots the brain.

GEORGE: You can say *that* again!

ARCHIE: They call this one "Chief Hollow Leg"…counta there's no end in sight for the precious brew…

GEORGE: Me? That's a laugh! This one, Marg: he's invested his life savings in Tap'a'Keg… *(Laughs.)*

ARCHIE: She don't know what you're talkin' about.

GEORGE: *(To Margy.)* Tap-a-Keg's out on Route One. You've never been?

MARGY: Yes, George, I must confess: in the matter of Tap-a-Keg, I have never been.

GEORGE: We could shoot down there one night, together, Marg. In your powder blue Studie.

ARCHIE: You makin' another move here?

GEORGE: What da ya mean?

ARCHIE: What do you mean "What do ya mean?" *(Imitates George.)* We can just shoot down there together, Marg…in yo'r powder blue Studie-doo… *(Imitation ceases.) Bullllllshit*, buddy! *Bullllshit!* That is a definite move you're makin' on my supper date and I don't like what I'm seein' at *all! Not at all!*

GEORGE: This one's seein' moves that aren't bein' made.

ARCHIE: *(Pulls rank.)* Why don't you knock off, George. I can finish up here…

GEORGE: *(Hurt; defensively.)* I'll knock off, but you won't get your bales wired or weighed or loaded on no truck for no uncle by no ha'pahst four in the mornin', and that's a definite *fact*…less you're figurin' Margy here's gonna do some of your work for you.

MARGY: I wouldn't mind.

ARCHIE: *(Laughs.)* Woman your size wouldn't get much pressed, Marg.

GEORGE: *(Laughing as well.)* This baler wants beef…like me and Arch…

ARCHIE: Bales weigh 800 pounds…some of 'em…

GEORGE: Minimum…

ARCHIE: Takes weight and muscle…

GEORGE: Beef…

ARCHIE: Be'n doin' this for years…

GEORGE: Archie's got a skill.

ARCHIE: This is *man's* work.

GEORGE: Man's work.

MARGY: I wouldn't mind helping.

ARCHIE: Doin' what?

MARGY: Why not?

GEORGE: Why not, Arch?

ARCHIE: Okay, no reason. Work beats just watching, huh?

MARGY: Working certainly does beat just watching, Archie.

GEORGE: *(Checking out Margy's breasts.)* Take your coat-sweater off, Marg…
   (George reaches for her coat-sweater, staring. Archie glares at George, staring him down. Margy smiles at each of them; slips out of her coat.)
   (To Archie; a child's defense.) I didn't mean anything there…
   (Margie hangs her sweater on a coat-hook, upstage of the baler. She turns and faces George and Archie. She stares at them, directly. She will now tell a story that is patently sexual. George and Archie will leer at her, somewhat dumbfounded, not only by what she says, but by her direct staring, and her direct smiling. By the end of her story, Margy will be in control of the men.)

ARCHIE: Here are some gloves. Grab a bundle, toss it on up to Kermit, and you're on the clock.
   (Margy goes into position; begins.)

MARGY: We used to have a four-on-the-floor stick shift. Old black DeSoto. Edgar said I'd never be able to press the stick down. It took a lot of weight and muscle. Beef. *(Pauses.)* I did it. I took the stick in my hand and I kind of stood over it. All my might…I pushed .. it gave…the gears meshed…We jerked forward. Burned rubber. *(Pauses.)* First to fourth in 15 seconds and that's no bull. We blasted off. Rubber all over the road. *(Pauses.)* Women can drive, when they want to. You'd be surprised. *(Moves to Archie, turns, beside him; faces baler.)* So? How does this thing work?
   (Archie and George are dumbstruck. Archie breaks the silence.)

ARCHIE: I take a sizable bundle in my hand and load in from the front for awhile…Then I pull myself up on to the lip and throw down from the top til she's ready…Then I start my down-strokes…pressing the shaft-head there by jiggling this wheel…squashing her down, notch by notch, which forces the shaft-head lower and lower. Once things get goin' good, I use long, smooth strokes, til she comes into shape. When the belly of the bale's as flat as she's ever gonna' be, I wire her up, tie her off, and I'm on to the next one.

MARGY: *(After a pause; smiles.)* That is…impressive, Archie. I am…impressed.

(Archie moves next to Margy, talks to her with some degree of confidence.)

ARCHIE: In what grade did Edgar go with Esther?

MARGY: Edgar and Esther? Go with? Oh, well…9th grade.

ARCHIE: I sure am a blank on your husband, Marg.

MARGY: Edgar wasn't very loud…not back then. Not recently, either, I suppose…

GEORGE: Couldn't'a be'n…

(Margy turns, looks at George.)

Loud. Couldn't'a be'n. I would'a heard him, if he'd'a made a noise.

ARCHIE: *(To George.)* What's the matter with you?

GEORGE: What do you mean?

ARCHIE: What do you *mean*, "What do you mean?"?

(Archie moves near bales. Margy counters to look at baler.)

(Angrily.) This girl is talking about a deceased husband, George. What you've got here is a sympathetic moment and you're talkin' really low class…*no* class! *(Pauses.)* Sometimes, I'm truly embarrassed to have be'n your friend…

(To Margy.) George Ferguson and I were formerly close friends, Marg…Not for years.

(Pauses; to George.) When you're a kid you take what's in the neighborhood. You don't think about it: you take it. You were in the neighborhood, so I'd figured we were friends and hung out with you. I mean, don't flatter yourself none, George. Now that I see you and I'm not a kid…well…I'm hardly comin' on to you like a friend, right? *You're* the one's runnin' over here to *me* to help…not the reverse.

GEORGE: Just what the hell're you sayin', Arch? You wouldn't help me if the chips were down?…

ARCHIE: *(Quickly.)* If the chips were down for you, George, I wouldn't be runnin' to you out of friendship. I'd run to you, alright, but it would be out of pity…out of feelin' sorry for you, yes, but certainly never…not ever…out of friendship. *(Pauses.)* You understand that? You follow?

(To Margy.) You see, Marg, sometimes people look the truth straight in the eye, but they see absolutely nothing like what's there. They see sugar where there's salt: that kind of thing.

MARGY: *(Cuts Archie off.)* Aren't you getting hungry, Archie?

GEORGE: *(Whoops as might a large bird.)* Whooooaaa, Archie! Your supper date's gettin' anxious here. Ohoooo-aaahhh oooooo!

ARCHIE: What are you? Soft in the head?

GEORGE: You getting a little hollow in the stomach, Margie?

ARCHIE: You're getting hollow in the head, George!

GEORGE: Munch, munch, hey, Marg?

ARCHIE: What are you? Talking dirty now?

GEORGE: This one can't take a joke at all, Marg.

ARCHIE: I'll bust your squash!

GEORGE: *(Laughing, as he shadowboxes with Archie.)*...Got no sense of humor, Archie! You got none!

ARCHIE: This'll put a smile on your face! *(Archie tries to butt George with the top of his head; misses and falls forward against bale. George laughs.)* What are you laughing at? *(Archie tries to butt George once again. This time, George sidesteps Archie, who races past George and falls on to the dune-like mound of loose newspapers, Upstage. George whoops with laughter.)* What's so goddam funny? *(Archie stands, goes to baler and slaps its side; then he goes to a bale and kicks it.)* God damn. God damn. God *damn!*
(Archie goes to Margy, looks at her. Margy laughs.)
What are *you* laughing at?

MARGY: You. Butting your head in the air like a goat...

GEORGE: *(Thrilled.)* A goat, Arch, a goat! She remembers! A goat!

ARCHIE: *(To George.)* I'll kill you!

MARGY: You always did that, Arch, even when we were in first grade. You butted your head in the air and made little goat-like noises...
(George giggles, happily.)

ARCHIE: *(To Margy.)* I don't like this...
(Archie goes to George and slaps him, with a fierce backhand.)

GEORGE: Hey, c'mon, Archie, huh?

ARCHIE: *(To Margy.)* Every time you make a smart remark that runs me down, I'm gonna hurt your friend here. You get me? You follow me?

GEORGE: No more smart remarks, Marg.

MARGY: To which smart remark, precisely, do you refer, Archie?

ARCHIE: Okay... *(Slaps George.) That* one..."precisely"...

GEORGE: *Hey, dammit!*

ARCHIE: *(He holds George in a hammerlock.)* I got feelin's here, ya know…

MARGY: Okay, Archie. No more smart remarks.

ARCHIE: Okay, good. *(Lets loose of George.)* You're free.

GEORGE: *(Sulking; humiliated; he throws paper into the baler. He gets a bundle, loads it into baler as well.)* Let's get some work done. I've got a heavy date tonight and I don't wanna be late.

ARCHIE: *(Laughs.)* You got a heavy what?

GEORGE: Let's get some work done, okay?

ARCHIE: No, no…C'mon, Georgie…I wanna hear that again: You've got a heavy *what?*

GEORGE: *(Quietly.)* I said "date"…

ARCHIE: Date? Is that dried fruit? Like a fig?

GEORGE: Yuh, Dried fruit. Like a fig.

ARCHIE: *(To Margy.)* You hear that? George has got to get out ta here count a big fig.

GEORGE: Yuh. Right. You got it, Arch. I've got ta get out ta here count a big fig, so let's get ta packin', okay? *(Turns to Archie, squares off.)* That okay with you, Arch, if we finish here?

ARCHIE: *(Giggles.)* I thought up a good one! You listening, George? Here it comes. Stay out ta the sun, George, 'cause if you stay in the sun too long, you yourself will be…a *dried fruit. (He whoops and cackles.)*

GEORGE: Wicked funny.

ARCHIE: *You get it? (Chuckling and rasping.)* You get it, George? A dried fruit! *You get it??*

GEORGE: No, I didn't get it. I'm a Mongolian idiot, so I missed the point. *(Turns away; then in a sudden back.)* A *course*, I got it, ya goddam goat! What da ya think I am? Thick in the head?? You coulda pulled that one on a wood fence, the fence woulda got it. *(Turns away; then in a sudden back.) God damn it, Archie! God damn it! (Then ever so softly; his feelings are hurt.)* God damn it, Archie. God damn it…

ARCHIE: What was it you called me? *(Pauses.)* Came in between the "Mongolian idiot" and the "wood fence"…You remember?

GEORGE: Uh, uh, I don't.

ARCHIE: Starts with a "G"…

GEORGE: C'mon, Archie…

ARCHIE: That really pisses me off, ya know that?…

GEORGE: Don't be dumb, Arch…

ARCHIE: Makes me see red…

GEORGE: Just 'cause I called you Goat?

ARCHIE: What am I hearing here?

GEORGE: Everybody calls you Goat…

ARCHIE: I'll break your back!

GEORGE: Goat's as much your name as Archie is…

ARCHIE: I'll rip your pecker off!

GEORGE: *Goat is your name, Goddam it!!*

ARCHIE: Oooooo! Ooooo-*ooooo!*

(Archie is now choking George.)

GEORGE: Tell him, Margie! Tell him! Tell him! *Tell him!*

MARGY: It is, Goat.

ARCHIE: I don't like this.

MARGY: Everybody knows you as Goat…

ARCHIE: *(Lets loose of George's throat.)* I don't like this at all…

MARGY: You've been Goat from the first grade on…Arnold…

ARCHIE: I never liked Arnold, neither…

GEORGE: For God's sakes, uh, Archie…Arnold is your God-given name! You were christened Arnold…not Goat or Archie…

ARCHIE: I've always liked Archie…

GEORGE: I can understand that…Archie.

ARCHIE: I'd rather not be called the other. Okay?

GEORGE: Sure. Sure thing…Arch. *(Worries.)* Is Arch okay? Or do you want the whole thing: Arch*ie.*

ARCHIE: Arch is fine. Arch is fine.

(Silence.)

MARGY: Edgar hated his name. That's why he picked "Moose"…

GEORGE: *(Comes the dawn.)* Moose! Moose, for God's sakes, *Moose!*

ARCHIE: *(The same dawn.)* Moose! Moose Burke! Goddam Moose god-dam Burke! Old stiff antlers Moose Burke! How come you didn't say Moose right off the bat?? Jez-us, Margie!!

GEORGE: Moose Burke! Hot damn! Moose goddam Burke! Hot goddam *damn!*

ARCHIE: I remember Moose Burke when he was four…No! Three! Little Moosie Burke! *(Cackles.)* Moosie Burke! Little Stiff-Antler Moosie!

GEORGE: I remember Moose when he could run the hundred in ten-two…

MARGY: That wasn't Edgar…

ARCHIE: That wasn't Moose?…

GEORGE: What are you? Kiddin' me?

MARGY: That wasn't him at all…

ARCHIE: No…That was Artie What's'it…the Jew. He won Longest-Distance-Traveled two three times…Skinny…

GEORGE: Artie? Yuh. I think so. *(Pauses.)* So who the fuck is Moose? *(Embarrassed.)* Pardon me, Marg, huh? My mouth, huh?

ARCHIE: Out ta control…like a freight train, huh? Say you're sorry to the lady, huh, George.

MARGY: I don't mind, really. Really, I don't mind…

ARCHIE: Let's *hear* it, toilet!

GEORGE: I said I'm sorry, Arch…
    (Archie glares at George.)
    Okay, okay. I'm sorry, Marg…I am.

MARGY: There's no need.

ARCHIE: There's need.

MARGY: There's no need. None.

ARCHIE: You mean that, or are you just bein' nice?

MARGY: I said there was no need. *(Suddenly angry; snaps at them.)* I said there was no need. Didn't you hear me?

ARCHIE: *(After an embarrassed moment.)* Okay, okay.
    (To George.) Take it back, George.

GEORGE: Huh?

ARCHIE: No need. The lady says no need. Take it back.

GEORGE: You mean the apology?
    (Archie nods; George stares.)
    You mean I should take back the apology?
    (Archie nods again.)
    This is dumb.
    (Archie glares.)
    You mean like, "I'm not sorry"?…
    (Archie nods; George turns to Margie, smiles.)
    I'm not sorry, Margie.
    (George giggles.)
    This is truly dumb…*(Pauses, straightfaced.)* I am not at all sorry, Marg…*(Giggles.)* I said what I said…*(Pauses; thinks.)* What'd I say? Oh, yuh. Oh, yuh. I'm not sorry I asked who the fuck Moose was…*(He laughs, looks at glaring Archie, who looks at smiling Margy and shrugs to George, who shrugs back to Archie and giggles.)* Margy *(Looks at watch.)* We should think about supper, hmm?

GEORGE: Me?

ARCHIE: Not him.

GEORGE: Not me: Archie, Marg…

ARCHIE: Not him: I'm the one you called for supper, not George.

MARGY: I didn't know George would be with us. George is one of the old gang, right, Archie. We're all in this together, right? All-for-one-one-for-all kinda' thing, right?

GEORGE: Now, that is real nice of you, Marg.

ARCHIE: I don't like this.

GEORGE: I couldn't accept.

(To Archie.) I didn't accept.

ARCHIE: He already has a date. You heard him...

GEORGE: True. True. I do. I do.

MARGY: With whom?

GEORGE: Who?

MARGY: With whom?

ARCHIE: With a fig.

MARGY: With whom, Georgie? Somebody we know? Somebody who might have been a cheerleader? A twirler? A top speller? A class clown? A most-likely-to-succeed? With whom, Georgie, whom? *(Pauses; moves to George.)* I am really quite curious, George. Really amazingly so. Strikingly so. I should even say *remarkably* so. *(Pauses; waits a moment, staring at the astonished George Ferguson; then, with a strong, studied Boston accent, she again speaks.)* I'm wicked awful anxious for yo'r answer, George! Let's hear it!

GEORGE: *(Stunned.)* What .. what are you...askin'?

MARGY: Who's your date, George? Who's the lucky...piece of fruit?

GEORGE: I...I don't have any, Margie.

MARGY: Any what, George? The antecedent to your pronoun is somehow quite obscure. Any date? Any fruit? Any what, George, hmmm?

GEORGE: Any date. I got no date.

MARGY: A good looking fellow like you? No date? What is this world coming to? *(Pauses.)* There's a Chinese take-out on Route Twenty-eight, George, down by the miniature golf. You have money?

GEORGE: Well, yuh...for what?

MARGY: Moo Shoo Pork and three pancakes...

ARCHIE: What's going on here?

MARGY: George is going out for food...for the three of us.

GEORGE: I'm not that hungry...

ARCHIE: You and I are going out alone, Margie. That's a deal.

MARGY: George is going out, Archie. Right now. You and I are staying here...alone.

GEORGE: What are you? Planning som'pim' while I'm gone, Margy?

MARGY: In what sense, George?

GEORGE: With Archie?

MARGY: Am I planning som'pin'? With Archie? While you're gone, George? *(Pauses.)* Such as what?

GEORGE: Oh, I dunno…hanky-panky…

MARGY: Am I planning hanky-panky with Archie while you're gone, George? Just maybe I am.

(Margy walks, wordlessly, around Archie. She now stands behind Archie, who looks at Margy as though she's just agreed to "hanky-panky"…and then some.)

ARCHIE: Write down our orders, George.

GEORGE: I don't like this.

ARCHIE: *(Takes pencil and paper.)* You write 'em out, Margy, so's George can just give 'em over to the Chinaman…okay?

MARGY: *(Thickly accented pronunciation here.)* Sure. *(She takes pad and pencil.)* My husband, Edgar, was an absolute fiend for the Oriental…especially Moo Shoo Pork. He loved to roll his own…

GEORGE: How come you like Archie, Marg? How come you picked him, say, over me?

ARCHIE: What's this I'm hearing?

GEORGE: I'm just curious, Arch! No sweat! No sweat here at all, huh? No *suh!*

MARGY: Picked Archie, George? How come? You mean over all the guys in our little gang?

GEORGE: Well, over, say, *me*, yuh.

MARGY: Picked Archie over you, ohhh…Well, for one thing, George, I forgot you, altogether. Nothing personal in it, mind you, but you'd just melted into the faceless pack…you were specifically forgotten, George. In fact, to this very moment, the best I can do is come up with a very porky, very mean little guy with a middle "K" like yours, but that couldn't've be'n you, right? *(Smiles, shrugs.)* As for "picking" Archie, we bumped into each other at Mals. I smiled, he smiled. I called him for dinner, he accepted. And that is the long and short of it, George. I am getting quite hungry. I would hate to return to my poor brother's deathbed, unfed. It's a tough enough vigil, as it is. Don't you agree? *(Suddenly angry.)* Don't…you…agree?

GEORGE: *(After a confused pause.)* Yeh, well, I lost a lot a weight right after senior year. Yuh…I did.

MARGY: *(Gets her sweater, starts upstage.)* Listen, you guys, I'll go off for dinner, okay? You keep working…you stay put. I'll go.

ARCHIE: Like hell you will!

(To George.) Like hell she will…huh?

GEORGE: I'll do it.

ARCHIE: Right. *(Archie shoves George toward door.)*

MARGY: Nonsense...I wouldn't want to split you two up...

GEORGE: No, I'll do it...

(Archie throws George's jacket at him.)

ARCHIE: Go, George!

GEORGE: I said I would... *(Starts to loading door.)* I don't know were. *(To Margie.)* Where?

MARGY: Chinese take-out. Route Twenty-eight, Stoneham. Is it still there? *(Writes out order.)*

ARCHIE: Yup. Chinese place, near the miniature golf...

MARGY: Here, George. Hand this note to the Chinese man at the counter, and, for God's sake, tip him fifteen percent! Go now, go, go... shoo... scat...

ARCHIE: You heard her!

GEORGE: *(Starts to loading door, stops.)* I really hate this... *(Starts again to loading doors; stops again.)* A nice girl like you, Margie. Swede'd be pissed...

ARCHIE: Will you get movin'? We're famished here! We want some grub, huh? You're keepin' us from it. George! That ain't nice or polite!

GEORGE: That's just bullshit! You're just tryin' ta get alone with Margie...

ARCHIE: I'll kill you, George. I swear ta God I will!

MARGY: Go, George... *(Smiles.)* It's alright... *(Pauses.)* Really...

GEORGE: *(Moves to door; stops.)* I'm gonna make this real fast. Don't you worry...

(Goes to door, stops, returns to locker, finds coat, slips it on, returns to door, stops, returns to Archie, makes universal "I've got no money" signal [rubs thumb and forefinger together]. Archie smiles, gives George $20 bill, George takes money. Exits. Archie looks at Margy and smiles. He moves to the loading doors, closes them.)

ARCHIE: Well, huh, well, look at us, huh, Marg...just the two of us, huh? All alone here...you and me. Wellllll... *(Smiles. There is a short silence.)* How's it goin'?

MARGY: It's going quite well, Archie. Quite well. I'm so glad to be back...to have seen you again...and George...in the flesh... *(Smiles, pauses. There is a short silence.)* We've got our work cut out for us, don't we, Arch?

ARCHIE: *(Motions to baler.)* This?

(Margy laughs.)

You mean baling?

(Margy stares at Archie, who shifts his weight nervously from foot to foot.)
Uh, Marg, if we're gonna…you know…we'd, uh, better, uh, well, uh, you know, right?

MARGY: I beg your pardon?

ARCHIE: Uh, well, there isn't a lot of time, Marg…

MARGY: For what purpose?
(Archie walks to her, wordlessly, embarrassedly. He puckers up his lips and waits to be kissed; his lips and face on the open air between them. Margy stares at him a moment; smiles.)
Oh, I see: kissing?

ARCHIE: Do you…wanna?

MARGY: Oh, well, no, Archie, I don't wanna…really. I think you and I have done enough kissing for one lifetime, don't you, Archie, really?

ARCHIE: I, uh, I can understand 'n all…really, sure. Yuh, well, I do, yuh, I do understand.
(Pauses.) I'm a *lunk*, right? A real lunk…

MARGY: No, Archie…That's hardly the reason…

ARCHIE: That's the reason. It's true too. I'm a lunk…a local…a lummox, too. I understand, I do, yuh, I do understand. You went away and you got yourself *terrific*…really…ya did, Marg: You look just *great!* Here I am: Archie Crisp. I mean, Christ! What've I got to offer a woman's traveled halfway around the world, probably? Maybe even all the way…

MARGY: All the way. Yuh. Twice.

ARCHIE: Ya see?? Twice. Jees, Marg, don't let it worry ya none, really. You don't wanna make love with old Archie Crisp, he's gonna understand, really. Call me crazy, Marg, but I really do understand. Really, I know that. I do, uh, well, I do kinda hav'ta ask a favor of you, though, Marg, if ya don't mind…

MARGY: What's the favor, Archie?

ARCHIE: I agree to your stipulation of no lovemakin' and hands-off and all, but Marg?…This is really important to me…*(He pauses; looks down and then to her directly.)* Don't tell George, okay?
(Margy turns from Archie, smiles. She pauses a moment. Her smile is gone. She faces Archie again.)

MARGY: I was seventeen, Archie. Seventeen…
(Archie averts his eyes; faces front, bows his head.)

(The curtain falls.)

END OF ACT ONE

ACT TWO

Later, same night. Lights up. If Act I light-source was daylight through shop's windows and skylights, Act II's lighting is from overhead electrical fixtures. George sits on chair, stage right, drinking beer, watching Margy paying rapt attention to Archie, who performs a story for her, enthusiastically. George watches, jealous of Archie's attention to Margy, and, at the same time, jealous of Margy's attention to Archie. Remains of George and Archie's eaten Chinese take-out meals visible. Many crushed beer cans (dead soldiers) near George's feet.

ARCHIE: When I was a little guy, I used to work here every Saturday. I got two bucks, which was a big deal then...wicked big. *(Smiles.)* Used ta be maybe seven, eight winoes used ta work here weekends...for my Uncle Max...before Spike the Loon worked with us...I was just a kid. *(Pauses; lost in a memory.)* "Lum" is what we called the big one. His name was Alfred, I think...Some people called him Allie. Most of us called him "Lumbago" on accounta he had it. For short, we called him "Lum." Dumbest, meanest son-of-a-bitch ten towns around, and that's a fact. *(Pauses.)* My particular specialty was to climb into the baler, counta I was a kid and little and all, and push the newspapers tight into the corners. A good bale has sharp edges. The only thing was, getting inside the press spooked me. Gave me the willies... *(Pauses.)* Lum always used to threaten me when I was in here. He used ta say he'd pull the top over me when I was inside. Then he'd say they'd press me in with the overissues and sell me in the bale and I'd get driven up to Fitchburg, to Felulah's Mill, and I'd get dumped into the acid bath with the overissues and come out ta the wet press up there, rolled into fine paper for stationery... *(Pauses.)* The miserable son-of-a-bitch! Tellin' that to a kid, huh? He grabbed me in a head-lock once Saturday, right here on this spot. Lum. No warning at all. He just grabbed me. I figured I was a dead kid, ya know. I mean, I was eleven and he was forty. The odds weren't exactly on *me*, ya know what I mean? But, I took a major shot and I whipped him around backwards.

(He looks at George, who averts his eyes.)

I ran myself forward as fast as I could, whipping him around backwards...and he flew! He *flew!* He hit the front of the baler so hard, it was like his face exploded. It looked ta' me like his head was half opened up. He landed on the stack, and just lay there, blood oozing out of him, staining the papers. *(Pauses.)* I figured I'd killed him. *(Pauses.)* Winoes grumblin', lookin' this way and that…They started fadin' outta the shop…the winoes. *(Pauses.)* I was scared shit. Just me alone and the body: Lum. *(Pauses.)* I figured the cops would give me the electric chair…or worse; hangin'…*(Pauses.)* I was scared shit. *(Pauses.)* I figured the only way was to get rid of the body, hide him. The winoes wouldn't talk. Nobody'd miss him, anyway, right? *(Pauses.)* I started coverin' him up with newspaper, but his blood kept staining through. So, I started draggin' him over to the baler…to throw him in. I was only eleven, Marg. Can you get the picture?

(Archie moves to baler to better illustrate his story. George will soon move in closer to Margy and this time, Archie will register jealousy. Without a break in his story-telling, Archie will shove George aside and complete his story.)

Me, eleven, draggin' this forty-year-old drunken corpse by the arm to the press here…*(Pause.)* This very very one…*(Slaps baler, pauses, smiles.)* You'll never guess what happened, Marg. You'll never in a million years guess…*(Laughs.)* Gave me bad dreams for about eighteen years…*(Pauses.)* Lum got up. I swear to God. He opens his eyes…blinks a bunch'a times…and then…then…*(He laughs.)* Lum gets up, as though from the dead. The cut wasn't all that deep, just bleedin' wicked. He must'a been out as much from the wine as from the hitting the baler. Blood dripping all down him…He comes at me. *(Pauses.)* I figured he was gonna kill me, Margy. Get even. He didn't. He shook his head a couple of times…moves to his chino Eisenhower jacket, and he goes away. No pay. No finishin' the day. No attempt whatsoever to do damage to me. *(Pauses.)* That was a big day in the life of this little Arnold "Billy-Goat" Crisp. I can tell you that. *(Pauses.)* Gaining respect is what life is all about.

GEORGE: *(From the chair.)* Lum ever come back?

ARCHIE: Huh?

GEORGE: Lum ever come back here? To work? To talk to you? Whatever?

ARCHIE: What the hell kind of question is that?

GEORGE: It's a question. It's a question. *(George stands, tosses food container and beer can into trash, walks around back of baler, arrives between Margy and Archie.)*

ARCHIE: You mean, did Lum ever come back here to *get* me? Is that what you mean?

GEORGE: I didn't mean that exactly. I meant, maybe, to work again, to just *be*…around here and all. Did you ever have to look him in the eye? Face to face…Did he ever…well. Yuh…I suppose…try to get you.

ARCHIE: Once, yuh, he did once…

GEORGE: When?

ARCHIE: I'm done talkin' on this subject.

(Archie slams down his packet of newspaper on to the floor instead of into the baler and storms off away from George and Margy. He exits through loading doors, slamming door as he goes.)

MARGY: What was that about, George?

GEORGE: He's still jealous.

MARGY: Of what?

GEORGE: Not what: *who.*

MARGY: Of who? *(Corrects herself.)* Of *whom*… *(Smiles.)* Sorry, George, but I've never been comfortable treating an objective pronoun like a nominative pronoun. I'm sure you understand my meticulousness. I do hope you forgive me…

GEORGE: How come you pretend like you're not a school teacher? Everybody knows that you are.

MARGY: But, I'm not.

GEORGE: But you are. It's a fact. Everybody knows…

MARGY: I work for a college, but I don't actually teach…

GEORGE: New York University?

MARGY: Well, yes. How did you know that?

GEORGE: Lucky guess. What do you do if you don't teach?

MARGY: What do I do? *(Smiles.)* I criticize.

GEORGE: Really.

MARGY: Really. .

GEORGE: What?

MARGY: What do I criticize? What other people write.

GEORGE: You mean like "good" or "bad" sort a thing?

MARGY: Approximately that, yuh…

GEORGE: Don't people get like *annoyed?*

MARGY: The people I criticize? Uh, well, sometimes, yes…

GEORGE: You get *paid* for that?

MARGY: I do. Yes.

GEORGE: Must be nice.

MARGY: Being paid to criticize? Nice? This is *exhausting! (Smiles.)* What do you do?

GEORGE: For money?

MARGY: Yuh. For money.

GEORGE: I, uh, well, usual thing.

MARGY: Really?

GEORGE: Yuh, well…yuh.

MARGY: What, uh, uh, what would that be, George: "the usual thing"?

GEORGE: I'm, uh, on the Town…

(He looks about nervously to see if Archie has heard him.)

MARGY: On the town?

GEORGE: *(Quietly.)* Yuh, well…yuh. I've be'n doin' it straight through… since high school and all: on the Town. *(Pauses.)* It's a steady thing, ya know. Not too exciting, maybe. I mean, not som'pin' like what yo're use'ta, for example, but, it's who I am and what I do…as far as money goes kinda thing…

MARGY: You're "on the town" for money? There was a musical comedy by that name…You're not telling me you sing and dance, *professionally*, are you, George?

GEORGE: I'm on the Town crew. Cleanin', sweepin', shovelin' sort a thing. Whatever's needed, kinda…I had longevity on the Gultch crew…ya remember? Guinea Gultch?

MARGY: Oh. Right. Italians…Water Street…Guinea Gultch…I'd forgotten that…

GEORGE: I was top dog on the Gultch crew for ten years. Seniority, that sorta thing. *(Suddenly.)* They laid me off. Just before last Christmas. Goddam town was near broke. They laid me off, and Porker Watson —'member him?—and Stoney Webster: the rotten three of us. Merry Christmas, huh? The whole goddamn town was very nearly bankrupt. *(Pauses.)* I don't care. I don't. I mean, who wants ta spend their life cleaning up Guinea Gultch, right? It's great when yo'r a high school kid, pullin' down maybe sixty-five a week. Hey, that's big bucks, right? But when yo're thirty-seven, goin' on thirty-eight, Marg, and they're still payin' ya the minimum wage, huh?

MARGY: You haven't worked since last Christmas?

GEORGE: A year ago last Christmas. No. Nothin'. Things are slim around these parts, Marg. It ain't the good old days, huh? *(Smiles.)* Hell, I ain't kickin' none…Give me a chance ta think. All them years, sitting on trucks with six seven eight other guys: no time to think: always laughin' and kiddin' around…drinkin' beers 'n all…acting like juveniles, really. It was a wicked awful waste a my time. I'm glad…*(Quietly.)* Buncha' blow'ahs. *(Pauses; then to Margy, smiles.)*

GEORGE: In the days when you and I were…ya know…intimately friends kinda'…well…ya know…money was easy…I mean, what did it take, huh? A couple'a bucks for this or that? Pizzas, dancin', maybe a tank of gas? *Shit!* Easy as fallin' off a log!

MARGY: When, George?

GEORGE: When what?

MARGY: When did I know you?

GEORGE: All our lives.

MARGY: Intimately. When intimately? When exactly were we "intimately friends kinda'"?

GEORGE: You've got to be kidding, Marg.

MARGY: I'm not, Georgie, I'm not. I don't mean to hurt your feelings, but I remember your name and that is, as they say, just about *it.*

GEORGE: H.M. Warren School, second grade, Georgie Ferguson. Look at me.

MARGY: Georgie Ferguson? Georgie Ferguson? Georgie Kermit Ferguson…Kermie…Kermie…Kermit…Georgie Kermie…G.K.…*(She looks up, hopelessly.)* A blank. I am shocked and amazed to announce a blank. *(She smiles.)* You made no impression on me at all, George. Not any. None.

GEORGE: Georgie Ferguson. Look at me.

MARGY: *(Angrily.)* I'm…looking…at…you!

(A short silence; Archie's voice breaks into the void, from way off-stage.)

ARCHIE: He walked you home and sent you notes.

MARGY: *(She looks about, amazed. Archie cannot be seen. She smiles at George.)* Sorry, but, I believe my silver fillings are picking up police calls.

(Archie enters, hops up on back edge of baler; repeats his announcement, flatly.)

ARCHIE: He walked you home and sent you notes.

GEORGE: *(Yells up to Archie, above.)* Don't start in, Archie. That was a long time ago.

MARGY: *(Also up to Archie, above.)* Me or Esther?

ARCHIE: *(Yells down.)* You!

GEORGE: You, too. *(He pretends to be ashamed.)* I kinda' had a knack with girls, I guess…

MARGY: George, is the implication here that you and I used to…*go together?*
(George nods.)
We *went* together?
(George nods again.)
Like a couple? Like let's double with George and Margy, Saturday

night, huh? *(Pauses.)* A couple? George and Margy, Margy and George? That kinda' thing?

(George nods.)

My God, I don't remember them at all.

GEORGE: I bought you a ball-point…Mrs. Card's store.

MARGY: No kidding?

GEORGE: No kidding.

MARGY: I use a fountain pen now, George. The world has changed. Didn't you hear?

GEORGE: You let me look down your blouse.

MARGY: Down my blouse? In second grade?

(George nods.)

In second grade you looked down my *blouse*…at my second grade breasts?

(George nods again.)

The world hasn't changed much in *some* sectors, has it, Georgie?

(George shrugs.)

ARCHIE: *(Roars.)* If this ain't the most goddam *disgusting display of smut* I ever heard! *(Archie moves to Margy; pointing his finger in the accusatory. He is attempting to control his anger, which is a considerable effort.)* I got feelin's, ya know! I got 'em!

MARGY: I beg your pardon?

ARCHIE: I was hiding back there the whole time…listening in. I heard every goddam thing the both'a'yas said! Didn't you know that?

MARGY: I had suspicions, yes.

ARCHIE: You knew that?

MARGY: I did, yes.

ARCHIE: A man doesn't hide unless he wants someone to come looking for him, right?

MARGY: I am simply amazed to hear your…incisiveness, your trenchance, Archie. I agree. I definitely agree. I am…in agreement.

ARCHIE: *(A hostile imitation.)* Well, I am simply amazed to hear that you agree, dearie.

GEORGE: Cool yourself down, Arch…c'mon…

ARCHIE: I'll cool yo'r ass!

GEORGE: Come on, Archie!

ARCHIE: You were lookin' down her blouse?

GEORGE: *Every*body was!

ARCHIE: Bullshit!

GEORGE: *Bullshit* to *you!* Everybody was, and you know it *full well!*

MARGY: Could I chime in here?

ARCHIE: Stay out ta this!

MARGY: But it's my blouse!

GEORGE: You listen to me, Billy-Goat Crisp, you got no right bringing up no dead issues, some twenty-five/thirty years after the fact, ya know what I mean? *Do ya? (Angrily.) God damn it!*

ARCHIE: Look at him, why don't ya? Ashamed, right? Isn't he ashamed? Isn't that the look of ashamed that's written all over the son-of-a-bitch?

GEORGE: *Up yours, I'm "ashamed!".*..that'll be some cold day in hell when you catch Kermie Ferguson "ashamed"!...and that's the God's-honest!

ARCHIE: As for you, sister, you got no shame! No shame! It's one thing for me to be coppin' a look: We were boyfriend and girlfriend and that is a fact. But for this Kermie Ferguson son-of-a-bitchin' bastard? No shame. Nooo...shame...

MARGY: Could we just hold here a minute?

ARCHIE: You start out dirty, you end up dirty. That's a fact.

MARGY: Could you close it down, please, Archie?

ARCHIE: Showin' your tits around in second grade and look at you now. Look at you now. Some filthy mouth, huh? And where did it start? H.M. Warren School, by the snow fence, second recess. That's where. And I'll tell you another thing...

(Margy slaps Archie's face. There is a stunned silence. George giggles a high-pitched giggle, covering his mouth; feminine, childlike.)

MARGY: Put a belt on that indecorous and milk-curdling giggle of yours, George. I find it far too girlish for our particular circumstance...

GEORGE: *What??*

MARGY: Better. *(To Archie.)* First off, the matter of my mammary glands...my breasts...my *tits*...my *boobs*...my *jugs*...my *knockers*...my *set*...my *funny valentines*...*(Smiles.)* My perfect little orbs...*(Pauses.)* They seem to be causing you some grief, my breasts. They've been quite something for me, too, over the years. I can't say I find them quite as...exciting as you two do...lucky for me. Imagine if I were caught up in the irresistability of my own breasts? Trying to brush my teeth, for example. I would fumble with tube and brush, unable to keep my hands from my fabulous *poitrine*. My teeth would green and decay: rot...Dressing: It would never happen. I'd just keep ripping my shirt away for another look...another peek...the cop of another feel. First, a bad cold, then pneumonia, then pleurisy...dread disease after dread disease...ending, no doubt, in death...*(Pauses.)*

What a pity she had breasts, poor thing. They did her in. *(Pauses.)* Thinking it over, Archie and George, I will gladly give my breasts over to you, for whatever purpose you choose. George, you would wear them on the odd days; Archie, on the evens. And I'll be free to get back to work...to get back to sleep at night...to end the constant and unrelenting fondling. *(Pauses.)* I want you to have my breasts, guys. I really do. You do so seem to envy them...*(She begins to unbutton her blouse—two buttons only—to show her breasts to the men; Upstage.)*

ARCHIE: What are you doin'?

GEORGE: What's a matter with you?

MARGY: You should look them over before you agree. It's a commitment, having breasts like these two beauties. You should have a look...in case you want to divvy them up, for example. I'm told they're not quite symmetrical. You might find one to be somewhat more exciting than the other...

GEORGE: Close your shirt...

(He looks away; as does Archie.)
Close it.

ARCHIE: You heard him.

MARGY: You sure?

ARCHIE: Close it up.

GEORGE: You sure are weird, Margy...

MARGY: You think so? Every time I've been in the right circumstances for comparison...you know...ladies' locker rooms...faculty physicals for group insurance...and other orgy-like nude gatherings of mine, the weaker sex...I've, well, compared. *(Smiles at George.)* I never found mine to be weird, George. Small, yes, but never weird.

GEORGE: I didn't mean your chest. I meant your attitude.

MARGY: Oh. My attitude. I see. Well, I'll just have to watch my mental step, won't I? *(Smiles.)* I do certainly beg your pardon, George. I do certainly. *(Fingers buttons on blouse.)* Last chance, guys.

GEORGE: Button it up, Marg! You're makin' a fool of yourself!

MARGY: Archie? Peeks?

ARCHIE: Button it up!

MARGY: *(Buttoning her blouse.)* Thirty years of laser-beam stares and innuendoes until finally I relinquish my greedy hold on the adored knockers and *my God! My God! (Imitates George.)* "Button it up, Marg. You're makin' a fool of yourself." *(Completes buttoning.)* There is much I would like to make of myself in the few spots of time left to make anything at all, George, but a fool, I must admit, is not on my list. *(Smiles.)* We've settled the breast question, yes?

(No reply. She asks again.) George?

(No reply.) Archie?

(No reply. She speaks with thick Boston accent again.) I don't hear an answer...I "shoo-ah" am wicked awful anxious to hear yo'r answer. Hmmmm?

(George and Archie turn away.)

Now, then...The matter of Archie's saying, "You and I were boyfriend and girlfriend," meaning, I suppose, you/Archie and I/Margy Palumbo. Is that a fact?

ARCHIE: What are you: cute or som'pin'.

MARGY: Me? Cute? Never!

ARCHIE: We were! Boyfriend and girlfriend.

MARGY: B.F. and G.F.?

ARCHIE: Yuh.

MARGY: Before tonight?

ARCHIE: You oughta' have your memory checked.

MARGY: *I* ought'a?

GEORGE: Archie's still smartin' 'cause you two were...ya know...sweethearts, you might say, and I split you up.

ARCHIE: Bullshit, buddy! *Bullshit!* You didn't split nothin' but the supper bill for your last date...

GEORGE: What's that s'pose ta mean? You callin' me *cheap?*

ARCHIE: Cheap? You: cheap? That's a laugh! You ain't just cheap. Callin' you "just cheap" would be like callin' the Pope "just Catholic"...You are more than cheap, pally-pal: You are cheap*est*...

MARGY: I don't think you mean "cheap*est*", Archie. I think you mean "cheap*errr*." When comparing two cheapskates, one is cheap and the other is cheap*er*. Only when comparison is made among three or more cheapskates does one find the cheap*est*. It's a small point, I know, but...*c'est la guerre de la lange Anglaise!*

ARCHIE: *(To Margy.)* I think we've both had enough smart remarks from you, Margy Palumbo.

(To George.) Right?

GEORGE: Right! Enough insults...

ARCHIE: High-falootin' airs...

GEORGE: Hoity-toity airs...

ARCHIE: College-girl bullshit...

GEORGE: You're really tryin' ta start trouble here...

ARCHIE: Between me and George…

GEORGE: Me and Archie…

ARCHIE: Split us up…

GEORGE: Yuh. That's it.

MARGY: Bullll*shit*, buddy!

ARCHIE: This is what you went to college for? To talk filthy?

GEORGE: Swede should be ashamed…

ARCHIE: *She* should be ashamed! It's disgusting. Honest to God…disgusting!

GEORGE: Great guy, Swede, huh?

ARCHIE: And I'm gonna' tell you something else: I never liked Swede. I never liked *any* handicapped kids too much, frankly. I've got enough problems of my own. You, leadin' him around like you were some sort'a *saint!*…All the kids pamperin' the two of yous…pretending he was normal and all…makin' him Class President and crap like that. "Peter Palumbo For President 'Cause He'll Get The Job Done." I never heard such crap, really!

(To George.) Where the hell do you come off sayin' you like him? Huh? You never liked Swede Palumbo. You hated him! Where the Christ do you come off makin' statements like that?

GEORGE: Just makin' conversation. Passin' the day. Makin' civil talk. It's only right.

ARCHIE: *(Imitates George.)* "Only right…"

(To Margy.) You shoulda heard what he was sayin' before you came in here. He "likes" Swede…hah? What crap. You *remember* what Kermie Ferguson did ta Swede? Do ya?

GEORGE: C'mon, Arch, huh?

ARCHIE: Bullshit, buddy. Bullshit! You don't go shovin' him inta line .. shovin' him hard and then come up with "I liiike Sweedie-deedie!" Bullllllshit…

(There is a sharp intake of breath from George and Margy: shocked.)

GEORGE: I can't fuckin' believe you just said what you just fuckin' said! I've be'n watchin' my tongue the whole night! Honest ta' Christ! *(Laughs.)* Makes me *laugh*. *(Roars.)* Makes me fuckin' laugh! Call me crazy, Margy, but this just makes me laugh!

MARGY: Call you crazy? Nawww. I'd never call you crazy, George. If you're crazy then what am I? Then what is Archie? *(Pauses, very upset.)* If I were large enough…physically…I would probably beat you. I would probably try to kill you. If I were large enough…physically…I would probably try to kill you and I would probably succeed. *(Pauses.)* But

I would never call you crazy, George. *(Pauses. Attacks George, punches him in a rage. They move onto dune-like mound of papers.)* If you aren't the most odious son-of-a-bitch I ever laid eyes on...*(She weeps a moment; punches her fist into her own thigh, twice, in self-disgust.)* Stop crying! Stop crying!

(She continues to weep. There is a pause. Margy's attitude will change here. She has lost ground. The menb will be, for the moment, stronger; more confident than they have been of late. George is the first to speak.)

GEORGE: Look at her. Cryin'...Weepin'...Sheddin' tears...Poor kid...

ARCHIE: God damn. I've hurt her feelings. I feel awful...

(To Margy.) Shushh, huh. C'mon now, Marg. I'm feelin' just terrible that I made you cry. Come on, huh?

GEORGE: Guys like us, Marg, we don't mean half the things we say. We're just talkin', ya know? Tryin' ta be cool, calm and collected, ya know? *(Moves close to her. She continues to weep.)*

ARCHIE: All kiddin' around straight ta' hell, Marg, you want a shoulder ta' lean on, kinda, you know you've got mine...Georgie's, too. I mean, we're, well...your pals.

GEORGE: Not just boys on the prowl...

ARCHIE: Nothin' like that...

GEORGE: We're shootin' straight with you now...

ARCHIE: I always liked you, Marg. And that's a fact.

GEORGE: He did. I can vouch for that. I remember.

ARCHIE: You liked her, too.

GEORGE: I did. I did. That's a fact. I did.

ARCHIE: Why are you crying?

GEORGE: She's unhappy.

ARCHIE: What's makin' you unhappy? What, specifically, Margy?

GEORGE: Us, defintely. What we said...

ARCHIE: About what?

(George shrugs.)

About what? *(Archie moves close to Margy.)*

About what, Margy, about what? I said something about what?

(Margy continues to weep.)

GEORGE: I think it was probably me.

(To Margy.) Was it, Marg? Was it something I said? God damn, I'm really sorry. I hope that you believe me, huh, Marg? I'm really sorry...I hate it when a woman cries...

(Margy sneezes into hankerchief. She moves away from the men, but they follow after her, crowding her, forcing her, finally, against the baler. She

will stay there a moment, regain composure, her crying will cease. Her strength will return.)

ARCHIE: Most annoying thing in the world!

GEORGE: Drives me crazy...

ARCHIE: Drives me nuts...

GEORGE: Makes me wanna take right the fuck off!

ARCHIE: Get out'ta' the house! Drive away...

GEORGE: *Move* away!

ARCHIE: Make a fist...*(Pauses.)* Hit...*(Hits his own chest.)* Hit...*(Again.)* Make a fist and hit...

(Margy moves to Archie, places her hand on his cheek. There is a short silence. Archie stops raving, settles into her touch, instantly and absolutely calmed.

George is wide-eyed, staring, left out.)

GEORGE: Hey, Marg...Arch?...Cut the kiddin' around, huh?

(The touch continues.)

Come on, you guys...

(A false laugh wanted here.)

ARCHIE: *(Short of breath; quietly.)* Ever since second grade, Margy...You were the only one. Honest to God...

(Margy turns from Archie; faces George, moves to him. He is frightened. She places her hand on George's cheek.

She groans, pained to feel George's cheek. He giggles, pulls back from her touch. He places his hand on her cheek. Margy doesn't resist. She moans, pained, somewhat slumped into George's hand.)

ARCHIE: What gives?

GEORGE: A touch! Just a touch! We were friends, too, ya know!

ARCHIE: Let loose, George...

GEORGE: Come on, Arch...

ARCHIE: Drop your hand.

GEORGE: Jesus, Arch...you got some kind of sharing problem, or what?

ARCHIE: Drop it, Georgie Ferguson, or I'll mop this place up with you.

GEORGE: *(Steps back from Margy.)* Okay? Okay?

ARCHIE: *(Quietly. His feelings have been somehow hurt.)* God damn, Georgie...God damn. *(Pauses, turns away.)* God damn...

(Archie is weeping. He turns his face away from George, who stares incredulously at him a moment, realizes; laughs.)

GEORGE: Look at that, Marg! Look at Archie! Whooo-eee!! *OOOO!!* The both of yous: *criers!* If that ain't the Goddam'dest thing I ever saw! *Whoooo-eee!*

(George giggles hysterically. Margy goes to console Archie.)

MARGY: Archie?…Archie, look at me…Arch?

ARCHIE: Goddam town'll bury ya…You got out, Margy…you and the Moose…Why'd you come back? Kinda' dumb thing to do, Marg, don't you think? *(Pauses.)* I heard you were comin' back. Spike the Loon showed me the *Item*.

GEORGE: *(Starts looking through the papers in his wallet.)*

ARCHIE: "Spike," I says, "No way. No way is Margy Palumbo comin' back to this armpit. No way. She's an educated woman."

GEORGE: I'll show ya…Look at this! I kept the clipping from the *Item*. Margaret Burke, *nee* Palumbo…this is you…Palumbo, and Burke is Moose.

ARCHIE: *(Grabs paper.)* Gimme that. *(Looks at clipping. To Margy.)* This is you, yes?

MARGY: That is me.

GEORGE: What's the picture in the Item for, Margy? Arch? It makes no sense. I read it but it makes no sense.

ARCHIE: *(Throws clipping into baler. Completely new attitude.)* Let's get this bale finished, huh?

GEORGE: Hey! Picture in the paper for what? What did you do?

ARCHIE: Come on, George! You're not gettin' paid to talk!
(Archie is now quite energetically loading the baler. He tosses a bundle of newpapers to George. George grunts under the weight of the bundle.)

GEORGE: Hey!

ARCHIE: I'm balin' paper. If you and this famous woman want to help…If you don't want to help, that's fine too. It's what I'm paid to do.

GEORGE: What'd she do, Arch? What'd she get her picture in the paper for? Explain it to me!

ARCHIE: *(Angrily.)* Will you kindly get the bundle in the baler?

GEORGE: I don't like this. *(Pauses.)* I'd like to point out to you, Archie, that this Margy Palumbo is tryin'…and succeedin'…in making goddam fools…idiots!…out ta the rotten two of us.

MARGY: Archie, I'm not doing that.

GEORGE: You think Archie Crisp is just some jerk kid you can fuck over, huh? Fuck him over for a laugh and then scoot, right out and spend the next fifteen/twenty years tellin' your high-fallootin' friends about this local, see?…this *local*…this townie asshole, Archie Crisp…and how he came on to her. Still likin' her and all, after all those years since the second grade. *(Imitates Margy talking to a cultured friend.)* This Archie Crisp, you see, is what you'd call a really steady boyfriend…

How steady? Second grade right up till age thirty-five/forty…How's *that* for steady, huh? Those locals stick like glue, huh? Not much goin' in those locals' lives, huh?…couple of farmers, 'ceptin' they got no *farms!* *(He bales furiously.)* She's insulting us, Archie! That's it—she's putting us down!

ARCHIE: Shut it up, George, huh? Huh? Huhhh? You got the brains of a cruller. *(Tosses a bundle into baler.)* Leave me out of this. I'm just doing my work.

GEORGE: You're her supper date, right? I mean she called you, not me?…I'm just being friendly and all…not comin' on or causin' trouble or nothin'…just bein' friendly and all…for old time's sake… *(Pauses.)* And for the sake of our old buddy, Swede…who's kicking off…

(Archie looks at George.)

…out of memory for the Moose…and her former junior high steady, our own Spike the Loon…dearly departed…and account a she's got kids, Raymond, et cetera, and her bein' unhappy and all…mentally fuckin' *depressed! (George is moving toward Margy now.)* We behaved respectably with you on account of all those things, Margy, and what I hear is that you can't stop laughin' at us and insultin' us and playing it smart…playin' it smart…*(He lifts bundle up over her head, menacingly.)* I've got muscle now, Margy. That's one change from the old day is, right? Me, rolley-polley and all…That's one change you might a noticed, huh? George Ferguson ain't rolley-polley now! Opposite: George Ferguson is a well developed man…He's strong…He can lift…He's got muscle…Uh huh. *(He throws bundle at Archie.)* You workin' or you watchin', huh? If you want a bale wired and out and ready for your fat uncle at four o'clock, you got ta move on it, same as me…*(To Margy.)* I personally never held with the idea that women are weak and along for a free ride. *(He throws a bundle to her.)* Up and into the baler. MOVE!

(Margy catches bundle and throws it at the baler's front door, screaming primal scream.)

I do not like the attitude you've got right now! I think your pronouns are fucked up, too! I can't follow your ante-fuckin'-cedents!

ARCHIE: Cool down, George. You're hot…

GEORGE: *I'm hot, alright…I'm hot.* Why not, huh? How'm I gonna stay cool with Miss Margy Palumbo blowin' in my ear like she does, huh? *(Turns to Margy, then to Archie.)* This pisses me off. This just pisses me off. *(Grabs two bundles, throws them into the baler.)* This just pisses me off!

(To Margy.) What you're after here is trouble between me and Archie. That's the way I got it pegged. You get your kicks outta' causin' us to be fightin' and crap with each other. That's the way I got it pegged... *(To Archie.)* And I got a good eye. I got a good eye.

(To Margy.) I don't like the way you call me and Archie here dumb or stupid for not gettin' our picures in the *Item* the way you do... *(Displays newspaper photo.)* What's this anyway, huh? Does this mean that if anything...you know...happened to you, that a lot of people would come snoopin' around on accounta' you're famous, so's they noticed you were missing kind'a thing?

MARGY: My children...Raymond and Rosie...they'd miss me...They'd "come snoopin'"...

GEORGE: I don't like you using your sex on us the way you do...to split us up...me and my best friend, Archie...

ARCHIE: C'mon, already, George...

GEORGE: Your fame and your power...

ARCHIE: You're talkin' stupid...

GEORGE: Your eyelids, blinkin' up and down like you didn't know they were... *(Reaches for and grabs Margy's breasts.)* I don't like the way you use these on us, neither...

MARGY: *(Breaking away.)* Please, don't, George.

ARCHIE: Keep back...less you wanna die young, pal...

GEORGE: It's a little late for neither of us "dying young," ain't it, Goat? Dyin' young at our age ain't no more...No more... *(George slips around behind Margy and fondles her breasts, from behind her.)* I don't like the way you've been usin' these on us...

(Margy pulls away from George, quickly.)

MARGY: George!

ARCHIE: Keep back from her, George, 'less you want to find your nose on your knee in the mornin'! You get me?

GEORGE: What's there to get, Arch, huh? What's there you're saying that's not to get? *(George holds Margy in front of him, gripping her tightly. She is his shield, his hostage.)* You wanna come at me, Arch, come on... *(Yells.)* COME ON!! *(George flips Margy to one side; squares off with Archie.)* Now come at me!

(Archie turns downstage, away from George and Margy. He seems paralyzed by his terror now, frozen. His eyes are wide open, but unfocussed: blind.

George is amazed and frightened by Archie's state. He snaps his fingers in front of Archie's empty eyes.)

GEORGE: What is *with* you? You see this, Marg? This one's all bark. All bark! Not me. Not me! I got no bark at all, right? No college-boy bullshit, I'm just dumb little Kermie Ferguson from over Gould Street... *(Pauses.)* Who gives a shit, huh? Who gives a shit?

(Pauses.) 'member how we used ta kiss, Marg? The way you used to *tongue* me. Let's show Arch, huh?

(He kisses her. Margy responds stiffly. She stands straight. George breaks away, finds can of beer, swigs; spits in pretended disgust from the touch of Margy's lips.)

GEORGE: You've turned into kinda' a dead fish, Marg...

(To Archie.) She's kinda turned into a dead fish...*(Smiles.)* Not like the old days, huh? You remember how hot she was in the old days, Arch?

(To Margy.) You remember how hot you were, Bunny?

ARCHIE: C'mon, will ya, George!

GEORGE: *(To Margy.)* You ain't in no hoity-toity *Worcester,* or no *Springfield,* or no *Nooo Yahwk,* or no *London, England,* or no *Paris, France...*You're in none of those high-fallootin', hoity-toity, swell places, now, Bunny Palumbo! You're home. *Home!* And when you're home, sis'tah, you are what you are. *(Pauses; angrily.) What you are!!* *(Pauses.)* Gang-banged at Fisherman's Beach and this one comes up smilin' and beggin' for more...beggin' for more!

ARCHIE: George, for the love of Christ...I...

(Archie takes a step toward George, pulls George's arm. George pulls away, violently. George moves to a bale and kicks and punches it several times. Margy leans against baler and watches.)

GEORGE: No touches! No touches! No touches! *(He punches bale; turns and faces Margy.)* Gangbanged! Gangbanged! The whole God damned Senior Class party and this one is still smilin' and beggin' for more... *(In a rage; throaty, whispered yell.)* Bunny Palumbo, Blind Swede's sistah...Bunny, Bunny, hop, hop, hop, huh? Right, right? *(Full voice.)* Fucks like a what? Answer me! Fucks like a *what?* ANSWER ME!

ARCHIE: *(From the baler.)* Leave her be, George! There's no need ta bring any of this back up!

GEORGE: It's up, it's up! It's already up. *(Moves to Archie in a rage.)* I'll be the one to say what comes up and what doesn't come up! I'll be the one! You get me? *You...get...me?*

ARCHIE: *(Almost begging, on the ground.)* I don't see the point, that's all. I just don't see the point...

GEORGE: Because this girl forgets who she is, that's why. This girl thinks she can come back to town and be new...and she can't...she can't. That ain't the way things are. This girl ain't no Princess Margaret... this is plain Margy...Bunny Palumbo...Blind Swede's no-titted sis'-tah...our stuck-up Salutatorian. That's who this girl is! This girl is Bunny, the one who got herself gangbanged, Senior Class beach party, Fisherman's Beach, up Lynn way...*(Smiles. He sings.)*
LYNN, LYNN
THE CITY OF SIN;
YOU'LL NEVER GET OUT,
BUT, YOU'LL ALWAYS GET IN.
(Moves to Margy.)
LYNN, LYNN
THE CITY OF SIN;
YOU'LL NEVER GET OUT,
BUT, YOU'LL ALWAYS GET IN.
(Laughs.) Man, oh, man! This is a girl with a *baaaad reputation*, ain't that right?...Fisherman's Beach, Bunny-Marg...up Lynn way...You remember who went first? You remember? *(Stares at Margy.)* Do you remember? *(No reply.)* I don't hear an answer...*(No reply.)* I don't hear an answer...*(No reply.)* I would like an answer! Do you remember who went first? *Do you remember? Do...you...remember?*

MARGY: *(Primal scream.)* You!

GEORGE: *(Triumphant.) Right! Me! Kermie! First! (Glares at her, again.)* Remember who went second? Do you remember?

MARGY: *(Weeping.)* No.

GEORGE: Think, Bunny, think...think. *(Pauses.) Think! (Looks at Archie.)* What's wanted here is the memory and name of the man who went second...number two...sloppy seconds...*Sloppy seconds...(Laughs. Looks at Margy.)* Who could that man be? Who, Bunny, who? Try to remember...try...Who? Who? I don't hear an answer...Who? Who? Who was number two? *(Sing-song; a cheerleader's rhythm.)*
Who? Who?
Who was number two!
Who? Who?
Who was number two!
Who? Who?
Who was number two?

ARCHIE: *(Moans.)* Me!

GEORGE: Another country heard from.

ARCHIE: Me. I was number two. It was me. Don't you remember, Bunny?...*(Softly.)* Marg? Margie? Don't you remember? *(Pauses.)* It was me, Archie, Billy-Goat Crisp...*(Pauses.)* I was talkin' to you all the way...all the way. I went all the way...talkin' to you...Whisperin' in your ear...Tellin' you "I love you, Marg." *(Pauses.)* I did. *(Bows his head.)* I do.

GEORGE: *(Laughs.)* This is terrific! Whooooo-eeeee! *(Pauses; softly, simply.)* This is terrific. *(George walks about in two large circles, forming a figure eight. He is quite pleased with himself. He turns to Margy suddenly.)* Three! Number Three!

ARCHIE: God damn you!

GEORGE: Three, Bunny, three!

ARCHIE: Don't do this, George.

GEORGE: Number three, number three.

Who d'ya see?

Number three...

Number, number three...

Who d'ya see?

Number three...

(Giggling.) I don't hear an answer, Bunny-baby...

MARGY: *(Simply, softly.)* Peter...*(Pauses.)* Swede...my brother...

GEORGE: You got it, Bunny! You got it! *(Laughs; walks in figure eight again.)* This is terrific, huh, Arch? Isn't this terrific?

ARCHIE: Yuh. You got it, George. Terrific. *(Archie looks at Margy. Their eyes meet.)* Why did ya have ta call me? Couldn't you have stayed away? *(Pauses.)* Jesus, Margy...*(Looks away, extremely upset.)* Jesus.

GEORGE: Number four, Margy?

MARGY: *(Softly.)* Cootie Webber...

GEORGE: Are you kidding me? Or what? Cootie Webber? Number four? Nothin' like that...Spike the Loon was number four. Porker Watson was number five and Stoney Webster was number six. *(Pauses.)* Cootie Webber was number seven. *(Smiles.)* Me and Spike the Loon went over the lineup, couldn'ta be'n more'n three weeks ago...I led off, Archie was sloppy seconds. Swede was numero trez, and Spike the loon was the definite clean-up...*(Pauses.)* Cootie Webber was number seven. *(Pauses.)* Cootie Webber was The Moose's best friend, Marg, you remember? Asshole buddies, first grade right up ta' Graduation, all twelve years. I myself personally always knew Moose Burke was a complete shithead, but who woulda' guessed he woulda' gone for the town pump, huh?

(To Archie.) Married her. Jee-*zus!* Goddam married her! What a shit-head, huh?

(Archie is extremely upset. George sees him and stops cold, staring.)

If that ain't the most disgusting thing I've ever seen! Billy Goat Crisp, crying like a girl. *(Whistles.)* God damn... *(Pauses: new attitude.)* God damn... *(George walks in a figure eight now. His bottom lip trembles as he fights back the tears.)* What I can't believe here is that you let this one do it to us over and over again...

(To Margy.) He couldn't stand it that I went first. Ya know what I mean? *(Circling her now.)* He pestered me for years. I don't know what for? I mean, ya can't take a true fact and change it...just to do away with somebody's jealousy, right? *(Pauses.)* I went first and he went second. Kermie was number one and Billy-Goat took what was left... *(Pauses.)* I foxed him, Marg.

(To Archie, who is still weeping.) Didn't I fox you?

(To Margy.) He was s'pose ta go first. It was all his idea...at Fisherman's Beach...the love-makin'...with you, Marg. That was all Archie's idea...You can read all the books you want and speak all the languages goin', Marg, and you ain't *never...never...*you ain't never gonna live that one down. *(Pauses.)* Ain't that a fact? Ain't it? *(Pauses.)* Sure...

(To Archie.) Ain't it a fact, Arch? She ain't never livin' that one down, right?

(To Margy.) See? Talking about it doesn't bother me at all, sistah!

MARGY: *(Quietly, at first.)* I'm hardly your sister, George. In respect to my dear family. I must say, the implication is just hideous.

GEORGE: I don't like your mouth.

MARGY: *(Sudden rage. She spits her words. Wakefield accent. She is the teenaged "toughie" she once was.)* THEN WHY'D YOU GO AND STICK YOUR TONGUE IN IT!? *(She dances her rage about.)* C'mon, ya blow'ah! C'mon, ya blow'ah! Ya wanna hit a girrlll? Huh? Huh? Huh? C'mon. C'mon, c'mon...Ya look wicked stooopid, George. *(She takes the stage. Her accent has suddenly returned to normal; as does her manner. Her rage is her own.)* I was seventeen, George, seventeen. Do you know how old seventeen is, George? Not very. *Not goddam very!* Do you have any idea what it was you stuck into my seventeen-year-old MIND, George? Do you? *Do you? (Pauses.)* Why'd they pick me? Was I too provocative? Was it the way I smiled? Did I look available? Did I look like an easy lay? *(Pauses.)* What was it, George? What was it about me that you hated…so deeply…so completely…so absolutely…that made you want to *make love*, hmmm? Years, goddam *years* of walking around like a zombie, wondering was I really, deep down, underneath it all, *lookin' for it?* I remember, ya know, George. I really do. I was kinda standing off by myself, pitch black out, no moon at all…and alls'a'sudden sombody turns me around and kisses me. I pull back from him, tryin' ta' laugh it off, I say, "No, thanks, really…" And he's giggling this kinda' high-pitched girlish giggle. *(She imitates George's giggle, then, suddenly moves to George, faces him, eyeball to eyeball.)* Weren't you giggling, Kermie, huh? And you hit me. You took your hand and you hit me. I square off with him…with this Kermie Ferguson blow'ah, 'cause I ain't a'scared of nobody. *No…fucking…body!* *(She is now atop mound of newspapers: the sand dune. She will punch bale to underscore her anger.)* Seventeen years old, five-foot-[four]-inches tall…and you hit me. And I whack you back and you *(punches bale)* hit me and you *(punches bale)* hit me and I fall over backwards and you hit *(punches bale)* me and then you and your kind did what you did. You line up…*LINE UP*…and you did what you did!

GEORGE: You loved it.

MARGY: *(Crosses to steps in front of baler; squares off with George. In a rage: Wakefield accent.)* I DID NOT LOVE IT! I HATED IT! I HATED IT! *(Crying as she screams, the Massachusetts accent thickens, dominates her speech.)* You know what I was doing, you jerks?! You know what I was doin' while you was doin' it to me? Huh? Huh? HUH? *(Laughs.)* I was thinking that I was getting run over…by a bus…by the *Hudson* bus. That's what I was doin', I swear ta Christ! That's how much I *loved it!* *(Dancing in her raging state, she imitates.)* "Ooooooooo, Arch!"…"Studie-doo"…I liked Swede…"Yo, Margyyyy! Open 'em up! Spread 'em out! Here comes *love!*"

GEORGE: Is this what you came back here for, ya bitch? Ta' get even with us?

MARGY: You bet your ass I'm gonna' get even! Yuh, George, yessireebob! I'm gonna' get even. I am! Wicked awful even! I'm gonna get sooo even with you, George, I can taste it! Taste…it! *(Margy turns her back. George giggles nervously, looks down. Archie calls out to Margy, quietly.)*

ARCHIE: The only reason I got inta' line, Margy, was 'cause I didn't think you'd have me any other way. I was never good enough, Marg…never smart enough…never sophisticated like you were…That's why,

Marg. Ever since the second grade I've carried a torch for ya...som'pin' wicked...

GEORGE: "Ever since the second grade..." Jesus!

ARCHIE: Nobody planned it, Margy. It just happened! Honest ta' God! I mean, well, boys are always talkin' about wantin' ta' do it with this one or that one...and *everybody* was always sayin' they'd love ta' do it with *you*, 'cause you were, well, beautiful. But nobody really *meant* it: jumpin' you. It's just when George, here, well, *started*, everybody...wanted to, too. Everybody liked you...

MARGY: You *"liked"* me, Arch?

ARCHIE: I did. A lot.

MARGY: And that's how you showed me you "liked" me?

ARCHIE: I was tricked out of first, I was. Otherwise, Margy, the first words you woulda heard whispered in your ear woulda been "I love you"...because I did and I do. I do still. Marg...som'pin' wicked...

MARGY: *(After a long pause; calmly.)* "I love you" would not have helped. Do you have any idea what my dreams were like for the first, say, three and a half years after our Senior Class Celebration? *(Pauses.)* You think I really missed our reunions, Arch? Really? I had one a night— in my dreams—for three and a half years...365 nights a year for three and a half years. That's a shitload of getting-together, don't you agree? *(Sternly.)* Don't you agree? *(No reply. She screams at them.)* Don't you agree?
(She stands her ground now, staring directly at Archie and at George. Archie bows his head; George giggles.
She swallows a sob; pauses. She speaks to Archie, quietly, excluding George at first.)

MARGY: I had no plan to get even, Archie: none. I took this trip home, because my brother Peter took what they call in the medical game "a turn for the worst." He's extremely weak, extremely frail, extremely close to the end. The doctors told me Peter wouldn't be able to talk to me. But, as soon as I sat next to him, he talked. He has a strong memory of our beach party. He wept, and he begged my forgiveness. I gave Peter my forgiveness and it made him feel "wick'id good." It made me feel "wick'id good," too. Call me crazy, but I kinda' figured you guys'd be begging my forgiveness, too. But, the truth is, after having this little First Reunion, fella's, I would like to kill both of you. I would very much like to watch both of you suffer and die: Be dead.
(Archie moans; George giggles.)

MARGY: It looks like Getting-Even is just the kinda' guy I am.

ARCHIE: I, uh, I, uh, I'm sorry, Marg. I really am. I never thought what was done was a good thing. I never thought that. I am...uh...well... ashamed. I wish it never happened. I wish there was a way of takin' it back, 'cause I would. I'm awful sorry, Marg, I am. But I gotta tell ya som'pin': What they did was *dirty*, Marg. What I did was *making-love*, and that's the truth. I've never loved another woman besides you, Marg. Not even one. I'm beggin' ya to believe me and to forgive me.

GEORGE: *(In disgust.)* He loves Bunny Palumbo, this Billy-Goat does.

MARGY: *(Glares at George, momentarily; then to Archie.)* I believe you, Archie...and I forgive you, Archie, I do. *(Margy cradles Archie's head, watching George as she does. She prods George into action.)*

MARGY: Do you see this, George? I've just forgiven Archie.

GEORGE: I don't like this...You're just forgivin' him: not me, too? *(Pauses.)* Stay back from him, Bunny.
(Steps toward them.)
You hear me?

MARGY: You're not splitting us up, George. I choose my date for the Twentieth, Archie: you. I do...

ARCHIE: Really?

GEORGE: *(Genuinely upset, runs at Archie and kicks him between legs, from behind. George nows faces Margy.)* You think you can just hop back inta town and be another person from what you are? You are who you are, Bunny, hop, hop, huh? Huh? *(George unhitches belt.)* What I want here is what you gave my friend about an hour ago. What's wanted here is more love-makin'...

MARGY: *(Hits George.)* Put it out of your mind, George...

GEORGE: It's already *in* my mind!
(He moves to Margy, who slaps his face, again, violently. He reels backward.)

MARGY: Don't you raise your hand toward me...ever...*ever!* Not a hand... not an eye...not a word...*(She slaps his face.)* From you...nothing is wanted, George Ferguson...*(She slaps his face.)* Nothing!

GEORGE: *(Feeling his cheek. He is next to Archie now, who is standing, head bowed.)* You hit me? Great! Now, I'm hitting this one...*(George backhands Archie, who screams in pain.)*

MARGY: God damn you! *(She slaps George.)*

GEORGE: *(George backhands Archie again.)* I don't even like you *talkin'* to me, Marg!

MARGY: What have they done to you, George? What have they done to you to make you so incredibly dumb? *(Margy hits George. George backhands Archie.)* Have they beaten you? Have you been tortured? *(She hits George, again. George backhands Archie, again.)* I'd like you to stop it now, George. Put your hand at your side…George? Did you hear me? I don't want you to raise your hand to Archie again. Put your hand down, George.

(George smiles. He suddenly, without breaking his stare at Margie, hits Archie with the back of his hand, dealing a terrible blow.)

George!

(Margy swings at George, who shoves her aside. Margy falls on to her back on the mound of old newspapers. It looks as though George will rape her.)

GEORGE: Nothin' changes, Margie… *(He pulls her up to her feet, her back to audience.)* Nothin' changes. Not around here. Nothin'…

(He rips her blouse open. She is barebreasted. Her naked shoulders glisten against the filth of the old newspapers, and against the filth of George's leering, hateful stare.)

GEORGE: I knew it! I *fuckin' knew it!*

(To Archie.) No underwear on top!…You see this, Arch? *(Yells.)* Do… you…see…this??

(To Margy.) No shame. No shame, you. No shame…

(Archie pulls himself up from the ground and moves toward George, stands square with him.)

Hey, Arch, c'mon, huh?…You look wicked awful pissed off at me…

(Archie grabs George. The two large men wrestle. George gains an advantage, shoving Archie atop a low bale. George runs to baler, finds tool box and grabs a hammer. He bashes head of hammer against front of baler, as Archie advances toward him: a warning.

Archie moves in. George swings hammer at Archie's head. Archie ducks under, lifting George high over his head.

The hammer crashes down on the baler's steel steps.

Archie rolls George on to floor, twisting George's arm, forcing George to drop hammer to cement floor.

Archie throws George across stage into bale of corregated cardboard, face first. George rolls on to mound of old newspapers. George rises up on his knees, confused. Archie butts George with the top of his head. George falls over backwards, stunned, hurt badly.)

ARCHIE: *(To Margy, with a mad-man's rational voice.)* Eight-hundred-pound bales…eight of 'em ta' fill Uncle Max's truck. Been doin' it for years now…since I was a kid. *(Archie moves downstage; talks again to Margy in a mysteriously calm fashion, given the situation.)*

ARCHIE: What we do is buy up old paper, bale it, and truck the bales up to the mills and sell them...up Fitchburg...Ayer...Shirley.

(Archie goes to George and kicks him in the stomach. He then chases George behind baler and kicks George with a terrible blow. George then flies back into the audience's view, upstage-right, into stack of bales. He returns to Margy, downstage, continuing his explanation of his quandry about his life's labor. He is terribly upset.)

They buy our paper and they process it, see? And they make it into paper. Use ta' bother me that I was workin' so hard takin' paper to people who were makin' paper...I mean, it never seemed like too much of a life bringin' paper alls the way up ta Fitchburg, just so's they could make more paper. I mean, what's the world gonna' do with so much paper, anyhow?

(Suddenly, silently, George pulls himself up and circles behind baler on catlike toes. He clears his blurred vision, focusses on Archie. He then runs straight at Archie, grabbing Archie in a headlock. Margy screams out.)

MARGY: Archie!

GEORGE: *(Desperately.)* Billy-Goat gonna die...

ARCHIE: *Leggo...my...head! Leggo!*

(Archie relives his prophetic story of Lum by running George backwards, Upstage, then flipping George into baler, face first. George's face "explodes," blood suddenly erupting, staining front door of baler. George falls away, upstage, face down on mound of old newspapers. Margy bows her head, leaning against a bale, facing the men. Archie runs in panic, ratlike, in quick little figure eights, from George to Margy and then to the loading door, all the way upstage. When he reaches the loading doors, he stops and calls to Margy. George's blood is visible on front of baler, like Oriental brush-painting.)

ARCHIE: George...all bloody, Margy...We're in trouble...Margy...run... run, Margy, run, run, Margy, run, run, run...

(Margy goes silently to George, looks at him. She then looks at blood on baler door. She touches blood, pulling her hand down through stain, enlarging stain. Margy goes to locker; collects her jacket, scarf, sweater, purse. Archie runs around back of baler, downstage, calls across to Margy, begs her to leave.)

ARCHIE: Please, Margy, run, run...run, Margy, please, run, please?...

(Margy moves a few steps toward Archie, stops when makes eye-contact with Archie; speaks.)

MARGY: *(Simply, clearly.)* I'll be back, Archie. It's a long list. *(Margy moves directly to loading doors, exits the play, slamming door behind her.*

Archie is stunned, unmovingly. He runs in ratlike half-circle to loading-doors, as if to prove to himself that Margy is really gone. He again moves to the fallen George.)

ARCHIE: Kermie? Kermie? C'mon, Kermie, we got ta run. Kermie? It's Billy-Goat, Kermie? *(Rolls George over; sees that George is dead. Groans.)* Oh, Jesus! Archie Crisp just killed Georgie Ferguson and ther's gonna be wicked awful hell-ta-pay…*(Returns to George.)* C'mon. Kermie, huh? We gotta run! Kermie! C'mon, Kermie…Don't be dead, Kermie, don't be dead. *(Archie lifts George's arm and tries to coax George back into life. He drags George by the feet to front of baler.)* This ain't funny, Kermie, ya dumb blow'ah…C'mon, huh? This here's wicked awful scarey, Kerm! Kermie! Don't be dead, Kermie…
(Archie covers George with old newspapers.) Oh, Jesus! Kermie? Don't be dead, Kermie…Don't be dead, Kermie…Don't be dead, Kermie… DON'T BE DEAD! *(Archie stands, back to baler, the mound that is George's newspaper-covered dead body at Archie's feet. Archie's breathing is loud, labored, rythmical. Archie stares straight out into auditorium. His eyes are dead, hollow. It is the stare of a blind man. He breathes deeply, four audible breaths. All lights fade out, but for single work-light overhead. Archie's breathing stops. There is a moment of absolute silence. Sudden blackout.)*

END OF PLAY

Park Your Car
In Harvard Yard

For Gillian.

AUTHOR'S NOTE

I have suggested sequences of action *between the scenes of the play* that will allow the play to continue in full light, rather than forcing the audience to wait trough black-outs between scenes.

Costume changes are really unnecessary in this play. It's possible for both Jacob and Kathleen to use old coat-sweaters, from time to time, to indicate the passage of time, or the changing of seasons. I recommend that the actors change clothing in full light. It is a mistake to make the audience wait in a black-out for costume or prop changes: neither will be visible to the audience...and, be warned: the steam will go out of the kettle if there are too many blackouts! I suggest that there be three or four blackouts at most, to indicate the changing of Summer to Fall and Fall to Winter...no more.

Another note: Sentimentality to be avoided at any cost.

And another note: The first scenes of the play should contain great mystery, great tension: Has Kathleen come to this house to kill Brackish? Why is she so hostile toward him? Why is he so strange with her? Mine this tension. It will deflect the audience's attention from the fact very little else is happening (for the moment).

A final note: When looked at from Kathleen's point of view, the play seems to me to be about gaining strength, courage and knowledge. At the start of the play, Kathleen has little of any of the above. By the end of the play, Kathleen has more than enough of all of the above. When looked at from Brackish's point of view, the play seems to me to be about sharing strength, courage and knowledge. But for the grace of (or lack of) an education, I think Jacob Brackish and Kathleen O'Hara are the same person.

Enough said.

I.H.
Paris, France—Gloucester, Mass.
1990-91

PRODUCTION HISTORY

Park Your Car in Harvard Yard was originally produced by Los Angeles Actors Theatre, and Bill Bushnell as Artistic Director and Diane White as Producer. The production featured Barbara Babcock as Kathleen Hogan and Stefan Gerash as Jacob Brackish and was directed by Bill Bushnell.

The Gloucester Stage Company (Israel Horovitz, Artistic Director, Ian McColl, Managing Director) production of *Park Your Car in Harvard Yard* featured Dossy Peabody as Kathleen Hogan and Thomas Celli as Jacob Brackish. The production was directed by Richard Hughes.

Subsequently, the play was workshopped at Manhattan Theatre Club featuring Ellen Burstyn as Kathleen Hogan and Burgess Meredith as Jacob Brackish. Michael McNamara was the radio voice of Byron Weld. The MTC production was directed by Lynne Meadow. Manhattan Theatre Club's premiere of the play was on February 28, 1984.

The French premiere of *Park Your Car in Harvard Yard* featured Jane Birkin as Kathleen Hogan and Pierre Dux as Jacob Brackish. The production, directed by Jean-Loup Dabadie, closed during the second year of it's run due to the death of Mr. Dux. Subsequently, the play reopened, and played for another two seasons, starring Sonia Vollereaux and Jacques DuFilho, directed by Jacques Rosny.

Park Your Car in Harvard Yard opened on Broadway at The Music Box Theatre on November 7, 1991, produced by Robert Whitehead, Roger L. Stevens and Kathy Levin; set design by Ben Edwards; costume design by Jane Greenwood; lighting design by Thomas R. Skelton, sound design by John Gromada; directed by Zoe Caldwell.

Kathleen Hogan . . . . Judith Ivey
Jacob Brackish . . . . Jason Robards
Voice of Byron Weld . . . . Christopher Plummer

CHARACTERS
    Jacob Brackish, 80(ish), a Yankee Jew, Gloucester native.
    Kathleen Hogan, 40(ish), an Irish Catholic Yankee, Gloucester
        native.
    Voice of Byron Weld, an elderly disk-jockey.

PLACE
    The action of the play is set in the upstairs and downstairs rooms
of the home of Jacob Brackish, East Gloucester, Massachusetts: a small
1850s wooden-framed, two-story Victorian house, with slightly Gothic
pretensions.

TIME
    From one Winter to the next: the final year of Jacob Brackish's life.

SEQUENCE OF SCENES
    Scene One – End of Winter.
    Scene Two – Spring/Summer. (Tourists in town.)
    Scene Three – Autumn. (Tourists gone from town.)
    Scene Four – Start of Winter.

PARK YOUR CAR IN HARVARD YARD

SCENE ONE
The End of Winter

The audience is seated. House lights remaining up, in auditorium. We hear Vivaldi, Concerto in A Minor, played over auditorium loudspeaker.

The voice of Byron Weld interrupts the music to make a small announcement—a plea for money for his one-man fm-radio station. As Weld speaks, Vivaldi fades under.

Byron Weld's voice is the quintessential sound of North Shore Massachusetts speech. It is the very essence of "wicked awful"…it hems and it haws. It is a veritable symphony of upper nasal croak and squeal, combined with splintery timbres of remarkably old age; years of poverty; a lifetime of frustration.

BYRON WELD: #1 *(Over loudspeaker.)* This is Byron Weld, WGLO- fm, Gloucester, Massachusetts, on Cape Ann. If you think Wint'ah's rough where you're sittin', try comin' 'round here by the transmitt'ah! You'll know what *rough* is! I got so many air- leaks around the windows, every time the wind blows, the curtains shoot out straight, parallel to the floor and the ceilin' which, by the way, stopped leakin', finally, 'cause it's so cold in here, the water that was pouring through the holes *actually froze up*...buttt, you'll never hear *me* complain! *(New, solicitous attitude.)* Donations can be addressed to me, Byron Weld, WGLO-fm, Gloucester, Massachusetts, 01930. Don't hold back 'cause you think what you're sendin' is too small. I'll take anything...

(The auditorium lights are black by now, and we begin to hear the sounds of a Winter storm.)

BYRON WELD: *(Continued)* Antonio Vivaldi lived from 1678 to 1741. He wrote five gorgeous cello concerti. This one is his Concerto in A Minor, RV422, on an RCA Red Seal Recording featuring Ofra Hanroy, on the cello, with Paul Robinson conducting.

(We again hear the agonizing sound of the Andante of Vivaldi's Concerto in A Minor, soft, baroque. Additionally, we hear the storm sounds, now increased. Music to full.

Note: The season is Winter. Any exterior foliage on set is without greenery: absolutely bare.

Lights up in rooms of late 19th C. woodframed "Gothic Victorian" house.

Upstairs, two bedrooms visible, but, dimly lit in this first scene of play. Downstairs, we see living room, dining area, and kitchen alcove. Overstuffed chair, Center; sofa, bookshelves crammed with books, stereo and speakers (prominent), substantial collection of records, CDs and cassettes on bookcase.

It is February, deadly cold; night. In the distance, the wind howls, the odd hound bays, the copious buoys sway, causing their warning bells to chime; the lighthouse foghorn bleets its endless caution; a seagull screeches out in hunger. A seasonal thunderclap claps.

Jacob Brackish and Kathleen Hogan stand near the door. Brackish is ancient and frail of frame, but he is powerful and immeasurably authoritative. By contrast, Kathleen is quiet and mousey. She is a strong-backed woman, around the age of forty. Both are quite tweedy. Brackish wears baggy trousers, dress shirt, necktie, and baggy wool coat-sweater. Kathleen wears wool skirt, black tights, and wool sweater. A swatch of black fabric is in evidence; pinned to Kathleen's sweater. She is in mourning. Brackish holds Kathleen's dripping wet raincoat and is about to find a hook on which to hang it. She clutches dripping wet boots.

Note: Hearing-aid in Brackish's right ear prominent.

Kathleen stares at Brackish each time he looks away. When he looks at her, she stares downward; frightened. He is animated. She is paralyzed. They are both intensely anxious. He goes to radio; turns off music.)*

BRACKISH: Kathleen I…I'm very happy you're here.

KATHLEEN: I…I'm very happy to be here, Mr. Brackish.

BRACKISH: I'm very pleased that it was a person like you who answered my advertisement. *(Notices boots hugged in her arms.)* You wouldn't believe how few people replied. You think nobody needed work around these parts. Not that you wouldn't have landed the job if dozens had replied. I mean…you would have…*(Pause)* It's not like I'll live forever, you know…You'll still be young when this is over, Kathleen. I can promise you *that.*

KATHLEEN: I'm not complaining.

BRACKISH: No, no, you're not…

KATHLEEN: *(Laughs, nervously; sees puddle on carpet caused by her boots.)* Gawd! I made a wickid big puddle on your carpet! *(Kathleen bends down, quickly, tries to rub out the wetness with corner of her scarf. She looks up at Brackish, laughs again nervously.)* Just rubbin' it up…

BRACKISH: Could you please let me take your *boots,* Kathleen?
(Kathleen removes a wadded packette of letters and money from her boot, pockets it.)

BRACKISH: Ohh, I see. Valuables…

KATHLEEN: Here. I'm really wicked sorry about yo'r carpet…
(Brackish goes to the doorway, hangs up coat and floors her boots. Kathleen stares about the room, intently. Her suitcase is near the door. Brackish lifts the same, returns to her proximity, smiles at her, nervously. Kathleen averts her eyes.)

BRACKISH: I imagine that your stomach's in knots, too, Kathleen… This isn't an everyday sort of occurrence.

KATHLEEN: I'm not complaining, Mr. Brackish…

BRACKISH: Oh, I know you're not…*(Pauses.)* I've resisted having a housekeeper, but, this last spell (I had) was a pip…I saw Doctor Chandler, up Addison Gilbert. He was my student, 2000 years ago. He gives me six months to a year, if I turn myself into the hospital for total bed-rest. But, I prefer to live it out in luxury, thank you very much, right here in my own house. So, you've got yourself a job, and I've got myself an employee.

KATHLEEN: I'm not complaining, really…What with my husband passin' on so sudden and leavin' me with next ta' nothin', I mean, really, I'm happy ta' be here…ta' be your housekeeper 'n all. Happy. *(Pauses nervously.)* Six months to a year is fine with me…

BRACKISH: Yes. I see…*(Hands suitcase to her.)* You're probably tired. You should go on up…I hope the room's not gonna' be too tiny for you…

KATHLEEN: Oh, Gawd, no! First time I ever had a room on my own! I always had'da share with my sis'tahs kinda' thing...Afta' I got married, a'course, I shared with my hus'bin. *(Smiles, nervously.)* This'll be my first room. My first bed, too...

BRACKISH: You never had a *bed?*

KATHLEEN: On my *own!* I always had'da share beds...before here.

BRACKISH: Ah, yes. I see what you mean...I think...Well, now...The things you dropped off, yesterday, are up there, already...I cleaned out four drawers for you. If you need more storage space, I can find the room, I'm sure.

KATHLEEN: Gawd, look at that! You've got about a million records. *(Smiles timidly; then looks directly at Brackish.)* I personally never saw the need for accumulation. It'll be fine.

BRACKISH: *(Looks up at her; confused.)* Accumulation of my records'll be "fine"? Your antecedent is unclear.

KATHLEEN: Oh, gosh, no! Not y'or records. I just meant my *stuff!* Four drawers will be more than enough for my stuff!
(Brackish senses Kathleen's deep discomfort.)

BRACKISH: We'll both be more relaxed with each other in short order. I know you're not complaining, Kathleen. It's just that the intimacy of the thing never occurred to me. These rooms have been mine, alone, for, well...*(Brackish pauses, uncomfortably; crosses to his chair.)* This chair has been my closest friend...my comfort and my company...my sole *confidant.* It's a hell of a thing when a man comes to depend on his chair not only to hold up his backside but, also, to hold up the other side of the *conversation...(He pats chair, lovingly.)* I've come to love my chair, Kathleen...Me and my chair...the two of us...against the world!
(He sits in chair, picks up writing-board, slots writing board across arms of chair: a perfect fit. Brackish now pauses. His eyes turn in. He is still and silent, totally lost in a memory. Kathleen turns away, looks up staircase, or at records. When she looks at Brackish again, She thinks he's dead.)

KATHLEEN: Mr. Brackish?...Mr. Brackish?...*Mr. Brackish!*

BRACKISH: *(Jostled out of his reverie.)* Hmmm?

KATHLEEN: I was just afraid maybe the doctor, you know, underestimated. I can bring the most wicked awful bad luck ta' people! I gotta' tell you: I have personally had all the death I can take for a while... *(Painfully embarrassed by what she's just said.)* I'd better go on up.
(Kathleen exits up the stairs. Brackish sits in his chair, looks out front,

extremely worried. We see Kathleen in her room, above. She goes to window, looks outside. She, too, is extremely worried. NOTE: *Escape-steps must be built into Kathleen's bedroom, leading into kitchen. When lights dim down in Kathleen's room, She immediately goes down escape steps into darkened kitchen. Continuous action must be felt.*

Lights crossfade to Brackish, downstairs. He goes to the radio, turns it on. Bach, emanates from the radio, filling the house. He then executes his morning routine, compulsively tidying living room... straightening papers and furniture, etc., etc., precisely. Bach is now interrupted by Byron Weld, who makes a second small plea for public funding.)

BYRON WELD: *(Over lightly playing music.)* This is Byron Weld, WGLO-fm, Gloucester, Massachusetts, on Cape Ann. You are listening to Johann Sebastian Bach, music that's been played continuously by music lovers ever since it was first written in 1725. Imagine! Music that's held up more than 250 years, when this music station won't hold up another twenty-five *days* if you don't send in some hard cold cash. This is a final warning!

(Brackish calls out, loudly, to Kathleen.)

BRACKISH: Kathleen? Hullooo?

KATHLEEN: *(Off.)* I'm in the pantry, Mr. Brackish!

BRACKISH: *Still?*

KATHLEEN: *(Enters.)* I've got about a half dozen more to go.

BRACKISH: Isn't it cold out there?

KATHLEEN: Oh, yuh, wick'id...It's freezing.

BRACKISH: I don't want you to freeze to death on your first day! Finish up in here!

KATHLEEN: That'll be alright?

BRACKISH: What'll be alright? Freezing to death on your first day, or finishing up in here?

KATHLEEN: To iron...in with you!

BRACKISH: It'll be fine.

KATHLEEN: I'll get my stuff. *(Kathleen disappears, and quickly re-appears, carrying ironing board. She knocks into furniture with ironing board; knocks pots off stove. She attempts to open ironing board. It won't. And then refuses to open. Finally, it explodes open. She sets up ironing board near desk in living room.)* Sorry for bangin' inta' everything...A strange ironing board can kill a woman. *(She giggles, nervously.)* No problem...*(Giggles again.)* I'll get the iron... *(She does.)* I'll plug in here...*(She plugs it in under desk; stands; touches iron; burns fingers.)* Oh, gawd! It's still hot!...No problem. *(She runs off, again, re-appears with laundry basket filled with white shirts about to be ironed, plus, an armload of freshly-ironed shirts; holds up shirts to iron.)* These are the ones to do...*(She now holds up armload freshly ironed shirts, on wire hangers.)* These are the done ones...They'll be much better over here by the grate where it's wa'm...*(Begins to hang the shirts from bookshelves, above the fireplace grate.)* They're still slightly dampish... The heat comin' out'ta the grate here will dry 'em nice.

(She now hangs freshly-ironed white shirts everywhere...The effect should be such that Kathleen's enthusiastic labor — and her boundless energy — changes the look of the room, absolutely. Brackish watches Kathleen, bewildered.)

KATHLEEN: Are you ready for another cup'pa tea yet?

BRACKISH: No more tea, Kathleen, please! I don't want to hurt your feelings, but I don't want to drown in my own living room, either! *(Suddenly, he whacks his hearing aid; yells at Kathleen.)* What?

KATHLEEN: *(Startled)* What?

BRACKISH: My hearing aid died out! *(Points to his ear.)* I can't hear you. I'm deaf as a haddock without this thing! *(He taps hearing aid twice.)* Just a minute...*(He crosses to small writing desk and rummages through drawers.)* I gotta' change my battery. I went dead on you...*(Searches for, and finds a new battery.)* Wicked awful thing, to hav' ta' depend on the likes of the Radio Shack to make the difference between hearing and not hearing. *(Changes battery.)* Ahhh...That fixed it. *(Suddenly, he is aware of the music.)* Ahhhh... Bach..."Concerto #2 in E Major".

BYRON WELD: *(On radio.)* Bach "Concerto #3 in D Major" played by the English Concert of London, under the direction of Trevor Pinnock...

BRACKISH: *(Overlapping.)* Goddammit, Byron, that was Number #2, E Major!

BYRON WELD: *(Overlapping.)*...This is Byron Weld, your host at radio station...

BRACKISH: *(Switches radio off, angrily; turns to Kathleen.)* Number #2 in E Major! You can take my word for it, Kathleen. The man knows *nothing!* *(He goes to his chair; sits. The moment his bottom touches down, Kathleen screams out.)*

KATHLEEN: Whoa!

BRACKISH: Somethin' wrong?

KATHLEEN: Iron's a little leaky. No problem.

BRACKISH: *(Looks at shirts everywhere. Looks at Kathleen ironing more shirts.)* You're not overdoing it, are you? I mean, there's no need to iron *all my shirts* the first day…I don't have any active *plan* for dress-ing-up…

KATHLEEN: I don't mind, really. I like ironing.

BRACKISH: Okay. Well, then. Iron. *(Brackish starts reading his newspaper: obituary page.)* Oh, dear…"Porker" Watson died. Scares me to open the paper, these days. 'Course, at my age, I'm runnin' out of possi-blilities. *(Reads a moment; looks up, again.)* Look at that! Crispy Franklin's son died. I'm so old now I've not only outlived my friends, I've outlived their *children! (Makes a noise.)* Fffhhh… *(Puts down the newspaper: enough awfulness: speaks to Kathleen).* You've seen some tragedy yourself? I don't mean to pry, but you did mention your hus-band's death…

KATHLEEN: Oh, well…no point in complaining, is there?

BRACKISH: Oh, well, I dunno'…I complain all the *time!*

KATHLEEN: I mean, nothin's bringing him back, right? Once you're dead you're dead…

BRACKISH: I suppose…

KATHLEEN: The worms crawl in, the worms crawl out kinda thing…
(He looks away disgusted.)
My Da use'ta say that…He also used'ta say that "all the complainin' in the world wasn't worth two-bits for a box'a clams, down Wood-man's…"

BRACKISH: Woodman's…You grow up local? On the North Shore, I mean? I thought you were living down the line in Woburn? Didn't you say you grew up in Woburn? ** (** *Pronounced "Wooobin"*)

KATHLEEN: Oh, noo. I was just staying up my husband's cousin's… She's married to a Woburn boy…McGrath…*(Suddenly.) Gosh darn it!*

BRACKISH: *(Stands; goes to Kathleen; inspects her labor.)* What now?

KATHLEEN: Leaked on the shirts, again…it's been doin' that on me all mornin'…

BRACKISH: Don't worry if you spoil a couple…I've got a life-time of white shirts. *(Looks around room.)* Looks like the Marblehead Regatta in here. *(He sees her fiddling about with the leaky iron.)* You can't fill it all the way. If you drain off some of the water, you'll be fine…*(Makes small joke.)* I think I bought that iron off President Taft…

KATHLEEN: Mmm…*(Thinks about Brackish's small joke.)* Oh… Got'cha!
(She doesn't drain off any water. She continues to iron. Brackish watches her.)

BRACKISH: Say, aren't you gonna'…*(She looks up.)*…drain it off?

KATHLEEN: No point in drainin' it off with just a couple of shirts to go…

BRACKISH: It'll only leak…

KATHLEEN: It's goin' better…

BRACKISH: Suit yourself.

(Brackish returns to his chair; sits. Kathleen completes ironing another shirt, buttons it on to a wire clothes-hanger, walks it past Brackish into living room, hangs it on an inappropriate place in living room. She manages to move furniture and papers, somehow undoing Brackish's compulsive morning routine. Brackish's space is clearly invaded. And he is clearly not happy.)

(Pauses; sighs deeply) This first day is probably the most difficult we'll ever have…together, I mean…

KATHLEEN: Oh, well, I guess, yuh…*(She crosses to get another shirt.)*

BRACKISH: *(His most practiced, most charming smile.)* You mentioned you had sisters.

(Kathleen is relieved. She chirps her answer.)

KATHLEEN: Oh, yuh…two, plus me, for three. Irish triplets. All three of us sis'tahs born in less than four years…They both went to Catholic school. I'm the only one got to go to public school. I'm the baby. *(Laughs.)* We're all "eens."

BRACKISH: I beg your pardon?

KATHLEEN: *(Steps forward to tell what is, possibly, thre best joke she knows.)* Me and my sis'tahs…We're all "eens"…Maureen, Doreen and Kathleen.

(Brackish doesn't laugh. Kathleen's courage withers.)

KATHLEEN: I guess they didn't have a lot of time for thinkin' up imaginative names or nothin'….

BRACKISH: It's quite difficult for me to follow the complexity of your sentences, Kathleen…the twistings and the turnings, so to speak "*We're all 'eens'*"…"*They* didn't have a lot of time for thinkin' up names"… The antecedents to many of your pronouns are not precisely clear…not as clear as they should be…*(Sees he's hurt her feelings.)*

KATHLEEN: I guess I should finish…up. *(She stands, goes to ironing board. She picks up iron. Water gushes out on to shirt and on to floor.)*

KATHLEEN: *God damn it!*

BRACKISH: What?

KATHLEEN: Oh, Lord! Sorry to be swearin' in the house!

BRACKISH: What happened?

(Kathleen lifts the arm of the white shirt that she has been ironing. It is brown, stained, ruined.)

KATHLEEN: The iron leaks brown rusty water…It's all over the floor…I can bleach this out…*(She puts shirt into laundry basket; starts to iron another.)*

BRACKISH: Aren't you gonna' mop it up?…The rusty water!

KATHLEEN: I'll get to it, later. No point in moppin' it up and havin' it leak again…moppin' it up, havin' it leak, moppin' it up, havin' it leak…over and over. I'll get to it later…

BRACKISH: It's your decision…

KATHLEEN: *(After a few moments of thoughtful ironing.)* I don't speak well, do I, Mr.Brackish? From a point of view of bein' understood quickly, or, you know, bein' a natural conversationalist kinda' thing…From a language point of view, I mean. *(Pauses; thinks.)* My husband cooked short-order. He never had much of a mind for long sentences. Just quick little ideas. "Hi. How's it goin'?" kinda thing. "I'm hot, I'm cold, I'm tired"…Those kinda' little quick ideas…I mean, the only thing he said to let me know the heart-attack was comin' on was "Heart!"

BRACKISH: "Heart!"?

KATHLEEN: That was *it!*

BRACKISH: Certainly not much warning there.

KATHLEEN: He was dead inside a minute. *(Irons; thinks.)* Coulda' be'n worse, I guess…

BRACKISH: I guess…

KATHLEEN: *(She stares a moment, lost in a memory.)* He hated music.

BRACKISH: I actually *taught* Music. Music Appreciation and English Literature…

KATHLEEN: Course, you did! You taught my husband.

BRACKISH: I didn't know your *husband* was local…His name was…?

KATHLEEN: Otto…Otto Hogan.

BRACKISH: Possibly…There were so many…Possibly…

KATHLEEN: Definitely! [*His name was*] Otto Hogan…We called him "Princie"…

BRACKISH: *(Sincerely.)* I'm afraid I don't remember your Princie, Kathleen. I hope that doesn't hurt your feelings any…

KATHLEEN: Oh, no, Mr. Brackish, really…it don't matter…

BRACKISH: Strictly speaking, I suppose it really doesn't.

KATHLEEN: I don't have any kinda wicked serious regrets .. if you get my message…

BRACKISH: I certainly do.

KATHLEEN: He was good to me.

BRACKISH: I'm sure of it…

KATHLEEN: We had our fun.

BRACKISH: No doubt of that…

KATHLEEN: *(Pauses; has a memory.)* He wore a bright orange shirt every day. Day and night. I don't even think they required it.

BRACKISH: I really don't get your message, this time, Kathleen. Syntactical! Who required the orange shirt?

KATHLEEN: Bob's Clam Shack. Princie cooked short order for 'em.

BRACKISH: *(He's had enough. He rolls his eyes to Heaven.)* Why should I want to remember this "Princie" person?…*(Realizes his gaffe.)*… Your husband, I mean…Was there anything unusual about him…?

KATHLEEN: He saved your life.

BRACKISH: In what sense, Kathleen?

KATHLEEN: It was years back, when you used'ta work summers givin' lectures on the tourist-boat, in the harbor…the Dixie Bell…Princie was havin' a cigarette out back'a Bob's, and he saw ya' flip over and he swam out…

BRACKISH: My God!

KATHLEEN: You were trapped under the boat with three tourists.

BRACKISH: Labor Day Weekend… *YES!* I was in a stupor from their endless questions about cheap lobsters and early Americana. A former student…swam out…saved us…and thank the Lord he did, they woulda' buried me with tourists!…I remember that he wore an odd uniform…orange…

KATHLEEN: That's what I've be'n tellin' ya!

BRACKISH:…He wasn't one of the good ones…students…I remember that. He wasn't one of the good students.

KATHLEEN: You flunked him in English and gave him a D+ in Music Appreciation.

BRACKISH: Really? I suppose I had to…

KATHLEEN: *(Moves to collect shirts froim shelves.)* It wasn't like he was dumb…retarded, or nothin'…

BRACKISH: Some were, Kathleen…some of them actually *were*… dumb, retarded. My memory-system has set up a kind of magical defense against remembering the failures: they fail, I forget. If "To Err is human" then "to forget is divine"…Forgiving is forgetting!…*Je ne me souviens pas, donc, je suis! Non momento ergo sum!*
(Brackish laughs heartily at his own arcane joke. On hearing his laugh, Kathleen wheels about and [accidently?] drops arm-load of Brackish's freshly-ironed white shirts, floorward, into the rusty water. An instant of shocked silence.)

You've dropped them in the muddy water! Oh, Kathleen! I told you six times to mop it up! Oh, Kathleen! What a shame! What a waste of effort! Oh, dear…Oh, dear…

(Brackish turns and goes to the radio, switches it on. Kathleen swishes stack of shirts around on wet floor, mops up water. Satisfied that he's found Byron's station, goes to chair, finds newspaper, opens same; sits; reads. Kathleen, in the meantime, has placed the soiled shirts in a saucepan to which she adds some bleach. NOTE: aroma of bleach wanted. Brackish sniffs the air; looks over at Kathleen, smugly.)

Brahms. Notice the contrapuntal shading…*(Hums along with music.)* Dah dee dah dummm…*(Calls to Kathleen.)* A composer of great sobriety. Don't you agree?

(Kathleen is nervously bleaching out the shirts. She fakes paying attention with false admiration for Brahms.)

KATHLEEN: Me? Oh, yuh…Marvelous.

BRACKISH: What the hell's that smell?

KATHLEEN: Bleach water. I could do it outside.

BRACKISH: In the snow?

KATHLEEN: I guess I won't…*(Nervous giggle.)* I forgot about the snow…

BRACKISH: It smell like more than just bleach…

(Kathleen suddenly realizes that pan on stove is on open flame, empty, burnt.)

KATHLEEN: Ah, shoot! The pot's burnt! *(She leaps to stove, burns her hand, she screams out.)* Ahhhh! *(She tries to pretend that she hasn't burned her hand.)* No problem! *(She does a little dance around kitchen after chucking hot pot loudly into sink and running cold water on to the thing, causing steam and sizzling sound in room. Brackish watches the entire sketch in astonishment.)*

BRACKISH: You okay?

KATHLEEN: Oh, yuh, perfect.

BRACKISH: It was an old pot. Not to worry…

KATHLEEN: Oh, no…pot's okay. It was only bleach water…

BRACKISH: In the pot?

KATHLEEN: Mmmm…

BRACKISH: In the pot that boiled away?

KATHLEEN: That's all. Nothin' black…

BRACKISH: Bleach was boiling away all that time…evaporating into the air we breath?

KATHLEEN: I s'pose. Yuh…

BRACKISH: That's Chlorine…

KATHLEEN: *(Corrects Brackish, lightly.)* Chlorox…

BRACKISH: When Chlorine evaporates into the air, it is deadly, Kathleen, deadly…

KATHLEEN: I'll crack the window…*(She opens kitchen window.)* There. That should be better…

BRACKISH: The German nation was censured by the entire world for using Chlorine gas in World War I…

KATHLEEN: You can hardly smell it now…

BRACKISH: Chlorine gas causes a slow, devastatingly painful death…

KATHLEEN: I'll crack open the back door, too…*(She cracks open the back door. She smiles.)* Smell's all gone in here. Really…
(Brackish coughs. Kathleen begins to scrub pot enthusiastically.)

KATHLEEN: I'll have this shining like a baby's bee-hind in no time at all.
(Brackish rolls his eyes to Heaven. He re-opens his Boston Globe; reads. The Brahms piece has concluded and now Bach's "Chaconne" fills the world, brilliantly. Brackish listens to the music a moment. He is embarrassed by his behavior toward Kathleen. He looks over at her; watches her labor a moment, silently. He tries to make calming small-talk, speaks.)

BRACKISH: I don't know why the Globe gives so much attention to the marathon runners. The sport requires no brains at all. It's just left, right, left, right. I mean what is the big deal, I ask you?

KATHLEEN: *(Absently, barely looking up.)* Hmmm?

BRACKISH: The Boston Marathon…

KATHLEEN: Mmm?

BRACKISH: It's weeks off, and they're already startin' to tout the thing…

KATHLEEN: *(Displays clean pot.)* See? Good as new.

BRACKISH: Why don't you take a break now, Kathleen…*(Pauses.)* You don't hav'ta' work day and night…It isn't as if we're goin' against any kind of deadline, here…*(Pauses.)* Sit down, Kathleen…Take a break…
*(Kathleen smiles. She enters the living room, nervously. She takes her quilting basket, sits on sofa, in corner of seat at furthermost possible distance from Brackish. Bach's "Chaconne" plays on, in spite of all.
Brackish looks over at Kathleen, who is now sitting on the sofa, intently working on a patchwork quilt. She is deciding among various patches which to applique and which to discard.)*

BRACKISH: *(Aware of the music; smiles.)* You hear this piece, Kathleen?

KATHLEEN: *(Intent on choosing quilting patches, doesn't look up. She fakes an interest; smiles and grunts, lightly.)* Mm.

BRACKISH: Bach. The "Chaconne."

KATHLEEN: Mmmmmm.

BRACKISH: The same few notes are repeated in different variations. Twenty-nine of them in all: variations. The untrained ear would never hear the repetition, but, I do. I hear 'em all. And they scare me silly...

KATHLEEN: Mmm.

BRACKISH: Over and over, nothing changes, sometimes faster, sometimes slower, sometimes broken into bits and pieces that accumulate in the memory and one day shock you with the realization "I've heard all this before!"...It honestly does scare me silly...
(Following speeches overlap.)

KATHLEEN: That's what scares me, too...the repetition...*(Pauses; Brackish barely looks at her.)* The waking up one morning and the realizing "I've done all this before...over and over again..."

BRACKISH: Even the beautiful parts of it irk and irritate...irk and irritate.

KATHLEEN: The seagulls screaming and screeching...The bed getting made and unmade...the food shopped, cooked, eaten, shopped, cooked, eaten...

BRACKISH: Twenty-nine variations in all...twenty-nine variations.

KATHLEEN: Huh? *(She looks at Brackish, absently.)*

BRACKISH: "The Chaconne," Kathleen...*(Annoyed.)* This Bach piece...
(Shakes head in schoolteacherish fashion; scolds her.) Don't you ever pay attention, Kathleen?
(Kathleen is devastated. She stands, takes her quilting basket and runs upstairs to her room. She sits on her bed. She is unhappy.
Downstairs, Brackish is thoughtful after Kathleen's exit from the room. He feels guilty. Upstairs, Kathleen sits on her bed; unhappy.
The "Chaconne" concludes. Brackish goes from his chair to the staircase. He pauses a while, as though looking upstairs. He listens, as well. He goes to bookcase and removes hearing-aid batteries from where he hid them, earlier; depositing same, in waste basket beside desk. He then covers them with waste paper. Brackish goes to the radio, carrying hearing-aid in his hand. On the radio, we hear Beethoven's "Diabelli Variations." He turns the volume up full blast, deliberately. Kathleen hears the change; perks up her ears.)

BRACKISH: Damn it, damn it, damn it! *(He moves to foot of stairs; screams up to Kathleen.)* Could you come down here? Hello? Helloooo?
(He now crosses to writing desk; begins fishing through drawers. He con-

tinues to call Kathleen as he searches for fresh batteries. Kathleen appears; top of stairs.)

KATHLEEN: Did you call me? *(No response; she screams over Beethoven blasting from radio.) Did...you...call...me, Mr. Brackish? (No response.) MR. BRACKISH!*

BRACKISH: I'll have to ask you to go out and buy some batteries for me...

KATHLEEN: Now? It's freezing out there!

BRACKISH: What?

KATHLEEN: Yuh, sure, why not...

BRACKISH: Be an angel, will you, and fire down to Radio Shack...Better still, try Tru-Value...yes, Tru-Value...*(Reaches into pocket, produces wallet and cash.)* Better buy two.

KATHLEEN: *(Makes an "okay" sign with her thumb and forefinger, three remaining fingers in the air above the circle.)* Fine. I'll buy two...right away...*(Kathleen takes overcoat from clothes-tree, puts it on. Takes hat from hook.)*

BRACKISH: Bundle up, now, young lady...I wouldn't want your catching your death on my conscience...

(Kathleen smiles. Brackish thinks she has spoken to him.)

What?

(Kathleen puts her cap atop her head; enroute to door, sneaks to radio; switches the station. We hear: jazz station, Miles Davis being played. Kathleen allows the music to play for a moment; checks Brackish. He doesn't hear: no reaction. She switches station, again, settling now on a raucous, caustic rap-song...MC Hammer, or, Ice T. Brackish does not seem to hear the music — thus, does not at all react to it. Kathleen smiles; exits, quickly, never looking back. Brackish, alone, engulfed in the dreaded music, sinks low in his seat. Dreaded music swells and then concludes.)

THE LIGHT FADES OUT

Scene Two
Spring / Summer

In darkness, we hear Byron Weld's voice, on radio.

BYRON WELD: This is Byron Weld, WGLO-fm, Gloucester, Massachusetts, on Cape Ann. You're in your wa'm house, with your heat turned back on, again, against this Memorial Day cold snap…no doubt toasty-warm, while I'm sittin' here on a metal stool, by the transmitt'ah, half-frozen ta' death for the want of heat. If you don't send in your contributions, this station's closin' down. No ifs, ands or buts. This next selection is on a Musical Heritage Society recording, "Symphony #40 in G Minor," K550, Wolfgang Amadeus Mozart…
(Brackish is at the stove, fussing with a hot pot of soup, bowls, cooking utensils. We hear Kathleen coughing, upstairs, off…three substantial coughs.)
BRACKISH: *(Calls upstairs to Kathleen.)* Are the vapors helping?
KATHLEEN: *(Calls from bathroom, off.)* I'm just now fillin' the bowl with hot water. *(She coughs; then, sneezes.)*
(Lights up in Kathleen's bedroom. Note: Season is now Spring/Summer. Exterior foliage now lush green. Kathleen enters bedroom; sits atop bed. She is bundled in gathering of bathrobes, towels, scarves; wears heavy stockings on her feet, over which are jammed slippers of the "mule" variety. She is a veritable symphony of pastels. Her head is swathed in terrycloth pastel toweling. There is a large steaming pot on her lap, producing vapors, which she inhales from time to time by means of an intricate system of toweling connecting the pot to her headdress. Chutes of toweling are employed to convey the vapors from pot to nostril. She coughs, six times.)
BRACKISH: *(Calls upstairs.)* A Memorial Day cold snap is just God's way of telling us that the tourists are coming, and that makes everybody sick. And that's no doubt why the good Lord invented chickens. So there'd by a cure. *(Burns his hand; screams out.)* Owwwwwwww! I burned my hand!
KATHLEEN: *(Calling downstairs; worried.)* Oh, God! Are you okay?
BRACKISH: *(He does a little dance, whisking his hand, flailing his arm. He calls out, enraged. A new voice: gentlemanly.)* You'll have to excuse this, Kathleen…*(He throws back his head, bellows.)* HO'SSSSSS-SSSSSSSSSSSSSSSSHHHHHHHHHHHHHHIIIIIIITTTTT!

KATHLEEN: *(After a short silence.)* Is your hand better?

BRACKISH: *(Calls upstairs.)* It feels just fine, now. "There's nothing so far gone that a little ho'ss-shit can't make it better." *(Brackish walks upstairs to her room carrying tray with soup, etc. Calls out, whilst on staircase.)* My father use'ta say that. My father use'ta say lots more than that, too. *(Enters Kathleen's room.)* If this old house could talk. What it's seen, huh? *(Pours chicken soup into cup, crosses to Kathleen. She coughs.)* My mother's secret potion. Many a chicken died so that you might live, Kathleen. I suggest that you drink this slowly and reverentially...It tastes like what it is.

KATHLEEN: *(Samples soup.)* Uggggggggghhh!...Dead chickens.

BRACKISH: *(Smiling his agreement.)* Dead chickens...Even honey tastes like medicine when it's medicine...My mother used to say that...*(Looks around room.)* This was my room. *(Smiles.)* This house was built by a stevedore...a lumper. It's a poor house. I imagine the original owner spent his life workin' the docks...

KATHLEEN: My father was a lumper...

BRACKISH: Hmmm?

KATHLEEN: Nothin'...Not important, really, go on...This house, built by a lumper...

BRACKISH: It's tiny, really, but me bein' an only child and all...it was spacious...a perfection. Imagine...living an entire life in one house... My father bought this house when he was 22 years old, with money he earned, sellin', door-to-door, off a horse-and-buggy. He was born over in Plum Cove—God!—over a hundred years ago! He was a Yankee Jew. Quite a rare breed. He spent his last cent educating me... wanted the best for me. *(Pauses.)* I always figured I'd move from here one day, when I married and had children, but, I didn't: none of those things. *(Pauses: another memory.)* Forgive me if you've told me this, before, Kathleen, but, did you and your husband have children?

KATHLEEN: Us? No. We never did.

BRACKISH: Understandable. It's already such a crowded planet.

KATHLEEN: I guess. All my friends were havin' em...Used'ta' trouble me, at first, worryin' why we were, you know, bein' passed over.

BRACKISH: I myself never wanted any...

KATHLEEN: Yuh, well, you weren't married, were you?

BRACKISH: Still and all, the choice is a basic human right.

KATHLEEN: Yuh, well, life's a lot different for Catholics.

BRACKISH: I suppose.

KATHLEEN: Princie was never bothered. He said he was glad to never bring any kid of his inta' this mess.

BRACKISH: My sentiments, precisely…

KATHLEEN: Sittin' with his body down ta' Pike's, I couldn't help but wonderin' if it might'a be'n different if we'd had 'em: kids…

BRACKISH: Only natural to wonder.

KATHLEEN: He was laid out four extra days, on account'a the ground froze up solid and they couldn't get a bite with the bulldozer ta' get his grave dug. I had a lot of time alone with him ta' think.

BRACKISH: Must've been grim.

KATHLEEN: Wasn't so bad. It was kinda' like havin' him asleep in front of the TV, only there was no TV. *(She shrugs.)* This cold is getting me mentally depressed. *(She smiles. Silence.)*

BRACKISH: I regret, Kathleen, that we have this odd coincidence between us…that your late husband was my student and that he…failed…

KATHLEEN: It wasn't like he was dumb or nuthin'…He was wicked unhappy when he found out he'd flunked English. He was supposed ta' repeat, in order ta' graduate, but he didn't…he dropped out. Since he didn't finish high school, college was out'ta the question…

BRACKISH: And you?

KATHLEEN: *(Kathleen looks up.)* College? Me? No.

BRACKISH: What held you back?

(Kathleen stares Brackish straight in the shoes.)

KATHLEEN: I'd have to say, more than anything, it was the grades.

BRACKISH: "The grades" in what sense, Kathleen? Antecedents.

KATHLEEN: *(Screws up her courage, as best she can.)* The grades you gave me in Music and English. They ruined any chance I had for a scholarship.

BRACKISH: You were my student?

KATHLEEN: Both subjects, yuh…

BRACKISH: But, I…My God, Kathleen! Why didn't you mention this before!?

KATHLEEN: No point…

BRACKISH: Of course, there was a point! I…I had no idea! *(He is shaken by this news.)* It's so perverse, Kathleen…really! You should have mentioned this to me, specifically…during our interview…You just let me ramble on and on and you never once mentioned this to me…My God!

KATHLEEN: I guess my feelin's got hurt, 'cause you forgot me kinda' thing…

BRACKISH: Kathleen, really. Do you have any idea of how many students passed through my life in fifty years of teaching two completely different subjects???

KATHLEEN: Lots, I guess...

BRACKISH: "Lots you guess"? Tens of thousands, Kathleen. Tens of thousands... *(Pauses.)* Did you fail?

KATHLEEN: Fail? Me? Oh, I wouldn't so much say I failed as I would say I was failed. Object versus subject kinda' thing...You gave me a C in English IV, and a D-plus in Music Appreciation, which, 'a'course, pulled my Senior average down too low for a scholarship, anywhere. I didn't even bother applyin', finally...

BRACKISH: Oh, Kathleen...I am sorry...

KATHLEEN: Doesn't bother me, Mr Brackish, really. No sweat...

BRACKISH: Oh, no, really, I am sorry...I don't really remember: that's the worst: I don't really remember. I'm sure I had my reasons...I was fair. I was demanding...hard, strict, but I was fair!...

KATHLEEN: I said that it didn't bother me, okay?

BRACKISH: There were so many...

KATHLEEN: Yuh. There were. In my family alone, there was a number. You might even say an astonishin' number...Mother, father, husbin'...

BRACKISH: That I taught?

KATHLEEN: That you failed. Good thing Maureen and Doreen went to Sis'tah school! You probably woulda' nailed them, too! *(She smiles at an astonished Brackish.)* You were the toughest teacher in Gloucester, Mr Brackish. Practically no one got away...from you.

BRACKISH: I was strict. It's true.

KATHLEEN: Listen, it's really no bother to me at all. Really. I hardly think about it. And I do understand. There are tests and kids either flunk or they don't. It just happens that most of the people in Gloucester that I was connected to, did: flunk. That's just the way it happened...the past is the past, right. Nothin's gonna change it.

BRACKISH: What was your maiden name, Kathleen?

KATHLEEN: O'Hara.

BRACKISH: *(Stands; stunned.)* Was it?

KATHLEEN: My father was Jebbie O'Hara and my mother was Francine Flynn...I'm in the Flicker with the green cover, tenth from the end, second shelf down, if you ever wanna' check it out...
(Brackish moves into window, bends forward, terribly upset. Kathleen is suddenly aware of his upset. Foghorn sounds.)

KATHLEEN: Mr. Brackish...

BRACKISH: *(Turns to her; suddenly.)* You lied to me!…What are you doing in my house? *(She turns away, terrified.)* Don't you turn away from me, Francine Flynn!…

KATHLEEN: What?

(Foghorn sounds again.)

BRACKISH:…Lying to me about who you are…tricking me into pleasant chat…*(He shivers.)* I feel cold. *(Tries to calm himself down.)* I will not have this terrible upset in my house! I never have and I never will…not here…not in this house. I simply will not! I'm going to my room. I want to be alone now. I should like to regain the sanctity of my home…I'm going to my room.

(A distant foghorn groans. Brackish moves quickly to his room, sits atop his bed, facing front, sadly. Foghorn groans in distance, again.

Brackish and Kathleen sit in their separate rooms, each facing front, each alone, but, inexorably connected to one another by their similar pride, similar guilts, their similar anger, their similar regrets.

Light fades down to spotlights on both…one moment…then, lights to black. In Black, tea kettle's whistle whistles.

Lights fade up again in Brackish's room. He is looking out of the window. He moves to his bedside chair, sits; reads. His hearing-aid sits atop bedside table, out of use. He has a headache.

Lights fade up in kitchen…and Kathleen is there, removing kettle from flame. Kathleen puts tea-pot and aspirin-bottle on to a tray, along with cup and saucer, glass, silver, etc. She sticks dust-rags and feather-duster under her arm; calls up stairs to Brackish.)

KATHLEEN: I'm bringin' your tea up!…*(No reply.)* Hullo?

(She climbs the stairs to Brackish's room, pauses at the door, seemingly unnoticed by Brackish, who continues reading, his back to Kathleen. She tests his deafness.) Hullo? Your hearin'-aid in or out or what? Hullo? *(No reply.)* Hullooooo!

(Kathleen enters Brackish's room. She slams door closed to test his hearing. He doesn't respond at all. She pauses, directly behind him, out of his line of vision. She stares at him, silently, five count. Satisfied that he cannot hear her, Kathleen speaks into his deafness.)

KATHLEEN: Sometimes, I am just amazed to think that I'm standing here and you're just there, within striking distance and all. You're like a legend to me, really…If my father could see me now. Wouldn't he'd a'b'en the jealous one, huh? I mean, he use'ta' dream a'bein' this close ta' you…and havin' a rock in his hand, a'course!…He was interested in marine biology, my father. He loved the sea and the boats and all.

He always loved ta' point out the different kinds'a weeds and name the fish and all…especially down the marshes. You'd think you were listenin' to some kind'a Hav'id professor, or somesuch. It really pisses me off ta' think that he spent his life, workin' the docks, lumpin', as he did. It killed him young, carryin' crates in Win'tah, and all. Deadhead stupid labor. Stupid, stupid useless!…He use'ta get tanked up, wick'id, down ta' Sherm's…he'd come home and beat my mother…I know he would'a loved to have beaten you, Brackish, but, the closest he could ever come was ta' beat my mother. The three of us girls cowerin' in the corner…like mice, scared shit so wick'id bad…Nobody havin' a life worth livin'…Every time I heard your name out loud, Brackish, it was in connection with somebody like my father gettin' their hearts broken, gettin' flunked, gettin' creamed. Nobody was ever good enough…smart enough…worth sendin' on inta' the world…You musta' hated passin' the ones you had'ta' pass: the John Connors and the Annie Bells…the naturally-smart-student-types. Most'a us scared little bastids, us poor lumpers' kids, we didn't stand a chance, did we? Not a chance!

(Brackish whirls around, faces her; suddenly aware of her presence in his room.)

BRACKISH: There you are! I was wonderin' if you'd taken a walk…forgotten me…my aspirin…

KATHLEEN: I didn't forget nothin'…

BRACKISH: *(Points to hearing-aid on table.)* I'm keepin' my hearing-aid out…Better for my headache.

KATHLEEN: *(Mouths the words, broadly.)* Fresh tea…your aspirin…
(She starts to pour a fresh cup of tea for Brackish. He pulls back, frightened.)

BRACKISH: Careful! You're gonna scald me!

KATHLEEN: Wouldn't I love ta', huh?

BRACKISH: Excuse me, are you saying something?

KATHLEEN: *(Startled; stiffens.)* Me? Nope…
(Brackish returns to his reading; deliberately ignoring Kathleen. Hostility abounds. Kathleen straightens Brackish's bed. He glances at her; returns to reading. She resumes talking to his back…to his deafness.)

KATHLEEN: I'm gonna' keep you alive until you apologize to us all…me, mother, father, husb'in…And after you do…then you can kick off…and I can kick off, too…'cause there won't be any reason for us two pathetic bas'tids not to…*(Kathleen goes to Brackish, touches his arm; gesticulates widely as She talks.)* I'm goin' back downstairs…

BRACKISH: Fine.

(Kathleen turns and exits his room, carrying tea-kettle, tray. She walks down stairs and into kitchen; begins chopping vegetables for a soup. Brackish sits alone awhile, worried. He puts down his reading, and, curiosity having gotten the best of him, replaces his hearing-aid in his ear; goes downstairs. He stops at radio, finds Byron Weld's station. A Bach cantata fills the room. Satisfied, Brackish goes to his chair; sits. He looks over at Kathleen, who is busying herself with the cutting and slicing of soup-vegetables. Brackish listens to the music a moment, smiles, takes his book, again; reads, again. Suddenly, Brackish looks up startled.)

BRACKISH: Oh, my God! I just went completely dead! It was cracklin' with static when I put it in. Now, there's nothin'! *(He whacks his battery pack.)* I'm taking this machine out of my ear, once and for all. *(Pops the hearing-aid earpiece out of ear; places battery pack on table; looks at Kathleen.)* Much better. *(Suddenly, yells out.)* What?

KATHLEEN: *(Rolls eyes heavenward.)* Oh, sweet Jesus! *(Yells to Brackish, pantomiming her message.)* I'll go downtown and get'cha some new batteries as soon as I finish my soup!

(Brackish stares dumbly.)

As soon as I finish my soup! *(Panto, with screams.)* As soon as I finish...the soup...*(Whacks pot with wooden spoon.)* The Soup! Lemme finish the soup, first!

BRACKISH: No, no, dammit! You finish your soup, first, and then head downtown for the batteries. No trouble ta' me ta' wait a couple'a extra minutes. *(Looks at Kathleen; sees her frustration.)* I'm a hard man to please, aren't I, Kathleen?

KATHLEEN: Sayin' you're "a hard man ta' please" is kinda' like sayin' "a rattlesnake's a hard animal ta' hug"!

BRACKISH: *(Looks up, suddenly, feelings hurt. Has he heard her?)* I beg your pardon, young lady?

KATHLEEN: *(Alarmed.)* I didn't say nothin'...*(Mouthes the words, carefully.)* I didn't say nothin', Mr. Brackish...

BRACKISH: Got'cha!

(Kathleen smiles. Brackish smiles. Kathleen chops the final vegetables and adds them to the soup stock. She smiles again. Brackish smiles again. She will now speak to him, into his deafness, simply, clearly, perversely...and without fear or hesitation.)

KATHLEEN: Well, that's it! Add some...fire and water...and, by magic, in 3 hours we shall have...seagull shit! *(She smiles at him again, as though she's just said something expected, such as "soup.")* I love it when you're stone deaf, Jake!

BRACKISH: It's no use, Kathleen.

KATHLEEN: *(Smiling deeply; sweetly.)* That's probably the hot roasted goat shit...We're talkin' hot roasted goat shit on a bed of clam shells, seasoned with the seagull dung that I just mentioned, and topped off, Mister stone-deaf-and-dumb Brackish, with Hound's pubic hair! *(She pats the pot atop the stove.)*...That is lunch, dearie!

BRACKISH: What's that you've got cookin'? Smells good...Looks good, too!

KATHLEEN: *(Smiles and nods.)* I live for these moments, Mr Bricklips, I truly do...

BRACKISH: *(Samples soup.)* Tastes even better! *(Sees and returns Kathleen's smile and nods.)* I'm delighted by your mood, Kathleen. Your spirits have lifted, haven't they?

KATHLEEN: *(Nods and smiles again.)* Goat shit, rat shit and my grandfather's leather boot up you arse, Brackish...

BRACKISH: *(Returns smile and nod, again.)* This does my old heart good.

KATHLEEN: *(Returning his nod and smile with still another nod and a smile.)* Oh, you are a foolish-lookin' turd, you are!

BRACKISH: While you're in such a jolly mood...Could I take up your offer to fire on down to Tru-Value?

KATHLEEN: I'll fire on down, alright. An hour away from you is worth more ta' me than a whole fuckin' day at the beach!

BRACKISH: Yes? Or no?

KATHLEEN: *(Nodding affirmatively; broadly.)* Oh, yes...Oh, yes... ohhhh, yesssssss!

BRACKISH: Oh, that's good of you! I'll be waiting right here.

(Brackish faces front, smiling. Kathleen seems to be leaving. She goes behind his back to the radio and switches the station. This time, she settles on Beastie Boys' "Hey, Ladies.")

KATHLEEN: Yuh, right, Mr. Backlash...You wait. I'll be back.

(Kathleen stops at the door; gloats. Brackish looks across room to Kathleen. She smiles, blows a kiss to him. He smiles, returns the blown kiss. She exits. Brackish sits a moment, not reacting to the music, which is loud and frenzied. He now rises from his chair and crosses to the radio. He picks up his hearing-aid from the table, tosses it in the air a few times, sets it back down on the table-top, in easy view of the audience.

A moment passes. He wipes his forehead, bringing his palm over his eyes, which he cups for a moment, masking his face. He switches dial… *"Hey, Ladies!" magically changes to Bach "Jesu Meine Freude." We hear: male singer singing sweetly. After listening a moment, Brackish sings along with the recording, in perfect German, word for word.*

We are now certain that Brackish is not at all deaf. He has heard everything we have heard.)

SINGER AND BRACKISH: "Duld ich schon hier Spott und Hohn, dennoch Bleibst du auch im Leide, Jesu, meine Freude…"

(Brackish has sung in perfect harmony with recording. The Motet ends, music fades. After a brief silence, Brackish bows his head.)

THE LIGHTS FADE TO BLACK.

SCENE THREE
Autumn

The auditorium is dark. Byron Weld's voice is heard in darkness.

BYRON WELD: *(On radio:)* It's just gorgeous out there, isn't it?…Could you ask for a better Autumn weekend? 'Course not. Perfect football weather. Or, perfect for just takin' a brisk walk along the Back Shore. But, 'a' course, I'm locked up here alone at the transmitt'ah…

(Lights up now in downstairs rooms. Kathleen is in the kitchen, cooking jelly. Fruit baskets and jelly pots, all around. Two huge corn pots steam away on the stove. Odor of jelly wanted in auditorium.

Note: Foliage blazen color: reds, yellow, browns, oranges. Some leaves already on ground.)

BYRON WELD: *(Continued.)*…I'm cooped up here like a man in prison, so's I can play for you the work of composers who are all deeply gifted…and this station better be gifted, too, and quick, 'cause without your gifts, we're gonna' fold faster than you can say "Wolfgang Amadeus Mozart"…speaking of which [sic], this is a Columbia Masterworks recording, #K172…Mozart "*Quartet in E Flat*"…

(Music up [on radio]: Mozart "Quartet in E Flat." Brackish appears outside of kitchen window, presses nose against glass, peers inside; sees Kathleen, smiles. He dissappears, momentarily, then, enters house through kitchen door.

He is a symphony of Fall colors, plaids and tweeds. His trouser-cuffs are tucked into his argyle socks, creating the affect of "Plus Fours." There is a pith helmet atop his head, for private reasons. He carries a basket of beach plums and rose hips in one arm and a fat, neutered male cat in the other. NOTE: Cat should be absurdly fat, friendly: no question of safety near the beast wanted.)

BRACKISH: *(Chirping gaily.)* There isn't a tourist left on the entire beach. It is a marvelous, marvelous, marvelous thing, the way the seasons change. It restores faith in the Deity. *(Smiles.)* March: the snow melts. April: the cellar floods. June, July and August: the cars all sport New York and New Jersey plates, and they weave from side to side, takin' in all the sights, threatening life and limb. *(Smiles, and pontificates.)* But, then, by God, Labor Day comes, and the tourists all pack up their dreadful greasy hot-dog colored bodies, and their Godawful charcoal sketches of Motif #1...and they vanish...like Greenheads and Mosquitoes: mystically, magically, they are...simply... gone... and it is a marvelous, marvelous thing... *(Nuzzles cat; sighs.)* Ah, it does please me: Autumn. I don't know why people insist on calling Autumn "Fall"...Autumn is Autumn...Fall is what you do from Grace!

KATHLEEN: Who's your friend?

BRACKISH: Ohhh. The cat's name is Nathaniel Hawthorne. Say "Hello," Nathaniel. The girl's name is Kathleen Hogan. *(Pretends to be the cat's voice.)* "Hello, Kathleen..." *(Laughs.)* Oh, did I get a phone call while I was out?

KATHLEEN: This phone? Ring? Uh uh.

BRACKISH: I thought maybe Nobby Ellis called. Nathaniel's Nobby's cat. I bumped into him...Nathaniel...back of Good Harbor Beach, near where Nobby and I used'ta pitch our ho'ss-shoes...so, I thought maybe Nobby was back home, seein' the cat and all...*(Pauses.)* We took a walk up to Nobby's house, up Brier Neck, but, it was still boarded up. *(Pauses.)* Kinda' a worrisome thing...*(Smiles; nuzzles Nathaniel, absently.)* He'll be callin' me...If it were bad news, I would have heard it by now. Nothin' spreads faster than bad news and cheap oleomargarine...

KATHLEEN: Are we gonna' boil Nathaniel down, too? Or, are we just gonna' eat him in the rough?
(Nathaniel squirms.)

BRACKISH: Oh, dear, I think Nathaniel heard you, Kathleen. *(Strokes cat.)* Easy, easy, easy, Nathaniel! Kathleen was just joking. She would never boil a wonderful cat like you. The girl just has a warped sense of humor! *(Nuzzles cat.)* I've known this beast for fourteen years…each human year is worth eight cat years…eight fourteens is a hundred and two…Nathaniel's a hundred and two, Kathleen. I'm just a kid, next to this old codger…

(Brackish first sets down milk, then cat. Cat knows exactly what to do with milk; does.)

KATHLEEN: A hundred and twelve…

BRACKISH: What's that?

KATHLEEN: A hundred and twelve. You said Nathaniel was a hundred and two…Eight fourteens is a hundred and twelve. You got it wrong…

BRACKISH: *(After a long pause.)* Well, my God!…You're quite right, Kathleen…

KATHLEEN: Yuh, I guess I am, yuh…

BRACKISH: *(Harumphs.)* Harumph…

(Kathleen turns away; giggles. Brackish flashes a playacted, over-acted, look of annoyance at Kathleen who giggles again.)

BRACKISH: *(Stops; worries.)* Where was I?

KATHLEEN: We'd both counted up Nathaniel's age. You got it wrong and I got it right.

BRACKISH: C'mon, Nathaniel, walk me to the mailbox. I'm gonna' get my paper.

(Brackish exits. Kathleen goes, immediately, to radio, switches it on, tries a few stations before settling on "Never, My Love." She lip-synchs and dances to music.

Brackish re-enters, without Nathaniel, carrying newspaper. He catches Kathleen dancing. She blushes, runs into kitchen, mortified.)

BRACKISH: Weather's changin'. I think we're in for it…*(Goes to the radio.)* What an odor comin' from the fish plant. Hard to believe the stuff they're bakin' is gonna' *be* food, instead'a havin' already *been* food!

KATHLEEN: *(Shrugs.)* Makes a lot of jobs.

BRACKISH: I s'pose.

(He switches station, finding Byron Weld's WGLO-FM. Byron has caught the cold of his life!)

BYRON WELD:…and it'll be yo'r fault, not mine. *(Coughs.)* This is Johann Pachelbel…*(Coughs.)…*"Canon in D Major" with Jean-Francois Paillard conducting his Chamber Orchestra… *(Coughs.)…*recorded in 1972 at Albert Hall…(Coughs.) I've got a wick'id cold…coughin'…the chills.

(The music begins. Brackish sits in chair, reading Gloucester Daily Times. *He suddenly yells aloud, middle of a thought, height of a rage.)*

BRACKISH: Scabrous son of a bitch! I knew when I saw his cat on the beach he'd pull something like this! Nobby Ellis was a scabrous son of a bitch, from the day I met him! I was five years old, Kathleen…five years old…and I could tell! He was competitive! To the point of somethin' very nearly illegal! Competitive! I would get an A, he would get an A+! I would buy a bike, he would buy a red bike. 'Course, as I knew he was pathologically competitive, it didn't really bother me when he beat me out for Valedictorian…'cause I understood the psychology of the situation: He, being from a broken home and all, and me, bein' from a wonderful family-oriented family… But, when he went into graduate school…graduate school…well…I knew he was directly competing with me. I mean, I got my B.A. from the finest, right? As did he? Two Gloucester boys goin' off to Harvard as we did? Hell, as far as I was concerned, the competition was finished: dead tie. Dead tie…But, no, not Nobby Ellis…He had'da keep competin'…M.A. from Yale in English Literature: isn't that just the most goddam absurd thing you ever heard of? I pick up my *Gloucester Daily Times* and I cannot believe my eyes! "Norbert Alvin Ellis the 2nd will leave tomorrow for New Haven, Connecticut where he will begin his studies for a Masters Degree in English Literature…"

(Kathleen tries to pour his tea.)

I didn't ask for that, did I?

(Kathleen backs off.)

I shoulda' let it go. I shouldn't 'a got down to his sick level and competed…BUT…I went back ta' Harvard…two miserable years of takin' the heart and soul out'ta' the likes 'a Byron and Keats and Shelly…learnin' lists of what Dr. Johnson had for breakfast on his two hundred mile walk with Boswell…makin' maps of goddam Wordsworth's goddam walks around the Lake District…I mean, really, is this the stuff that's gonna' get the fire lit on a cold winter's morning? *(Pauses; disgusted.)* No sooner do I get back ta' Gloucester and back ta' teachin'…bang! I pick up my *Times* and there's Nobby…off to Trinity College, Toronto, Canada, for a Ph.D. in guess what? Right! English Goddam Literature…This still gets my nipples up, Kathleen, if you'll pardon my anatomical reference… Ph.D. in E.L.….Great! Off I go into Cambridge. You'd think I was working for the M.T.A., I rode it so often…Back I come ta' Gloucester…four years older, carryin' more letters after my name than a post-man could fit in his goddam sack! A Jewish Ph.D. teachin' High School Music and English in Gloucester, Massachusetts. What I was, was something that happens every two hundred or three hundred million years! And Nobby Ellis goes off ta' England, to Oxford University, to teach English to the English…Isn't that a kettle of fish you'd call "just fine"?…It never ended, Kathleen!…Never! They retire the Son-of-a-bitch at age sixty-five, same as they retired me, but, where does he come for his twilight years? Does he stay in Merry Olde You-know-where? You know he doesn't! Right back ta' Merry Olde Gloucester, where I have'ta' pitch horseshoes against him at Good Harbor Beach every wa'm day, and play Gin Rummy against him every cold day, right here in my own dining room…for eighteen years, until they take the stupid bastid away ta' Rattray's Old Age Home down Wakefield, because Nobby ain't got the brains, nor the guts, ta' simply say, "No, I ain't goin' ta' any old age home, anywhere, under any condition!" His half-wit son-in-law speaks and he obeys, like he was still in goddam graduate school. I begged the pencil-brain ta' move in here with me…I offered free rent, the works…We were practically even in gin games and I was way, way up pitchin' horse-shoes…but, he went. He goddam went… *(He is desolate now.)* Over a year and not a single word…until this… *(He picks up Gloucester Times and slams it down.)* First-ta'-Die Award. Nobby wins it, huh? The stupid bastid, leavin' me like this. He was two months and a week older'n me, Kathleen, so, you know what that makes me now, huh? I am offically the oldest livin' man in Gloucester, Massachusetts, U.S. of A. Nobby was it, but now, it's me. I outlasted him. I took the title. I…win.

(Kathleen re-offers cup of tea to Brackish. This time, He picks up cup, sips. NOTE: Pachelbel piece must be timed out to conclude precisely as speech concludes. Repetition of small section of music needs to be added just prior to ending. The lights fade to black.

Lights up in the kitchen. Kathleen has prepared a tray with "vapours"…bowl, toweling, etc. Brackish pulls on bathrobe, puts thermometer under tongue. She calls over to Brackish, softly, gently.)

KATHLEEN: We're ready for you…

(Kathleen sets vapours-bowl and toweling at table. Brackish has thermometer in his mouth.)

BRACKISH: You'd better check on Nathaniel. Make sure he's peeing in his box instead of in my bed, again…

KATHLEEN: Don't talk with the thermometer in your mouth…

BRACKISH: What's hell's the difference? We know I've got a fever! A thermometer's a waste of time, if you ask me! *(Brackish goes to calendar.)* Same damn thing as a calendar! If you don't know what date it is, already, a calendar's no use at all! I mean, really, try starin' at one when you really don't know the date! All a calendar will give you is 365 guesses! *(Turns on radio, flips through stations, finds Byron Weld, who is also ill.)*

BYRON WELD: *(On radio; coughs twice.)* Robert Schumann lived from 1810 to 1856…*(Coughs twice, again.)* Excuse me, I'm sweatin'. I'm wick'id sick…

BRACKISH: You hear that? Byron's sick, too…*(To Kathleen.)* This sickness you caused is goin' through the town like wild fire! I'm one foot in the grave…Nathaniel's up there, half-dead…sweating away, incontinent…

(Music in: Schumann's "Bach — Op. 60." Brackish walks, slowly, to the dining table, under Kathleen's watchful eye, overacting his illness, badly, as might a child. He stops enroute to the table and sticks a finger in the frosting of a partly-eaten Halloween cake, orange frosting, samples same; doesn't respond to the taste.

He hands thermometer to Kathleen; sits. Kathleen moves the vapours-bowl in front of him.)

BRACKISH: We'd better use the blackboard. Last time I took the vapours with my hearing-aid in, the steam rusted the damn thing brown…Get the blackboard…*(Brackish takes hearing-aid out of ear, places it on table.)* What?
(Kathleen fetches a largish blackboard from kitchen, sets it up, propping same against stack of books. Music continues, under.)

KATHLEEN: Get under the towels.

BRACKISH: What?

KATHLEEN: *(Pantomimes his getting under toweling.)* Go under…towels.

BRACKISH: What's my temp?

KATHLEEN: (Under her breath.) I thought you weren't interested. *(Reads thermometer.)* Ninety-nine-one…

BRACKISH: I can't hear you, dammit. Write it!

KATHLEEN: *(Writes same on blackboard.)* Ninety-nine-point-one…

BRACKISH: Ninety-nine-one? That's nothing! I'm burning up! I'm way over a hundred! Goddam thermometer's useless!

KATHLEEN: Go under the towels…

BRACKISH: That s'pose ta' be funny?…Talkin' ta' me when I can't hear?

KATHLEEN: *(Exasperated; pantomimes.)* Go under...the towels!...
   (He goes under and comes right back up; glasses steamed opaque.)
BRACKISH: Great! My glasses steamed up! Now, I can't see what I can't hear...*(Rubs glasses, puts them on.)* Did you say something?
KATHLEEN: Nothin'. I didn't say nothin'...
BRACKISH: *(From under towel.)* I cannot bear this.
KATHLEEN: Yuh, well, tough luck.
   (Kathleen walks to radio and switches it off; pops in cassette of Phoebe Snow singing Paul Simon's "Something So Right." *She allows music to play in room, softly. She returns to kitchen and work. Brackish continues his complaint, sans fin.)*
BRACKISH: *(Pops out from under towel.)* Philosophically speaking, the ultimate danger for a deaf man in not hearing a tree fall in the forest isn't that the sound doesn't exist! It's that the goddam tree will fall on your head! *(Goes under the towels, again; pops out, again.)* Where the hell is United Parcel with my records? Did you call them?
KATHLEEN: *(Nods an enormous nod.)* Yes, I did...*(Holds up three fingers.)* Three times, three...one, two, three times...
   (Kathleen writes "3 times" on the blackboard.)
BRACKISH: There's no need to write that! I counted your fingers, dammit! I'm not blind, ya' know! I'm deaf! *(Sneezes; coughs.)*
KATHLEEN: *(Exaggerated bowing and scraping.)* Sorry, sorry, sorry... SOR-RRY! *(Writes word on blackboard.)*
BRACKISH: Don't act mousey with me, Kathleen. *(She shoves him under the towels.)* I hate this. Damn it! I am an educated man! I don't want to die face-down in a bowl of Vick's Vapo-Rub! *(Pops out from under.)* This is your fault, really. All that damned opening and closing of the door for trick-or-treaters. That's what did me in...One of their horrid little killer snot-noses brought us the trick and the treat of this virus, that's what. *(Sips tea.)* Encouraging them with cup-cakes! Gimme one of those!...
   (Kathleen places cup-cakes on table.)
BRACKISH: *(Fingers frosting; tastes.)* Why's this frosting orange? What did you use to color it? It tastes weird.
KATHLEEN: Carrot juice.
BRACKISH: What?
KATHLEEN: Carrot juice!
BRACKISH: I can't hear you. You forget?
KATHLEEN: *(Writes "carrot juice" on blackboard.)* Carr...ott fucking

joooosss! *(Picks up hearing aid.)* Will you please put yo'r Goddam hearing-aid back in!

BRACKISH: Carrot juice? Carrots are vegetables! *(He shoves cupcake aside in disgust.)* You feed 'em carrots, they'll be able to see in the dark! They'll be comin' around every night! *(Coughs; listens to music, a moment, forgetting his alleged deafness.)* Is this your idea of music? This isn't music! *(Brackish stands, walks to cassette deck; switches music off. Kathleen stares at hearing aid in her hand, and then at Brackish. She is amazed to catch him hearing without his hearing-aid.)*

KATHLEEN: *(A voiceless whisper.)* Oh...my...God...

BRACKISH: *(Snaps at her; meanly.)* I'm talking to you, young lady! *(Kathleen turns and faces him.)* I need some tea. What you put in front of me is cold...You have a simple job to do here, young lady...to keep things hot...(*Kathleen doesn't move.*) I must insist that you keep your half of the bargain, I provide wages and a place for you to hang your hat; and you provide assistance...as I need it...And I need it now, please! *(Yells, full voice.)* Now, please!
(There is a silence.)

KATHLEEN: Lemme just put a record on, first, Mr. Brackish...One a' your favorites...a'course, you won't be able to hear nothin', what with your hearin' aid out'ta your ear and on the table...Right? *(Walks to phonograph, pulls out an album, at random.)* Pablo Casals...Bach... "Suite For Unaccompanied Cello"...1936 to 1939...
(Kathleen puts phonograph record on turntable, starts the music, lightly. It is indeed Casals playing Bach's "Suite For Unaccompanied Cello." We hear the gentle sound of Casal's cello...until...Kathleen: pulls the arm of the record player and needle across the record. A terrible scratching sound is produced. Brackish looks away. Another pull, another scratch. Another and another. Brackish finally talks to Kathleen through clenched teeth.)

BRACKISH: Stop it!...Stop!...STOP!...STOP THAT!
(After a long pregnant pause.)

KATHLEEN: It's kinda' a miracle your hearin' improved so much, ain't it? Ain't it??? *(Kathleen throws hearing-aid into wastebasket. A moment's silence.)*

BRACKISH: *(Mortified.)* I'd better check on Nathaniel.
(He stands; gets away from Kathleen as quickly as he can...He switches radio back on, defiantly, childishly...then switches on light on stairs. He then runs up the stairs, into his room. He picks up Nathaniel, rolls his

eyes to Heaven, places cat lapward as he sits; smiles. He is beyond em-
barrassment: mortified.
We hear: Beethoven's "Symphony #1 in C Major, Opus 21."
Kathleen goes to kitchen, sits at table, begins writing a letter.
The music stops, suddenly. The lighting dims. We hear Byron Weld. His
voice is incredibly weak, near death.)

BYRON WELD: *(On radio.)* I'm sorry ta' hav'ta shut down shop for a
while...*(Coughs.)*...I'm sick as a dog...*(Coughs.)*...I'm just gonna'
hop up ta' Addison Gilbert and get myself looked at...*(Coughs.
Coughs, again.)*...This is Byron Weld, signin' off...*(Coughs.)*...
WGLO-FM, Gloucester, Massachusetts, on Cape Ann...
(Suddenly, dead air: Silence. In his room, Brackish hears this, sits erect,
alarmed. We now hear: Voice of young man replacing Byron.

NEW VOICE: *(On radio.)* This is Arnold Weld, Byron Weld's nephew. Uncle Byron died last night, up Addison-Gilbert. Before he died, he told
me to tell ya's that he thanks none of ya's. I'm takin' over the station,
for the moment, and WGLO-FM, Gloucester, Mass., is gonna' be
playin' more 60's-70's-80's-and-90's rock'n'roll than other station
north of Boston. From the 70's, here come the Buzzcocks...
(Music in: Buzzcocks "Mad, Mad Judy" crashes in. Brackish, without
cat, rushes down stairs, shuts off radio.)

BRACKISH: I sent the bas'tid six dollars a week, fifty-two weeks a year for
forty-one years in a row, you know that? And do you think he ever
once mentioned my name on the radio?! Even just once?! I cannot
tolerate his ingratitude!...I cannot tolerate the ingratitude of my former students, either! Not a one of them calls, comes around. Not a
one of them. I never married because of my students, you know...I
mean, did I have need for children? I had...thousands, right?
(Kathleen ignores him; doesn't answer. Instead, she sits at kitchen table,
writing letter, intently.)

BRACKISH: Don't you know that non-verbal non-communication reveals
an ignorance? If you have a thought to express, express it in language...Speak English words!
(Kathleen ignores him; contunues writing letter.)
So? Here I sit, alone, except for the likes of you, Kathleen O'Hara,
and Nathaniel Hawthorne, a fat, half-blind, half-dead, neutered
male housecat! So? What added up? What accumulated?
What...mattered? *(With self-pity, but aimed at Kathleen.)* A lifetime
of teaching in Gloucester High School. A lifetime! Thousands of stu-

dents and not a single one of 'em can come around and say a "Hello." Not a single one of 'em!

KATHLEEN: *(Speaks without looking up.)* You oughta' be thankful nobody come around and stuck a knife in your heart. You oughta' be thankful. Thankkkfulll.

BRACKISH: I might remind you that my hearing is working just fine, young lady. Your obscenities are coming in loud and clear. Loud and clear!

KATHLEEN: Really?

BRACKISH: Really.

KATHLEEN: Kathleen O'Hara shoulda' gone ta' college and be'n somebody, but, you crapped it up!

BRACKISH: Jacob Brackish shoulda' stayed at Ha'vid and taught some real students…but, you crapped it up! *(Screams.)* Who are you writing to, God damn it! Sittin' in that mousey way, scratchin'… scratchin'…Who? Who? WHO?

KATHLEEN: None of your damn bis'ness!

BRACKISH: I don't wanna' sit in this chair! *(Brackish throws his leg-blanket onto floor, leaps up, enraged.)* I don't want these terrible flashing pains inside my head…under my arms…I don't want my gums pulling back and my teeth falling out in the sink! And I don't want you sitting there in that mousey way, scratching those letters in my house. *(He moves to her and raises his hand; strikes her. She pulls back from him, stunned.)*

KATHLEEN: Oh my God! You hit me. You old bast'id! You hit meee! *(Leaps up.)* I'm writing to my mother and father!

BRACKISH: They're dead!

KATHLEEN: I'm still writin' to them! I'm writin' to my husband, Princie, too…all of 'em, Brackish! I'm tellin' all a'them!

BRACKISH: You're squealin' on me, Kathleen???

KATHLEEN: I am! I'm tellin' 'em everything I know…every goddam thing about you I've picked up…and I seen it all, Brackish, I seen it all! *(Kathleen runs upstairs and into her room.)*

BRACKISH: You don't know a thing about me!

KATHLEEN: *(Screams to him, downstairs.)* Lonely, miserable old Fuck! Lives alone with a half-dead cat, and a Scrooge-voice that drops dead on the radio! They're all leavin' you, Brackish! Every last one of 'em! Same way I'm gonna'be cuttin' out'ta' here, myself!

BRACKISH: Ungrateful little bitch! You deserve to flunk!

KATHLEEN: Yuh, sure! I deserve ta' flunk and so did Mama and Da and

Princie and Josie Evangelista and Floey Rizzo and Fast Eddie Ryan and Ruthie Flynn!…You wanna' hear the whole list? I got it all written down! Every last one of us you ruined!

BRACKISH: You know what a sick waste of your time it's been makin' a list like that?

(Kathleen runs downstairs; confronts Brackish.)

KATHLEEN: Ohhh, you're really som'body ta' be talkin' ta' me about a "Sick waste'a time!"! How's about the sick waste'a yo'r time never marryin', huh? Nobody in this town was never good enough for you, Brackish? You were too smart, too sophisticated, too worldy for any of the local crop, right? So, you coop yo'rself up in this pathetic hovel for fifty-sixty-seventy years! You coop yo'rself up, pissed off and gutless, and you flunk the whole goddam Town of Gloucester…and you talk to meee about "a sick waste of time"? What are you? Crazy?

BRACKISH: I did not, young lady, flunk the "whole Town of Gloucester." I did nothing of the kind!

KATHLEEN: *(Counting on her fingers.)* Mother, Father, Hus'bin, me…

BRACKISH: You failed! Your family failed! I may not be proud of much else in my life, but, I am pretty goddam proud of my teachin' record, so, don't you attack it! And don't you attack the way I lived my life, either! I've got no regrets! Not one! All's I hate is the bein'-old part of it…bein' trapped inside a body that doesn't work. I hate it! But most of all, I hate bein' trapped inside a house with the likes of you! I just hate it!

KATHLEEN: Then what did ya' beg me ta' come here for?

BRACKISH: You answered an ad…for money! I have never begged anybody for anything in my life!

KATHLEEN: THEN TRY IT! IT'LL DO YA' SOME GOOD! Try sayin' "Thank you" and "You're welcome" and "You ain't so smart, but you ain't nothin'…you ain't a piece'a tossed-out goddam lobstah' shell on the beach!" TRY SAYIN' THAT, BRACKISH! Try sayin', "You ain't Einstein, but, you certainly do deserve a pat on the back for gettin' through the win'tah', 'cause, it's miserable wicked awful cold and lonely…and it's tough…It's TOUGH! *(Chokes back her tears.)* I ain't gonna cry I ain't gonna cry I ain't gonna cry! I ain't gonna mouse out-'ta this! *(Looks up at Brackish. Square in the eye, now, no tears.)* I may've be'n a D-Plus dodo in Music Appreciation, Mr. Brackish, but I knew how'ta give a hug and a kiss and I knew how to get a hug and a kiss…and you didn't! Now look at you! You got no friends at all. Cooped up alone with the goddam radio, and this half blind neutered cat, who by the way, ain't fakin' his blindness, Brackish. He ain't fakin' a handicap like some SICKOES I know, tryin' to' win sympathy, stead'a love, hidin' behind fake deafness, spyin'! Pretty fuckin' pathetic, if ya' ask me! I'll give you another dose of the truth: I came here to watch you die. I came here to enjoy your death. I open the paper ta' see the Obituary I phoned in for my Princie and it ain't there, Brackish It ain't in the paper! I call Nan Cobbey, who I've known since Girl Scouts, and she's now some kinda' deal down the *Times* and she don't know and she calls back an hour later and says the *Times* is "...sorry they left it out...that the little blank hole on the page is where it was s'pose'ta be, but after the paper was pasted up, Princie's ahhhticle fell off, somehow...Princie fell off the goddam page! She asks me did I know "A white hole on a newspaper page is called a 'widow?' And isn't this a 'gross irony?' And then she gives me her 'sympathy'"...The next thing I see in the paper is your ad, which stuck ta' the page like God-himself glued it down. And I knew I hadda' take your job. I knew I hadda' do it...There was nobody at Princie's wake, down Pike's Funeral Home, Mr. Brackish. Just me and nutso Buster Sheehan, who'll sit with anybody's body over-night, so long as you give him the Guinea Red...I felt relief when Princie died, Mr. Brackish. I did. I felt relief. He wasn't very nice ta' me. *(Sobs openly.)* They start you out in 5th grade with a nickname like "Tit-mouse" and it don't do a whole lot for your spine. They tell you when you're seven that "you'd better learn ta' typewrite, K.O., 'cause you ain't goin' ta' no college, or endin' up intellectual or even hopeful"! *(Ruefully.)* K.O. Great little set of initials ta' start out with, huh? K.O.'d at birth! K.O.'d right at the 1st round bell!

BRACKISH: I've never heard such self-pitying paranoic ho'ss-shit in my en-tire life! The world was out to get Kathleen O'Hara, right? Even me: out ta' get'cha', right? I gave you a D-plus, not because it was what you earned, but, because I was perverse...vindictive...whimsical! It had nothin' whatsoever to do with your actual achievement, right?
(Kathleen starts to run upstairs. Brackish stops her with his voice.)
Am I correct? Am I correct? AM I CORRECT???
(Kathleen covers her ears, as might a child. She turns, screams at Brack-ish and to the world.)

KATHLEEN: I did it all ta' myself: me! *(She slaps her own face, three times, powerfully.)* I did it myself, okay? *(She now punches her own hip to pun-tuate her guilt.)* I only got myself ta' blame. Okayyy? *(Punch.)* I been my own worst enemy. Okayyyy? *(Punch.)* Okay? Okay? OKAYY???

(Final punch. She weeps, turning her face away from Brackish. She leaps into chair and buries her face in pillow on the chair-back, so as to muffle her sobs. Brackish chokes back his own tears, now. He speaks to her, compassionately.)

BRACKISH: Oh, Kathleen...Kathleen, please...tell me what I can do for you. I want very much to help you. I want to know that this time you've spent with me was worthwhile. Please...tell me what I can do...for you.

KATHLEEN: *(Looks up at him: front.)* A make-up test in Music Appreciation. I want private tutoring and I want another chance...to raise my grade. A make-up test in Music Appreciation. That's what I want.

(Music in: lights build as music by Strauss fades in...swells. Kathleen runs upstairs. She appears in bedroom wearing Walkman earphones; studying sheet-music. Brackish goes to desk, gets his bluebook, crosses to bookcase, arranges albums for test, then puts one record on to turntable. The Strauss piece is the first of a medley of Bach, Debussy, Brahms, Chopin selections, ending with Mendelssohn's "Symphony No.4 in A Major."

Kathleen runs downstairs carrying bluebook and pencil. She goes to coffee table, writes her answers in bluebook.

When final piece (Mendelssohn) in medley has played, Brackish drops the needle arm of the phonograph on to the record. The lights come up to scene level. Schubert's "Unfinished Symphony" is heard. The make-up test is underway.)

BRACKISH: There's a time limit.

KATHLEEN: I know, I know...

BRACKISH: Enough?

KATHLEEN: *(Panic.)* One sec, one sec...Oh, God... *(Yells, relieved.)* Okay! Okay! Got it!

BRACKISH: Three to go...

(Brackish plays a snippet of Mozart. Kathleen bites her pencil and, suddenly, remembers. She writes an answer, stops, thinks better of it, punches fist down on table-top, three sharp blows.)

BRACKISH: Ready?

KATHLEEN: One sec, one sec...Oh, God, oh, God, oh, God... *(She writes her answer into her notebook.)*

KATHLEEN: Okay. Ready...

BRACKISH: The final pair...Here's the penultimate...

(Brackish places arm of record-player into groove and Bach's "Chaconne," played by Nathaniel Milstein, plays in room. After a few mo-

ments, during which Kathleen smiles and writes her answer, Brackish switches the record and plays a final piece.) Last one. *(Brackish allows the arm of the phonograph on to the record and Rachmoninoff's "Symphony No. 2 in E. Minor" fills the room.)*

KATHLEEN: *(Worried.)* Oh, God, oh, God, oh, God, God, God…*(She thinks she's got it. She writes her answer into her book.)* Done. *(Brackish turns from stereo and faces her.)*

BRACKISH: Done.

KATHLEEN: My brain's inside out…

BRACKISH: You wanna' check over any of 'em?

KATHLEEN: I heard 'em once. Fair's fair…

BRACKISH: Would you like a cup of tea before you turn em' in?

KATHLEEN: What are you so nervous about?

BRACKISH: Ready when you are, Mrs. Hogan…

KATHLEEN: Number one was Strauss…definitely…late Romantic period…Strauss…Number two is Bach…Baroque…G-Major… The Brandenberg concertos…Number three was hard…Impressionistic. Debussy. My guess is one of the *"Nocturnes"*…I'll go with that: Debussy *"Nocturnes."* Number four was Romantic…Brahms…fairly easy. Number five was a gift, thank you very much for the birthday present, Chopin *"Ballade in F-minor"*…Six was Romantic, I'll have ta' say Mendelssohn…Number seven was another piece of cake, thank you for the birthday present, Schubert *"Unfinished Symphony"*…number eight was sneaky, but I'm gonna go with Mozart, and I think it was *"No. 40 in G-minor"*…I dunno, but I'm relatively certain it was Mozart, so, that's my answer: classical period, Mozart…number eight. And number nine was Baroque: Bach's *"Chaconne."* No doubt about it. And number ten was a wicked awful sneaky thing for you to pull on me 'cause you know I don't really know much about Rachmoninoff, I would say Rachmaninoff… Maybe not, but my hunch is Rachmoninoff…*"No. 2 in E-Minor"*…And that's it. Oh, and I'm wicked awful sorry I scratched your Casals record…How'd I do?

BRACKISH: That was precisely the I.D. section of my Freshman General Music "drop the needle" midterm at Harvard. I got six out of ten, which was good enough to pass, but just. I saved my bluebook. Here…*(He opens a dog-eared "Bluebook"; reads.)* I missed Rachmaninoff. I also missed Mendelssohn, Bach's *"Chaconne,"* and that piece of cake: Chopin *"Ballade in F-Minor,"* thank you very much…You didn't miss anything. You went ten for ten.

KATHLEEN: I did. Yuh. I knew I did.

BRACKISH: The I.D. section counted only 50%.

KATHLEEN: What?

BRACKISH: The other 50% is all on Section Two, which I have decided to make oral: one question. You ready?

KATHLEEN: I am. Yuh.

BRACKISH: Here goes, then. Final question…worth 50%. This is probably the most important question you'll ever hav'ta' answer in your entire life about classical music!…Ready?

KATHLEEN: Yes. I'm ready.

BRACKISH: Did you enjoy the music, Kathleen?

KATHLEEN: I did. Very much, Mr. Brackish. I did.

BRACKISH: *(Pause)* Congratulations. A perfect score.

KATHLEEN: Oh, my God! That was the question?!

BRACKISH: Oh, yes, as you suggested, I listened to your Miss Phoebe Snow singing the Paul Simon song, *"Something So Right,"* and I do see what you mean…homophonic…romantic…reminiscent of English Court Ballads…in the sonata form…lyrically quite sound, really. *(Smiles, simply.)* I…liked…it.

THE LIGHTS FADE.

SCENE FOUR
The Start of Winter

Music in: Albinoni "Adagio for flute and strings" plays under entire scene. The season has returned to Winter; foliage is, again, barren, bare. Snow is falling, heavily.

Lights fade up in downstairs rooms again. It is Christmastime. Christmas lights, hidden in book-shelves, around room, around window-frames, etc, now twinkle, gaily.

Kathleen hangs a string of Christmas lights over the mantle.

Brackish reclines on the sofa. At his feet are stacks of papers that have come from a storage trunk, old-fashioned variety, that has probably been in evidence, throughout the play, Upstage. There is also a large waste-basket, overflowing with papers, nearby the trunk.

Brackish takes sheet music and book written in Greek from trunk; considers them.

BRACKISH: I regret never having the vision, the talent, or the discipline to compose beautiful music. I also regret never learning to read Ancient Greek...This is Euripides... *(He tosses sheet music and book into wastebasket. He finds Chinese primer.)* Or Chinese... *(He tosses primer in wastebasket. He finds a small oil painting kit and palette.)* I also regret never having an ounce of talent as a painter. Winslow Homer's paintings of Niles Pond and Brace's Cove still thrill me silly! *(He tosses kit and palette into wastebasket.)*

KATHLEEN: I was conceived on the Niles Pond sandbar...I'm blushin' ...I must be beet-red...

BRACKISH: No need to be embarrassed...Not with me.

KATHLEEN: My mother told me that towards the end, just before she passed on...I was dozin' off beside her bed...She was sleepin' all the time...all's a'sudden I hears her say, "Kathy, you were started inta' life on the Niles Pond Sandbar. Your father and I lay together there and I knew a child would come of it, and you did...I had a lotta' trouble goin' over there after I found out...Took me maybe a year, but I went there...Two big dogs, Labrador Retrievers, were, uh, well, they were...

BRACKISH:...Doin' it?

KATHLEEN: Doin' it! They were! Right there on the same spot...Well, relatively the same spot! It made me laugh! Oh, God, it made me feel good! *(She chortles, then, suddenly, she sobs. Brackish watches her weep for a moment, then he speaks to her, soothingly.)*

BRACKISH: It's the worst thing in life, Kathleen...outlivin' the ones you love. It's the worst thing. It strikes a terrible loneliness, and a terrible fear of dyin'...I always loved takin' morning walks across the Niles Pond sand-bar...especially in Summer...wearing shorts...feeling the tall wet Goldenrod and Angelica against my naked legs...smellin' the wild roses, the Honeysuckle...Nuns and priests from the Catholic Retreat on their dreamlike prayer walks, scarin' the piss out'ta' the birds and the berries with all that spooky holiness... *(Watches Kathleen regain her composure.)* Let your memories make you happy, girl...Otherwise, they'll cripple you...turn you to stone.

KATHLEEN: *(Wipes eyes dry; looks up at Brackish, smiles.)* Any other regrets to chuck out?

BRACKISH: *(Pauses; thinks.)* Yup. I regret never sleeping with certain women.

KATHLEEN: Which women, specifically?

BRACKISH: Oh, uh, well, Grace Kelly, the movie actress. I've seen "High

Society" nine times. And Agnes Virgilio, from the bread store. She married Cosmo who'sis…

KATHLEEN: She's about eighty!

BRACKISH: This is not a recent regret, Kathleen. We're talking about a lifetime of regret! Agnes Virgilio had eyes that stopped you from thinkin'…deep, happy, full of promise…And breasts that stopped your breath. Agnes would walk into my class and I would turn, look at her, and within the countin' from one to six, I would suffer the loss of vision, of logic, of all pulminary functions!

KATHLEEN: You ever sleep with her?…Oh, no, right. This is a regret list.

BRACKISH: And right at the top of my list, Princess Grace Kelly and Agnes Virgilio.

KATHLEEN: What held you back? From sleepin' with her?

BRACKISH: She married Ranier!

KATHLEEN: I mean Agnes Virgilio.

BRACKISH: She saw through my hearing-aid, same as you…Both my mother and my father went deaf, early on…I was so sure I was going deaf, I started to wear my father's hearing-aid. I started wearing it to school. I could hear a pin drop!…One day, in front of my sophomore English class, it fell out. I said "I'm deaf without my hearing-aid, class. I can't hear a thing!", and one of the little sons-a-bitches up the back of the room yells, "You're a wicked arsehole, Brackish!"…From that day forward, I had my own secret way of knowin' exactly what was on my students' minds…They told me themselves…same as you!

KATHLEEN: Oh, God, I'm sorry about my swearin' and my sayin' bad things about you and all… *(Remembers things she's said.)* Oh, God-ddddd!

BRACKISH: Don't apologize. I deserved every word of it. Any man who peeks through a keyhole deserves ta' get a key in his eye…
(He laughs, she laughs. There is a pause.)

KATHLEEN: I have a regret. I regret never asking my mother about something before she died. I remember bein' home alone and getting a call from Sherm's, the bar, down by the head of the harbor…My father had caused a commotion…a fight…

BRACKISH: He'd…struck somebody?

KATHLEEN: Opposite. He'd got himself creamed by some big "mukka."

BRACKISH: Oh.

KATHLEEN: They called for Mama to come get him,…Mama wasn't in the house and I felt panicked somethin' wicked. I rode my bike down there in about a minute flat…down over your hill. We were living top of Mt. Pleasant, just near here…

BRACKISH: Yes…

KATHLEEN: Papa was layin' on the floor, drunk…all bloody…singing "Red Roses for a Blue Lady"…I can't ever forget it…me comin' inta' this dark pit of a bar-room, seven yars old, wearin' a powder blue dress with little tulips printed on it…findin' my Da singin' away, drippin' his blood, nobody payin' the slightest attention ta'either of us. I don't think Papa knew who I was. I try ta' lift him but I can't and he keeps singin' the very same words over and over again. *(Sings.)* "I got some red roses, for a blue lady…I got some red roses, for a blue lady." *(Speaks.)* The cops came in…Papa stood up and started walkin' …I followed him. Up Haskell Street hill here…He just kept singing the same words, over and over 'til we got ta' your yard here…Mama had taken our car, and it was parked out at the end here…*(Kathleen screws up her courage. She will now, for the first time in her life, admit to a connection between Brackish and her mother.)* Mama parked her car in yo'r yard, Mr. Brackish!

(Brackish looks away, Kathleen watches him, she continues speaking, again, softly.)

Papa walked up to our car, face still all bloody, and he rubs his fingers in his own blood, after spittin' on 'em, and he takes his hands and does like finger painting, on the windshield…*(Pauses.)* He painted red roses…all in his blood…about a half dozen of 'em, maybe…Then, Papa walked off home. I cleaned off the windshield so's Mama wouldn't get scared when she got into the car and all…

(Kathleen and Brackish allow their eyes to meet, for a moment.)

Mama parked her car in yo'r yard, Mr. Brackish. *(Pause.)* Did you sleep with my mother a lot?

BRACKISH: *(Nods.)* Yes, I would have to say "a lot." Francine and I began seeing each other long after you and your sisters were born. Your father had hit her, and for some reason she came here to me. After that I was here whenever she needed me. *(Pauses)* Being with your mother was the most terrifying and exciting thing I've done in my *(entire)* life.

KATHLEEN: Poor Da…

BRACKISH: *(He pauses.)* Poor Da…poor everybody. He was bellowing his song about the roses out by my gate…Your mother and I went to my window, looked down, and there he was…You, too…tiny little thing, off to one side, as scared as we were…*(He pauses.)* She never came back to me after that day...I never saw her again. *(Sighs.)* I adored your mother, Kathleen...

(Kathleen goes to Brackish, hugs him.)

KATHLEEN: So, why'd you flunk her?

BRACKISH: Why'd I flunk Francine Flynn? Are you kidding? Your mother was a terrible student, Kathleen. How could I pass a student like Francine Flynn? Just because I would choke for oxygen when she walked into my class? Just because my vision darkened and dimmed when I tried to look at her? These are not reasons to pass a poor student. A man's got to have some standards! *(Laughs.)* Oh, God! If the man I am met the man I was, there would be a fist-fight!

(They share a laugh.)

KATHLEEN: If I walked into your class today, would ya'...you know...feel a little blind and dumb? Hard ta' breathe kind of thing. Would ya'?

BRACKISH: Oh, Kathleen...if I could live my life over, I would have you walk into my class and I would behave like an animal! I would choke for oxygen...You would cause a spontaneous pneumothorax... blindness, deafness, mental lapse...I would deliquesce: melt...

(There is a substantial silence.)

Ah, Kathleen...Gloucester! I've got to get some rest, now. *(Brackish stands, bracing himself against Kathleen's arm. He recites a schoolboy poem, softly.)*

Gloss-tah bo'hn...

Gloss-tah bred...

Couple'a days, I'll be

Gloss-tah dead.

(Looks at Kathleen. His accent is now exactly like Kathleen's accent.) I'm wicked awful tired. *(Starts up stairs, falters; falls.)*

KATHLEEN: *(Runs to him.)* Mr. Brackish...?

BRACKISH: I went weak. I'm short of breath.

(Kathleen goes to him. She helps him towards chair as lights fade out.)

BRACKISH: Yuh...Maybe my chair...

(The lights dim down. Kathleen goes to Brackish and leads him slowly, painfully, to his chair. He sits.

Albinoni "Addagio" swells to conclusion, and Pachelbel "Canon in D Major" plays softly.

Lights swell to full. Kathleen is discovered at the phone, ending conversation. She hangs up; goes to Brackish. He is incredibly weak; obviously near death.

Kathleen chirps, happily, as if to pump strength into Brackish's failing spirit.)

KATHLEEN: I had some really great news from Mrs. Dallin down at the High School. They're naming a prize for you. It's official: The Jacob Brackish Prize for Outstanding Scholarship in English Literature and Music Appreciation. Mrs. Dallin is workin' out the final details with Mick Verga, who's president of The Gloucester National Bank, now. Do ya' ba-leeeve that? If the graduate goes ta' Ha'vid, he or, she gets double. Great news, huh? *(She sings Paul Simon's song* "Something So Right," *softly. Brackish is unresponsive. Her smile fades.)* They've all be'n callin', from ten towns around. You'd think it was the Pope himself that was sick, honest ta' God! Some of them wanted ta' run right over here now and give ya' their get-well-quick wishes in person, but, I told 'em all ta' wait till you're feelin' a bit less punk... *(Pause.)* Maybe I better call Dr. Chandler, huh? I won't let 'em take you to any hospital. I'll keep my promise on that, but, maybe he better come over and just have a look, huh?

(She stands and starts to the telephone. The rattle of Death rattles. Brackish dies. Kathleen turns around, in a sudden, looks across to him.)

You say som'pin? *(She goes to Brackish; stares a while before realizing that he is dead. She "crosses" herself.)* Oh God. Oh, God. Oh, God. Oh, God... *(Kathleen removes his glasses, "closes his eyes." She talks to Brackish as if to comfort him.)* You remember Snoddy Timmons from my year? He called. They all called: August Amoré, Franny and Evvie Farina, Harry and Margaret Budd, John Sharp, the Shimmas...God! Everybody! You're really respected around these parts, Jacob. You can't imagine. *(She sits holding his hand, watching him, waiting. They are both at peace. She smiles at Brackish. She holds his hand. She looks at him admiringly. She removes her locket.)* This was Mama's locket. My baby-picture's in one side. Mama, herself, is in the other...from when she was, ya' know, young. I was thinkin' you might want it. I've got other stuff of her's ta' keep for myself... *(Presses locket into his hand.)* Thanks, Mr. Brackish...Jacob. I'll always be grateful. *(Kathleen stands, listens to the music, just one brief moment; she speaks, softly, to a world.)* Pachelbel... *"Canon in D. Major".*..18th Century... Baroque...Beautiful. *(She walks to the telephone, dials the police station.)* Hullo...I wanna' report a death.

THE LIGHTS FADE TO BLACK
THE MUSIC ENDS

END OF PLAY

Henry Lumper

For Grey Johnson.

PRODUCTION HISTORY

Henry Lumper was first presented at the Gloucester Stage Company in Gloucester, Massachusetts (Israel Horovitz as Artistic Director, Ian McColl, Managing Director). The play was subsequently presented in New York by the Working Theatre (Bill Mitchellson as Artistic Director) and the Gloucester Stage Company in association with the Actor's Outlet Theatre on January 31, 1989, directed by Grey Cattell Johnson. The set was designed by David Condino, costumes by José Rivera and lighting by Douglas Kirkpatrick. The Stage Managers were Elizabeth Keeden, Douglas Gettel and Elaine O'Donnell. The New York cast was as follows:

Father O'Malley, Gus, Dan	Rober Arcaro
Mark Lissa	Ralph Bell
Patty Percy	Carol Bradley
Young Henry Boley, Hal Boley	Brian Delato
Ensemble	Michael DellaFemina
Alberta Fusco, Midgy	Beverly Dretzel
Fabiano, Packy, Dr. Berkowitz, Mort Shimma	David Wolos-Fonteno
Angelo Catalano	Randy Frazier
Scroop, Bardolf, Bobby, Cookie, Artie	Kilian Ganly
Young Lissa, Porker, Barry	Anthony J. Gentile
Guido Vega	Billy Gillogly
Pasta	Luis Guzman
Tom Percy	Joseph Jamrog
Allie Richards, Frank Percy	Cullen Johnson
Mrs. Nelson	Mary Klug
Dr. Nagoa, Henchman II, Townsperson	Ben Lin
Jack Silva	Jordan Lund
Ellen Percy, Alice Quigley, Agnes Virgilio	Honour Molloy
Young Tom Percy, Harry Percy	Paul O'Brien
Mary-Ellen Percy	Courtney Peldon
Mrs. Boley, Emily Fusco, Dolly	Cathy Reinheimer
Young Angelo, Petey	Monte Russell
Vernon Koski	Rocky Santo
Henry Boley	Roger Serbagi

CHARACTERS

Henry Boley, leader of the Waterfront Workers and
    Fishermen's Benevolent Association, 70's. *(N.B. to be played
    in Prologue at age 35 by the same actor who plays Hal Boley.)*

Thomas Percy, retired co-leader of WWFBA, Boley's
    contemporary. *(N.B. To be played in Prologue at age 35 by same
    actor who plays Harry Percy .)*

Hal Boley, son of Henry, 30's.

Harry Percy, son of Thomas, 30's.

Patty Percy, wife of Harry, 30's.

Jack Silva, Hal Boley's closest friend, fat; small-time gangster;
    a/k/a Tubby Silva, 30's.

Mark Lissa, 2nd in charge of WWFBA; Hank Boley's closest
    friend; 70's. (To be played in Prologue by 35-year-old actor.)

Petey, Dan & Fitzie, Hal Boley's friends.

Angelo Catalano, 3rd in charge of WWFBA; chubby and
    bald. *(To be played in Prologue by 35-year-old actor.)*

Vernon Koski, Harry's young cousin.

Dr. Nagoa, 2nd in command of the Church of the New Way,
    in Glossop, Mass., a/k/a the "Lillies."

Alberta & Emily Fusco, sisters; two of Hal's many girlfriends.

Guido Vega, Cookie Evangelista, Mort Shimma; various
    Captains

Mrs. Nelson, Hank Boley's housekeeper; kindly; old.

Dolly, Jack Silva's mistress.

Mary-Ellen Percy, Harry's young daughter, age 6.

Bobby, Gus, Mowbray, Hastings, Pasta, Porker, lumpers

Fabiano, a gangster.

Gadshill, Lazzaro, Bardolph, cronies of Silva.

Various Lumpers, Fishermen, Townspeople, Shopkeepers,
    Policemen, Koreans, "Lillies", Doctors, Nurses, etc.

Note: Essential that cast be racially mixed.

PLACE

Various locations in Glossop, Massachusetts, on Cape Ann, including Waterfront Workers and Fishermen's Benevolent Association Hall; homes of Henry Boley, Harry Percy, Thomas Percy, and Jack Silva.

TIME

The play begins thirty years ago, and then leaps to the present.

ACCENT

North Shore Massachusetts ("Pah'k Yo'r Ca'h In Hav'id Yah'd") accent required.

HENRY LUMPER

PROLOGUE

Thirty years ago. Auditorium in darkness. Drumbeats, singly, softly, muffled; funereal. A groaner-foghorn is heard in distance. Lights up (murky, color-filtered to support flash-back) to soft glow on Townspeople, in semi-circle, all reading newspapers with "banners" that feature words "Glossop Chronicle." Townspeople wear tweed caps, workingman variety. Their faces are covered by their newspapers. Semi-circle is upstage of Allie Richards, who is centre-stage, blindfolded, hands tied, facing into auditorium. Two young men, Boley and Percy, stand at either downstage corner of stage, in pin-spots. Both wear oversized oil-skin foul weather gear, and scarves pulled across their faces, masking them. Both hold pistols. An old man, Mark Lissa, steps forward from among the Townspeople and speaks directly to audience as narrator full-voiced; a story-teller.

LISSA: Once upon a time, long, long ago, there was a bustling, lively village in Massachusetts, called Glossop. Glossop was on on Cape Ann, not far from Gloucester, but not quite it.

RICHARDS (*Calling out, suddenly.*). Hankie...Tommy...come on, will ya's! Please, you guys! I'm beggin' ya's? Look? (*Richards falls to knees.*)

LISSA: Glossop was a powerful seaport, without a single condominium on its shore. It was a working port, with livings being made by a thousand lumpers and fishermen; with ships coming in from all over the world.

RICHARDS: *(Pleading.)* Please, Hankie...There's plenty of room for all of us. We know each other. This is crazy!

LISSA: Something happened in Glossop...

TOWNSPEOPLE: *(Whisper in unison.)* Murder.

RICHARDS: Think of yo'r kids! You guys both have kids...they're gonna' hav'ta' grow up with this! *(Suddenly; he yells his plea.)* Tommy! Hankie! For God's sakes, pleeease!

LISSA: *(Points to men as he names them.)* That man, *(Points.)* Allie Richards, inherited leadership of the Waterfront Workers and Fishermen's Benevolant Association...the Union for Glossop's fishermen, fish-plant workers and lumpers...from his father, Alfred Richards, Senior, by Union Law, upon the elder Richards' death...

DOLLY: The elder Richards was an honest man and a good leader, but his son, this younger Richards *(Points.)* was a racketeer and a thief...

LISSA: In no time, young Richards stained the Glossop waters, opening the port to drugs and easy money. Two young Glossop men...Henry Boley: *(Points.)* him...and Thomas Percy: *(Points.)* him...set out to stop him.

RICHARDS: Jesus, Hank! Listen to me!

PRIEST: They singled Richards out, cornered him, shot him dead.

RICHARDS: I got friends, ya' know! I got plenty of friends! Tommy! Hankie! Come onnnnn!

DOLLY: They hid his body in an ice house...

RICHARDS: Your kids will hav'ta live with this!

TOWNSPEOPLE: *(In a whisper; in unison.)* Murder.

PRIEST: Young Henry Boley and young Tom Percy carried Allie Richards' dead body, frozen solid in the center of a block of ice, on to a lobster boat, which they sank off Bass Rocks...after chaining the corpse to cement blocks...

RICHARDS: Jesus, Hankie, don't!

TOWNSPEOPLE: *(In a whisper.)* Murder.

LISSA: A town turned its eyes and tongues inward. Jaws and front doors slammed shut. Hearts burned secretly in great gratitude to the two young men...

RICHARDS: Jesus, Hankie, Tommy, please, no, no, nooooo!

(Boley and Percy each raise an arm now, pointing pistols at Richards.)

TOWNSPEOPLE: *(They turn upstage; backs to the crime. They whisper, in unison.)* Murder.

(Suddenly, four drumbeats. Boley and Percy shoot Richards, who is in-

stantly dead, pitching forward, on his belly, legs and arms splayed every-which-way. Boley and Percy drag the dead Richards, by the feet, in a full circle of the lower stage, finally pulling him through the crowd of Towns-people, upstage. Lissa looks at the audience. He speaks softly.)

LISSA: The fish is fried. Long live the cooks.

(*The lights fade out.*)

END OF PROLOGUE

ACT ONE
Scene One

In the darkness, we hear laughter; cheers. Uptempo popular period song is playing on record-player; probably Eddie Fisher, singing "Oh, My Papa." Lights up in Waterfront Workers and Fishermen's Benevolent Association Hall. N.B. lighting remains color-filtered to support flashback. Turntable used to glide actors into scene, if possible.

Henry Boley and Thomas Percy are being sworn in as co-leaders of the WWFBA, They will be co-Number Ones. Both men are in their early thirties. They face Mark Lissa, who is officiating: leading the ceremony.

A row of men in tweed sport coats and cloth caps stretches across the edge of the stage: the footlights. Women stand in a row in front of men. Children beside women. The scene begins with a young Mark Lissa, 35, admonishing the spectators good-naturedly.

LISSA: I asked ya's all, nicely, ta' quiet down, now, I'm gonna' hav'ta insist: quiet it down!

MAN #1: Quiet it down!

MAN #2: Shut it up!

MAN #3: We're starting!

LISSA: I'm gonna' start the swearin' in ceremony…

MAN #1 Cover yo'r kids' ears. There's gonna' be some swearin'!

(*Laughter from all. Ruth Boley, calls down to Baby Hal Boley, 3.*)

RUTH: Can you see okay, Hally?

LITTLE HAL: Uh uh, I can't! Lift me up!

(*Baby Harry Percy, also 3, calls out from opposite side of stage.*)

HARRY: I can't see either, Mama! I can't see! Lift me up…

(Ellen Percy lifts her child into her arms. Ruth Boley lifts Hal into her arms. A young Angelo Catalano 35, points and calls out.)

ANGELO: Hey, Hank, watch out! The co-Sons-of-One are itching ta' take over, already!

HANK BOLEY: Bring 'em both up here! Give Hal to me Ruthie.

(Boley reaches out and takes his son from his wife, setting Little Hal down beside him.)

TOM PERCY: Come on, Harry, you, too! Gimme him, El…

(Cheers and laughter as Tom Percy now holds his son's hand in the air, as well.)

HANK BOLEY: *(Calls out to all.)* You got the next hundred years of union leadership in front of ya's!

(All cheer and laugh. Lissa raps gavel, six sharp raps, calling the ceremony back to order.)

LISSA: This is serious stuff!

LUMPER IN BACK: *(Calls out, heckling.)* Markie's in a hurry. He must be hungry!

LISSA: Goddam right!

(Laughter from all, Lissa suddenly remembers clergymen nearby; shows them his palms.)

Oh, Lord, sorry, father…*(Lissa raps gavel again. The gavel is small, gold, antique.)* Both of ya's, touch the gavel at the same time, to-gether…

(Boley and Percy try to fit their large hands on to the gavel's tiny han-dle.)

HANK BOLEY: Our hands don't fit…

(Laughter from all.)

LISSA: We're gonna hav'ta' get ourselves a bigger gavel…

(Laughter from all. Lissa stands facing Boley and Percy, awkwardly, and begins the formal ceremony. They stand awkwardly touching the gavel's handle at the same time.)

LISSA: For the first time in the one hundred year history of the Waterfront Workers and Fishermen's Benevolent Association, we are swearing in a Number One who wasn't born to it: who wasn't a Son of One.

(Boley turns out front and smiles to his wife. Ruthie waves to her hus-band, smiling.)

This starts a new line of command for the WWFBA and a new line of leadership…*(Nods to Angelo.)* Our Business Agent, Angelo Cata-lano, has the next thing to say here…

(Angelo Catalano, a young black man, steps forward, nervously, for his

spot of public speaking. Percy turns out front and smiles and waves, discreetly, to his wife. Ellen waves back to Percy.)

ANGELO: If there is any dues-paid-up member who wishes to lodge a complaint against either Thomas Percy or Henry Boley, let him do so at this particular time, 'cause these men will be in charge here for years and years to come...

(Applause and cheers from all after a small silence and a couple of giggles. It is all good cheer. Lissa raps the gavel four times, officiously, bringing quiet to the room, once again.)

Save your applause for afta'...*(Pauses.)* Do I hear no complaints?

(Silently, each person in the line looks to the person next to him. Angelo nods to Lissa.)

Blessing.

LISSA: Both Father Scroop, from Our Lady of the Good Voyage Church, and Father O'Malley, from St. Ann's, have agreed to bless this swearin' in...bow your heads.

(Two Priests step forward. Both are youngish. O'Malley is skinny; Scroop is thick. O'Malley talks.)

O'MALLEY: We start here with a silent remembrance of Alfred Richards, who led this waterfront, as did his father and grandfather before him, until his tragic and premature death at sea...

(There is a small silence. Boley looks at Percy, who looks away and down. Townspeople whisper, softly, a single word.)

TOWNSPEOPLE: *(severally)* Murder.

O'MALLEY: We ask Jesus Christ to walk beside Henry Boley and Thomas Percy to help them be gracious and thoughtful leaders...

(O'Malley nods to Father Scroop.)

SCROOP: In the name of the Father, the Son and the Holy Ghost...on this day, March 31st, in the year of our Lord, Nineteen Hundred and Fifty-Nine (*N.B. Adjust date to 30 years prior to performance*)... Amen.

O'MALLEY: *(Overlaps.)* Amen...

ALL: Amen...

(A cheer goes up from all assembled. Lissa hands the gavel over to the two men. There is an uncomfortable moment and each wonders who will hold the gavel. Percy relinquishes his grip and hands the gavel over to Boley. The lights narrow to a spotlight on Boley and Percy. Crossfade to a spotlight on Fabiano, a thin, mean-faced gangster, backed by two stubby henchmen. Fabiano is enraged. He screams, loudly.)

FABIANO: What the fuck is going on here? What the fuck is goin' on here? What the fuck is goin' on here??? *(Shrieks.)* I wanna see the new Number One! Where is he? WHERE...IS...HEEE?

(The lights widen now to fill the stage, changing color. We are now on State Wharf, still in flashback. N.B. If a turntable is used, Fabiano and henchmen will walk downstage at the same time the turntable turns a one-third turn, upstage. The women and children have turned upstage. The men stand together in two clots; behind Percy and behind Boley. Each man carries a crate on his shoulder.)

BOLEY: You're lookin' at him, Fabiano...

PERCY: Right over here, Fabiano...

BOLEY: *(Softly, clearly.)* You were warned not to expect Glossop lumpers to handle this load. This port is closed to you and yours, Fabiano. This is a fact of life...

FABIANO: Do you know who you're talkin' to?

BOLEY: Alfred Fabiano, a no-brained Palooka who ain't gonna set foot in Glossop for the rest of his life, unless he wants to float like his box of goods there...

(Fabiano starts to reach for a gun in his pocket.)

Don't! It'd be a shitty way ta' die, Fabiano. Don't.

(Every man on stage, except Boley and Percy, holds a pistol pointed at Fabiano and two henchmen.)

HENCHMAN #1: Don't, Alf!

HENCHMAN #2: Hold off, Alfie.

FABIANO: That box of goods in the water's got eight to ten pounds, un-cut. That's worth about $9,000 to us on the street... *(A sudden smile.)* Listen up, you guys, huh? We can do business, yes?

BOLEY: We ain't doin' business, Fabiano. Glossop's closed to you and yours. *(Boley nods to the Lumpers, who, one by one, dump their crates into the "harbor." It is the Boston Tea Party reincarnate. Note: Possible to set wading pool, O.S., filled with water, for authentic splash.)*

FABIANO: You guys crazy? You know what that's worth? *(Sees guns, realizes.)* Hey, what the hell are you doing, huh?

BOLEY: Swim...straight across. It's only fifty yards from here to the wharf in front'a Sherm's, Fabiano...Nothin' to it...

PERCY: Nothin' to it...Swim!

BOLEY: What's a'matter? You ha'hd of hearin'?

(Fabiano and his henchmen look at one another. Boley nods to Lumpers who extend their arms, pointing their guns now directly at the gangsters.)

Swim, and live to tell about it. Or, don't. You got a choice.
(Suddenly, Fabiano and the two henchmen turn and run to the "Harbor." They leap into the space where the Lumpers dumped the crates, earlier. There is a splash, another, another; and then the Lumpers cheer. Boley and Percy embrace.)
We did it! We goddam did it!
(Sudden silence. Tableau. Lissa, Boley, Percy, Angelo, arms around one another, frozen in place.)

END OF SCENE ONE

Scene Two

N.B. From now on, the action will take place in the present. Thus, lighting should be brighter and less obviously stylized, to support a sense of reality: time present. Further, costumes should now be contemporary, as should all background music to individual scenes. It would be greatly helpful if some small, easily-recognizable link were found between the Boley and Percy of 30 years ago and the Percy might smoke a pipe and older Tom Percy might still smoke the same pipe. Or a particular article of clothing may be worn. Or Boley might own a gold pocket watch, which is prominent through the play, ending up in Hal's possession at the end of the play.

Old Mark Lissa moves to the four young men frozen in tableau. He speaks to audience, directly.

LISSA: Thirty years have passed. *(Pauses.)* Lumpers grow old, early, too early. And there's no turnin' back.
(An Old Hank Boley and an Old Tom Percy now "take over" from the Young Hank Boley and the Young Tom Percy. They are both in their 60's. Boley is dying of cancer. He is boney, hawklike. There is a ritual passing of the gavel, from Boley to Boley, and a rain-slicker from Percy to Percy. The YoungBoley and Young Percy exit, arm in arm.)
Thirty years have passed. This is Henry Boley, now...
(Old Boley crosses to table, where Old Angelo sits, drinking coffee.)
And that's Tom Percy.
(Old Percy, carrying gardening tools, exits. Old Mark Lissa enters; crosses to Young Mark Lissa, who puts his arm on the old man's shoulder; smiles to audience.)

This's Angelo Catalano now. And this is me: Markie Lissa. Old men: all of us.

(Young Lissa exits. Old Lissa walks to table, across stage, joins Angelo and Hank Boley at table; sits. The lights crossfade with Lissa. SFX: Possible to have Music on juke-box in b.g., probably Springsteen, contemporary labor song, playing lightly, under scene. Boley sits at a tiny table in a small pastry shop, with Angelo and Mark Lissa. Possible that other men might be around other tables, drinking coffee, eating pastry, talking softly.)

LISSA: *(To Angelo)* You tell him yet? *(Boley looks up at Lissa.)* Somebody dumped a couple'a Hefty bags full'a Pogies onta' the Mayor's front steps...

BOLEY: You kiddin' me?

ANGELO: They were chucking some dead fish all over up around Haskell and Hammond, too...

BOLEY: How come?

LISSA: Gettin' back at some of the neighborhood people up there who got the Board of Health to close the plant down...

BOLEY: What's the matter with our boys? Neighborhood people didn't get any plant closed down. Nobody at the State House is listenin' to neighborhood people. It's the condo developers got Glossop Protein shut...who's gonna' plunk down a quarter-of-a-million for a l-bedroom condo with a view of the harbor and the stink of the stuff Glossop Protein's producing.

LISSA: Gurry...

ANGELO: If that's protein, I'm stickin' with carbohydrates. Beer, bread, pasta...That's what Carmella says.

BOLEY: It's always the lumpers and the fishermen that lose out...and neighborhood people and local politicians always catchin' hell... takin' the blame. I'm sick of it. *(To Lissa.)* Markie, I wanna' set up a meeting, say, Thursday, with the top ten condo developers and plant-owners. Tell the plant men we wanna' talk about a new contract. Tell the developers we've got some waterfront property we're thinkin' of letting go...They'll all be anxious to meet with us...

(A younger man, Guido Vega, has entered; stands to one side waiting for Boley to acknowledge him. Angelo pokes Boley.)

ANGELO: Hank, I think Guido's waitin'...

(Boley looks up.)

GUIDO: Hi, Hank. How goes it?

BOLEY: Yuh, sure, sit. *(Calls out to shop-owner.)* Hey, Mike, another round of coffees. Four…*(To Guido.)* You hungry? Anybody want another pastry?

(They indicate "no.")

GUIDO: Just coffee for me, thanks, Hank.

BOLEY: *(Calls out to shop-owner.)* Just the four coffees! *(To Guido.)* So, how come you look nervous?

LISSA: Two guesses…

BOLEY: Well, I know damn well you ain't the one's been throwin' Pogies around the mayor's house, so, my guess is you wanna' bring another cousin over.

GUIDO: I do, yuh. He's 18. He's speaking a little English, already, too. He's a good kid. Yuh, I do.

BOLEY: You got room in the house?

GUIDO: Yuh, sure, there's room.

ANGELO: Your sister-in-law must have a good nature, huh?

(All laugh.)

GUIDO: There's room.

LISSA: Maybe she likes young cousins livin' in!

(All laugh, heartily. Guido is annoyed.)

GUIDO: I said "There's room"!

BOLEY: *(Seeing Guido's anxiety.)* Can we make him your responsibility, direct?

GUIDO: *(Breaks into a smile.)* I swear to God.

(Boley nods a "yes" to Lissa.)

LISSA: Okay. Call Sally Morella down at North Shore Fish as soon as the kid's boat gets in. He'll start him lumpin'. When do you expect him?

GUIDO: His boat left Lisbon, three days ago. He should be here Saturday.

BOLEY: He left Lisbon, already?

GUIDO: Yuh, well…*(Shrugs.)*

BOLEY: *(Smiles.)* No wonder you were nervous…*(To all, smiling.)* No wonder he was nervous, huh? *(To Guido.)* How come he ain't flyin' a jet plane? It's 1989.** People don't take boats anymore…

** *(Change to year in which play is being performed.)*

GUIDO: Gettin' paid to work crew on a freighter's a hell of a lot better than buyin' tickets on a jet plane, huh?

BOLEY: Smart. It'll be good ta' have another Vega lumpin' in Glossop.

ANGELO: Oh, yuh, right…We only got a hundred and ninety-nine Vegas on the books, so far. It'll be great ta' have an even hundred!

GUIDO: *(Happily; pumps Boley's hand.)* Thanks so much, Hank, huh?

Markie, Angelo…thanks. *(Guido exits; yells to cousin awaiting him.)* He said 'Yes'!

BOLEY: Good kid: Guido, huh?

LISSA: Oh, yuh, excellent. Hard-workin', family-oriented…

ANGELO: Family? Sure thing, Lissa…Nothin' but family!

BOLEY: You related to Guido?

ANGELO: All the Porteguees are related! You kiddin' me?

LISSA: Yuh, well, if Porteguees don't help each other, we ain't gonna' catch much help… *(Boley looks at his watch.)* Not around these parts, anyhow…

BOLEY: Whoa, I'm late. I'm s'pose ta' bring Mrs. Nelson her St. Joseph's roll by noon…

(Boley stands, walks to the other side of stage. Lights crossfade with him to line of People waiting for fresh bread, in shop. As people see Boley, They step out of his way, usher him forward, to head of line.)

YOUNG MAN: Hey, Hank. Great day, huh?

BOLEY: It's a pip…

OLDER MAN: Hey, Hankie, you're lookin' good!

(Young man and young woman exchange a grim glance. Young woman silently mouths the word "Cancer.")

YOUNG WOMAN: *(Cancer.)*

BOLEY: Hey, Austin. How's the family?

OLDER MAN: Everbody's excellent, Hank. Hear Hal's home…

BOLEY: Yup, he's back…

(Agnes, an older woman, enters carrying tray of freshly-baked rolls.)

AGNES: Who's first? *(Sees Boley.)* How many, Hank?

BOLEY: The usual.

(Agnes puts two rolls in a waxed paper bag, and hands them to Boley without looking for or taking any money. Boley takes one of the rolls out of bag; nibbles and eats, as he talks.)

BOLEY: How's Frankie's wedding shaping up?

AGNES: Don't ask. *(Boley smiles.)* I see Hal's livin' back home.

BOLEY: He's back in Glossop, yuh…

AGNES: You're lucky. Must be nice ta' have him back.

BOLEY: Definitely nice, yuh.

AGNES: Frankie and his wife's gonna' live down Swampscott…I'll never see them!

BOLEY: You'll be seein' them plenty. Don't you worry.

AGNES: I guess. See ya', Hank.

(Boley exits. Man steps to head of line; speaks to Agnes, as woman joins in.)

MAN: He looks rough...

WOMAN: He's getting worse...

AGNES: Cancer...

ANOTHER OLDER MAN: *(Whispers.)* Cancer...

(The lights crossfade to Mrs. Nelson a kindly older woman, Boley's house-keeper. She calls out to Boley. She carries a few plastic bags, filled with her belongings.)

BOLEY: You done, already?

MRS. NELSON: You didn't mess it up much this week...

BOLEY: That's what you said last week...

MRS. NELSON: You didn't mess it up much last week, either... *(Smiles.)* The kitchen floor's still wet. If you wanna, you could walk in that way and make a hell of a mess... *(Laughs.)* Guess Hal ain't stayin' home, huh?

(Boley looks at her. She shrugs.)

MRS. NELSON: His room ain't been touched.

BOLEY: Oh, yuh, no. He's stayin' with a friend... *(Boley takes remaining St. Joseph roll in its bag and hands it to Mrs. Nelson.)* Brought you your roll. Guess you ate something already. I got talkin' down to Mike's. I'm pretty late... You need a lift home?

MRS. NELSON: Kathy's on her way... *(Looks at St. Joseph's roll.)* Sure you don't want it yourself?

BOLEY: Nope. It's yours...

MRS. NELSON: It'll save me goin' downtown, later...for my supp'ah roll. Traffic's a mess, 'counta the goddam Lillie restaurant...

BOLEY: Yuh, I saw that just now. About fifty or so pickets...

MRS. NELSON: Foolishness.

BOLEY: The picketing?

MRS. NELSON:...The sellin' the place ta' Lillies ta' begin with. Imagine: the Catholic Church reads that Dr. Lill and his whole cult-following of Jesus-haters and child-kipnappers wanna' buy a building in Glossop to set up their world-wide headquarters. What do they do? Do they warn their Parishoners to lock their doors? No! They sell Lill a building! Sell Lill a building! Catholics are as crazy as bedbugs, if you ask me.

BOLEY: Catholics?

MRS. NELSON: Shoo-ahh! Now we got Lillies everywhere you turn! And who's to blame? The Catholics! Makes me want to spit! *(She makes a spitting noise.)* Ptwieeuu! They're wreckin' the fish business and the whole goddam waterfront, if you ask me!

BOLEY: The Catholics?

MRS. NELSON: The Lillies! They're undercuttin' everybody's prices! *(Boley smiles. Mrs. Nelson smiles.)* Ahhhhhh... You're always pullin' my leg. *(Lifts one leg.)* It's a wonder it ain't ten inches longer than it is... *(Laughs; then suddenly.)* Oh, God! 'Course you're a Catholic yo'r-self !!!

BOLEY: *(Smiles.)* Oh, yuh, well... not devout...

MRS. NELSON: I'm always shooting off my mouth... This Lillie business has everybody nuts! My nephew Gus says we ought'a band together like an Army and run the Lillies up 128 and right the hell out'ta' this town!

BOLEY: Yuh, well, there's enough fish out there ta' go around for every-body...

MRS. NELSON: Yuh, well, I guess...

BOLEY: And this kidnapping-of-Glossop-kids business never seemed to materialize, did it?

MRS. NELSON: Yuh, well, I just don't like the look of 'em! They wear funny clothes... and, let's face it: they're not white, are they?

(The sound of a car's horn blowing, off-stage, in the distance.)

MRS. NELSON: There's Kathy. I gotta' scoot...

BOLEY: I left your check on the table. You get it?

MRS. NELSON: I did. Thanks. Give Hal a big hug for me, okay?

BOLEY: See you next Saturday, Mrs. Nelson...

(N.B. If turntable is used, Boley and Mrs. Nelson are taken upstage as Patty Percy and Mary-Ellen are brought on-stage. Hal should enter, walking past his father and Mrs. Nelson, crossing past Patty, then stop-ping, looking back, going to her, as turntable stops.)

END OF SCENE TWO

Scene Three

The lights crossfade to Patty Percy, 30, with her 6 year old daughter, Mary-Ellen. She is frozen in place, staring across at Hal Boley, also 30. Patty and Hal are both extremely good-looking; both unusually so.

PATTY: *(Giggles.)* My Goddd! *(Giggles.)* Is that really you?

(Hal walks to Patty, without speaking. He and Patty circle each other, giggling, like high-schoolers. After a few seconds, Patty remembers her daughter; steps back.)

This is Mary-Ellen. She's mine...

HAL: Hi-ya, Mary-Ellen. You're nine?

MARY-ELLEN: Yuh, right. I'm a dwarf!

PATTY: *(Laughs.)* I didn't say "she's nine": I said she's mine...

MARY-ELLEN: I'm six.

PATTY: She's six.

HAL: Hi-ya Mary-Ellen. You look very tall...for a dwarf. *(To Mary-Ellen; babbles a story, drunkenly, rapidly.)* I knew this kid once who totally freaked when saw his first dwarf...a little fat one, leaning up against a building, smoking this big cigar. The kid says to his mother "Ma, what's that?" The mother goes: "That's a dwarf." The kid goes "What's a dwarf?" Mother says: "A dwarf's an adult who never grows. Everything else is normal, except his size." After about five minutes, the kid goes: "Hey, Ma, am I a kid, or am I a dwarf?" *(Hal smiles at Patty and Mary-Ellen.)*

PATTY: I married Harry.

HAL: You married Harry. That's great. Well...that's great. I've, uh, gotta' go...See you later, Mary-Ellen. Don't smoke cigars, okay?
(Exits.)

MARY-ELLEN: *(With a professional comic's timing.)* Who the hell was that?

PATTY: He's an old friend of your father's. We went all through school together...

MARY-ELLEN: What's his name, so I can tell Daddy we saw him?

PATTY: Let's not do that right away, Mary-Ellen. We'll tell Daddy later...

MARY-ELLEN: When?

PATTY: How's about ten years?
(Patty laughs. The laughter is joined by the laughter of three Lumpers: Bobby, Porker, and Gus, across stage. Hal passes them, nods a greeting. The lights crossfade.)

HAL: Bobby...Porker...How goes it, Gus?

GUS: Good. How goes it with you?

HAL: Good.
(Hal exits. The Lumpers exchange an astonished moment.)

GUS: Was that...Hal Boley?

BOBBY: Looked like 'im...

PORKER: Was. He come into the diner, end'a last week...

GUS: You sure?

PORKER: 'course, I'm sure. He was the only one come in all mornin'...
Quarter-pa'hst-six, ordered two eggs over easy and home fries.

GUS: Couldn't've finished 'em, huh?

PORKER: What's that s'pose'ta mean, asshole? Some kind of smartassed
diner-putdown?

GUS: I just meant 'cause the man's wicked skinny. He couldn't'a ate
nothin'...

PORKER: Oh, yuh. I see what ya' meant.

GUS: Ivy League bullshit, probably. All them top colleges make ya'
promise ta stay skinny, or they won't graduate you...

BOBBY: Juicy Reed was sayin' Hal moved back home...

PORKER: Two weeks now.

GUS: The man's a waste...

BOBBY: He musta' changed some, if he's gettin' up for breakfast at quarter-pa'hst-six...

PORKER: He wasn't gettin' up. Opposite. Just headin' home. He's stayin'
over with Fatso, Tubby Silva.

BOBBY: Oh, yuh.

GUS: *(Laughs.)* People don't change...

PORKER: He was pretty wasted. I had'da call 'im a taxi.

GUS: Imagine takin' taxies in Glossop? My-my, isn't that sophisticated?
Must be tough bein' the Son of One and the Son of God, both at the
same time!
*(The three Lumpers laugh. Their laughter is joined by the laughter of two
women: Alberta & Emily Fusco. Lights crossfade now to opposite side of
the stage. Patty and Mary-Ellen are gone and replaced by the women,
who are in bed with Hal Boley. Hal and the two women are all extremely
drunk. Hal kisses one and then the other. They all laugh.*

*N.B. If turntable is used, a one-third turn should have carried Patty
and Mary-Ellen off-stage prior to scene with Hal, Porker, Bobby, etc.,
and another one-third turn should now replace the Lumpers with the
Fusco sisters, allowing Hal a fairly natural walk from one scene to the
next, with the change in locale supported by a lighting change and introduction of music, in a new scene.)*

END OF SCENE THREE

Scene Four

SFX: Music, probably Madonna song: "Get In The Groove," off, in background softly.

HAL: Don't go, huh?

EMILY: We gotta' go, Hal. We're both workin' the nightshift this week. Really, we gotta'...

HAL: You don't gotta'...Stay with me, huh? Come onnn ..

ALBERTA: What for?

HAL: What for? For me, that's what for. For me, for your sister Alberta...

ALBERTA: I'm Alberta. She's Emily...

HAL: Of course, you're Alberta. You think I didn't know that? I knew that...

EMILY: You already slept with us. What's left?

ALBERTA: *(Giggles.)* Emmmileeee!

HAL: *(Loudly.)* I have NOT slept with you! I have been awake with you. Fornicating!

ALBERTA: *(To the neighborhood; good-naturedly.)* Excuse me, neighbors! Could everybody hear that?
(They all laugh.)

EMILY: What did Tubby Silva tell you about us, anyhow? Did he tell you we did doubles?
(The sisters giggle, but Hal is oblivious to what they're saying. He is staring up at the sky.)

HAL: Shhh! *(The girls look at him, puzzled.)* How come it's dark?

EMILY: Uhhh, lemmme' guess. 'Cause it's night?...

HAL: Night! I gotta' go!

EMILY: Why? Heavy date?
(SFX: Music now electronic; mysterious. The lights crossfade to spotlight on Jack Silva, 30, enormously fat.)

HAL: Heavy date? *(Laughs.)* That's funny...*(Whoops with laughter, drunkenly.)* That's hilarious!
(Silva is directing three cohorts, Barry, Bardolph and Gadshill, in the stealing of computers and computer parts, stacked in clean carton boxes, under a canvas. They carry the cartons offstage, quickly, and return for others. Silva is not doing any actual/visible labor. N.B. If turntable is used, full turn will carry Hal, et alia, off, and Silva, et alia, on.)

SILVA: Careful, careful...

BARDOLPH: Grab an end...

SILVA: I don't grab ends...

BARRY: Aren't you gonna' help?

SILVA: Absolutely not. *(To Gadshill.)* Careful with that, Gadshill! That's not your wife, you know, that crate is worth something!

GADSHILL: Fuck you, Silva, okay?

(Lazzaro, a stump of a man, enters.)

LAZZARO: What's this I hear, Silva? 600 a crate?

SILVA: I know. I'm too generous...

LAZZARO: Wiseass! I wouldn't give my mother 600 a crate...

SILVA: I don't know your mother...but, if you say she's not worth 600, your word's good enough for me. But, 600's our price, Lazzaro.

LAZZARO: 400's my limit...

(The lighting shifts to Hal leaving the Fusco sisters. Petey calls out to him from their you.)

PETEY: Hey, Hallie! Let's go!

HAL: This is my pal, Petey. This is either Emily Fusco or Alberta Fusco. And this is either Alberta Fusco or Emily Fusco.

PETEY: *(Kisses theirs hands; speaks French.)* Enchanté, Mesdemoiselles...

ALBERTA: What's with the French. You Canadian or something?

PETEY: I'm something. I'm not Canadian.

HAL: Petey's my good friend. He's not my best friend. We're about to rob my best friend.

EMILY: Tubby Silva? You're gonna' rob Tubby Silva? He's your best friend, right?

HAL: Well, it's not exactly robbing. It's more like whale-watching, only with guns.

(Petey and Hal laugh.)

ALBERTA: What'cha' gonna' do to Silva?

HAL: It's Tubby's birthday...

PETEY: We're giving him the surprise party of his life!

(Petey and Hal laugh again. The light shifts back to Silva. Two other Lumpers stand behind Lazzaro: his helpers.)

LUMPER: How many more cartons are goin'?

(From the opposite side of the stage, suddenly, two men call out from the shadows. It is Dan and Hal, voices gruffly disguised. They wear comic masks. They appear to have handguns, one in each hand.)

DAN: Everybody lay face down on the ground!

HAL: You heard him! DOWN!

BARDOLPH: Aww, shit.

GADSHILL: God damn it…

PETEY: *(Offstage.)* You heard him!!! All 'a' you's!!! LAY DOWN!!!
(Blinding white quartz light is switched on; shines on to audience, obscuring the stage.)

BARRY: What the fuck gives???

SILVA: Oh. My God. Oh, my God…

HAL: *(Offstage.)* Lay down and shut up!
(Everybody lays down on the ground. Petey, voice disguised, calls out.)

PETEY: We want the keys to both trucks, now! NOW!!
(Lazzaro stands, throws car keys, which Dan catches. Bardolph throws another set of car keys which Hal catches. A blinding light also shines on Lazzaro and Bardolph, preventing their seeing the "robbers." The light shines from a video-camera in the hands of a light attached to the camera in the hands of a fattish man, Fitzie, who is video-taping the entire proceedings. Hal screams in a disguised voice.)

HAL: Listen! All of ya's: take off! Sta'ht runnin'! I said "Sta'ht running!"
On yo'r marks…get set…and don't a one of ya's look back, neither!
GO!
(The men behind the voices begin to laugh. the three Lumpers stand, look at one another quizzically, and, one by one, run off. Silva now stands and he begins to run. Barry stands and follows Silva. Now, Bardolph does the same. Now, Gadshill follows, as well. All exit. The lights on audience are switched off.

Hal, Petey and Dan move to centre-stage, laughing uncontrollably. They turn and face Fitzie and his video-camera, "filming" the event. They each hold bananas, one in each hand. They laugh uproariously, waving their bananas: their "guns.")

HAL: Get our bananas! Get our bananas!

FITZIE: Got it…
(Hal, Petey, Fitzie & Dan are crippled with laughter and self-congratulations.)

PETEY: Oh Goddd…Did you hear himmm?

HAL: *(Laughing; to Dan.)* We'd better get a move on. You and Fitzie head over to the Rigger and set up. Petey and I'll put this stuff back….
(Dan and Fitzie exit and Hal and Petey quickly restack the cartons. As they work, Mark Lissa enters and stands watching their labor.)

PETEY: That's it…

HAL: Great... *(Hal turns; sees Lissa; jumps.)* Jesus! You scared us, Markie...

LISSA: What the hell are you doing here, Hal?

HAL: You know Petey Parnell? Petey's Maxie Parnell's boy. *(To Petey.)* You know Markie Lissa? Markie's my father's oldest and closest friend, aren't 'cha', Markie?

LISSA: *(To Hal.)* You're a fuckin' disgrace, you know that?

HAL: *(Smiles.)* Okay, well, listen, great seein' you again, Markie. Hell of a night, huh?

LISSA: I'm gonna' get your ass for this, Hal. I'm tellin' ya', face-ta'-face.

(Lights crossfade to Jack Silva, opposite side of stage, telling his version of what happened that night: he was robbed. N.B. If turntable used, full turn wanted to change scene.)

SILVA: They were humongous, but, the leader was off the charts. Six eleven...the one they called "The Little Guy" was maybe six-two, six-three...Maybe even bigger.

(Lights widen to include Hal, Dan, Fitzie, and Petey, facing Bardolph, Silva, Barry, and Gadshill. A TV-video monitor is in evidence. All men are holding back laughter.)

HAL: *(False amazement; overly innocent.)* Jeepers, Tubby, what was it? A basketball team that held you up?

SILVA: I'm tellin' ya's: they had'da average six-six, with the leader six-eleven. On my mother's grave...I swear!

HAL: This happened on your mother's grave?

GADSHILL: *(Embarrassed.)* He wasn't six-eleven...

SILVA: *(Angry.)* He was! He was pointing a stun-gun in my face!

(Petey and Hal roar. Gadshill laughs, as well. Silva yells at Gadshill, first; than, at Hal)

SILVA: What's so funny? What are you laughing at? What's so funny? What's so funny? What is so goddam funny?

HAL: Let's watch a little TV, Tubby, huhhh?

(Dan and Fitzie start the "playback" of the tape on the TV monitor. N.B. Possible to overhang TV monitor over stage, facing audience, to use for screening "robbery" sequence, as well as screening tape of actual settings, scene for scene. For example, an interior of a barroom's back room could be featured going into the present scene; an interior of a Board Room could be used to set up Boley's WWFBA Hall scenes; etc. If using an actual TV monitor isn't feasible, it is possible to use a flickering light to indicate a TV monitor adding in a sound recording of the "robbery" as playback. Silva reaction is more important than the actual videotape.

Silva and others stand watching the tape play back. Everyone other than Silva is hysterical with laughter.)

BARRY: You look great on TV, Tubby!

HAL: So?

PETEY: So?

BARDOLPH & BARRY: So?

GADSHILL, DAN & FITZIE: So?

SILVA: *(After a pause.)* Nice, really nice…

GADSHILL & PETEY: *(Sing.)* "I'm Chiquita Banana and I'm here to say…"

HAL: Happy Birthday, Jack…

BARDOLPH: Happy Birthday, Tubby…

FITZIE: *(Appears with creamy-frosted birthday cake, which all get behind and march toward Silva.)* Happy Birthday, Jack…

ALL: *(Sing.)* Happy Birthday to You…Happy Birthday to You…Happy Birthday, dear Jackieee *(N.B. Some sing "Tubbyyy")* Happy Birthday to you…

HAL: I wanna' make a small speech here. I wanna' thank Jackie Silva, a man who's been my best friend since 1st grade…a man who took me back into his life when I came back from the big city…destitute, friendless, drunk out'a my gourd! I wanna' now do for Jack Silva what I have done for no other man…

(As they near Silva, he realizes that they are about to hit him in the face with the birthday cake. He backs away.)

SILVA: You wouldn't dare!

(They dare. The birthday cake is added to his face. Blackout.)

END OF SCENE FOUR

(Uptempo music in. N.B. If turntable used, full turn wanted here to change scene, totally. New lighting wanted, as well.)

Scene Five

Bright, white morning light up, opposite side of stage, on three men, in line: Gus and Pasta and Porker. They are joined by a fourth man, Bobby.

GUS, PASTA AND PORKER: Hey, Bobby…Bob…etc…

BOBBY: Hey, Pasta. How goes it? Gus...Hey, Porker. Sorry about the diner.

PORKER: Oh, yuh, well, thanks...

GUS: What's with the diner, Porker?

PASTA: Big fuckin' piece in the fuckin' paper last night...

PORKER: We're closin' down...

GUS: No kidding?

(Hal enters, opposite side, at the same time another man enters. He is a burly lumper, Salvie Reed. Both Hal and Salvie are signing in for work. Sal and Hal suffer from hangovers and from not getting to bed as of yet. They chat and then join the line together.)

SALVIE: Hey, Hal. Big head?

HAL: Oh, yuh, both of them. I gotta' sign in and get myself home ta' bed...

SALVIE:Must be nice.

(Hal and Salvie join the line behind, Pasta, Porker, Bobby, Gus, who do not notice Hal, who is the sole "feather-bedder" among them all.)

PORKER:...What with my Pa and me workin' long hours and takin' nothing out'ta' the place. Makes no sense to keep it open...

PASTA: The fuckin' Lillies are packin' 'em in up ta' their fuckin' place...

PORKER: They don't hav'ta' pay their help like Americans do...

GUS: Look'it this: quarter pa'hst Nine, and none of us workin. Shit!

PORKER: The cancer's rotting Boley's brain, if you ask me! Harry Percy's got the right idea: dump Boley and the Lillies into the harbor and start out fresh!

PASTA: *(Sees Hal first.)* Yo, Porker, chill!

(Porker turns to look; bumps into Hal. Eye contact. There is a silence. the men all look from one to the other, realizing that Hal has overheard everything.)

PORKER: How goes it, Hal?

HAL: Hey, Porker.

GUS: How do you like bein' home?

HAL: It's okay, Gus, it's okay.

GUS: Ain't much like Princeton, huh?

HAL: Well, gosh, I dunno', Gus...I haven't been in Princeton since college. About 12 years now.

PASTA: You been livin' down fuckin' Noo Yaw'hk City, right? That's what the fuckin' paper said...

HAL: Yuh, I was livin' in Noo Yaw'hk, yuh, this is true. *(Smiles.)* But, I'm home, now.

(Angelo enters; holding clipboard. He calls out to the men who are waiting in line for assignments.)

ANGELO: That's all the work we got for today. You guys still out here can get your Unemployment Cards stamped and head down to Salem to collect…

(The men respond, grumbling, taking out their proper forms and crowding forward.)

PORKER: This union's a joke!

PASTA: I ain't had fuckin' work in three weeks.

GUS: We ought'a try inta' Charlestown. I hear they're lumpin' Russian boats…

PASTA: I'll lump anybody's fuckin' boat. I don't give a fuck!

(Hal seems confused. He moves forward to Angelo.)

HAL: You never called me, Angelo. I never signed.

ANGELO: Yuh, that's right.

HAL: I gotta sign.

ANGELO: No go, Hal.

HAL: Hmm?

ANGELO: You ain't signin'…

HAL: How so?

ANGELO: Your father's orders. You gotta see him if you wanna' straighten it out.

(Lights crossfade to opposite side of stage to Hank Boley.)

BOLEY: I don't own the goddam Union, ya' know?

(Hal turns around and moves to his father, cautiously.)

HAL: Yes, sir, I know that you don't…

(Hal is blurry-eyed: hung-over. He squints and grins, falsely, trying to seem alert. Boley pauses from time to time, noticing Hal's condition with disgust. Beyond them, through the glass window overlooking the harbor, we see the morning's boat traffic: the flurry of activity; pulsations of labor, of men earning their keep…all in contrast to Hal's sleepy-eyed concentration, and Boley's steely-eyed disgust.)

BOLEY: So, what do you expect?

HAL: Well, it's just that since I came back here, I've been signin' in every morning…you know…for work and all…*(Boley stares at Hal, who looks down, ashamed, as he continues.)*…and, well, this morning, I…

BOLEY: *(Interrupting.)* For "work"?

HAL: Hm?

BOLEY: You said you "signed in for work"…

HAL: Yuh, well, I went to sign in…

BOLEY: Are you drunk?

HAL: Drunk? No, it's morning…

BOLEY: You don't drink in the morning?

HAL: No.

BOLEY: I'm a sick man, Hal. People know this and it makes them nervous…

HAL: I can understand that, yes.

BOLEY: When people heard you were divorced and all and movin' back him, they figured something different… *(Pauses.)* Princeton man…educated…comin' home…me bein' sick and all…Nobody figured you were just a drunk and a whoremaster, comin' home to wait it out…

HAL: To wait what out? *(There is another pause, longer. Boley stares at his son.)* To wait what out, Pa?

(There is a knock on the door. Boley and Hal turn and watch door open; Mark Lissa pokes head inside; talks.)

LISSA: Sorry to interrupt, Hank, but, Dr. Nagoa and some others are waitin' already.

(Boley nods to Lissa, who in turn nods to Hal.)

Hal…

(Lissa exits. Boley looks at his son and gets to the question.)

BOLEY: Were you involved in the robbery over at State Wharf?

HAL: What robbery?

(Boley stares, silently.)

HAL: Nobody stole anything!

BOLEY: But, you were in on it, yes?

HAL: It was a joke, that's all: for somebody's birthday. Nothing was stolen.

BOLEY: A joke?

HAL: I was the one who put the stuff back…(Pauses.) I guess you know that already, huh?

BOLEY: I get reports, yuh. *(Pauses; stares at Hal.)* I'm putting you on three months' suspension. No work, no signin' in for pay, no nothin'.

HAL: For puttin' stuff back?

BOLEY: For knowing about the robbery in advance and doing nothing to stop it! *(Pauses.)* For thinking that jeopardizing union-protected property is some kind of joke…something funny… *(Pauses.)* I got people waiting. Get out of here.

(The lights crossfade to Dr. Nagoa, a Korean. In the shadow, behind Dr.

Nagoa sit other Korean businessmen, silently, straight-backed, in a row, as might birds sit on a telephone wire. Dr. Nagoa speaks in broken English.)

DR. NAGOA: We haven't gone to the police and we don't want to...

BOLEY: We appreciate that.

DR. NAGOA: Our people mistrust the police...Our presence in the community causes misunderstanding.

BOLEY: Yes, there's been a great deal of misunderstanding... *(Pauses.)* I'm sure you know some of the fears people have about your being in town...

DR. NAGOA: They think we're going to steal their children.

BOLEY: That's a big one, yuh...

DR. NAGOA: The Church of the New Way has been in Glossop for three years. Are there any children missing?

BOLEY: I know that...

DR. NAGOA: Glossop is our home...

BOLEY: Dr. Nagoa, Glossop was never a rich man's town, but, a fisherman or a lumper could count on makin' a buck here...feedin' his family... *(Pauses.)* The Canadians have been comin' in here with fish prices about 50% lower than ours... *(Pauses.)* Now, you guys are here, with tuna prices that are gonna' put our dealers out'ta' business... *(Pauses.)* You really think people here are gonna welcome you with open arms? It's just economic. You challenge a man's pocketbook; he fights...

DR. NAGOA: Forgive me, Mr. Boley, but, it's not "just economic." Nobody ever sank a Canadian boat. There are very few yellow-skinned Canadians. And whoever heard of white people going to jail for a tax discrepancy? We've come to you, Mr. Boley, in trust. We think that we have an understanding with you...with you. Either you stop whoever's sinking our boats, or we do.

BOLEY: Leave this to me. You can trust me.

(Nagoa bows and exits. A light fades up on Harry Percy, opposite side of stage.)

HARRY: You guys have questions for me, yes? Tell Boley I haven't got all day. Some of us hav'ta' actually work for a livin'...

(Boley turns and faces front. He is enraged. He changes his tone of voice totally from the tone used with Dr. Nagoa. The lighting on Boley changes color: new scene.)

BOLEY: *(Authoritative; enraged.)* We've been too easy-goin' with this kid for way too long! I don't give a fuck whose son he is? I intend to make a stand on this and I don't want anybody thinkin' they can buck me here!

(Lights widen to include full Executive Board of WWFBA. N.B. Dr. Nagoa and the other Korean businessmen should exit and re-enter to "become" new characters in this new scene. They should not, simply, turn into the scene. Therefore, if turntable is used, full turn required to create exit and entrance of same actors, different characters. The primary turn of turntable will carry on Harry, Tom and Frank Percy.

Harry Percy stands facing the men of the Executive Board and Boley. Harry's father, Tom, and Harry's uncle, Frank, stand just behind Harry and now move forward, into the inner circle, to join the others at the conference table.

The men sit around the table in the following order: Mark Lissa sits next to Walter Blunt and Angelo Catalano, alongside Boley, as lieutenants, of sorts. Around the table are four other men: Mort and Artie Shimma, Eddie Bell and Timmy Johnson. These four men are young and tough: blue-collar workers. Lissa, Angelo and Blunt are closer to Boley's age. All of the men wear sturdy clothing. Flannel shirts are worn under tweed sport coats, by the older men. The younger men wear work-clothes: flannel shirts, chinoes, boots.

Tom Percy, Harry's father, like Hank Boley, has grown older in appearance than his actual years. Unlike Boley, Percy is now slightly puffy and slightly soft. He is a pleasant fellow, well-dressed and clean. He and Boley exchange a knowing glance and a smile. Tom Percy seats himself opposite Hank Boley.)

PERCY: How goes it, Hank?

BOLEY: Fine. Give us half a minute. *(Exits with Lissa.)*

PERCY: Eddie, hi. *(Motions to Frank and Harry.)* Sit here. Over there, Harry. *(Frank sits. Harry doesn't move. Tom nods to others.)* Mort, Artie, how's your dad?

MORT: Pretty rough still, Tom, thanks.

PERCY: Sorry to hear that. How is the family, Timmy?

JOHNSON: Not so bad, Tom. How's yourself?

PERCY: *(Smiles.)* We'll tell you in about ten minutes, huh, Harry? *(Percy smiles at his son. Harry remains silent and stern: unmoving. There is an embarrassed silence and then chatter.)*

PERCY: You younger guys all know my brother, Frank, or no?

MORT: I don't. I'm Morty Shimma. This here's my brother, Artie...that's Walter Blunt...

(Frank smiles. Blunt nods.)

FRANK: Pleasure...Frank Percy...

ARTIE: You live local?

FRANK: Used'ta'...

PERCY: Frank's down from Worcester...

ANGELO: You guys want a coffee and cruller?

(Percy and Frank nod a "no." Boley re-enters with Lissa.)

BOLEY: Let's go!

LISSA: You wanna know this: you're not being charged here, formally. Not yet, anyway. We wanna' just hear your side of it then the Executive Board can make its decision...

PERCY: We're confident that the Board will see that this has all been a mis-understanding...

LISSA: We hope so, Tom...for everybody's sake. In the meantime, the WWFBA's got government contracts to protect, and we mean to pro-tect 'em at all costs...we can't have people scared to pull into Glos-sop harbor...

FRANK: So, you're gonna' set up another Percy as a sacrificial lamb. Is that it?

BOLEY: Frank?

FRANK: Just seems to me every time you need a patsy to stick this or that on, one of us gets it in the neck.

BOLEY: *(Interrupts.)* Get out of here, Frank.

FRANK: Hmmm?

BOLEY: You heard me: out.

FRANK: What gives?

BOLEY: *(Pauses.)* You weren't invited to this hearing, Frank, so, go: out.

HARRY: *(Loudly.)* I asked my uncle here!

BOLEY: *(Louder.)* Hardly your place to, fella'!

(Harry is enraged. Percy puts his hand on his son's arm to quiet him. Frank stands, looks each man in the eye, turns, wordlessly; He exits the meeting.)

What the Lillies claim is that you rammed their boat, deliberately...

HARRY: *(Interrupting.)* You takin' their word over mine?

BOLEY: *(Continuing angrily; not allowing Percy's interruption.)*...that you rammed their boat and told 'em your name...and warned 'em that you'd be sinkin' more boats...

HARRY: *(Interrupting again.)* I asked you if you were takin' the Lillies' word over the word of one of your own...

BOLEY: *(Again not allowing interruption; not recognizing that question has been asked.)*...and told the Lillie-kids to tell their leaders they had'da get off Cape Ann.

HARRY: *(Angrily; loudly.)* I asked you a question!

BOLEY: *(Yells; angrily.)* You didn't ask a question! You interrupted a question: my question...

(There is an embarrassed silence. Percy flashes a worried look at his son.)

HARRY: What's your question?

BOLEY: Did you sink the Lillie boat, Percy? *(Harry smiles; takes envelope from his pocket and tosses same on table.)*

HARRY: I heard you'd be tryin' to hang this on me, so, I saved ya's all some trouble...*(Pauses.)* Inside is a sworn statement that I was nowhere near the Lillie boat sinkin'. *(Shoves statement closer to Boley.)* Here...The statement tells you where I was and It's signed by moren' fifty witnesses...all paid up WWFBA members. *(Smiles; pretends to reach for envelope.)* Want me to read it out loud, or you guys wanna' read it to yo'rselves, later on...? You got a choice!

BOLEY: No need for you ta' ham it up, Percy. We'll read what's in there and make our decision. You done? Anything else we should know?

HARRY: Yuh, there is. I wanna' add that I love Glossop and while I ain't myself personally be'n sinkin' no Lillie boats, I'm glad somebody has. The Lillies are out ta' destroy fishin' on Cape Ann, and I'm glad that somebody's takin' a decisive and manly action against the bas'tids. That's what I want to add.

(Boley stares steely-eyed at Harry Percy.)

BOLEY: It's my feeling that you're hopping on to this so-called "Lillie-issue" for other purposes, Percy...

HARRY: That's yo'r feeling, huh? Well, that is just fuckin' fascinating...

BOLEY: You keep that mouth of your's shut, and do some listening! *(Pauses.)* We've got waterfront to protect here and the livelihoods of a hell of a lot of men to protect, too! *(Pauses.)* I hope what you say is true. The Executive Board will meet and vote and decide. You'll get a fair shake. *(Pauses.)* Now, you have a moment's think, Harold, and you decide if there's anything else you want to say here...

HARRY: I said it all.

BOLEY: Okay...*(Pauses.)* In the meantime, if you've got any possible influence in this, you see to it that no more of Dr. Lill's boats are bothered. Do you understand? *(No reply. Boley yells, pounds table.)* Do...you...understand???

(Harry nods his "yes," wordlessly, through clenched jaw. He is furiously silent. Boley raps the gavel, three raps.)

BOLEY: This meeting is over.

(A light comes up on Frank Percy, downstage.)

FRANK: You just smile at the bas'tid and keep your mouth shut, Harry! You hear me?

(Harry Percy moves to Frank, as lights fade out on all others. N.B. If turntable is used, Harry simply steps off downstage edge of turntable as it turns upstage, causing all others to exit.)

HARRY: It just fuckin' galls me!

FRANK: Just cool down, Harry. You're hot...

HARRY: Goddam right I'm hot! I got the likes of Hank Boley screaming at me, and his pussy-son Hal Boley back in town, blowin' in my ear...these things get me hot...wicked hot.

FRANK: *(Snaps at Harry; angrily.)* You keep a lid on your temper! When it's time to fight, we'll fight fine. It didn't hurt me to leave the meeting then, did it? Didn't I keep my dignity? Didn't I keep a lid on my goddam temper? You think I wasn't burning up?

HARRY: Yuh, okay...

FRANK: Trust me...

HARRY: I trust you. If it were just you I had to trust, there'd be no trouble here...

(Lights fade out.)

END OF SCENE FIVE

Scene Six

Lights fade up in Boley's office. Boley sits atop his desk, feet on floor, facing Tom Percy.

BOLEY: You're gonna' hav'ta control your son, Tom.

PERCY: How's about you controlling your son?

BOLEY: My son ain't out sinkin' boats. Nor is he threatening to take over...

PERCY: That ain't what I hear.

BOLEY: What's that?

PERCY: Nothin'... *(There is a pause.)*

BOLEY: Why's Frank here?

PERCY: I asked him to. *(Pauses.)* To help out with the boy. Harry has a great respect for Frank.

BOLEY: *(Shrugs.)* Frank's not the right influence on Harry.

PERCY: Lay off, Hank. The kid's justifiably very upset by what's goin' on here. You know it and I know it.

BOLEY: How so?

PERCY: You know.

BOLEY: How come you say I know? I don't know. I really don't know. Why don't you tell me, Tom? Then I'll know.

(There is a long pause. Tom Percy speaks.)

PERCY: I never had any interest in bein' Number One...You did, not me...

BOLEY: Yuh? And?

PERCY: What we did, we did because it was...right. We did what we had to do. For the good of the town...

BOLEY: We had reasons, yuh...Tom, does your son know anything?

(Boley and Percy hold a moment of eye-contact.)

PERCY: Absolutely not. Yours?

BOLEY: 'course not. A sacred promise was made.

PERCY: Henry. Listen to me. This is the honest-ta' God truth I'm speakin' here. I was happy to let you take over the gavel for yourself.

BOLEY: You made out okay.

PERCY: Am I complaining?

BOLEY: *(Yells; suddenly.)* Tom! You got a kid out there sinkin' other people's boats like some kind of war's been declared!

PERCY: *(Angrily.)* And you've got a kid who's drinkin' and fuckin' around with women and signin' in for pay without a lick of work and my boy, like the rest of the waterfront, is very pissed off.

BOLEY: Why? Why's Hal anybody's business?

PERCY: 'Cause, everybody knows you got cancer, Henry. Nobody wants the gavel to pass from you to your son.

(Boley turns and faces Percy, silently. They are both old men, proud and worried. The lights crossfade to Harry Percy, addressing a group of Lumpers and Fishermen. Frank Percy stands to Harry's right. Among the group is Gus, Pasta, Porker, Bobby, who all stand listening, paying rapt attention.)

HARRY: Boley was never given leadership of the WWFBA on his own. My father, Tom Percy, and Henry Boley were given an equal share. Boley wasn't born to it any more than you or me. He grabbed it for himself…(Pauses.) Okay, fine. We all know it's survival of the fittest, and the meek get shit…Okay, fine, but, just 'cause my father's willing to give in his rights doesn't mean I, his son, am willing to, too. I'm tellin' ya's that I'm not…*(Pauses.)* If Hal Boley's a Son of One by some kind of birthright, then so's Harry Percy…Tom Percy's son…me. *(To Frank.)* My uncle Frank here was on the scene when Boley and my father took over. Am I right in saying they were equals?

FRANK: Absolutely.

HARRY: Am I right in saying that I've got as much claim to being the next Number One as Hal Boley does?

FRANK: No question.

BOBBY: This has got nothin' ta' do with sinkin' Lillie-boats, Harry…

HARRY: You wanna' try to make your livin', inland, away from the water, Bobby, huh?

PASTA: You can't tell me the fuckin' Lillies set up fuckin' George's Bank, can you? That's fuckin' ludicrous, Harry!

HARRY: I'm only telling ya's we could make a living if the Lillies were outta' Glossop!

PASTA: I don't know, Harry…Seems to me, fuckin' Glossop's fucked! Fishin' and lumpin' are fucked, fuckin' Lillies or no fuckin' Lillies!

BOBBY: Cookie Evangelista pulled the plug on "Bessie II," yesterday, ya' know…

FRANK: *(Interrupting, suddenly. False voice.)* Okay, boys, let's get back to work!

(All turn face Markie, Lissa and Angelo, side-by-side, eavesdropping on everything that's been said.)

HARRY: Markie, Angelo. You guys some kind'a Commie KGB, here, now, or what?

LISSA: You're diggin' your own grave, Harry… *(To all.)* If you guys are his friends, you'll stop him. *(Nods to Frank Percy.)* Frank. Good to see you on the docks again. Guess you can't keep a good lumper off the docks, no matter how old he gets, or how far away he lives…he comes back, huh?

(The men "break up" and move away, not wanting to be associated with Percy as Percy's "gang." Lissa and Frank Percy stare at one another. Frank nods. Harry Percy laughs aloud, out of context. Lissa stares at him. Lights

shift, slightly. Lissa stands Centre. Light opposite side of stage. Light on Lissa remains on throughout lighting shift. Lissa turns and faces Boley as Frank and Harry Percy exit slowly, in darkness.)

LISSA: What the hell has Frank Percy got such a hard-on for you for, anyhow, huh?

BOLEY: What? Are you kidding me? Frank Percy was Allie Richard's messenger boy! Frank hates my guts for takin' over Number One. Tom Percy and Frank Percy are like night and day. Always were. *(He pauses.)* Tom's boy, Harry, and my Hal, same thing. Night and day. They were born five minutes apart, you know that?

LISSA: I knew they were close in age and all...

BOLEY: Within five minutes of each other, up Addison-Gilbert... *(Pauses.)* Tommy and I used'ta' stand side-by-side, every night, up the hospital...starin' in the nursery windows at our boys... *(Smiles.)* Ruthie and Ellen used'ta' link arms and walk up and down the corridor while Tom and I would be standin', starin', makin' big plans for our sons... *(Pauses.)* Funny, the way it turns out...Ruthie and Ellen both gone... *(Boley pauses; lost in memory.)* I used'ta' wonder if maybe they switched 'em...the babies...up Addison Gilbert.

LISSA: He's still young. He'll come around...

BOLEY: I guess. *(Smiles at Lissa.)*

(Lights crossfade to Harry Percy, on opposite side of stage, on telephone. He is enraged.)

HARRY: What are you givin' me, Matza? Either you're in or you're out? Which is it?

(Patty Percy stands in shadows, eavesdropping on her husband's telephone conversation, discreetly.)

Listen to me...LISTEN TO ME!...If you don't wanna', don't. That's cool. Just keep your trap shut about it, okay? Yuh, well, you better mean it, Matza... *(Harry slams down the telephone.)* Fuckin' stooge!

PATTY: *(Calling to Harry, surprising him.)* Something wrong, Harry?

HARRY: What were you? Listening in?

PATTY: I just heard you yelling.

HARRY: That was private stuff.

PATTY: I wasn't listening. I didn't hear...

HARRY: You sure?

PATTY: What's with you, anyway?

HARRY: I just don't want you listening in on private stuff. That's all...

PATTY: *(Goes to Harry .)* You tired?

HARRY: I gotta' go out…

PATTY: Now?

HARRY: *(Starts to exit.)* Yuh, well, I gotta'…

PATTY: *(Without warning.)* Did you sink the tuna boat, Harry?

HARRY: What's this?

PATTY: I hear this around town. People say you were the one who sank the Lillie boat and that you're threatening to sink more. *(There is a small silence.)* You're my husband. I gotta' wait up for you. I ought'ta' know these things, don't you think?

(Mary-Ellen enters frightened, upstage behind Patty. Harry sees her.)

HARRY: What are you doing up?

MARY-ELLEN: You woke me up, fighting.

HARRY: We're not fighting. We're talking.

MARY-ELLEN: Then how come Mama's crying?

PATTY: I'm not crying. Go back to bed, now.

HARRY: Go back to bed. Your mother and I are talking…

PATTY: Go on, Mary-Ellen. I'll come right up…

MARY-ELLEN: I don't wanna'…

PATTY: Mary-Ellen…

MARY-ELLEN: Okay. Okay…

(Mary-Ellen exits. Patty faces Harry; speaks softly, clearly.)

PATTY: A simple yes or no, Harry. I got a right to know.

HARRY: What?

PATTY: About the boat. Was that you?

HARRY: Who sunk it? Me? Nope. I didn't.

PATTY: Good.

HARRY: Did you?

PATTY: Did I what? Sink the Moonie-boat?

HARRY: Mmm.

PATTY: *(Laughs.)* No.

HARRY: Good.

(Patty and Harry embrace.)

You still in love with me, or what?

PATTY: 'course I'm still in love with you? Why'd you ask me a question like that?

HARRY: No reason.

PATTY: You still in love with me?

HARRY: What's with the "still"? When did I ever tell you I was in love with you?

PATTY: That was me, in the church, "til death do us part"…Remember?

HARRY: That was you? In the white dress?

PATTY: Yup.

HARRY: A promise is a promise, I guess.

(They kiss.)

HARRY: Your old friend Hal Boley's back in town. You know that?

PATTY: Yuh, I know. I, uh, saw him…

HARRY: You what?

PATTY: In the car. He was goin' one way, I was goin' the other.

HARRY: He saw you?

PATTY: Huh?

HARRY: That's simple enough: did Hal Boley see you?

PATTY: Me? *(Pauses.)* No.

(Lights out on Patty and Harry. N.B. If turntable is used, Patty and Harry step on, at same time as Boley and Angelo step off.)

END OF SCENE SIX

Scene Seven

BOLEY: How do you know this Angelo? How?

ANGELO: Hank, come onnn. What the hell was Guido Vega doin' out there on a boat that needs a ten-man crew, the minimum, with just his brother?…They couldn't'a been fishin'!

BOLEY: Maybe they were pickin' up crew somewhere…

ANGELO: Hankie, come onnn…

BOLEY: Guido Vega's hardworking, Angelo. He's a boy I've known since he was twelve…

ANGELO: Yuh, so? I knew him in the crib and I'm tellin' ya still: Guido pulled the plug.

BOLEY: Bring him in here. Just Guido. I don't want anybody to know I'm talkin' to him…round up some of the other Captains, too.

ANGELO: The Irish kid from the paper's been snoopin'…

BOLEY: Where?

ANGELO: Here. He was out front an hour ago…

BOLEY: Tell Guido to come by my house, 3 o'clock. The others, too.

ANGELO: I dunno if I can find Guido…

BOLEY: He's got two dozen cousins workin'. There ain't a one of 'em with decent papers. You find him.

(Drumbeat. Light shift. Guido, Cookie, Mort Shimma and Salvatore Reed in semi-circle, facing Boley. Each wears Lumper's clothing and a cap with gold braid signifying ownership of a boat: rank. Each is a captain. Note: Angelo has exited.)

GUIDO: I haven't made expenses in twenty straight weeks, Hank. I ain't even come close. My insurance premium's due in a month and I ain't got a hope in hell of meeting it. My mortgage on the boat's four thousand a month, alone. I grossed $3800 last month and that was my best month outta the last six... *(Pauses.)* I used to gross $3800 a week. *(Pauses.)* I'm sorry if what I did makes you look bad, Hank. You've been wonderful to me and I don't want anything to make you look bad...

(Drumbeat. Light shift. Mort Shimma speaks.)

SHIMMA: I could'a lied to you. I could'a told you we caught fire, like I told the Coast Guard...but, well, I didn't...I'm tellin' you the straight goods. I got eight mouths ta' feed. Eight. I love fishin', but, well...how? They raised my insurance premium from $14,000 a year to $41,000 a year. I tried to find a second company, you know, to change. I couldn't. Nobody else even wanted to insure me...I can't pay $41,000 for insurance, Hank. You know that.

(Drumbeat. Light shift. "Cookie" Evangelista speaks to Boley.)

COOKIE: My boat's worth a hell of a lot more to me under the top of the water. I can sell my pier to Phil Duffy for a hundred and sixty thousand, no questions asked, all's I gotta' do is pick up the phone. He's developin' condo's...So, what am I gonna' bust my balls for, huh?

BOLEY: I don't get it, Cookie. I don't get it. *(Pauses.)* I've known you all my life, right? Your father, your grandfather...

COOKIE: I've known you as long as I can remember. It's true.

BOLEY: I look at all the problems here on the waterfront: Canadian prices, Georges, the Lillies, all of it. Look, I understand when somebody pulls the plug on an old boat to get a new boat. We turn a blind eye to these things. But 40 trawlers? I do not understand, also, why half our goddam waterfront's bein' sold to condo developers. Families who've be'n fishing 4 or 5 generations are sinking their boats and selling their wharfs out from under themselves and WHY??? I do not understand these things!

COOKIE: I can't talk to you anymore on this, Hank. Don't make me lie to you. I'm not the right one ta' be askin' these questions to…I got 8 kids.

(Drumbeat. Light shift. Boley moves to Sally Reed, slaps him, suddenly.)

BOLEY: Answer me, Salvatore, God damn you!

SALLY: I can't, Hank!

BOLEY: I brought your whole family across, Salvatore. I did that: me! Now, you open your mouth and you speak words, God damn you!

SALLY: *(After a long pause.)* Cocaine, mostly.

BOLEY: What the fuck are you tellin' me here, Salvatore?

SALLY: It's big, Hank.

BOLEY: How big, Salvatore? Why is this shit startin' up, again? And since when, I wanna' know! I cleaned this waterfront up with my own hands! I did that! Talk!

SALLY: I can't, Hank, I can't…

(Drumbeat. Light shift. Boley returns to Guido, slaps him.)

BOLEY: Tell me, you little fuck!

GUIDO: I can't hit you back, Hank! I can't raise a hand!

BOLEY: *(Threatens a fistfight.)* Come on, Guido, raise a hand! Raise one! Come on!

GUIDO: *(Backing down.)* What don't you know?

BOLEY: Let's say I know nothing, huh?

GUIDO: I could wind up dead from this…

BOLEY: Fucking "A", Guido. Let me hear some words…

GUIDO: I don't know how many boats are runnin' heavy, exactly. It's a lot, I know that. Once the Coast Guard has solid word on a ship, they get their impound orders goin'. You know the rest…

BOLEY: You forget? I don't know nothing. Talk…

GUIDO: Once the Coast guard impounds a boat, it sits at dock for maybe eight or nine months, waiting for trial. The owner can't make a penny fishing while his boat's tied up. The boat's worth maybe a million or two, and it's just sittin' there, tied up: dead…Mortgage, insurance, interest keeps clickin'…So, they pull the plug…Don't ask me who's runnin' the show, Hank, 'cause I swear to you, I don't know…

BOLEY: How many of our boys are wired, Guido?

GUIDO: I dunno'…*(Pauses.)* Most everybody's fishin' for a livin'. The boats go down, the insurance goes up, the rest of use get trapped in the middle…Any goddam shack we own that's close to the water, we can sell like that *(snaps fingers)* for more'n any of us'd clear in two years of fishin' or lumpin' or cuttin'. It's a tough situation here…

BOLEY: I must be gettin' stupid! I figured newcomer-Yuppies and Boston-

Mafioso, yuh, sure! But not our people...not Glossop people. I thought I cleaned this place up, once and for all. I must be gettin' really stupid. Tell me something, Guido. Do you carry drugs?

GUIDO: Never. Not once. I swear on my children. Not even once. All I tried to do was fish. I couldn't make it. *(Pauses.)* Maybe, if I carried drugs, I could have...

(A spotlight, opposite side of stage, fades up on Harry and Frank, as end of Scene Seven overlaps starts of Scene Eight.)

HARRY: I ain't sayin' Boley's on Lill's payroll, but, it sure wouldn't change things any if he were. Would it?

FRANK: Lumpin' gone sour, too. A lot of boats are avoiding Glossop, these days—they're goin' down ta' Beverly, into Gloucester, Salem...Glossop's finished.

BOLEY: What are you gonna' do now, Guido...for a living?

GUIDO: I dunno', Hank...*(Pauses; smiles ironically.)* I was just gonna' ask you...

END OF SCENE SEVEN

Scene Eight

Sunset. Patty Percy stands staring at the sky, lost in a memory. HAL calls out from across the stage, softly; startles her.

HAL: You told me to wait here for you, and here I am.

PATTY: What? How long have you been standing there?

HAL: About 17 years.

PATTY: What are you talking about?

HAL: When we were in high school. Right there...on that spot. You said "I'll always meet you here if you need me to. Just wait for me. I'll show up." So, here I am.

PATTY: I said that?

HAL: You don't remember saying that?

PATTY: I do. I remember. *(Smile; embarrassed.)* I come here almost every day. I like to watch the sun go down and come up: both of those things. Gives me hope. *(Smiles.)* Yuh, 'course I remember. I'm just surprised you did.

HAL: I remember everything you ever said to me, Patty. *(Hal moves to Patty; stares lovingly at her. It seems as though he might kiss her.)*

PATTY: I'd better get home. I've got a supper to get in. I've got this family…*(She starts off. Hal calls to her; softly.)*

HAL: I'll be here waiting for you tomorrow night. Same time, same place. I need you to meet me…

PATTY: I, uh, I better get home and get my supper in…*(Patty runs off.)* *(Lights crossfade to Jack Silva, who calls out to Hal.)*

SILVA: The word is you're seeing Percy's wife.

HAL: Maybe I am, maybe I'm not.

SILVA: I wrote you a poem on the subject, this morning, while I was on the toilet.

HAL: You redefine the word "gross," you know that? Your humor is gross. Your mind is gross! Your ass is gross! You are "gross," from top to bottom! You are gross, inside and out! You are gross incarnate! You are twelve dozen!

SILVA: *(Silva takes hand-written poem from pocket.)* I don't usually wax poetic, but, ècoute, mon frère…*(Clears throat.)*

HAL: What's this?

SILVA: It's your poem. *(Unfolds paper, clears throat; reads title.)* "On My Best friend's Screwing His Worst Enemy's Wife", A Salacious Sonnet of Sexual Insinuendo, by Jack Silva, A Saint." *(Looks up at Hal; smiles.)* Wanna' hear it?

HAL: What happens if I say "no"?

SILVA: Read my lips. *(Hal leans in to read Silva's lips. Silva speaks aloud.)* I will put beach-sand in your condoms. *(Clears throat; prepares to recite poem.)* Eat your heart out, T.S. Eliot. *(Clears his throat, again; waxes poetic: recites poem.)*
I admit it's your own degenerate Life to lead,
But, it's crazy Harry Percy's Wife with whom you breed.
And, as crazy Harry has a 12" Knife to heed,
It's Jack's unfathomable mental Strife, indeed!
As poor Jack Silva simply doesn't want to bleed.
So, for the sake of Jack's Mental Health,
Put the Questionable Lady-in-Question back up on Percy's Shelf,
And act with Wisdom! Act with Stealth!
And get Lady Patty-Cake out from under Yourself!
Think of it as a Favor for your plump, old pal, Jack,
But, get the fuck off'a Percy's Wife's Back!

HAL: Get off of her "back"? Are you calling me a "bugger"?

SILVA: You know what rhymes with "front"?

HAL: *(Shows Silva his fist.)* You know what rhymes with "dread"?

SILVA: 'course I know what rhymes with "dread"! Why do ya' think I wrote the poem?

HAL: I'm being totally discreet.

SILVA: "Totally discreet," yuh. About sixteen different people told me they saw you being totally discreet with her, under the footbridge at Good Harbor Beach, 6:30, Sunday Night.

HAL: One small lapse in otherwise total discretion. Hey, I'm only human. *(The lights crossfade to Harry and Frank Percy, in a meeting in Harry's house with three Lumpers: "Foggy" Hastings, 30; Freddie Mowbray, 30; Harry's cousin, Vernon Koski, 18, all sit around dining table. Harry is the consummate organizer.)*

HASTINGS: I don't know if sinkin' Lillie boats is any answer, Harry...

HARRY: Definitely not! Not one boat at a time, anyhow. But what would you say to sinkin' the entire Lillie fleet.

(Frank and Vernon and others all laugh.)

FRANK: We ain't blamin' the Lillies for all our troubles here. We're blamin' one man and one man alone: Henry Boley. He's the one sellin' Glossop down the river...

HASTINGS: So, why are you talkin' about sinking Lillie boats? You're running the risk of bringing every cop and every TV camera in the world inta' Glossop. I mean, that's kinda' gonna' make us pretty stupid, right?

FRANK: Exactly right, Hastings! You got it! It's the one thing we can do that's gonna' pull Henry Boley off his ass and out'ta' the Number One's seat...And put Harry here at the helm where he belongs, so the WWFBA can have proper representative leadership from the workers themselves...not from the elite rich, and not from outsiders! *(Patty Percy is now visible in the shadows. She carries a tray with a coffee pot, mugs, coffee cakes. She stops short of entering the room. She stands in the shadows; listens.)*

HARRY: You know the Tuna Contest that Lill sponsors? The entire Lill fleet is gonna' be in a straight line, single file headin' past Dogbar, leadin' the contest boats out'ta Gloucester harbor. It's a beautiful chance to make Boley look like the horse's ass which he is, and run some of his yellow friends right the hell out'ta Glossop along with him!

MOWBRAY: When?

HARRY: Same day as "Greasy Pole"...

FRANK: Right smack in the middle of Fiesta...

(The lights fade out on all but Patty. She stands alone, in dim light. She pauses; backs up another stop; pauses; turn; exits. Blackout.)

END OF SCENE EIGHT

Scene Nine

A light fades up on Jack Silva, standing on a stool, reading a listing, an inventory...sort of a score-card of the "take" for the evening. Enthusiastic applause greets each new list-item.

SILVA:...17 VCRs, 21 CD players and 25 stereos...39 TVs...23 computers, monitors and printers...and more than 37 hand appliances, such as 6 gaily-colored blow-dryers and 5 friendly feminine personal vibrators!
(We hear applause, as the lights widen to include everyone in Silva's apartment. There is party in progress, celebrating a successful night's looting. Among the happy guests are; Emily and Alberta Fusco; Silva's girlfriend, Dolly; Barry; Bardolph; Petey; Gadshill; Dan; Fitzie and a woman who is sitting on Hal's lap named Alice Quigly The mood is all drunken good cheer. There is a mound of cartons, etc: the stolen goods. Silva continues.)
We had a great, great night, tonight...a totally successful looting...*(Applause.)* But, while we are all winners for just playing the game, every game has its Champion. And Champions must be rewarded...*(Applause.)* I would like to announce tonight's MVP, ladies and gentlemen, the MVP for tonight: our own Kenny Bardolph!
(All applaud enthusiastically. Hal seems drunker than usual; peers out from under Alice Quigly, who sits on his stomach.)
HAL: What's the noise?
ALICE: Everybody's clappin'...
HAL: Who sang?
ALICE: Silllyyy. Tubby just gave Bardolph MVP for stealing more than anybody else tonight...They hit the summah' houses, over Long Beach...
HAL: Ohhh.
ALICE: Why didn't chu' go?

HAL: Stealing? Me? Never. I'm not a crook. I'm a bum. Big difference, what's-your-name…What's your name?

ALICE: Alice Quigly, sillyyy. Rememberrrr? Afta' the Cape race? We snuck upstairs at the O'Malley School…

HAL: Of course. *(Pauses.)* I don't remember you, actually. Look, could you not sit on me? You're making me sick. I'm sick.

ALICE: You wanna' heave?

HAL: I wanna' leave! You sicken and disgust me…

ALICE: Right, well, fuck you very much. *(Hal stands, dumping Alice; starts across room. Silva threatens Dolly with stickpin. They wrestle, playfully.)*

SILVA: For my dearest Dolly, here, I have appropriated this elegant Emerald stickpin, for her to stick…

HAL: *(interrupts.)* You disgust me! You both disgust me! You all disgust me! You are all disgusting!

(Hal falls over, dead drunk. Everyone laughs. Hal stands, falls again, Everyone laughs again. Hal feels his way across the room and moves to opposite side of stage, in shadows, to front door. Light shifts to exclude party and include Patty, standing in the shadows at Silva's front door, about to ring the bell. Hal rubs his eyes, hugs his knees and looks up at Patty.)

HAL: Hiii…

PATTY: I've been standing here about ten minutes tryin' ta' get up the courage to push it…

HAL: To push what, exactly?

PATTY: Your bell.

HAL: Ohhh, of courssse…my bellll…*(Hal tries to be sober, but is incredibly drunk. He smiles out of context.)*

PATTY: Can I come up? Are you busy?

HAL: You wanna' come upstairs? There? Whatever for? You wanna' get debauched? *(Laughs.)* Nobody ever wants ta' get bauched, right? everybody wants ta' get rid of bauch…get themselves de-bauched, right? *(Hal giggles; tries to kiss Patty.)* Wha's'a' matter, Patty-Cake Palumbo? Don't 'cha know who I am? *(Stands erect; nearly falls backward.)* I am Henry Boley, Jr., the team Captain, and you are Patricia Palumbo, Head Cheerleader, Glossop High…I am Quarterback, you are "G"…Wait a minute? are you "G" or are you "L"…*(A pronouncement.)* I made it with "G," "L," "O," "S," and the other "S," but, I drew the line at #2 "O:" Rose Mota. She was a dog…*(Hal tries to kiss Patty again.)*

HAL: Play Patty-Cake, Patty-Cake, will yaaa'? Look at meee! I'm handsome Hal…I'm gonna' run this town, some day. I was born to it!

PATTY: Don't, Hal, please…*(Hal gropes Patty, belching and teetering, sloppily.)*

HAL: A kiss, that's all. Maybe a little tongue…Come onnnn, Pattyyy…
(Without warning, Patty hits Hal. It is not at all a girlish swat, or even a lucky punch. Patty hits Hal as if to knock him from the face of planet Earth. It is a stunning blow. Hal flies backwards, out of control. He is betrayed by his very substance, which, once rolling backwards, gathers a terrible momentum. Hal smashes into the front door pillar, and falls, in a heap.)
Jesus, Patty, that really hurt!
(Patty walks to Hal and kicks him, cruelly.)

HAL: Uggghhh…*(Hal rolls to one side, feebly trying to protect himself.)*

PATTY: I used to have dreams about you! *(Quietly.)* I was "L". Agnes Vergillio was "G," Carolyn Russo was "O," and Rosie Mota was #1 "S" not #2 "0." She married Tommy Grilk and they live up Lynnfield and I hear they got four kids and they're wicked happy…
(Patty turns away, stops; looks at Hal again. He is down, and out.)
You shouldn't'a come back. You should'a died…*(Patty exits, crossing stage. The lights crossfade with Patty standing facing a woman her own age, Midge, who holds imagined door open.)*

MIDGIE: What gives? It must be ten o'clock…

PATTY: I gotta' talk to somebody, Midgie…

MIDGIE: *(Quietly.)* Gus's home.

PATTY: You know what Gus and Harry are planning?

MIDGIE: *(Alarmed.)* Call me in the morning, Patty, I…can't now…really.

PATTY: I've got to talk to you, Midgie! When can we talk?

MIDGIE: Gus is home, Patty! For God's sake, I got'ta be careful!
(Midgie closes imagined door, turns and faces her husband, Gus, who has been standing upstage, watching Midgie and Patty; eavesdropping.)

GUS: What's she after?
(The lights crossfade again back to Hal, who stays on the ground a moment. Then he sits up, slightly. Then, he stands and walks back into Silva's party. The lights widen, on Hal's arrival, to include all party animals. Hal goes as directly to Silva as he possibly can, given his state of drunkeness and upset. As party animals see Hal weave and bob, they laugh.)

HAL: I need the keys to the van, Jack…

SILVA: It's empty. All the stuff's here…

HAL: *(Yells, enraged, totally out of context; drunkenly.)* I need the fucking keys to the fucking van!

(There is a small silence. Then everyone goads Hal with the same line, passed rhythmically from person to person.)

PETEY: Hal needs the keys…

BARDOLPH: Hal needs the keys…

DOLLY: Hal needs the keys…

BARRY: Hal needs the keys…

GADSHILL: Hal needs the keys…

FITZIE: Who needs the keys?

DAN: Hal needs the keys…

ALICE: Hal needs the keys.

(Silva stops forward, wordlessly hands keys to Hal. Everyone laughs. Hal staggers slowly to opposite side of stage. The lights shift with him, as he goes; feeling his way down imagined stairs to an imagined front door, across an imagined driveway and into an imagined automobile.

We hear: The sound of a car's engine, revving, on tape.

Ensemble now holds lit flashlight, one in each hand. Hal begins to circle the stage, runs faster and faster and faster. Flashlights roam the audience, slowly at first and then madly.

We hear: The sound of a car, out of control: tires squealing, horn blaring, brakes screeching. And then we hear a terrible car-crash.

Hal rolls across the stage, madly. He is now drenched in his own blood. The flashlights fly out on to the stage, still lit, and come to rest, where they will. Hal and the flashlights have stopped moving.

After a moment's pause, Bardolph runs center-stage, screams out his message, directly to audience.)

BARDOLPH: Hal Boley just totaled the van! They think he killed himself!

(Petey runs on, opposite side of stage; screams out his message as well. NOTE: Everyone should repeat message in overlap/cacophony of alarm.)

PETEY AND OTHERS: Hal Boley just missed runnin' down four tourists, over Bass Rocks. He flipped the van over, just missed 'em!

BARDOLPH AND OTHERS: The van flipped over on to the rocks!

PETEY AND OTHERS: Hal jumped out!

BARDOLPH: They got him up to Addison-Gilbert, over Gloucester!

DOLLY: They got him on a machine! They're tryin' ta' save him!

(We hear Hal's breathing, amplified, over speaker in auditorium. Silva, Barry, Bardolph and others now circle Hal, looking out at audience.)

SILVA: Did you hear?
DOLLY: Did you hear?
BARDOLPH: Hal.
PETEY: Hal.
GADSHILL: Did you hear?
BARRY: Did you hear?
ALICE: Hal.
EMILY FUSCO: Hal.
ALBERTA FUSCO: Hal.
ALL: HAL!!!

(Drumbeat. All sounds and lights snap off, suddenly, but for the still-lit flashlights on the stage next to Hal, and a single, tight white spotlight, up on Lissa, center stage. He talks directly to audience. Hal still lies nearby, in pool of blood.)

LISSA: Sometimes, seeing the difference between the force of Life and the force of Death is like seeing the difference between a wave coming in and a wave going out. You've got to pull back and look at the whole beach to know what the tide's accomplished: to figure out which way it's moving. With people, sometimes, you've got to pull back and look at the whole life…to see if the person's trying to live, or trying to die.

(Two white-coated stretcher-bearers walk to Hal, place him on a board-stretcher, carry him off.)

LISSA: Some people dedicate their precious time on Earth to one thing; some to the other. *(Pauses; smiles.)*

END OF ACT ONE

Act Two
Scene One

Lights up on Hal, preparing to leave hospital. Dr. Berkowitz stands stage right. Reverend Scroop stands opposite, stage left. Patty stands facing Hal from across stage.

PATTY: *(Tears streak her face.)* I couldn't have beared it…if you died…and we never talked…and you died…

HAL: *(Touches her teardrop with his fingers.)* Oh, yuh, that makes two of us! I would've hated that myself, if I died!
(Dr. Berkowitz enters; talks to Hal, sternly. Patty turns upstage.)

DR. BERKOWITZ: It's a miracle you made it through, Hal. I saw the car after they fished it out. It's a miracle. Maybe you can stay away from the bottle, now, hmmm? Next time, you won't be so lucky… *(Pauses.)* I've signed you out. You can leave anytime this morning. See me in the office next Thursday or so. Call Hazel for an appointment. Okay?

HAL: Okay. Thanks, Dr. Berkowitz…
(Reverend Scroop enters. He is old; talks to Hal, gravely. Dr. Berkowitz turns upstage.)

REV. SCROOP: God wanted you to stay alive. He must have some real purpose other than drinking and womanizing.

HAL: I guess, yuh…

REV. SCROOP: You're not a child any more, Hal.
(Silva calls out from the shadows, opposite side of stage. Silva is shaving, looking in imagined mirror as he shaves.)

SILVA: Look, I'm not saying you're immature, but most of us pulled out of the Fuck-Me-Suck-Me-Rubber-Duck-Me Stage when we were about 13 or 14…

HAL: It's genetic. I was born very young.
(Hal walks next to Silva, starts to shave, as well. The two men play the head of this small scene standing side-by-side, looking into an imagined mirror, shaving.)

SILVA: One way or the other, you're lookin' to lose your ass, right?

HAL: How so?

SILVA: Petey said he saw you makin' out with old "L" between "G" and "O-double-S-O-P," over near Salem Willows last night…

REV. SCROOP: Pray with me. Hal…

HAL: What? *(Looks over his shoulder. Scroop's still there, being reverential.)* Oh, yuh, sure, father...*(Scroop bows head. Hal bows head; looks over to Silva, whispers.)* What's the implication here, anyway, Jack-off?

SILVA: You seein' Percy's wife, again, or what?

HAL: Why do I feel this question is rhetorical? Is there a rumor around that I'm *not* seeing Percy's wife?

(They laugh. They finish shaving. Hal changes his shirt; "dresses up.")

HAL: Did I ever tell you about right after my wife and her money dumped me, down in Noo Yawk City? I was broke, so, I took this job, servicing this rich old impotent dude's young, fat wife. When I got tired of her, after about four house-calls, the old dude comes around to my place, totally pissed off at me, rings my bell, grabs me, and goes: "I hear you're not sleeping with my wife!"

REV. SCROOP: *(Interjects.)* In the Name of the Father, Son, Holy Ghost...

SILVA: Take my advice. If you gotta' keep seein' Harry Percy's wife, be smart about it: play it safe and meet her somewhere out of town...like maybe Argentina!

HAL: What are you so afraid of, anyway?

SILVA: My blood on these Dhurrie rugs, basically...

(Music in: Otis Redding singing "Sittin' On The Dock Of The Bay." The lights brighten on Hal and Patty; fade out on Silva. Rev. Scroop still stands nearby, praying; head bowed. Hal and Patty sit cross-legged on stage, facing front, as if sitting on a wall overlooking the sea.)

PATTY: I could sit, starin' at the ocean like this, for all my life...

HAL: I dunno', the ocean's always spooked me: it's too big...

PATTY: Humbling. That's what my Dad used'ta say all the time: The Ocean is Humbling."

HAL: I totally agree. Many's the time I've looked at the ocean and said "I never could drink that much, I am humbled..."

DR. BERKOWITZ: Stay off the bottle and you might stay alive. *(Exits.)*

PATTY: What's with you?

HAL: In what sense?

PATTY: How come you are like you are?

HAL: How come I'm how? How am I?

PATTY: A drunk. Pissing your life away.

REV. SCROOP: *(Punctuates Patty's pronouncement.)* Amen...*(Exits.)*

HAL: Gimme a break, will ya'? I stopped drinkin', ya know?

PATTY: Oh, yuh? When?

HAL: *(Looks at watch.)* 31 hours, 10 minutes, 48 seconds...49...

50...51...I'm digital! I like it when you worry about me. It's... chah'ming.

PATTY: Chah'ming?

HAL: Mmmm.

PATTY: Fuck you.

HAL: That's chah'ming, too. What a mouth! *(Smiles.)* I always liked that mouth...*(He touches Patty's cheek, gently. They kiss.)*

PATTY: You got kids? I've been meaning to ask you about your marriage and all...

HAL: Me, personally? Nope. The woman I was married to...Deborah Coe...she had two kids from her first husband...*(Smiles.)* She used to introduce me to people as "Harold, my second husband, by marriage." She could make a very dry joke, old Debbie could...and a Martini to match! *(Pauses.)* I worked for Deborah's father, setting up tax shelters for rich investors. I took a salary from his firm, slept with his daughter, drank his whiskey, babysat his granddaughters, drank more of his whiskey, sailed his boats, drank more of his whiskey, drank more of his whiskey...Eventually, Deborah and her two daughters and Deborah's Daddy all got really pissed off cause'a my constantly getting pissed...I'd constantly get pissed, they'd constantly get pissed off. Fearful symmetry.

PATTY: Is that why you left her?

HAL: I didn't exactly leave her.

PATTY: You left "Noo Yawhk"? **...

** *(Translation from North Shore Massachusetts dialect: "New York.")*

HAL: That's it: I left "Noo Yawhk"...

PATTY: And came home...

HAL: That was the one thing in life I was trying not to do: come home, come back to Glossop, come back to bein' known most of all as Hank Boley's son, the Son of One, buttt, home I came...twenty years older...my brain pickled...

PATTY:...Much better-lookin'...Mmmmmm, s'true...

HAL: Boy, you haven't changed at all, have you? One thing on your mind. Always the same. One thing on your mind, all the time...two things, actually: sex and lust.

PATTY: Yuh, right...You got it.

(Hal stares at Patty, smiling.)

What'cha' lookin' at?

HAL: Somebody.

PATTY: *(Simply, clearly.)* I've never loved anybody but you in my whole life. I'm ashamed to admit it, but, it's the God's-honest-truth... *(Smiles, shrugs.)*

HAL: Same goes for me, too, Patty. There's only been one woman I've ever really loved and you're it.

PATTY: I've never cheated on Harry, before tonight. Not even close. I want you to know that.

HAL: Before tonight? Really?

(Patty takes Hal's face in her hands and kisses him. It is a gentle kiss.)

PATTY: I've got to careful about Mary-Ellen. She's only little. I've got to be careful...

HAL: I promise... *(Hal starts to take Patty in his arms; thinks better of it. He is frightened. Patty looks at Hal; smiles. She takes Hal's face in her hands. They kiss. She is in control. It is a passionate kiss.*
Gus and two Lumpers step out of shadows, watch a moment.)

GUS: Where's Harry?

LUMPER: He should be over Sherm's by now...

GUS: Let's head over. This's gonna' make his night..

(Lights fade out.)

END OF SCENE ONE

Scene Two

Lights up on Angelo, carrying clipboard, facing a large group of Lumpers.

ANGELO: I got two ships, so there's work for all a'ya's...

(The men cheer. Angelo steps to one side, revealing a stack of crates. Some crates are smallish, others are enormous.)

ANGELO: This first load's frozen goods, but there's a ten percent pay override. Who wants it?

(One by one, men step forward to start carrying crates. Hal is among the men. They all face Angelo.)

Packy, you're on. Tommy D., you got it. Gussie, go for it. *(Sees Hal.)* What do *you* want?

HAL: My suspension's time's up...

ANGELO: Yuh?

HAL: Today's the day.

ANGELO: Okay, sign in…

HAL: Uh uh. I'm workin'…

ALL: *(Mocking.)* OOoooOOOOOoooOOOOOO! Hal's working!

ANGELO: Yuh?

HAL: Yup.

ANGELO: *(To older man.)* Okay, Gussie, you're Boss Lumper. Hal Boley says he's working…

GUS: *(Smiles.)* Okay, Hal. Let's see what ya' got…Grab that top crate. It goes on the stack…there.

(The top crate is enormous. Hal steps forward and "lumps" the crate, carrying it from one side of the stage to the other. Hal's knees nearly buckle under the strain of his load. N.B. Turntable can be used as treadmill.)

Oh, God, Hal, I screwed up. It doesn't go on that stack. It goes on this stack.

(Points to stack near the one from which Hal took the crate in the first place. Hal moves crate, again. He is exhausted, but won't quit. SFX: Music in: Probably Springsteen work-song. NOTE: Possible, young lumper sings. All jeer. As soon as Hal succeeds in getting the crate moved, Gus breaks new and worse news.)

GUS: Oh, my God, Hal, I am definitely Shitforbrains, himself, huh? I was right the first time. That crate goes there! *(Points to stack from which Hal just moved crate.)*

HAL: You're the boss, Gus…*(Hal cannot budge the crate, at first. And then he does. He lifts the crate on to his shoulder. His legs start to buckle under him. A young lumper, Bobby, steps forward before Hal can fall; grabs an end.)*

BOBBY: Gimme an end…(To all; in disgust.) We got a boat to unload here, yes?

(Hal and Bobby carry the crate to its stack. The other Lumpers resume their work. Hal has, in a small way, begun to gain their respect.)

HAL: Thanks, Bobby.

BOBBY: Hey, no sweat, huh?

(Lights now crossfade to Percy, sitting, watching TV. Patty enters, crossing quietly along back edge of stage, behind Percy, who speaks to her without turning, without actually facing her.

Harry speaks with obvious hostility.)

HARRY: So? You decided to come home? How come?

PATTY: I had to go over to Liberty Tree Mall to exchange something…

HARRY: Really?

PATTY: Yuh, really.

HARRY: I heard you were over there...

PATTY: Over where?

HARRY: Liberty Tree Mall.

PATTY: What else did you hear?

HARRY: All of it.

PATTY: All of what?

HARRY: You planning to go out again, tonight?

(The lights widen—to Silva's apartment. Silva and Dolly sit together, watching TV. Hal crosses through the room wearing a terrycloth robe, towel on his head; just showered.)

SILVA: I asked you if you were goin' out...You gettin' deaf, or what?

HAL: Yes, to your first question. I couldn't hear the second part.

PATTY: I gotta', yuh. I promised...Midgie.

HARRY: Okay. *(Nods.)* Okay.

(The lights fade out on Patty and Harry; brighten on Silva.)

(N.B. If turntable used, Harry should exit on turntable. Patty should hesitate a moment and then walk off.)

SILVA: Mrs. You-know, again?

HAL: Yup.

SILVA: Yup?

HAL: Yup.

SILVA: You're lookin' ta' get your balls shot off!

DOLLY: Nice talk...

(Doorbell rings.)

HAL: Get that, will ya'? I'm late...

SILVA: I'm s'pose'ta' walk downstairs? For you?

HAL: *(To Dolly)* Do you like Jack?

DOLLY: I admire Jack.

(Doorbell rings again. Hal exits into bedroom.)

DOLLY: She's nervous.

SILVA: She should be nervous. She's married to a certifiable lunatic...

DOLLY: What does that make me?

SILVA: I don't quite make the connection?

DOLLY: Keep eating Rings Dings and Devil Dogs, and you won't even come close to making the connection.

SILVA: You have such a remarkably joyous way with words.

(Doorbell rings again. Hal yells from bedroom.)

HAL: *(Yells from offstage.)* Come on, will you? Somebody let her in!

DOLLY: I'll get it…

SILVA: Nooo, sit. I'll go…*(Turns to Hal.)* You owe me for this!

HAL: *(Yells from offstage.)* Tell her I'll be right down!
   (The doorbell rings again. Silva stands, yells.)

SILVA: Keep your knickers on, you horny old trollop!
   (Silva crosses the stage. The lights crossfade with him. He descends an imagined staircase, opens an imagined door. He looks around in the darkness: shadows. No one there. Suddenly, a hand pulls him out, further, into the shadows. Gus and Harry Percy stand in front of Silva.)

SILVA: Hey!

GUS: Who's this?

HARRY: The fat friend…
   (Harry and Gus each hold knives against Silva. Gus holds a knife against Silva's throat; Harry against Silva's stomach.)

HARRY: Tell your pally-pal, Hal, my wife ain't able ta' visit tonight, okay? And tell yourself something: if you ever see her come to visit and you let her into your house, I'm going go even deeper…Okay? *(And with that, Harry allows his knife to pierce Silva's shirt…and the skin on his stomach.)*

SILVA: Oww!

HARRY: You follow? You get my point?

SILVA: Yuh yes yesss.

HARRY: Good deal.
   (Lights crossfade back to Dolly, watching TV. Silva staggers back into room, holding his stomach, which is covered with blood. Dolly sees blood; covers her mouth in terror.)

SILVA: I'm gonna' be sick.

(Hal walks out of his room, smiling; sees Silva and Dolly and his smile vanishes. Lights fade out.)

END OF SCENE TWO

(N.B. If turntable is used, Silva and Dolly should be aboard, for their exit, whilst Hal remains off to one side, staring after them. The St. Peter's Parade Marchers then enter, on the turntable. There should be a moment of silence as Hal watches. Then parade-music in, and Hal runs off, into blackness.)

Scene Three

The lights fade up on a statue [or photograph] of St. Peter, carried by Fishermen. Alongside them, Lumpers, Older men, and St. Peter's Club Members, 'walking' in place. Boley, Lissa, Angelo and others parade behind the statue, 'walking,' in place. Boley, Lissa and Angelo wave to imagined crowd. We hear the sound of cheers in auditorium, as well as cheers from all actors.

CHEERLEADER: *(In bastardized Portuguese.)* "Usseee mussee tutti muttay??? *(Translation: "Is everybody deaf?")*

OTHER VOICES: *(In response; 3 repetitions.)* Viva San Pietro!

(Boley and Lissa and Others are smiling, shaking imagined hands. All sing "God Bless America." Suddenly, Boley weakens, sickens, collapses to ground. Angelo and Lissa don't notice him at first.)

BOLEY: Markie!

(A woman screams. Lissa turns and sees Boley on ground.)

LISSA: Angelo! ANGELO!

(All sounds fade under, lightly. Lights crossfade quickly to Harry Percy, in front of map of Gloucester Harbor. Frank Percy stands beside him. They look out front, using the theatre audience as their own assembled audience.)

HARRY: I hope ya's all can see the map okay...On Sunday, Greasy Pole will start at 5...(Points to map.) Here. And the Lillies'll gather their boats and all the contest boats just inside Dogbar...here. They should be in full force at about 1:30, as they're all getting briefed at ha'pahst noon over East Glossop, then comin' across to nest...

(Vernon, Harry's cousin, screams up at Harry from the rear of the auditorium.)

VERNON: Hank Boley just collapsed in the middle of the parade. They rushed him up to Addison-Gilbert!

(Harry Percy looks up; amazed. Sirens suddenly blare out. The lights crossfade to Boley, lying in hospital bed, in soft spotlight. Percy exits in dark. Angelo, Lissa & Others, stand in line, in imagined corridor outside Boley's room. The amplified sounds of a life-support system are heard in the auditorium. Hal enters, on the run; sees the men; stops.)

HAL: There you are...Where is he?

ANGELO: They got him on a machine. It spread to both his lungs!

ARTIE: He's sleeping…

HAL: *(Quietly.)* He's alive?

LISSA: No thanks to you… *(Lissa walks to Hal and spits on him. All are amazed.)*

ANGELO: Hey, Markie! What are you doin', huh?
(Lissa turns and exits. All look at Hal, who lifts his face, head up. All men but for Hal back up, one step. Hal speaks to his father.)

HAL: Pa? It's me: Hal…

BOLEY: *(Lifts his head, looks at Hal).* I feel awful.

HAL: It's gonna' be different, Pa. I swear to you. *(Hal turns; exits. The lights brighten. All men step forward, two steps. They surround Boley's bed. Mort Shimma is first to speak. Once he does, others join in, speaking rapidly.)*

MORT: He's got more than twenty boats…

ANGELO: He's got a lot of support, Hank…

BOLEY: When?

ANGELO: *(After a pause.)* Sunday.

BOLEY: I don't know when that is.

ANGELO: Sunday…during Greasy Pole…It sounds like he's gone totally nuts! He's makin' his move right in the middle of Greasy Pole…

BOLEY: What's today? I've been asleep.

LISSA: Tuesday night. We've only got two and a half days…

BOLEY: Ask Tom's kid to come in and talk to me…ask him to come in.

MORT: He won't come in, Hank.

ANGELO: We tried already.

BOLEY: Get Tom in here.
(Drumbeat. There is a lighting change. All turn their backs to Boley. Tom Percy enters, slowly, looks at his old friend.)

PERCY: I'm sorry, Hank.

BOLEY: It's not your doing. I know that…

PERCY: I tried to talk to him, but, he won't come near me…

BOLEY: He knows you're against him. That's why.

PERCY: *(Quietly.)* He's my son.

BOLEY: Who can get to him, Tom?

PERCY: Nobody.
(Drumbeat. Lighting change. Hal speaks softly, from opposite side of stage. Tom Percy turns upstage.)

HAL: Angelo came and got me…

BOLEY: I may have to ask you to share something you may not be prepared to share…

HAL: Okay…

BOLEY: This involves Harry Percy…

HAL: *(After a pause.)* Tell me what you want me to do, Pa, and I'll do it.

BOLEY: Tom?

(Drumbeat; lighting change Tom turns to Boley; Hal turns upstage.)

PERCY: What, Henry?

BOLEY: Jesus, I feel awful. I don't have much time, Tom…

PERCY: What can I do for you, Hank?

BOLEY: Where's your brother?

(Tom Percy turns his back, upstage. A drumbeat. Frank Percy and Vernon Koski enter, move to Boley's bedside. N.B. If turntable is used, Boley should be set at exact centre.)

FRANK: I'm sorry you're feelin' punk, Hank.

BOLEY: Thanks, Frankie. Me, too…

FRANK: You know my nephew, Vernon Koski? This is my sister's boy, Vernon. He's visiting from Australia.

VERNON: Good to see you, Mr. Boley…

FRANK: Vernon's been driving me here and there. My eyes are no good. We get old, huh?

BOLEY: You got to stop him, Frank…

FRANK: Stop who?

BOLEY: Frank, it's ridiculous to play games, with me in this condition. I know that Tom's son is going to hit the Lillie boats on Sunday. I know where, when, who's with him. I know it all…*(Pause.)* It's a small town, Frank. People know things.

FRANK: What do you want from me?

BOLEY: Stop him, Frank. *(Pauses.)* I talked it through with my son, Hal…and he's willing to share the gavel with Harry…co-Number Ones.

VERNON: Really?

(Boley looks at Vernon: smiles.)

FRANK: I'll tell him.

BOLEY: Good.

(Drumbeat. There is a lighting change. Frank Percy and Vernon stop downstage, two steps. Frank grabs Vernon roughly.)

FRANK: He's lying.

VERNON: *(Looks at his uncle.)* You think so?

FRANK: I know so. I go back years and years with Henry Boley. It's the same as it was with your Uncle Tom. Is he co-Number One?
(Vernon looks down.)
Boley's in like this…*(Knots fingers.)* with the Coast Guard. Every last one of us will end up in Federal Court…

VERNON: Jesus, Uncle Frank! What do we do?

FRANK: We just shut up about what Boley said to us. We don't say nothing to Harry. We let Harry go ahead and take over…his way.
(Drumbeat. Lighting change. All men turn and step forward to Boley's bedside again. Hal is among them. Frank Percy and Vernon exit, in darkness.)

LISSA: This meeting is official. We have a quorum…*(Lissa carries a small wooden box, which he opens and from which he removes the small, solid-gold gavel. He hands same to Boley, placing box on bed.)* Hank.

BOLEY: *(Taps the gavel down on the wooden box, producing a fairly meek thud.)* I asked for this meeting and I'm glad you all could come…

ANGELO: Excuse me, Hank, but, do you think Hal should be in here now?

BOLEY: Hal's the Son of One.

HAL: I know how you all feel and I, uh, hope I can change your opinion of me…

MORT: This is very touchy…

BOLEY: I'm dying, Mort. I got no time for what's touchy and what isn't…Hal stays in the meeting. *(Pauses.)* Anybody hear from Frank Percy, yet?

ANGELO: The word's very bad, Hank…

LISSA: Frank double-crossed you…

ANGELO: Whatever Frank said to Harry changed nothing. The word is that Percy's got more than a hundred men with him tomorrow…
(Boley stares disappointed.)

MORT: The thing is snow-balling…

ANGELO: The word's very bad, Hank…

HAL: I've got an idea…If I were to go one-on-one with Percy, early… tonight…tomorrow morning…I could bring this thing to a conclusion…

BOLEY: What kind of conclusion?

HAL: I happen to think I can handle Percy. I happen to thnk I can take him out…

LISSA: Takin' out his wife ain't like takin' out the man himself, Hal. You want to be careful.

HAL: You want to be careful, Markie. I know you like to think of me as wet behind the ears, as you just spit there, but, I got'ta warn you: I play to win…and I have an excellent memory as to who played on my team and who played against me team. You follow?

ANGELO: That ain't necessary, Hal. Mark Lissa's put his name on the line, many's the time, for your father…

BOLEY: None of this is necessary. I won't have you goin' against Harry Percy, Hal. I forbid it. Okay? This matter will be resolved peacefully…We wait to see if Harry takes up the offer to share control…

MORT: We've got no time, Hank…As soon as the tuna-contest boats start out of the harbor, Percy's gonna' move against them…

BOLEY: Do the Lillies know what's comin'?

HAL: Don't you think if we know, they know?

BOLEY: Markie, go see Dr. Nagoa. Find out what he's planning.

MORT: Aren't they Pacifists?

BOLEY: Oh, yuh, sure. Go see, Markie…*(To all.)* Let's reconvene after lunch, after Markie's got an answer. *(Pauses.)* Hal, I want you to find out what Frank told Harry. Find out if Harry even knows my offer…
(Vernon enters; dribbling basketball.)

HAL: You think that Frank will be straight with me?

BOLEY: No, no, don't waste your time talking to Frank.
(Light shift to Vernon Koski, opposite side of stage. Vernon turns, sees Hal, starts to run. Hal tackles Vernon. They wrestle and roll about, but, the boy is no match for Hal who is older, larger, stronger and far more determined.)

VERNON: Get off me!

HAL: What did your uncle tell Harry?

VERNON: I don't know nothin'!

HAL: You answer me, Koski!

VERNON: I don't know nothin'!

HAL: *(Whacks Vernon, roughly.)* Talk!

VERNON: I got nothin' to say!
(Vernon starts his exit, as Guido Vega enters, upstage.)

HAL: Did Harry get our offer?

VERNON: I don't know nothin'! Ask Harry yourself!
(Guido Vega walks slowly across the upstage edge of the stage, head down, trying not to be seen by Hal. Hal spots Guido and runs after him. Lights shift with Hal. Vernon exits in darkness. Hal catches up to Guido who throws a punch at Hal, hitting him.)

HAL: Don't, Guido! Talk to me!

GUIDO: Pound sand, Hal!

HAL: My father's dying, Guido!

GUIDO: I can't do nothin' about that Hal,…I'm sorry. Leave me be!

HAL: My father's been lookin' after you how long, Guido? How long? HOW LONG? *(There is a long pause.)*

GUIDO: It's big, Hal. We could both get killed over this. It's big.

HAL: Tell me, Guido.

GUIDO: I can't, Hal. I'd like to. I would. Your father's like my own to me. Honest to God…

HAL: I'll play the fuckin' violin, Guido. My father's layin' in a bed near dead and he's countin' on you. Don't tell me what you'd "like" to do! Open your mouth and talk, Guido!

GUIDO: I can't, Hal.

HAL: My father's from the old times, Guido. He's naïve. He thinks Glossop people are all clean-living, all family. He reads the paper and he doesn't believe it. He doesn't know what goes on here with drugs and money. Don't forget: I've been on the inside here, Guido. I know. *(Pauses.)* Frank Percy's running Cocaine through Glossop, isn't he? *(Pauses.)* Isn't he? *(Pauses.)* Isn't he, Guido??? *(Pauses.)* If my father dies knowing you lied to him, Guido, it'll be on your head forever…

GUIDO: Come onn, Halll. I was one of maybe a hundred boats. I only carried goods for Frank three times, total…

HAL: Is Harry Percy in on it?

GUIDO: I don't think so…

HAL: So, what the fuck gives? Harry Percy's about to turn Glossop into the worst place on the map of Massachusetts, and that includes Woburn, Lawrence and East Boston. Why's he doing this?

GUIDO: I dunno', honest ta' Christ, I…

HAL: *(A sudden explosion.)* Who are you protecting, Guido? What are you? On Frank's payroll?

GUIDO: 'course not! I did maybe three jobs for Frank, total. I made some pin money — chump change — that's all. I got no other connection.

HAL: Why'd you pull the plug?

GUIDO: *(After a pause.)* Frank told me to. He's got somebody on the inside, with the Coast Guard. They were on to me, that I carried packages for Frank. *(Pauses; sadly.)* So, I got a few bucks, now…no boat…

HAL: Nobody'll ever insure another boat for you, right?

GUIDO: Yuh, right: nobody…

HAL: You help me, Guido, I'll help you. I swear on my mother's grave…(*There is a long pause.*)

GUIDO: Frank's using Harry to pull the Coast Guard's attention off him. Between the Fiesta and what Harry's plannin', nobody'll be lookin' in Frank's direction…

HAL: Shit! 'course, he is! Perfect!

GUIDO: Frank's bringin' in enough to retire on. He's buying and sellin' the Protein plant, for condos. We're talkin' millions here! He's got a good bunch of us in on it. We're talkin' very big, very major bucks, Hal. A lot of guys are makin' big. That's why you gotta' promise to never let anybody know I talked. You gotta', Hal…I gotta' hold you to that, or I'm gonna' float up somewhere, some day. I'm scared, Hal.

HAL: Trust me, Guido.

(*Hal, like his father before him touches Guido's shoulder. Guido, so touched, smiles, as he has before. Hal turns from Guido and moves across stage. Lights shift with Hal, at Silva who now faces Patty Percy.*)

SILVA: You can't come in!

HAL: Let her in, Jackie.

SILVA: Mother of Christ! I've still got a scab on my stomach from her maniac husband!

HAL: (*From behind Silva.*) I said let her in, Jackie!

SILVA: You promised me, shit-for-brains! You gave your sacred word!

HAL: I did nothing of the kind. (*To Patty.*) Does he know you're here?

PATTY: He knows I'm somewhere.

SILVA: Oh, God…he knows she's somewhere! You hear that? We are talking Death, here. D.E.A.T.H!!(*Silva exits, backing away, slowly; terrified*).

HAL: (*Moves to Patty.*) Frank Percy never gave Harry our offer to split Head of the Union with me. Harry never heard this. I think it's best if it comes from you, now…Maybe he'll still listen, if it comes from you.

PATTY: I'll try. (*Pauses.*) We all thought it was complicated when we were sixteen, didn't we? (*Pauses.*) Right now, I don't feel like I'm living inside my own life!

(*Patty moves across stage, slowly. The lights crossfade with her. Hal backs off into the shadows. She joins Gus and, together, they move to Harry Percy. Two other men are with Percy.*)

GUS: It's your wife.

(Percy turns and faces Patty. He nods to men, who exit the office, leaving Harry and Patty alone.)

HARRY: Why don't you leave me the fuck alone?

PATTY: Please, Harry, listen to me.

HARRY: Yuh, so, what? What do ya' want from me?

PATTY: Hank Boley offered you Co-Head with Hal. Hal agreed. Your uncle never told you the offer.

HARRY: What are you givin' me here?

PATTY: While you're out there attacking the Lillie boats, your Uncle Frank is bringing a shipment of drugs in. He's using you as a diversion. It's a big shipment...

HARRY: Uncle Frank? That's bullshit!

PATTY: *(Pauses.)* Your Uncle Frank lied to you. He carried an untrue message from Henry Boley...

HARRY: How come you know this?

PATTY: Hal told me.

HARRY: You saw Hal again?

PATTY: Yuh, just now.

HARRY: You in love with him, Patty?

PATTY: *(Looks at her husband, answers quietly.)* Yuh, I am, Harry...
(Harry walks to Patty and slaps her.)

HARRY: I'm sorry.

PATTY: Me, too.
(They kiss. Patty turns and exits. Harry turns upstage and punches his hand through an imagined window. We hear: the sound of glass shattering. Harry, blood capsule concealed in his hand, now turns and faces audience, blood dripping from hand. Gus re-enters on the run.)

GUS: Something break? *(Sees Harry's hand.)* What's you do?

HARRY: I fucked up my hand...*(Wraps bandana around gun in hand.)*

GUS: What's with the gun? What the hell are you doing?

HARRY: Where's my uncle?

GUS: I dunno'...

HARRY: Find out!
(The lights crossfade to opposite side of stage, now including Tom Percy staring across at his son. Lights out on Gus. Harry moves to his father. Upstage, Frank Percy sits watching TV. Light of TV flickers; sound of the David Letterman Show, in progress, lightly under the scene. Harry has bloody bandana around hand, runs across to Tom, yelling "Pa!" Drumbeat.)

PERCY: What is it?

HARRY: Is he here?

PERCY: Who?

HARRY: Uncle Frank…

PERCY: Yuh, he's in watching TV. I was just upstairs, doin'…
  (Harry shoves past his father. Tom Percy follows his son.)
  What's up, Harry? What's the matter?
  (Frank Percy, watching television, hears commotion, turns and looks; sees Harry standing in doorway. There is a bloody towel covering Harry's hand. Sound effect: Television program, continuing: Letterman interviewing a writer.)

FRANK: Hey, Harry, how goes it? I was comin' over right after Letterman. What's the matter? What happened to your hand, Harry?

HARRY: Uncle Frank's been telling me all about the old days… *(Pauses.)* How you and Boley made plans for me to run the Union… *(Pauses.)* How Boley bought you off…

PERCY: Nobody bought me off…

HARRY: With this…this house, the freezer plant…half a million dollars…

PERCY: What's this? Hank Boley never bought me off. Whatever I have, I earned…

HARRY: Uncle Frank's been tellin' me different, hasn't he?

FRANK: What gives, Harry?

HARRY: Uncle Frank's been tellin' me everything. How my wife's fuckin' Hal Boley…how the Lillies are fuckin' Glossop…how I'm gettin' fucked out'ta my just desserts… *(Smiles savagely.)* Uncle Frankie tells me lots! *(Pauses.)* Uncle Frankie's been pushin' me…pushin' me…really givin' me the kinda' support you'd expect from family…It's been great…Uncle Frankie and I have some enormous plans…

FRANK: What's the matter, Harry?

HARRY: Uncle Frank's got a shipment of coke comin' into town tomorrow that would sink a battleship, don't ya', Uncle Frankie? Uncle Frankie's wired like a goddam pinball machine!

PERCY: What are you sayin'?

HARRY: Uncle Frankie's buyin' and sellin'. He's found himself quite a parcel. Ain't that what they call it when you put the pieces together, Uncle Frankie: a parcel? Quite a parcel Uncle Frankie's got: you're in it, Pa, I'm in it, half'a fuckin' Glossop is in it!

PERCY: What the hell is he talkin' about, Frank?

HARRY: What? That wasn't clear?

FRANK: That was clear…*(Frank takes a gun from his pocket, suddenly, which he trains on Harry.)* Wicked clear!

PERCY: Jesus, Frank, don't…

FRANK: Back off, Harry…

HARRY: Uncle Frank's been plannin' ta' use me like some kind of stooge…some kind of dumb decoy, right? Right?

FRANK: Yuh, Harry, that's right.

PERCY: Jesus, Frank…

HARRY: He's got me out there raising hell with the Lillies, while Uncle Frank's runnin' himself a double-reverse play, right under our noses…Look at me, Uncle Frank…*(Points at Frank w/bandaged hand.)* I said look at me!

FRANK: I'm looking at you, Harry.

(Harry has a pistol hidden in the bandage wrapped around his bloody hand. He now fires the gun, four consecutive shots, killing Frank Percy. We hear: Four drumbeats.)

PERCY: Frank…Jesus, Harry…Frank's dead…

HARRY: Uncle Frank…all bloody…

PERCY: This is my fault. Get out of here, Harry. I'll take care of this…This is my fault. You leave me the gun. Get out of here!

HARRY: I'm not stopping, Pa. I want Number One! It's mine!

PERCY: Let it go, Harry…

HARRY: No!

PERCY: Let Hal Boley have it, Harry. You take your wife and your daughter and you live your life!

HARRY: I got no life to live! *(Waves pistol.)* This here's my life! *(Motions to Frank.)* He's your brother. Bury him…*(Harry turns and exits, running past Boley. The lights crossfade with him.*

END OF SCENE THREE

Scene Four

N.B. If turntable is used, Tom and Frank should exit on turntable as Boley is brought on. Harry Percy should stop off and exit, running, after Boley is on. In the darkness, we hear the amplified sounds of a life-support system, along with the amplified sounds of Boley's labored breathing. The lights fade up on Boley, asleep, alone, in the throes of a murderous memory: a nightmare.

TOWNSPEOPLE: *(A low whisper; many voices, in unison.)* Murder.
(Boley stirs, groans, his labored breathing continues along with his haunting nightmare. The townspeople whisper again.)
Murder.
(Boley groans again. Angelo enters, suddenly; waking Boley.)
ANGELO: Hank? Sorry.
BOLEY: *(Wakes; startled.)* What? What is it?
ANGELO: Frank Percy's dead.
BOLEY: When?
ANGELO: An hour ago…gunned down.
BOLEY: Who?
ANGELO: Tom's boy, four bullets, cold blood. He's started.
BOLEY: You sure of this?
ANGELO: Dead sure.
BOLEY: Who's the source.
ANGELO: Usual: our man inside.
BOLEY: Where is he now: Tom's kid?
ANGELO: Back at the wharf, his place, gearin' up…
BOLEY: Oh, Jesus!
ANGELO: What do you want me to do, Henry?
BOLEY: Get my son, Angelo. Bring him here…
ANGELO: Why, Hank? There's no time…
BOLEY: Angelo, bring Hal here!
ANGELO: Sure thing.
(Angelo exits. Drumbeat. Lights shift to Hal, downstage of Boley.)
HAL: Angelo told me about Frank Percy. Tell me what to do, Pa. I want to help…
BOLEY: There's something terrible…something you have to know. Listen to me…We can't have the police in on this. We have to handle it ourselves…*(Hal looks at Boley, surprised Boley speaks with great difficulty.)* Years back, when I was your age, lumpin', Allie Richards was wired, runnin' drugs in through Glossop at a time when most of us didn't have a clue what the hell drugs were, even…It took us no time to figure out what heroin was, what it was doin' to people…*(Pauses.)* Tommy and I made a vow to stop him, no matter what. Allie had no

wife, no kids, nobody to hand the gavel over to…so…*(Pauses; groans out his confession.)* We killed him, Tommy and me, we killed Allie Richards…It was my idea…Tommy and I were co-heads…co-number ones, just for a while, just for appearance-sake, but Tommy never wanted any part of it. He stepped down I stepped up, and that's how I got Number One.

TOWNSPEOPLE: *(In a low whisper; in unison.)* Murder.

HAL: Pa, I…never put the pieces together. Your being Number One always seemed so…natural…

BOLEY: I've changed my mind. I need you to stop Harry Percy…

TOWNSPEOPLE: Murder…

BOLEY: I can't handle it myself…

TOWNSPEOPLE: Murder…

BOLEY: Just you and him, like you offered, nobody else. We can't have the police in on this…*(Groans.)* It's a lousy goddam time for me to be dying. I'm leaving things in a mess!

HAL: You're not dying, Pa, you're just weak, that's all…

BOLEY: I don't need that! Don't, Hal, please! What is is! Listen to me, Henry. When the Italians first came to Glossop, everybody said they were gonna' ruin the fish business. The same with the Irish, the Finns, too. The same with the Porteguees, when they came. The Lillies are no different from any of us. They're just people come to fish. *(Inhales from pain.)* Nature is supply and demand. When a mother stops nursing her baby, the milk dries up in her breast. As long as she keeps nursing, the milk keeps flowing. That's what life is, Hal…Somebody's got to fish, Hal. If there are no fishermen, the fish themselves will die.

HAL: I'll try, pa. I'm scared shit, but I'll try.

BOLEY: Good. Get Markie and Angelo and the others…

(Lissa, Angelo, Shimma, and others all turn in face Boley and Hal.)

BOLEY: I don't want to wait. I want the gavel to pass along to Hal, my son, now…

LISSA: That's not the rule…

BOLEY: It's what I want, Markie! We got certain things that need to be done right away. We've got no time…*(Pauses.)* We've got a quorum here. This is what I want. This is probably the last thing I'll ever ask from any of ya's. *(There is a small silence.)*

ANGELO: *(Softly.)* I move that Hal Boley take over duties as Number One,

as of now, acting for his father, Hank Boley, who is Number One so
long as he lives…

MORT: Second.

BOLEY: All in favor?

(*All hands go up. As each man raises his hand, he says "aye" and there is
a drumbeat. Finally, Lissa raises his hand and the vote is unanimous.
Boley hands gavel to Hal. The power has passed to Hal. Lights fade out.*)

END OF SCENE FOUR

Scene Five

Lights fade up on Harry and Gus. Harry is slightly drunk; drinks beer.

GUS: Easy with the brew, huh? We got some work ahead of us, huh,
Harry…

HARRY: Fuck off, Gus, will ya'…

(*Harry laughs; drinks from a bottle of beer. Vernon enters.*)

VERNON: Can I talk to you, Harry?

HARRY: Who's that?

GUS: It's your cousin…

HARRY: I got no cousin…

VERNON: (*Looks furtively at Gus, who is also alarmed.*) Harry, I've talked
to Boley.

HARRY: (*Turns and faces Vernon.*) And?

VERNON: Boley wants to go one-on-one with you…

HARRY: What are you? Shitting me? Hank Boley's s'pose'ta be layin' in a
sickbed up Addison-Gilbert!

VERNON: Hal Boley. (*Pauses.*) He took over as Number One, last night.
Hank Boley's nearly dead. They got him on some kind of machine.
Hal's Number One…

HARRY: (*He inhales, sharply. He turns away; laughs. He faces Vernon.*)
What'da'ya' mean "one-on-one"? S'that a joke? Number-One-on-
Number-One?

VERNON: Just the two of you, nobody else. Someplace private. To figure
out who's got control…

(Percy goes to Vernon and puts a hammerlock on the boy, twisting his arm painfully.)

HARRY: I put four bullets into your uncle. You can only get the chair once. Killin' a little pisser like you's nothin' ta' me. Nothin'! *(Twists.)* Is it true? Is this a true offer?

VERNON: Ten Pound Island, 2 o'clock. It's a true offer...

HARRY: Are you working for Boley?

VERNON: I ain't working for nobody but myself, Harry. I swear to God.

HARRY: *(Lets the boy go.)* Me neither, Vernon. *(Smiles.)* That's the first smart thing I ever heard you say...

GUS: What about our plan, Harry? We're gonna' get damn close to a hundred men out there!

HARRY: Let 'em surround Ten Pound Island. If Boley's got some kind of funny shit goin', he'll have a war on his hands... *(Smiles.)* If he don't, he'll have a battle, just what he's askin' for: one-on-one... We go back all the way to the crib together... *(Smiles.)* I should'a done the bas'tid back then... *(Laughs.)* You spread the word, Gussie: circle Ten Pound Island and wait for me. Then we go for the Lillies.

(We hear: the sound of an Announcer's voice excitedly, over amplified sound-speakers, off in the distance, and the sounds of an excited crowd.)

ANNOUNCER: Salvy Benson, ladies and gentlemen... The undisputed champion of the Greasy Pole... making his second attempt. Salvy Benson...

(The lights crossfade to Hal, Silva, Petey, Bardolph.)

HAL: I'd better be alone in my boat going out there...

(N.B. the sounds of the Greasy Pole Contest, and of the boats' engines, should be played under the scene, just barely audible, but, present.)

PETEY: You sure?

HAL: If Percy thinks I'm not alone, he'll use his men, too. He's got 100 piratical lumpers backing him up, and all I got is you, Bardolph and tubby Jack Silva, so what's the point? If I show up alone, maybe he'll show up alone. One-on-one's my best shot. I know you're devastated by the news...

SILVA: What news?

HAL: You won't be able to go hand-to-hand with Percy and Gus...

SILVA: I won't? *(False disappointment, badly playacted.)* Damn. *(Shrugs.)* I'm going back to bed...

PETEY: What do you want us to do?

HAL: Just stay back... Lemme do what I hav'ta... *(Pauses.)* If it doesn't work out…if Percy, well…*(Pauses.)* You guys come and get me…*(Pauses.)* Ten Pound Island's covered with rats. I'd rather have a less ignominious parting. *(Pauses.)* If it goes wrong, you tell my father, okay, Petey? Get over there fast, so it's you who tells him…

SILVA: Why are you doin' this?

HAL: It's a matter of honor.

SILVA: Honor? Honor is just the opposite of "off her." If it were me, I'd be on the shuttle to LaGuardia: now…

HAL: I've been on the shuttle to LaGuardia. That's the difference between us…that, and about 187 pounds…

SILVA: You wouldn't want what you just mouthed to be your last words, would you?

HAL: Maybe I would. *(Change of attitude.)* Jack?

SILVA: What?

HAL: If I do have the last word…if I come back from this…things have got to change?

SILVA: In what sense?

HAL: In every sense.

(Hal starts boat's engine sound of same increases. The lights crossfade to Patty. Patty moves upstage into shadowy light, calling out to Tom Percy.)

PATTY: Dad? *(Patty stops, looks about worried. She smiles and calls out again.)* Dad? *(Patty takes one more step forward, then looks upstage and screams.)*

(NOTE: All women in cast should echo Patty's scream, so that the sound carries from women to women, and surrounds the audience/auditorium. If scenically possible, lights fade up, dimly, upstage. We see shadow of Tom Percy, hanging by the neck, dead.

Patty walks to grave and takes note from ground, opens same, reads same aloud. The lights cross to Harry, opposite side of stage. Patty turns and faces her husband.)

PATTY: *(Reading.)* "I claim full responsibility for the death of Alfred Richards and for the death of my brother, Francis Percy. I killed them both with my own hand and by my own hand I take my own life and end this murderous rampage. whatever I own, I leave to my son, Harold Percy, who I pray will forgive me…" *(To Harry.)* And he signed it… *(Weeps.)* Oh, God, Harry, I'm so sorry…

HARRY: At least, he found some courage…

PATTY: You've got to stop now, Harry. You've got to…

HARRY: Opposite…What is is! Nobody can change it. Nobody can take it away…*(Harry goes to Patty and kisses her, roughly. He turns from her suddenly, leaving her alone, weeping; resolute. He calls to opposite side of stage.)* Hal Boley!

(Drumbeat.)

HAL: *(Off-stage, in shadows.)* Right here, Percy…

(Drumbeat.)

HARRY: You ready, Boley?

HAL: *(Enters.)* Ready.

HARRY: What's your poison?

HAL: How's these? *(Hal holds up two curved fish-knives, high over his head.)*

HARRY: Fine with me.

HAL: Ten Pound Island, ten minutes, just us…

HARRY: Ten Pound Island, ten minutes, just us…

(Hal and Harry walk in opposite circles, full perimeter of stage. Lights dim. SFX: We hear in auditorium the increased sound of Greasy Pole Contest, on shore.)

ANNOUNCER'S VOICE: *(Over amplifier.)* This Greasy Pole Contest is holding for the pleasure boats out there! Somebody tell them pleasure-boat operators we ain't gonna' have another walker 'til they move them pleasure boats away from under the Greasy Pole…

(Lighting shifts to extremely dim lighting, three edges of stage, allowing audience their view from front. All cast members, except Boley and Tom Percy and Frank Percy, stand in shadows, not recognizable, making sounds of rats. A slight glow now appears, stage center. Hal enters from stage right. He kicks at the imagined rats. Drumbeats will punctuate this entire scene, henceforward.)

HAL: Not me!

(Harry enters from stage left. He kicks at the rats as well.)

HARRY: Not Harry Percy! I got a whole 'nother meal planned for you rats: it's called Hal Boley! *(He flashes knife at the imagined rats. We hear the sound of the rats squealing, increase with their excitement, as stone is hurled.)*

HAL: *(Looks across, watches Harry, calls out.)* Harry Percy…

HARRY: Hal Boley…

HAL: Long time…

HARRY: Long time…

(Harry Percy and Hal Boley begin to fight, as might two savages. A life-time of misunderstanding spurs each of them on. The advantage changes and changes again. First, Hal is on top; then, Percy. Their sounds are an-

imal-like, joining with the sound of the rats. The fight carries them in and around the audience up and down ramps and platforms. Suddenly, Harry mis-steps, loses his footing; falters. Hal stabs Harry in the stomach. All sound stops. Loud drumbeat.)

HARRY: Oh, Jesus!

ALL OTHERS: *(A whisper.)* Oh, Jesus Christ!

(The two young men fall to the ground together. Blood oozes from Harry's chest. Hal cradles Harry's head.)

HAL: Oh, God, Harry, I'm sorry. I am, I'm really sorry…Harry?

HARRY: It hurts wicked, Henry…*(Pauses.)* Am I gonna' die from this?

HAL: It looks bad.

HARRY: You remember our parents used'ta take us all up Derry, New Hampshire, to the water slide?

HAL: I do, yuh.

HARRY: I was thinkin' about that. It was fun…*(Pauses.)* Take me off'a here, huh? The rats…

HAL: I will.

HARRY: You…win. I'm goin' ta' sleep, Hal. You win…

HAL: *(Sobbing.)* I do, Harry. I win…

(Harry Percy dies. We hear the sounds of the rats squealing. Hal screams.)

HAL: Noooo! *(Hal kicks at the rats. he tosses stones at them. He turns and sees that rats are close to Harry's dead body. Hal screams again.)* Noooooooooooooooo! *(Hal picks up Harry as best he can, and carries Harry in a circle, slowly.)* I'll leave you in the water, Harry. You'll be safe…*(Hal "buries" Harry Percy at sea. He kneels and says a prayer. May the soul of the faithful departed, etc.)*

ALL: *(They all sing "The Requiem," in Latin.)*

(Hal stands and moves to the full group of spectators, now stand, in a cluster, hands at sides. Hal runs in circle, ending, center, at Angelo. The lights brighten to hot white light.)

HAL: Did anybody tell my father?…

ANGELO: He's…gone, Hal.

HAL: When?

ANGELO: Noon. It was…peaceful.

(Hal stands straighter. He does not weep. Angelo embraces Hal. Lights fade out.)

END OF SCENE FIVE

Scene Six

In the darkness, we hear drunken laughter; followed by Silva's voice bois-terously.

SILVA: Come on, party-people! We will own this town!
(The lights snap on. Silva, Dolly, Bardolph, Barry, Gadshill, Alberta and Emily Fusco and others, dance on, in the throes of great celebration. Singing as he runs on.)
You've got to fight...for your right...to parrrrrtyyyyy!...
(They arrive in a party-cluster, upstage-left.)
I kid you not! I will be to Hal Boley what Spiro Agnew was to Richard Nixon...
DOLLY: Spiro Agnew was Jackie's main hero...
SILVA: Spiro Agnew was a God!
(All look up to see: Hal, standing, facing them. Silva grins from ear to ear, calls out to Hal. All cheer and call out with Silva. Hal, cuts them off.)
SILVA AND OTHERS: Halll! Hallieeee! Hallll!
HAL: I don't want any of you living or working in Glossop, or anywhere on Cape Ann...*(All laugh; cheer.)* You've got two weeks to move out...*(Laugh.)* I know everything about everybody here...
(Everyone laughs. And then they don't. One by one, grins fade into some-thing serious, as Hal makes his pronouncement.)
HAL: Glossop's going to change...If anyone of you is still here after two weeks, the police will get a full report from me about whatever I know...and I know a lot...Glossop's off limits to every one of you. No exceptions, two weeks...No exceptions. (All *turn away, but for Silva. Silva and Hal make eye-contact. Hal makes his final pronounce-ment, quietly, sadly.)* I don't know you, fat man.
(Hal backs away from Silva and the others, never breaking eye contact. All turn, exit. The lights crossfade to Patty across stage, inside of her house. She is dressed in black dress, her face tear-stained.
Hal should scream his lines from off-stage, behind the audience, if possi-ble. Patty should be alone on stage, calling off to Hal)
Patty!?
PATTY: What?
HAL: Where are you?

PATTY: Here. Inside…

HAL: I'm coming in!

PATTY: No!

HAL: Did you hear?

PATTY: Vernon came by.

HAL: There was no other way, Patty.

PATTY: There's no way I'm gonna' make you feel better about this. What you did, you did…*(Pauses.)* What I did, I did…*(Tragic scream.)* It's a shame, that's what. A wicked awful, terrible fuckin' shame!

HAL: I know. I agree. But what is is. I can't change it. *(Pauses.)* Do you wish Harry killed me?

PATTY: No.

HAL: I'd like to see you…talk to you…when you're ready…Do you want to never see me again?

PATTY: *(After a pause.)* There's a lot I've gotta' get done first, with my daughter…Maybe in a year. I dunno'…*(There is a small silence.)*

HAL: *(Calls out to her; softly.)* Will you see me then? In a year?

PATTY: Yes.

(Lights crossfade to opposite side of stage, where Markie Lissa and Angelo Catalano enter from Boley's graveside. All others surround audience singing prayer in Latin. Angelo and Markie stand facing each other, center stage as the others continue and complete the Latin prayer: The Requiem.)

ALL: Ahhhh-mennn…

ANGELO: Hard to believe..

LISSA: Yuh.

ANGELO: Guy like Hank shoulda' lived to a hundred…

LISSA: Yuh, I s'pose…

ANGELO: It's gonna' be different. At least we've got Hank's boy…

LISSA: What are you? Kidding me? The kid hasn't spoken a civil word to me in months! I'm the one who got him suspended…

ANGELO: Yuh, that's tough!

LISSA: An hour ago, at the cemetery, I tried to shake his hand, an he pushed me aside like I was a nobody…

ANGELO: He's a kid still…Hotheaded…

LISSA: Yuh, well, he may be a kid, but, he's running the show now, Angelo…

ANGELO: He is popular, yuh…

LISSA: I'm 71, Angelo. I can't start up fresh. I'm too far gone for lumpin'…
(Hal enters.)

PASTA: *(Calls out.)* The new boss, everybody!

(Everyone turns, sees Hal; applauds and cheers. Hal smiles, waves. Lissa walks to Hal and offers a handshake. It is a courageous act on Lissa's part, as the gesture is now totally public.)

LISSA: I tried to shake your hand at the grave, but, you didn't see me Hal…*(Pauses.)* I want to offer you my total support…

HAL: *(Smiles; looks over at Angelo.)* "Total support"? That's quite an offer, Markie?

LISSA: I know you hate me, 'counta' my causin' your suspension…but, what you did slurred your father. It was a slap in the face of this Union and all of us, and a slap in your father's face, most of all…*(Pauses.)* When you have a son, if he breaks the rules in the same way, he'll be treated by me in the same way. It's a promise I make to your father, years and years ago, and I make it to you right now. Even if you hate me for it, Hal. I know right from wrong…

(There is a silence in the room, as everyone stares, somewhat embarrassed, deeply aware of what is being said.)

HAL: I pray to God that I'll have a kid, someday, who'll be lucky enough to have a guy like you around with his eyes on things, Markie…

(Hal hugs Lissa, kisses his cheek. There is a delighted silence, All applaud. We now hear a constant drumbeat.)

ALL: Hal Boley! Hal Boley! Hal Boley!

END OF SCENE SIX

Epilogue

Lissa moves downstage, into a pool of light in front of the Townspeople. Hal moves up on to a small high platform, into a firecely white light, gold gavel in his hand.

HAL: My father believed that any man, woman and child who wanted to live in Glossop and work hard for a living, should and would have that chance…

(Lissa speaks to audience, as he did in the play's Prologue, now in counterpoint to Hal.)

LISSA: The worst and the best of men and trees finally fall forward, dead, to fertilize an Earth, so that men and trees might rise and have their time...

HAL: ...No matter if they are Porteguee, Irish, Finnish, Italian, Korean, Protestant, Catholic, Jew, hard-working people will have their chance. I promise this.

(All Townspeople cheer. The cheer ends unfinished, suddenly clipped.)

LISSA: Glossop is gone, but for the odd scrap, the odd vestige, a blade of an ice-skate, a handle from a glazed ceramic coffee mug. Otherwise, Glossop is gone...

HAL: There are plenty of fish in the sea, enough for everybody! My father believed that and I believe that. And I am ready to defend that ideal against any one and any thing...

LISSA: Ideal, like honor, is just another word. A holy war is finally, nothing but a war. And murder, in the name of goodness is nonetheless murder. And fisherman who sink their boats or sell their piers in the name of money can never again call themselves Fishermen. They are, simply, ordinary men with pockets full of paper money...

HAL: I swear upon the memory of my father to run this waterfront in my father's way. Glossop will be great again!

(All cheer. The cheer ends, suddenly clipped.)

LISSA: The only Lillies left on Cape Ann grow on graves. Where Glossop was, now stand a thousand towers: condominiums staring out over a filthy fishless sea...

HAL: I am my father's son. Whatever my father began, I will...continue...I promise, with my blood, Glossop will be great again...

LISSA: For we, the living, now, there's still time to take down our "For Sale" signs...and to live.

(Drumbeat. The Townspeople cover their faces with newspapers, reading as they did at the start of the play. Lissa now covers his face by opening a Glossop newspaper, too, and reading. Five drumbeats, softly. A moment of silence and then the lights switch out.)

END OF PLAY

Gloucester - London - New York City,
March, 1985 - February, 1989.

ADDENDUM: AUTHOR'S NOTES for *Henry Lumper*
PROGRAM, NYC PRODUCTION.

By way of background for this specific play, Gloucester was for some 300 years, first and foremost, a working-class city, an international seaport. Livings were made "on the water," hunting fish or lobster, or "workin' the wharfs," cutting and packing fish in the processing plants.

During the past decade, Gloucester gained national attention for three local commodities: "Moonies," waterfront real estate and hard drugs. The hottest issue by far was what the newspapers called "The Moonie Issue." Boston's beloved Richard Cardinal Cushing somehow approved (if not engineered) the sale of a massive piece of Gloucester property to Rev. Moon, leader of the Unification Church, a world-wide religious organization best known for its mass weddings, and for the sale of more canned tuna fish than any other producer on the planet earth. Gloucester people were at once certain their innocent children would be drugged and kidnapped by the "Moonies." On the side of Reality, the "Moonie" fishing fleet actually did undercut local fish prices, and by a lot. Racism exploded. T-shirts appeared on the chests of otherwise sane Gloucester family folks headlining such legends as "Save Gloucester— Shoot a Moonie!"

But Time does have its way. No Gloucester children were drugged or kidnapped. Fish prices came into (relative) balance. T-shirts and picketlines faded and the other two Gloucetser commodities worthy of nationwide media attention stepped forward in Gloucester people's hearts and minds. According to the *Boston Globe,* in 1986, Gloucester real estate prices were reckoned to be the "most inflated in the nation." And according the *Boston Globe,* in 1987, Gloucester's drug problem, was "the worst in the nation."

In the simplest possible terms, local real estate prices and local wages became absurdly disproportionate. A local person could sell his house, instantly, for an amount equal to ten years' wages. No local young couple could possibly afford to buy a first-time home. A fisherman could earn more money carrying a cigar box filled with cocaine than he could earn in a month of fishing.

And any local business that happened to be housed on the waterfront could be sold to condo developers for ten times its actual worth. Businesses sold. The fishing industry was damaged beyond repair.

What happens to people's dignity when their work is no longer useful or available?

In frustation, a shocking number of Gloucester people sold their homes, sold out. And an even more shocking number of Gloucester's young people began selling drugs...and using drugs.

About the play, specifically. A Lumper is a stevedore. It is said that the term came into usage 200 years ago, when Gloucester Lumpers, anxious to have ships tie up at port (rather than in neighboring ports such as Salem or Newburyport), gained a reputation for being ready and willing to carry any lump of anything that need be loaded or unloaded from a visiting freighter.

Lumpers work from 4 A.M. til just after Noon, six days a week, year in, year out. They are hard working, hard living men. They are paid by what they carry, not by the clock. The top Lumpers are called "A-list" or "Preferreds" and get first crack at available work at morning "shape up." Whatever work is left over goes to the casual day workers, called "scallywags."

Control of the Union is held by the "Boss Lumper." One of the colorful myths surrounding the history of Gloucester Lumpers tells us that ultimate control of the union (a/k/a "the gavel") always passes from father to son, as in a monarchy. Apocrypha well worth dramatising!

And yes, *Henry Lumper* does purposefully parallel *Henry VI-Parts 1&2*. My apologies to Mr. Shakespeare for giving my fabricated high-adventure tale of a war for control of Gloucester's waterfront a piggy-back ride on the shoulders of his good great masterpiece.

In the matter of writing about life as it was and is being lived, we are, all of us, fair game.

I.H.
Sydney, Australia,
January, 1989.

Post Script: A sad update. Gloucester's work force of 1000+ lumpers has dwindled to a half-dozen men, barely earning a living.

I.H.
New York City
July, 1995

North Shore Fish

*To the memory of
Gail Randazza.*

PRODUCTION HISTORY

North Shore Fish was given its world premiere on August 24, 1986, at the Gloucester Stage Company (Israel Horovitz, Artistic Director/Producer, Ian McColl Managing Director.) The production was directed by Crey Cattell Johnson with sets by David Condino, costumes by Jeanine Phaneuf Burgess and lighting by B.N. Productions. The cast, in order of appearance, was as follows:

Alfred "Porker" Martino . . . . Mark Rogers
Florence Rizzo . . . . Geraldine Librandi
Arlyne Flynn. . . . . Mary Klug
Ruthie . . . . Judith McIntyre
Salvatore (Sally) Morella . . . . Theodore Reinstein
Josephine Evangelista . . . . Michelle Faith
Maureen Vega. . . . . Karen Crawford
Marlena . . . . Teade Gormley
Catherine Shimma. . . . . Tara Dolan

Subsequently the play had it's New York City premier at the WPA Theatre (Klye Renick, Artistic Director), on January 12, 1987. Directed by Stephen Zuckerman, sets by Edward T. Gianfrancesco, lights by Craig Evans, costumes by Mimi Maxmen, sound by Aural Rixation. The Production Stage Manager was David Lawrence Folender and the cast was as follows:

Alfred "Porker" Martino . . . . John Pankow
Florence Rizzo . . . . Christine Estabrook
Arlyne Flynn. . . . . Mary Klug
Ruthie . . . . Cordelia Richards
Salvatore (Sally) Morella . . . . Thomas G. Waites
Josephine Evangelista . . . . Michelle Faith
Maureen Vega. . . . . Elizabeth Kemp
Marlena . . . . Laura San Giacomo
Catherine Shimma. . . . . Wendi Malick

CHARACTERS

Alfred "Porker" Martino, 30's, small, sadly comic.
Florence Rizzo, 30's, once a high-school bombshell.
Arlyne Flynn, late 50's, thin, nervous; Ruthie's mother.
Ruthie Flynn, 30's, adorable; enormously pregnant.
Salvatore "Sally" Morella, early 30's; lean, handsome.
Josie Evangelista, 30's, strikingly plump.
Maureen Vega, 30's, tall, thin, bespectacled.
Marlena Vega, 30's, Maureen's cousin; quite beautiful: the new girl.
Catherine Shimma, 30's, slightly up-market look.

PLACE

Assembly-line and main plant, North Shore Fish, a frozen fish processing company in Gloucester, Massachusetts.

TIME

A work-day in Summer, the Present.

ACCENT

Massachusetts North Shore accent, as in *Park Your Car in Harvard Yard.*

SET

The set should be primarily stage scenery, but combined with components of actual assembly-line machinery.

Generally speaking, the machinery that would be correctly used for *North Shore Fish* would be outmoded, obsolete. The feel of the plant should be 1950's: out of date.

Although only one assembly-line is functional, there might be another assembly-line in view.

There is a large glass-windowed office overhead, probably centre-stage, housing the Inspector's Kitchen. The office is kitted-out with desk, typewriter, scale, stove. The office should have a solid door, so that a full-blown argument in the office, upstairs, would only present an angry murmer of sound to the Workers, downstairs, on the "line." Anyone in the Office, however, is totally visible to Plant Workers and Audience alike. The overall effect of the Office is that of a 2nd stage (or a gigantic movie screen or television monitor inhabited by live actors, acting) suspended over the primary stage.

North Shore Fish Processing Co., Inc. has seen better days, in years past. This fact should be made clear by the shabbiness of the plant, and by its accumulated clutter.

Each station of the assembly-line is personalized with a small open box upon which the name of the worker has been magic-markered. Thus, there are boxes marked "Flo," "Ruthie," "Arlyne," "Josie," "Trish," "Zoe," "Carmella," Slugger," and "Hazel."

Trash containers are clean corrugated-cardboard cartons, tall, lined with clear plastic bags that are collared around the topmost edge of the cartons, awaiting filling and closure. There is a carton at every functional station of the entire "line" and there is a stack of stock cartons forming a huge mass on the upstage wall.

Pipes, ducts, chains, cables and other "high-tech" trappings are in evidence everywhere.

The assembly-lines have two major conveyor systems: one to bring raw product to the workers; the second to bring finished product to the wrapping table.

COSTUMES

White or pastel dresses and aprons, rubber or disposable plastic gloves, hairnets and netted visor "caps," for the women. Porker wears short-sleeved chino shirt, matching chino pants, high rubber gloves, white apron, rubber boots, Red Sox cap. Sally wears tight-fitting blue gabardine slacks, black loafers, striped shirt and tie, long white coat. He sometimes wears hard-hat. Catherine wears skirt, blouse, sweater, white coat over all.

North Shore Fish

ACT ONE

Lights up on line of machinery, interior of fish-processing plant. 1950's assembly-line fills stage. Aluminum vats, white-rubber conveyor belt, cement floor, vast space all around. A glass-windowed office overlooks the "line" from above, centre-stage. Porker Martino, early 30's, mops floor. As he mops, he sings "Strangers In The Night," taking liberties with song's lyrics. He wears chino pants and shirt; Red Sox cap.

PORKER: Strangers in the night…
   Exchanging glances…
   Strangers in the night…
   Taking our chances…
   We made out all right…
   Because of lovvvve…
   How would we have guessed?…Dum duh dah…
   Dum dahhh (*Forgets lyrics completely.*)…
   I forget the rest…*(Improvises.)*
   Love was just a glance away…
   A warm romantic chance away…
   (Heading toward a big finish.)

We made out all right...
Taking our chances...
Lovers at first sight...
Take off your pants-es...
She wasn't too bright...
But, we were strangers in the *nighhhhhtttttt!*
(Florence enters, wearing shorts, bright blouse, sunglasses, carrying two largish pocketbooks, cigarette in her lips. She rubs her hands together, warming them. She listens to Porker's big finish before commenting. Her comment startles him.)

FLORENCE: Jesus, Porker, that you *singin'?* I thought they were stranglin' fuckin' *dolphins* in here! I never would'a guessed you were stranglin' fuckin' "Strangers In The Night."

PORKER: You sound like a *toilet*, you know that?

FLORENCE: You *are* a toilet! What a sketch, Porker! Moppin' and singin' like whathisname...Andy Williams...*(Pulls her blouse over her head. She wears a lacey bra or not.)* Turn your head around! I'm changin'!

PORKER: *(Looks away.)* Frank Sinatra, dumbbell...

FLORENCE: How old's he? Eighty?

PORKER: Yuh, right, eighty, you got it...
(Florence goes to closet and removes freshly ironed pastel-green smock, which she pulls over her head. She puts her sweater in closet.)

FLORENCE: I'm takin' my pants off...

PORKER: What am I? S'pose'ta'get *excited?*

FLORENCE: Just turn your head around! You're s'pose'ta be moppin', that's all, so *mop!*

PORKER: Hard ta' get anything much worked up around your pants comin' off, I can tell you that! It's kinda' like gettin' excited about a wave hittin' Good Harbor Beach.
(Florence folds her slacks into the closet with her sweater, neatly. Porker continues.)

PORKER: First couple'a waves, you yell "Oh, wow, lookit! A wave!" But, after fifty or sixty thousand waves, it's kinda' hard ta' get anything much worked up in the excitement department, if you follow my message...

FLORENCE: What the Christ are you talkin' about, Porker?

PORKER: Your *pants*, Florence! After you take your pants on and off fifty or sixty thousand times, it don't make much of no impression on anybody...

FLORENCE: Oh, right, I get you, Porker. It's a *jokkke*...about me takin' my pants off a lot counta' I'm in and out of bed...

PORKER: *(Adds an "s".) zssszzz...*

FLORENCE: Bed*ssszzz*...Well, I guess you must be jealous, bein' left out and all, counta' you got no dick...

PORKER: I do okay...

FLORENCE: Is that a fact?

PORKER: What's a *dolphin*, anyhow? Like in the circus kind'a thing?

FLORENCE: Dolphins are grey mammals. Dolphins are smart. They got brains. They talk to each other. They got their own language. They *frolic!*

PORKER: I frolic...

FLORENCE: Bullllshhhittt you frolic, Porker. You're a hundred per cent glum all the time and you know it! You are next ta' pathetic! What's with the air-conditioning? It's freezing in here.

PORKER: I already turned it down...

FLORENCE: What's Markie planning? Ta' freeze the help and cut us up inta' *fillettes?*

PORKER: I already turned it down!

(Arlyne enters with Ruthie, who is enormously pregnant. Both women are smoking. Both carry coffee thermoses under their arms, drink from plastic coffee cups as they enter. They walk directly to their lockers.)

FLORENCE: *(Sudden sweetness; to Arlyne.)* Mornin', Arlyne. How's the hip?

ARLYNE: Rough, still, thanks, Floey. How's yo'r Mum?

FLORENCE: Doin' better, thanks...

ARLYNE: Mornin', Porker. Freezin' in here...

PORKER: I already turned it down...

FLORENCE: He already turned it down. Mornin', Ruthie.

PORKER: Mornin', Ruthie...

RUTHIE: Mornin', Floey...Mornin', Porker...

FLORENCE: No change, huh?

RUTHIE: Nothin'. I'm ten months, as of this mornin'. Dr. Benoit's definitely got my due date wrong. I'm thinkin' of changin' doctors, to tell you the truth...

(Ruthie stops talking, suddenly, as Sally Morella enters. He is thin, handsome, thirty. he wears a white shirt, tie, long white coat, open; hard-hat. Without noticing or acknowledging anyone, he runs up the staircase into Kitchen in glass-windowed office above the "line." He tidies up the place, fussing about, nervously readying Kitchen for new Inspector. He Windexes

the Kitchen window. he plumps pillow on desk-chair. he arranges pens on desk.)

RUTHIE: What's with Sal?

PORKER: New government inspector starts today…

RUTHIE: Oh, yuh, right. So, how're the kids, Flo?

FLORENCE: Ungrateful, late for school, usual stuff…Bradley said he had a headache, so, I said "You're seven, Bradley, you can't have a headache 'til you're ten…" He says "Who says?" and I says "It's a fact, everybody knows it, boys don't get headaches 'til then and girls don't get 'em til twelve, 'cause they're smarter…" Then, Emily screams "You hear that, Breadloaf? Girls are smarter!" And Bradley throws his goddam egg at her!

ARLYNE: Nooo!

FLORENCE: Yesss!

ARLYNE: Little boys can be very mean to little girls.

PORKER: Raw?

FLORENCE: What's this?

PORKER: The egg: raw?

FLORENCE: Scrambled, shitforbrains! What? You think I feed my kids raw eggs?

ARLYNE: This mornin'?

FLORENCE: Less than an hour ago…

RUTHIE: What'd Emily do? She muckle him, or what?

FLORENCE: No, not much. Bradley's got her scared. I think he hits on her when I'm not home yet…*(Pauses.)* She cried…
(There is a pause.)
Either of you see the dolphins on TV, last night…?

RUTHIE: With the guy speakin' French or something?

FLORENCE: Jock-something, yuh. You see it?

RUTHIE: I switched over. I couldn't stand the foreign words…

FLORENCE: There was a simultaneous translation…in English…a guy was translating over the French…at the same time.

RUTHIE: Yuh, but, I didn't like it…And Earl gets really pissed off when they talk foreign on the TV.

FLORENCE: The dolphins were so wicked smart…

ARLYNE: I remember, years back, there was a TV show every week. What was it called?

RUTHIE: I don't know why they don't just put American shows on the TV? I don't know who they think they're tryin' ta' please by puttin' all this

French crap on. I'll bet we don't have more'n two Frenchman livin' on Cape Ann, period...

ARLYNE: Uncle Ben?

RUTHIE: That's rice, Ma...

ARLYNE: Something like that...There was a show with a "Ben"...

PORKER: "Gentle Ben"...

ARLYNE: That's it! That was great!

PORKER: *(To Florence, confidentially.)* Stupid fuckin' show...

FLORENCE: *(Sees that Arlyne is embarrassed.)* Will you watch your tongue, cesspool?

PORKER: If that ain't the teapot callin' the fryin' pan black...

(The three women giggle. Porker is perplexed.)

PORKER: What's funny? What's so goddam funny?

(Sally pokes head out of upstairs office. he calls down to the women.)

SALLY: Mornin', girls ..

ARLYNE AND RUTHIE: Mornin' Sally...Hey, Sal...

SALLY: Hey, Florence, you got a minute?

FLORENCE: In front of everybody?

(Giggles from all.)

SALLY: Very comical.

PORKER: Big day, huh, Sally? You ready for this, or what?

SALLY: What's this?

PORKER: You kiddin' me?

SALLY: That? No big deal there ta' *me!*

PORKER: You seen her yet?

SALLY: Makes no nevermind to me, whatsoever! *(To Florence.)* Can I just see you, please?

(Sal exits into Inspector's Office, again, closing door behind him. Florence laughs, goes up the stairs to Sally. She enters Office, closes door behind her. Note: Sally and Florence are now visible to audience through Office window. Maureen and Marlena enter, all in late 30's. Maureen and Marlena cross and exit off-stage, to changing-room, smiling to Porker as they go.)

MAUREEN: Mornin', Porker...How's the weekend?

PORKER: Not bad, not bad. Yourself?

MAUREEN: Good. It's freezing in here.

PORKER: I turned it down already. *(Sees Marlena.)* This her?

MAUREEN: Yup.

PORKER: How's it goin'?

MARLENA: How's yourself?

MAUREEN: Where's Floey? She sick again?

(Arlyne and Ruthie point straight above their heads, as if pointing to Heaven.)

PORKER: Company business.

(Maureen looks up at office window. Note: We now see Florence and Sal are in a passionate embrace.)

MARLENA: Wow! Who's that?

MAUREEN: I'll tell ya' later. Come on...

(Maureen and Marlena exit. Josie enters. She is strikingly plump.)

ARLYNE: Morning, Josephine...

RUTHIE: Morning, Josie...How goes it?

JOSIE: Morning, Arlyne. Morning, Ruthie. It's cold in here...Where's Florence? Sick again?

(Everybody points straight up. Josie looks up and shakes her head in mock disgust.)

JOSIE: They were doin' that when I left here, Friday. They been there all weekend?

(Josie crosses to her locker, touching Porker's shoulder as she passes him.)

JOSIE: Mornin', Porker...

PORKER: Yo, Josie, what's up?...I turned the air-conditioner down already. New shirt, huh, Jose?

JOSIE: It's not a shirt, Porker, it's a blouse. Boys wear shirts, girls wear blouses...

(Florence re-enters; goes to line, sets up for work.)

FLORENCE: Mornin'...

JOSIE: I hope you kept your mouth closed when you kissed him!

FLORENCE: You got it: mouth closed, legs open.

RUTHIE: Nice talk!

(Sally re-enters, whisk-broom in hand, sweeps steps to Kitchen, vigorously brushing his dirt-findings into dustpan. He checks his work, satisfied that steps are spandy-clean, goes down steps to hand truck, exits in freezer. Everyone pauses to watch him come, work, go.)

JOSIE: What's *with* him?

FLORENCE: New government inspector starts today...

JOSIE: What happened to Haddie?

FLORENCE: She was just a fill-in temp...

JOSIE: No kidding?

PORKER: Absolutely. She was just fillin' in 'til the Feds found a full-time replacement for Dorothy...

ARLYNE: Poor Dorothy. Hard to believe...

JOSIE: Hard to believe…

PORKER: Un-believable…

RUTHIE: I still can't believe it, myself…

(Josie and Florence exchange a private glance. Florence breaks the eye-contact; moves upstage. Sally re-enters with hand truck. He sets down pallette with crates of frozen product at head of "line," ready for processing.)

MAUREEN: Mornin', Sal…

SALLY: Mornin', Reenie…

JOSIE: *(Pulling sweater off over head.)* Boys, close your eyes!

SALLY: You're supposed to be usin' the big room!

JOSIE: *(Wears lacey bra; "flashes" the men.)* Cheap thrills!

SALLY: Very comical! *(To All.)* I'm tellin' her and I'm tellin' ya's all: you made me set up the big room downstairs with changin' booths and a cot and a Mr. Coffee and bullshit, and if ya's ain't gonna' use all that, I'm gonna' return the merchandise and use the space for something profitable!

JOSIE: Ain't nothin' profitable goin' on around North Shore Fish…

SALLY: I can use it for storage…

JOSIE: Keep runnin' the front office the way it's bein' run, you'll be able ta' use the whole plant for *storage!*

SALLY: You wanna' watch that mouth of yours, sis'tah, huh? Jobs are gettin' scarce.

JOSIE: I wonder who we get ta' blame for that particular turn of events, huh?

SALLY: What's this I'm hearin'?

JOSIE: What's yo'r problem, Sally? Waxey ears? You can't hear clear what I'm sayin'? *(Closer; loudly.)* I'm sayin' North Shore Fish is goin' *down the tubes!*

(Sally blanches white, raises the back of his hand as though he might hit Josie. Florence steps between them.)

FLORENCE: *(Stares him down, eyeball-to eyeball.)* Stay back from her.

SALLY: *(Sally puts his hand to his side.)* I'm gonna' tell ya's all somethin' straight: This is not the day!

JOSIE: What's your plan for the new Inspector, Sal? You gonna' grab her in the freezer for a cold quickie, or are you gonna' go for a long and meaningful relationship? Hmmm?

SALLY: Just watch your ass.

JOSIE: *(She looks down to her derriére.)* Okay, now there are *three* of us watching my ass: me, you, and Hotlips Martino.

(Sally walks to end of "Line," moves blocks of frozen fish into position for processing. He then exits into refrigerator.)

PORKER: I got that, you know.

JOSIE: Why shouldn't you have got that? Was anybody speakin' in complex sentences you mightn't comprehend?
(To All.) I'm goin' to the big room to change. I wouldn't wanna' be the cause of Sal bringin' our Mr. Coffee back ta' Zayre's!
(Josie exits. Porker goes to Florence.)

PORKER: What was the implication s'pose'ta be there? That I'm *stupid* or something?

FLORENCE: That was no implication, Porker. That was a *fact of life!*

PORKER: Me: stupid? I ain't the one callin' no TV-dolphin "Gentle Ben." Gentle Ben was a goddam grizzly bear, you dodo! The TV dolphin for about a hundred years, as everybody knows, was "Flipper"!
(To all.) Right? Is this not right? Is this not a perfectly right fact?

FLORENCE: That wasn't me, ya' nincompoop! I was just goin' along 'counta' I didn't wanna' hurt Arlyne's feelin's. If your memory ain't eaten away by the drugs, you might recall it was Arlyne who come up with Gentle goddam Ben and hardly myself! I said nothin'…I just went along…

ARLYNE: *(Eavesdrops; interjects.)* Yuh, I think I did, and you're definitely right, Porker. Gentle Ben was a bear. Flipper was the porpoise…

FLORENCE: Dolphin…

RUTHIE: Same thing, if you ask me. They look like big hairy slugs…

PORKER: What do you mean "slugs"?

RUTHIE: Slugs. Slugs are slugs…

PORKER: Like in a gun in a gangster movie "slugs"?

FLORENCE: Jesus, what a dork!

PORKER: I'm just askin'! I'm just checkin'!

FLORENCE: She don't mean "slugs" like in a gangster movie. She don't mean "slugs" like after you make a bad smell, neither, dork!

PORKER: Will you get off my goddam case!

RUTHIE: What I mean is slugs like you get when you grow your own lettuce…in the vegetable garden…black fleshy hairy slimey disgusting slugs!

FLORENCE: See?

PORKER: I know that!

RUTHIE: Porpoises are like big bloated-up slugs! Used'ta'make me sick when we used'ta go into North Station to Barnum & Bailey's Circus, when I was little…

PORKER: Porpoises?

FLORENCE: *(Confidentially; to Porker.)* Don't you correct her, you!

PORKER: Did I say nothin'? *(He shows his palms to Florence.)*

RUTHIE: *(Continuing; quite disgusted.)* These porpoises would come out (big hairy slimey fleshy things with whiskers) and they'd kinda' *flop around*...all fleshy and slug-like! The trainers would feed 'em live fish, which they'd kinda' *suck up*, then they'd bark some kinda' weird kinda' dog-like soundin' bark, and then they toot out something on car horns or somesuch. I usually had my eyes closed at that point, and had my legs clamped together tight, in case they got loose and came at me, and, you know, tried to get under my skirt or anything...
(There is a small astonished silence.)

ARLYNE: Jeffrey once put five or six slugs in Ruthie's underpants to scare her, when she was little. She was about then, maybe eleven...

RUTHIE: Gawd, Mama, Jesus!

ARLYNE: ...I'm never suppose'ta mention it out loud...

RUTHIE: Gawd!

ARLYNE: Little boys can be very mean to little girls...
(There is another small silence. Sally re-enters with a hand truck with several fresh blocks of frozen fish-product stacked neatly on a pallette, ready for processing.)

SALLY: What is the *matter* with you people? Do you see the clock? We're just about to have a bell! S'posin' Markie comes in early? No saws on, no batter mixed and ready! A new inspector startin' today and nobody set up ta' work! This is brilliant, people, huh, with what's goin' down here, huh? Huh? Am I talkin' for my own good here, or am I talkin' for the good of all'a ya's, huh?
(Porker walks wordlessly to the band-saw and flips the on-switch "on." Arlyne walks to the wrapping-sealer and flips the on-switch "on." Florence walks to the batter-tank and flips the on-switch "on". Ruthie moves along the "line" to the hot-plastic-wrap station; hits the "on" switch. Josie re-enters with Maureen and Marlena. They re-join the "line" at their various work-stations.)

SALLY: Where *were* you people? You're not even set up!

JOSIE: We were just givin' the new girl the lay of the land.

PORKER: *(Guffaws.) You ought'a know! Haggghhh!*

JOSIE: What's that noise just come out'ta Porker? Sounded like a trained *seal!* Somebody throw Porker a fish! *(Guffaws.)*

SALLY: Get set up, okay?
(Maureen and Josie exchange a private glance.)

JOSIE: Sorry I razzed ya', Sal. I know you're feelin' pressured.
  (Maureen and Josie exchange another private glance. Maureen smiles approvingly.)
SALLY: I accept. *(Sally pats Josie's bottom.)* Don't sweat it.
JOSIE: *(Smiles.)* So, how's Carmella and the kids doin'? Okay?...
SALLY: Great, great, terrific. *(To Maureen.)* Get your cousin set up, too, okay? This is her...she...right? *(Smiles flirtatiously at Marlena.)* We ain't been officially introduced yet. I'm Sal.
MAUREEN: Sorry, Sal. This is Marlena, Sal. Marlena, this is Sal. Sal's foreman.
SALLY: Very pleased ta' meet'cha...
MARLENA: Likewise...
SALLY: Maybe we can meet up later and I can show you some tricks...how ta' handle product kind of thing...
  (Marlena and Sally exchange a flirtatious glance. Florence flashes an angry stare at Sally.)
SALLY: *(To Maureen.)* Get her set up...
  (He exits into office. They all set up to work: get ready for the bell.)
FLORENCE: What gives here?
MAUREEN: I'm just breakin' Marlena in, so's she can cover for me next month, when Anthony and I are travelin'. She's my cousin...That there's Florence Rizzo: she batters...
MARLENA: Hi.
FLORENCE: Hi.
MAUREEN: These two here are Ruthie and her mother, Mrs. Flynn...
ARLYNE: Arlyne...
MARLENA: Hi...
ARLYNE: Hi...
RUTHIE: Hi...
MAUREEN: *(To Marlena.)* Get boxes off the stack...about so many. *(Indicated amount with her hands.)*
MARLENA: *(Enroute to box-supply; to Ruthie.)* How far along are you?
ARLYNE: She's overdue.
RUTHIE: *(Pats her stomach.)* I'm ten months. *(Munches her donut; laughs.)* I'm eating for two.
JOSIE: *(Pats her own stomach.)* I've been eating for two all my *life!* Anybody got any extra food?
ARLYNE: I've got a ricotta pie from Mike's. You hungry already? Didn't you eat breakfast?
JOSIE: A'course I ate breakfast! That's my point. I was just checking for

later. If I eat my lunch, early, around ten/ten-thirty, which is my plan, I'll get hungry again around eleven/eleven-thirty...

ARLYNE: I'll save you half...

JOSIE: You're the best, Arlyne! Honest ta' God.

RUTHIE: My doctor got my due-date wrong, on account of I'm never regular. I think I probably wasn't even pregnant when I first went in for the check-up, but, we all figured it was a definite, 'counta' I missed two months straight 'n all...So, Earl and I relaxed our system and next thing I know...

ARLYNE: *(Completes the sentence.)* Pregnant!

JOSIE: Earl and Ruthie use the Basic Cape Ann Catholic System.

RUTHIE: Oh yuh, what's that?

JOSIE: *(Shrugs; explains simply.)* Getting Pregnant.

RUTHIE: That's about the size of it...

JOSIE: *What's* about the size of it?

(Reasonably raunchy laugh from all.)

JOSIE: Gloucester men have it down to a science: they drink til about 3 A.M., and then they come in making enough noise to wake all the kids up. Then they roll you over and come, faster than you can say "I ain't got my diaphram in!" Then they drop dead asleep. You miss your period. They get pissed off. They meet young out-of-town girls who take aerobics, and they move out of the house.

(There is a long embarrassed pause.)

MAUREEN: Josie's goin' through a bad time.

MARLENA: *(Smiles at Ruthie.)* You'll probably deliver soon. You're carrying low.

RUTHIE: I dunno'...

ARLYNE: She always carries low. I used to carry down around my knees somewhere.

RUTHIE: I got a lot bigger the last two times. I hope you're right. I'd hate to stay pregnant for thirteen or fourteen *months!* Jesus, that'd be *awful!*

PORKER: *(Looks at Marlena admiringly.)* So, this is the cousin, huh?

MARLENA: Yuh. Hi. I'm Marlena...Reenie's cousin.

MAUREEN: That's Porker. He's on the band saw. I wouldn't walk too close. It could kill you...

MARLENA: His saw?

FLORENCE: His *breath!*

(The women laugh. Porker is disgusted.)

MAUREEN: I hope you don't mind Marlena coverin' for me while I'm gone. Keeps the money in the family....

FLORENCE: I don't mind...

RUTHIE: It's fine, great, no problem...

MAUREEN: I checked it out with Markie...

FLORENCE: Sure, no problem...

JOSIE: Maureen worried you might be p.o.ed about it, 'count'a yo'r Mum...

FLORENCE: Naw, what the hell, huh? If Markie okayed it, huh? 'Sides, my Mum's got a million things ta' do. She doesn't miss any of this, I can tell you that...

JOSIE: Florence's Mum worked here nearly thirty straight years.

MARLENA: Ohhh...

FLORENCE: Laid her off, a couple of months ago. Bloodless fuckin' people run this place...

(Sfx: The work bell rings. Full sound of machines, on tape. All work, feverishly. Sounds fade under, work continues.)

RUTHIE: Whose side of the family you on?

MARLENA: How's that?

RUTHIE: Maureen's Da's side, or the Mum's?

MARLENA: Oh, neither. I'm Anthony's cousin...

RUTHIE: Oh, yuh, right...

(Sal re-enters from office.)

SALLY: Anybody gonna' pack fish here, or what? *(To Florence.)* Could I see you, private. *Now!*

(Sal exits into upstage kitchen; Florence follows.)

MARLENA: Boy, he works ya, huh!

MAUREEN: Yuh, well, business is a little off.

JOSIE: Right! Business is a "little off" and Ruthie is a "little pregnant"!

PORKER: Yuh, well, we can turn it around if we hustle!

(While nobody actually answered Porker in words, they have all now begun their day's labor, and seriously.)

MAUREEN: You'll be settin' up boxes, like so...tight corners, like so...

(Maureen demonstrates setting up a box. Marlena watches, imitates.)

ARLYNE: They've gotta' be tight and trim.

MAUREEN: *(Smiles; imitates Arlyne.)* Tight and trim.

RUTHIE: Earl says he heard some Boston Mafioso's interested in buyin' Markie out...

(We now see Sal and Florence, upstairs, in office, through window. They are arguing. Work continues, full tilt.)

JOSIE: They're fighting again.

RUTHIE: They're either fighting or...you know...doin' the opposite.

JOSIE: *(Laughs at Ruthie's euphemism.)* How come Earl's gettin' this secret information about Markie and all? *(Josie smiles at Maureen knowingly.)*

RUTHIE: When Earl was pickin' up here, yesterday, he saw some big muscleman bodyguard Mafioso-type hangin' around Markie's office — fifth day in a row…

MAUREEN: *(Filling Marlena in.)* Earl's Ruthie's husbin'. He picks up our garbage every night…

RUTHIE: *(Interjects; corrects, instantly.)* Refuse!

MAUREEN: *(Smiles, allows herself to be corrected.)* Refuse.

RUTHIE: He seen this humongous bodyguard type hangin' around five days straight…

PORKER: I seen him myself.

JOSIE: What's this?

PORKER: There's been this muscleman type—like Ruthie says Earl says— a Mafioso bodyguard kind of person…hangin' out with Markie…

MAUREEN: *(To Marlena.)* Markie owns the plant…

JOSIE: Markie Santuro's got a bodyguard?

PORKER: Nobody said that! I just said this big jamoca's be'n hangin' out in the front office…

JOSIE: What the hell does Markie Santuro need a bodyguard for? This place is gettin' weird!

(Note: Through office window, we see Florence and Sal are again in a passionate embrace.)

JOSIE: They stopped fighting. Now they're back to *[imitates Ruthie here]* "…you know…doin' the opposite," again.

PORKER: *(Eying the work-load.)* We'd better keep it movin', huh?

MAUREEN: C'mon, Porker! We musta' already packed more this week than we did last whole month!

(To Marlena.) Everybody's feelin' the pressure…under-the-gun kind of thing, about the plant bein' in trouble'n all…

ARLYNE: North Shore Fish was a wonderful place to work, years back…

MAUREEN: *(To Marlena.)* Arlyne's worked here years and years…

ARLYNE: Use'd'ta be if you got on a line at North Shore Fish, your worries were over…

(Note: At this point in the conversation among the workers, labor should be at fairly brisk pace. It should be obvious that the workers have sped up the normal pace of their normal labor: that there is concern about the possibility of the plant's closing: that all conversation is simultaneous to labor, but, at no time does labor ever stop for conversation. Florence re-enters, goes down the stairs to her machine.)

FLORENCE: I'm runnin' out'ta bricks, Martino!

PORKER: What are you givin' me here…

FLORENCE: If this place goes under, it ain't gonna' be *my* fault, I can tell you that! *(She re-stocks the "line.")*

JOSIE: I'm out'ta cartons, Porker.

PORKER: Sure thing, Jose.

(To Florence.) I'm givin' Josie a hand.

ARLYNE: When my mother first started workin' a line here, it was a very respectful occupation…kinda' like equal almost to a job a school-educated woman might get. Right up there.

FLORENCE: Hurry it up, Martino! If those blocks melt, the fish'll come back ta' life and they are very pissed off about what we've be'n doin' to 'em, I can tell ya' that!

PORKER: Hold yo'r hosses!

JOSIE: He's helpin' me!

(Sally exits office, hops down stairs, passes through all, inspecting work-progress enroute to freezer. He stops at Marlena, checks her box-making.)

SALLY: Excellent!

(He touches Marlena's cheek, affectionately, setting up a jealousy; a competitiveness. Everybody looks at them.)

Good looking, and smart, too!

(Florence looks over, annoyed and hurt. Sally exits into freezer; off. Josie and Porker are working together, downstage. The lights shift to them slightly.)

JOSIE: So, how's Rose and your fatha'?

PORKER: Rose is fine. My fatha's fine.

JOSIE: Good weekend?

PORKER: Yuh, we did stuff. How's about yourself, Jose? Good weekend, too?

JOSIE: Well, you know, it ain't the same…

PORKER: Cookie's a good guy, really. I'd call this temporary insanity, more'n anything else…

JOSIE: Yuh, well, I guess…

PORKER: I guess it's toughest on the kids, huh?

JOSIE: Yuh, well, they know he ain't around, that's for sure. They're fightin' all the time…

PORKER: Temporary insanity. He'll be back…

JOSIE: Why? You hear anything?

PORKER: Me? No.

JOSIE: You seen them?

PORKER: Together?

JOSIE: Yuh, well, yuh...

PORKER: Down the Rigger, just the once, last week. And down the Blackburn, a little more recent...

JOSIE: Saturday night?

PORKER: Yuh, well, yuh...

JOSIE: Everybody's been tellin' me that. If my fatha' hears, I can't be responsible for what he'll do...

PORKER: To Cookie?

JOSIE: A'course to Cookie! *(Leans in; confidentially.)* You tell him something for me, Porker. You tell him if my fatha' hears, he's gonna' cut his balls off and feed 'em to the seagulls... *(Pauses; nods.)* You tell him that.

PORKER: Anything else?

JOSIE: Yuh. Tell 'im the kids are fine, not to worry. Tell him I'm startin' ta' look around myself, ta' see, you know, who's available and who's unavailable sort of thing...

PORKER: You want me to *say* that?

JOSIE: Are you my friend or what?

PORKER: Come on, Josie, you know I am, since how many years?

JOSIE: So, you'll tell him?

PORKER: Cookie's my friend, too...

JOSIE: Who's closer?

PORKER: Well, you know...we were a thing, you and me. Me and Cookie were never a thing...

(Josie is aware of everyone eavesdropping, she makes a "public" private statement.)

JOSIE: When I start doin' it again, with other men, you'll be among the first...

PORKER: I know that... *(Leans in to steal a kiss. Josie sees everybody is watching; pulls back.)*

JOSIE: What are you? Crazy?...

(Florence and Ruthie and Maureen exchange a smile. Maureen resumes explaining the labor to Marlena. The lights re-widen to include all.)

MAUREEN: It's pretty much like cuttin', only different.

(To Arlyne.) Marlena used'ta cut, up Essex.

ARLYNE: I used'ta work live fish, myself.

MAUREEN: Smells better workin' live fish.

FLORENCE: Oh, yuh, the batter's a killer...I think they put formaldehyde in it, to keep the fish lookin' tasty!

(Sally re-enters with palette-trunk; He arrives at the end of the "line" with crates of already-packaged frozen fish, in individual boxes.)

SALLY: Porker! Gimme a hand here, Pork...

(Porker goes to Sally. Together, they stack the individual boxes on the end table.)

PORKER: Where are these goin'?

SALLY: I dunno', back to Japan. Label's all Japanese. Some Chicago broker called it in...

PORKER: Crazy goddam thing, huh?

SALLY: What? Sendin' it back ta' Japan? Yuh, well, it's business...Who cares?

MAUREEN: See how Porker cuts those big blocks down into bricks? The machine is shaping them fish-like and Floey breads them...you and me set up the boxes, then Ruth and Arlyne box 'em...and Josie wraps and that's it...

MARLENA: How come they gotta' shape 'em so they're fish-like?

MAUREEN: So, they look like fish. You wouldn't wanna' eat a fish that looked like a brick, would ya?

MARLENA: Yuh, but, if they're already fish, how come they're not already *shaped* like fish?

MAUREEN: 'Cause they're really about a million fish all smashed to-gether...

FLORENCE: It's more like a family of fish than just a fish...*(Holds up slab of fish.)* See, look close. Piece of a middle, piece of a neck, another piece of middle, little tail...

MARLENA: Wow, is that ever *gross!*

FLORENCE: It's nothin' compared to the breading...

MARLENA: Is the fish local?

FLORENCE: God, no. The fish is from Boston, mostly...

MARLENA: That's where they catch it?

FLORENCE: That's where they buy it. They buy it in auctions, like...al-ready frozen. Some of it's Canadian, some of it's Japanese. It comes from all over.

MAUREEN: All the *live* fish is local...

MARLENA: Oh, yuh, I know that...

PORKER: See these blocks we're cutting up. They're from Japan, 6,000 miles away. All we're doing is cutting them up, spraying a little bat-ter on them and sending them right back to Japan: 12,000 miles round trip. Don't ask me. I only work here.

MARLENA: No kidding? That is *weird....*

FLORENCE: Your cousin puts notes in the far-away stuff...

MAUREEN:...Yuh, well, I do. So what?

(The women laugh at Maureen, affectionately. Maureen checks to see if Sally is listening.)

MAUREEN: Sometimes, if stuff is goin' to, you know, Japan or Australia, someplace really *far*, I like to toss in a couple of words. Nothin' too much...Maybe "Hi, I'm Maureen Vega from Gloucester, Mass., U.S. of A. I'm thirty-one and I like Sylvia Plath and summers." That kind of thing.

(The women continue their labor, as they chat. The fish-bricks are moved along to the various stations and the fish is shaped, breaded, wrapped, packed and labeled. Unnoticed at first, at the furthermost end of the room, Catherine Shimma enters. She wears a coat, collar up, high-heeled shoes. She is extremely attractive, far more worldly-looking than the other women. She moves to center, pauses; watches.)

ARLYNE: I can remember workin' here some years back when we were still cuttin' live fish, we used'ta have two three four Japs standin' lookin' right over our shoulders, makin' bids right then and there, you know, against each other and all...

MAUREEN: They are great fish-eaters, the Japanese...

ARLYNE: Oh, you don't have to tell me! I've seen Japs with my own eyes: They have a true respect for fish...I wish they didn't bomb Pearl Harbor, but, they must have had their reasons. That's all I'm going to tell ya's...

SALLY: *(Re-enters with hand truck; sees Shimma.)* Can I help you?

SHIMMA: I'm looking for Salvatore Morella.

FLORENCE: *(In childish schoolgirl sing-song chant.)* Salll-vaaah-torr... Close-the-doorrrr!

SALLY: *(To Florence.)* What are you? Demented?

(To Shimma.) I'm him...he...this is me: Sal Morella...Plant Manager...

FLORENCE: *(Interjects.)* Sal Mo*nilla*...the disease!

SALLY:...Who are you?

SHIMMA: Catherine Shimma...

SALLY: Oh, well, good.

(Sally flashes look of anger at Florence. Everyone has stopped work and is staring at Sally and Florence and Shimma, openly. Sally flashes angry looks to all. He then turns again to Shimma, smiling boyishly.)

SALLY: Let's go up the front office, and meet Markie. He's the owner. Then I'll show you your kitchen...

(Shimma walks directly to the breading vat, allows breading to flow on to her finger.
She tastes the breading.
Then she picks up a wedge of frozen fish and breaks it into its component pieces: a few sections of fish-necks, etc. She tosses pieces into tray.
Then she looks at Sally; nods.
Sally leads her off; she follows.)

SALLY: This way…

SHIMMA: After you…

SALLY: No, this way…After you…

SHIMMA: No. You first.

> *(There is a moment of silence.)*
> Go.
> *(Sally obeys; leads the way off. They exit. Everyone stares after them; astonished.)*

FLORENCE: She look like anybody?

PORKER: Everybody looks like somebody…

FLORENCE: I know she looks like *some*body, wiseass. I mean, does she look like anybody we know?

PORKER: Not ta' me… *(Shrugs.)*
She looks kinda', I dunno', *sophisticated*…

FLORENCE: I dunno'…She's got somethin' familiar goin'…

JOSIE: She looks like me, before I discovered the blueberry muffins down the Glass Sailboat. Thinnish, small knockers… *(She stacks a supply of empty boxes in front of her; continues talking as she continues wrapping frozen breaded fish.)* I dunno' why I bother to put the muffins in my mouth. I ought'a just apply them directly to my hips…

ARLYNE: *(As she labors.)* You have a nice shape, Josie…

JOSIE: Yuh, right, so did last year's Dodge Vans. They had a nice shape, too!

MAUREEN: You read that book about the guy who ran Dodge? What's'-name…funny name…"Coke-head," somethin' odd like that…

JOSIE: Sounds great.

MAUREEN: No, it was. Different. Interestin', really. All about how they spied on him and all. Made you think.

JOSIE: I'll have to pick it up and read it.

> *(They labor a while. Suddenly, Maureen calls out.)*

MAUREEN: Iococca!

PORKER: What's with her?

MAUREEN: Name of a book.

PORKER: What kind of book?

JOSIE: Squarish, paper pages, with printing all over 'em...

PORKER: I love a good joke. I wish somebody would tell me one.

FLORENCE: You *are* one! C'mon, Martino, I'm out of batter!

MAUREEN: Fantastic thing, big business, really...

(Porker brings new supply of batter to Florence.)

PORKER: What are you doin'? Throwing it on the floor?

FLORENCE: When I work, I work...when I party, I party...'cause, that's the kinda' guy I am... *(She playacts being a man: she scratches her crotch and pretends to spit on the floor.)*

MAUREEN: Iococca took Dodge and turned it around...

FLORENCE: Whose Dodge?

MAUREEN: The whole company. It was goin' out'ta business. He put it back into profits, almost by himself...

FLORENCE: He know anything about the fish-business? Maybe we can set him up here, huh?

(Laughs. Porker brings her new supply of bricks batter.)

PORKER: We got no problems here, so long as we get the product out.

(Everyone labors more enthusiastically, somehow inspired by Lee Iococca.)

ARLYNE: North Shore Fish has seen good times and bad times. We survive 'em both.

RUTHIE: Where were you born?

MARLENA: Me?

(Ruthie nods.)

MARLENA: Up Newburyport... *(Pauses.)* We moved down Burlington, when I was nine, but, soon as I was old enough to do it on my own, I moved back on the water.

ARLYNE: Oh, I agree! When you're born on the water, you never can live anyplace else!

RUTHIE: My mother and fatha' broke up over water.

ARLYNE: That wasn't the only reason, but, it was *one* of 'em.

RUTHIE: That's the way you always told it to *me!*

ARLYNE: Well, her father was livin' with, you know, another woman and all...

RUTHIE: He was workin' up Needham...

ARLYNE: He took a place up near his plant and wanted me to move up with him. I couldn't do it...I was 6 months pregnant with Ruthie...

RUTHIE: My grandmother and grandfather and aunts and all were in town...

ARLYNE:...My mother and fatha' were here in Gloucester...my sisters, too. I couldn't just pick up and leave all that! Kids, too...
(Josie, Florence and Ruthie recite Arlyne's oft-spoken thoughts with her, in unison, lovingly. Arlyne never notices.)
RUTHIE AND ARLYNE: His job wasn't permanent.
(Simultaneously.)
> FLORENCE: She commuted up weekends.
> ARLYNE: I commuted up weekends
> JOSIE: Weekends!
(Simultaneously.)
> ARLYNE: He wanted me there full-time.
> FLORENCE: He wanted her there full-time.
(Simultaneously.)
> ARLYNE: He took another woman...
> RUTHIE: Weekends...
> JOSIE: Mondays through Fridays...
(Simultaneously.)
> ARLYNE: Two-timer! They're all alike!
> FLORENCE: They're all alike!
> JOSIE: At least, I'm still in Gloucester, on the water.
ARLYNE: At least I'm still in Gloucester, on the water...
(There is a short silence.)
RUTHIE: We live out on the Fort...
MAUREEN: Ruthie and Earl live upstairs, over Arlyne.
MARLENA: Can you see the water?
RUTHIE: Oh, God, No! We face in, over the freezer plant. But, we can drive over to Good Harbor Beach in—what?—ten minutes. A'course, you gotta' go at *night!*
MAUREEN: Traffic's wicked, summ'ah'time...during beach hours...
FLORENCE: I tried to get over there, day before yesterday, on our lunch-break...
MAUREEN: *(Smiles.)* I remember...
FLORENCE: I never fuckin' made it...*(Politely.)* Sorry, Arlyne...
ARLYNE: I don't mind. I know you're angry...
FLORENCE: Two million summah people, one to a car. I dunno why the hell they don't just *team up?* I mean, *none* of us got there! We just sat on Bass Avenue maybe thirty-five minutes I turned around. Took shit from Markie for bein' late comin' back, too...
MAUREEN: We all ask "How's the beach?" 'cause we all figure Floey's beet-

red from laying out in the sun. A'course she's beet-red with a fever and all from sittin' in her car in traffic on Bass Ave!

(Sally and Shimma exit front office and enter kitchen, closing door behind them. Sally makes "Keep it down" signal to all before closing door. Porker slides upstage, plants himself under window to kitchen in order to spy on Sally and Shimma, inside.)

FLORENCE: This new one ain't gonna' buy his greaseball charm, I can tell ya's all *that!*

MAUREEN: If our product's good, what's the diff? She's not inspectin' Sal; she's inspectin' product, right?

FLORENCE: Yuh, so, if that's true, what's he tryin' ta' get into her pants for? Answer me that?

RUTHIE: Nice talk, huh...

FLORENCE: Yuh, well, I'm just not up for bein' out'ta work all next year, that's all...

PORKER: Come on, Florence. Sal can handle thisss...I'm gonna' watch closer.

(Porker moves upstage; spies on Sally)

MARLENA: What's she sayin', Maureen?

MAUREEN: Florence is a little negative, on account'a this and that.

MARLENA: Which and what?

FLORENCE: I heard that, Reenie. I ain't a "little negative." I am *very fucking negative!* Look around you! You see how empty it is here? This place looks like a fortune cookie, after somebody got the message! There's nobody here, Reenie! This is a dead place. The fish business has had it! *Absolutely definitely had it!*

ARLYNE: Florence Marie Rizzo, you close that mouth!

FLORENCE: *(Sincerely; childlike.)* Sorry, Arlyne...

ARLYNE: What if your mother heard you...?

FLORENCE: I know...

ARLYNE: Businesses have ups and downs...

FLORENCE: It's true...

ARLYNE: The fish business just has fewer ups and more downs, that's all...

FLORENCE: I suppose...

ARLYNE: We are fish people. We are doing what we were born to do...

FLORENCE: I don't think that...*(Thinks better of it.)* I guess...

(Florence and Ruthie and Arlyne, in unison, complete Arlyne's oft-spoken thoughts.)

ARLYNE AND OTHERS: "Negative criticism will only bring the very thing you dread right down onto your head..."

(Florence smiles at Ruthie, gratefully.)

ARLYNE: That's what my mother used ta' say ta' me, and she was right. That's all I'm gonna' tell ya's...
(Ruthie and Florence exchange another conspiratorial glance and smile.)
She was a smart woman, my mother. We worked together...
(Simultaneously.)

    ARLYNE:...elbow to elbow, side by...

    ALL OTHERS:...elbow to elbow, side by side...

ARLYNE: *(Alone.)* It's a wonderful thing when you can earn your livin' workin' side-by-side with people who care about you...

FLORENCE: I know...
(Florence moves upstage with empty stock-tray, which she will replace with full stock-tray.)

ARLYNE: And it's a wonderful thing to live your life overlookin' the water.

MARLENA: Oh, I agree. There's something so special about livin' on the water...

RUTHIE: Definitely! The water gets in yo'r blood...

MARLENA:...Takin' walks on the shore...

FLORENCE: My fatha' used'ta be able ta' name all the flowers over Braces' Cove...Dropwort Shoots and so forth...Angelica and stuff. You'd think you were hearin' some kind of Ha'vid professor, honest ta' God!
(We see Sally, above, in office, touch Shimma's cheek. Florence sees as well. Shimma pulls back, angrily.)

FLORENCE: Ah, shit...

RUTHIE: That's the thing: knowing you know everything about the ocean, because you've lived your life on it...Naming all the fish right. That sort'a thing...

MAUREEN: I like thinkin' about what's out there...across from us...

JOSIE: I got enough trouble thinkin' about what's right under my nose...
(Eats a Snickers Bar.) Oh, God, I ate it! I was gonna' save that for afta' lunch!

MAUREEN: You know, if you go straight out from here across the northern part of England, there isn't a single mountain range between us and the Ural Mountains in Russia...
(Simultaneously.)

    MARLENA: Is that right?

    JOSIE: No kidding?

MAUREEN: If you could blow hard enough, you could blow out some-body's birthday candles in Russia, and that is a fact...
(Shimma is clearly annoyed with Sally.)

PORKER: I think they're fighting...

FLORENCE: You say something?

PORKER: I think Sally's yellin' at the new inspector...

(They all turn and look. Sally storms out of the kitchen, slamming the door. He runs down the stairs. Each worker busies herself with her labor. Sally moves directly to the refrigerator, about to exit. He stops, thinks better of it; talks.)

SALLY: I want every fifth fillette weighed. I want no light product. And check the batter. I want no thick breading. If this bull-dyke wants to play it by the rules, I say "fine"! I say we give her perfect product and let her break her own dyke balls and if anybody here says different, let them bread their own ass too thick and find work elsewhere, 'cause this plant is not goin' under! *(And with that, Sally exits into the freezer. After a pause, he re-enters.)* Porker, I want sixty crates of the Howard Johnson's out and ready to rewrap with Stop'n'Shop!

PORKER: That order ain't due for three and a half weeks...

SALLY: I give *no shit!* The second that vicious mother of a bitch rejects one miserable underweight or triple-breaded fillette, we go off the fresh-frozen and right the fuck on to re-wraps. *Bang! (Punches crate, violently.)* I got Stop'n'Shop rewraps, I got Jap rewraps, I got next year's Daitch-*Shopwell* rewraps. I do not give a shit. Is this okay?

PORKER: It's okay.

RUTHIE: It's okay.

MAUREEN AND JOSIE: Okay...

SALLY: I apologize sincerely for my filthy mouth, Arlyne, but, as you can see, I am overwrought...

ARLYNE: That's no excuse...

SALLY: Arlyne!

ARLYNE: "A filthy mouth speaks the thoughts of a filthy mind!"

SALLY: *(Head down, he "mouths" precise sentence with Arlyne, in unison.)* "...of a filthy mind..." *(He goes to Arlyne.)* Arlyne, we have trouble here! I think I have to warn nobody. I think you can see from the three closed-down lines and the many laid-off close friends and loved-ones, this plant is on no solid ground and should she fuck us over, we could go down if not under. *(He spots Shimma walking down staircase from her office.)* Here she comes! *(He runs into freezer. Shimma walks to "Line," carrying a tray; wordlessly. She smiles at everyone, officiously. She places six samples of breaded fish on her tray. Shimma purposefully exits the "Line" area, and re-enters her kitchen. Sally peeks out from behind the freezer door.)*

SALLY: What I smell here is not good...Porker, come here...

    (To Porker.) I'm goin' in to Markie. Any kind of move at all: report. You follow me?

PORKER: Yuh, sure...

SALLY: What'd I say?

PORKER: I got you...

SALLY: *What'd I say?*

PORKER: I'll get you...

SALLY: Martino, I am in no fucking *mood!*

PORKER: You're in with Markie. If she makes a move, I'll come get you...

SALLY: No, this is exactly what I do not want! *(Moves to Porker.)*

    You know Markie's position here, which I am laboring to change, yes?

PORKER: I have a good idea, yuh...

SALLY: What the fuck do you mean "I have a good idea, yuh"? I *told* you exactly what his position is on this, right?

PORKER: *(Looks around; worried.)* Yuh, well, shhh, yuh, okay, Sal...

SALLY: If she makes a negative move or a rejection-like move involving product, this is what you come get me for...But don't...

PORKER: *(Finishes the sentence.)*...let on to Markie!

SALLY: *Exact!*

    (He realizes that everyone stands, staring.)

    Hello? Are you being paid to work, or is this the company clambake, huh, people? Thannnkkk youuuu!

    (Everybody starts working again. Sally looks up at Shimma, through window. He then looks over at Porker; exits. Through the window, we can see Shimma, in her office/kitchen, cooking the frozen fish in a microwave oven. She opens the oven, takes out a filet of cooked fish, replaces it with a filet of frozen fish, shuts oven, hits "ON" switch. She weighs cooked fish. She tastes cooked fish, chews it awhile, spits what has been in her mouth into a plastic-bag-lined garbage container; begins to write a report.)

MARLENA: Look, Reenie, she's eating our fish!

MAUREEN: That's how they do the test: they cook it up and taste it...

MARLENA: Hey! She spit it out!

JOSIE: They always spit it out...They taste maybe eighty, ninety pieces of fish a day. Imagine what they'd weigh if they didn't spit it out? I never spit it out. I swallow everything.

PORKER: *Everything?*

JOSIE: You're an embarrassment to the Italian race, you know that?

MARLENA: What if she rejects it...the fish?

RUTHIE: We have to throw out the batch...

ARLYNE: ...Clean the breader, make new batter...

JOSIE: That's what Dotty did...

ARLYNE: Poor soul...

JOSIE: She was rejecting everything, at the end...

MARLENA: Who's Dotty?

FLORENCE: Dorothy Fabiano. She was Government inspector here for seven years, nearly eight...

MARLENA: She quit?

MAUREEN: She was the one I was tellin' you about...

MARLENA: Oh...

FLORENCE: She died...She was having a serious thing with Sal for the last four years or so...

JOSIE: Then, Sal got interested elsewhere...

FLORENCE: What's this, you?

JOSIE: Just talkin'...

RUTHIE: Sal's married...and he got Dot pregnant...

MARLENA: Reenie was tellin' me...

FLORENCE: The way people around here see it, Sal was the definite cause of Dot's dyin'...

ARLYNE: *(Shocked.)* Florence Marie Rizzo, I am not going to let you incriminate Sal so viciously. We are all Catholics here, mostly, and this sort of incrimination is hardly the way we were taught!

FLORENCE: I'm entitled to my opinions, Arlyne. Even though you're Ruthie's mother, I am...

(Porker and Florence exchange a glance. Porker shakes his head in disgust. Florence returns to her battering.)

FLORENCE: I'll stay out of it...

JOSIE: For the last couple of months or so, Dotty'd wait 'til we got set up with a fresh batch of batter, then she'd come out, get a fish, cook it, shake her head, come out and put her thumb down. No words, nothin', just her thumb down. Sally used'ta' fuckin' *burn...(Laughs.)* Sorry, Arlyne...

ARLYNE: I know it's something that angers us all...*(Pauses.)* Dorothy was a lovely, lovely, lovely girl...Local, too. We all knew her family... motha', two brothers, sis'tah. Her sistah's teachin' up a O'Malley School right today. Very lovely family, honest ta' God...

PORKER: She's comin' out!

(Shimma enters; looks about; speaks to Porker.)

SHIMMA: Where is he?

PORKER: Front office.

SHIMMA: Get him.

(Porker pauses a moment; then runs to door to Markie's office; exits. Shimma looks at Florence and others.)

SHIMMA: Beautiful day out there. Beach weather. Shame to be trapped inside…

JOSIE: Ain't I seen you drivin' around town with the "GOLF" licenseplate?

SHIMMA: Oh, yuh, that's me, yuh…

FLORENCE: What's this? You live local or something?

SHIMMA: Oh, no. I live up Woburn.

FLORENCE: Oh, yuh? Woob'in? *(To all; sarcastically.)* Figures.

SHIMMA: Why? You got somethin' against Woburn?

FLORENCE: Me? Naw. So long as I don't hav'ta' drink the water…

JOSIE: She's got a plate with "GOLF" on it.

SHIMMA: I do, yuh…

MAUREEN: There's a blue Duster out in the lot with "GOLF" on it!

JOSIE: That's *her.*

SHIMMA: That's me.

MAUREEN: You play golf?

SHIMMA: Me? Uh uh. It's my husbin's plate. It's mine, now, but, it *was* his…

FLORENCE: Don't I know you?

RUTHIE: *What?*

FLORENCE: I'm not talkin' to *you,* Ruthie, I'm talkin' to the new inspector: her. *(Steps toward Shimma.)* You look wicked familiar to me.

SHIMMA: We met. My husb'in's got cousins who are yo'r husb'in's cousins. He told me ta ask after you when I sta'hted out this mornin'…

FLORENCE: Is that a fact?

RUTHIE: She's Floey's Cousin! See? You never know…

JOSIE: You *always* know! Everybody's related to everybody else around these parts. We're even cousins, distant, right, Arlyne?

ARLYNE: I don't think so…

JOSIE: Aren't you related to the Asaroes?

ARLYNE: No, that's Florence.

FLORENCE: That's me, cupie doll.

JOSIE: If there's anything I hate more than bein' fat, it's bein' *wrong!*
(To Shimma.) So, how come you got "GOLF" on your plate? Yo'r husb'in some kind'a big golfer?

SHIMMA: My husb'in? Uh uh. He's never played any golf…

(There is a pause.)

I got him a vanity plate for his birthday and it came through with "GOLF" on it...

JOSIE: You didn't ask for "GOLF"?

SHIMMA: Not really. There was a bunch'a spaces for choices .. I asked for "Billy," first, on accounta' that's his name; then "Bill"; then "Willy"...his brother used'ta call him "Willy"...but, then, there was this fourth empty space for a choice. I shoulda' thought ta' put down "William" but nobody ever calls him that and I guess I forgot that was in the runnin', even. I used'ta drive by this golf club every day when I worked over Wakefield...

RUTHIE: Bear Hill...

SHIMMA: That's the one, yuh. I always thought it would be really—I dunno'—sophisticated if he took up golf, so, I just wrote it in in the empty space. I guess "Billy," "Bill" and "Willy" were taken and when the plate came through I got fuckin' "GOLF"! *(She laughs embarrassedly.)*

MAUREEN: He doesn't *ever* play golf, your husb'in?

SHIMMA: Naw, never, no sports at all. He used'ta bowl before I met him...

JOSIE: Didn't he get pissed off, when you gave 'im the plate?

SHIMMA: Oh, yuh, *wick'id!* That's why *I'm* drivin' the car. He won't *touch* the thing!

(Sally runs into room, followed by Porker. Sally doesn't see Shimma at first, as she is among the workers.)

SALLY: Where is this dyke?

PORKER: *(Sees.)* Oh, my God...

SALLY: *(Sees. His attitude changes entirely. He smiles seductively.)* Alfred came got me. You sent him? *(Motions to Porker.)* Him.

(Shimma stares wordlessly at Sally.)

SALLY: So? What's up? *(Sally smiles his most boyish smile at Shimma.)*

FLORENCE: *(Disgusted.)* Jesus!

(Shimma walks silently into her kitchen; leaves door open. Sally looks around at the women.)

SALLY: What gives? What were you jawin' about with her? *(He looks them over, one by one.)* We got a plant ta' protect here, ya' know, so's don't any of ya's play it too *sma'ht*, if you're able ta' got my point...

FLORENCE: A good couple'a us have *had* your point, Salvatore! It don't look like it's gonna' work with this one! *(Motions toward Shimma.)* You might hav'ta'use yo'r *brain* for change, ladykiller.

(Sally walks to Florence, slowly, angrily. He stares at her a moment,

silently, then turns, moves up staircase to kitchen, tentatively. He then en-
ters kitchen, closing door behind him.
We can now see Shimma and Sally in conversation.
Porker moves to Florence, subtly; silently. When next to her, he speaks
quietly.)
PORKER: What's the matter with you?
FLORENCE: *(Choking back anger.)* Fuck off…
PORKER: You lookin' to get smacked, or what?
FLORENCE: *(Angrily.)* Leave me alone… *(Turns upstage; moves off from*
others, alone. She paces; angrily; enraged.)
JOSIE: What'd you say to her, Porker?
PORKER: Oh, yuh, sure… *me!*
ARLYNE: Just leave her be. Let her collect herself… That's the best.
RUTHIE: It's embarrassing when you cry…
ARLYNE: It's better to stand off, alone, get a grip…
RUTHIE: Collect yo'rself…
(*Pauses; Florence paces like a caged cat, upstage.)*
RUTHIE: Get a grip…
(*Pauses; Florence continues to pace.)*
Stand off, alone… It's embarrassing when you cry…
(*Marlena looks to Maureen for an explanation. Maureen speaks to Mar-*
lena quietly, but, certainly not discreetly.)
MAUREEN: Florence and Sally there are on-again/off-again kind of thing…
MARLENA: Oh, yuh? Her, too?
JOSIE: Italian men are the worst…
MAUREEN: Italians, "Portegees," Irish and English: the worst!
RUTHIE: I'd say Jews were the best.
JOSIE: You've never *seen* a Jew!
RUTHIE: I know Mr. Linsky…
JOSIE: I mean a young Jew: a Jew under thirty…
RUTHIE: Oh, no, I don't know anybody like that.
JOSIE: *(Smiles.)* Mr. Linsky must be seventy-five…
ARLYNE: *Sixty*-five…
MAUREEN: Everybody's nice when they hit sixty-five. They get kinda'
beaten into it!
ARLYNE: I wouldn't say Linsky's so nice… *(They all look at Arlyne.)* I could
tell you a couple'a stories about Linsky!
(*They all smile, enjoying their game.)*
RUTHIE: *(The widest smile of all.)* She's still mad at him over something.
ARLYNE: It ain't money, neither!

RUTHIE: She went out with him once…

ARLYNE: I wouldn't get too close to Jews if I were you!

RUTHIE: I always bring it up ta' get her goat…

ARLYNE: They're loose with their hands! That's all I'm gonna tell ya's…

RUTHIE: *(Giggles.)* Never fails me…

ARLYNE: They can sweet-talk you, all right, but, when push comes to shove, stay clear of Jews. That's all I'm gonna' tell ya's…

RUTHIE: *(Imitating her mother's voice.)* They can break yo'r heart, too…

ARLYNE: *(Exact same voice, but, tearfully.)* They can break yo'r heart, too…

RUTHIE: *(Giggles.)* Never fails me!

(Sally and Shimma argue, in kitchen, upstairs. Florence paces away, upstage, alone. She is extremely upset. She watches Sally and Shimma, through kitchen's window-wall, above.)

JOSIE: So, that rules out Jews, Italians, Portegees, Irish, English…What's left?

MAUREEN: Frenchmen.

MARLENA: Frenchman?! You soft in the head? Frenchmen'll fuck *lobsters* if you hold their claws open! Frenchmen are the *worst!*

MAUREEN: How about Frenchmen from Montreal, or from up Vermont? How do you feel on *them?*

MARLENA: That's what I'm *tellin'* ya's! *(Pauses.)* We had a shed built once. Six Frenchmen, all brothers. *(Pauses.)* My husband's upstairs, shavin'. One of the Frenchmen asks me if he can use the downstairs toilet. Another one wants a glass of water. He has his own *glass!*—I shoulda' known something funny was comin', right? —I'm in my housecoat still, 'counta' it's maybe 6:30, 6:40…

RUTHIE: In the mornin'?

MARLENA: A'course in the mornin'! My husband only shaves in the mornin'! *(Takes a breath.)* The one with his own glass comes up behind me and like presses himself against me. The older one—with the muscle-shirt—he presses himself against me, in front, kisses me. The younger one reaches under and up, around front…

MAUREEN: *(Interjects.)* You are *kidding* with this!

MARLENA:…and I, of course, cannot make a *peep…*

MAUREEN:…'cause'a Frank…

MARLENA:…'cause my husband's upstairs, shavin', not thirty feet away. *(Pauses; then smugly.)* So, you wanna' tell me about Frenchmen?

(There is a long astonished pause. Porker is first to break the silence.)

PORKER: So, what did you do?

(They all look at Porker, as if surprised by his participation.)

MARLENA: I didn't know he was listenin'...

JOSIE: Jesus, Porker, you got no *shame?*

(To Marlena.) Porker's a tell-me-a-story freak.

PORKER: I wasn't listenin'...

(To Marlena.) I wasn't listenin'...

(To all.) We need more bricks!

(Porker goes to saw; saws down blocks into smaller brick shapes. The women continue their labor, wordlessly. After a while, Maureen talks to Marlena.)

MAUREEN: You ever tell Frank?

(We become aware again of Florence, upstage, stopped now, watching Sally and Shimma in kitchen-office, through window. Sally touches Shimma's cheek again. Shimma slaps Sally's hand.)

MARLENA: You kiddin' me? I'd hav'ta have been lookin' to get beat black and blue.

(There is another flurry of wordless work. Josie breaks through.)

JOSIE: So, what did they do?

(Marlena looks at Josie.)

The Frenchmen...

ARLYNE: Josephine!

RUTHIE: Jees, Josie...

JOSIE: *Why?* Am I the only one interested?

MARLENA: They just kinda' groped around for a while and then they left...

(Simultaneously.)

> JOSIE: That's it?
>
> RUTHIE: That's all?

(Marlena shrugs, shows her palms. Porker cannot resist a question.)

PORKER: *(Upstage; cannot resist asking.)* Did you pay 'em?

(Marlena and all look at Porker. He explains quickly.)

For the shed...

JOSIE: What is *with* you, Porker?

PORKER: It's just a question, that's all! I'm just interested!

(Marlena is done with her story, done talking on the subject. Porker shrugs, shows his palms, sets stack of bricks in front of Florence, at breading machine. Florence is back at work, but still not in commune with the others.)

JOSIE: Porker forgets from time-to-time. He thinks he's one of *us.*

MAUREEN: They say that dogs do that. Somebody dies in a house, the dog gets depressed. Divorce, too, does the same thing. I read that...

(Sally storms out of the kitchen, swaggers down stair-case. He is in a rage.)

SALLY: Burn the crop! Dump it all! I don't want no arguments here, just dump the whole batch! Porker, I want all the HoJo crates...all of 'em...*(Screams at Porker.)* MOVE!

(To Arlyne.) Get the Stop'n'Shop labels, Arlyne, and I want ya's all ta' hear this: the only way this plant's stayin' open is if we can cover our asses for this loss and the losses for the last four months, and even then I'm promisin' nobody nothin'...except for that leaky douche-bag, who I am promisin' that I will process no fish whatsoever, if that's the way she wants it. I will find orders on rewraps and rewraps only. And if she wants ta' turn down our rewraps, she can sue the Federal Inspector who approved 'em in their last wrap, 'cause they are all approved, all registered, and I don't care if we spend the rest of our lives takin' Howard fucking Johnson labels off'a fish and puttin' Stop'n'-fuckin' Shop labels *onta'* fish...if that's what she's lookin' for, that's what she's gonna' find...'cause I say "fuck the dyke!"...and what I say *goes!*

(Screams at Porker.) MOVE!

(To all.) You all heard me: dump the product, clean the breader. I ain't havin' her fault us on no fuckin' cleanliness...

ARLYNE: Is she going to test you on *language*, Salvatore...

SALLY: Oh, gimme a fffff...a *break*, Arlyne, will ya'!? You *see* what I'm goin' through here?

ARLYNE: This is not an excuse!

SALLY: Ar*lyyyyynnnne!*

ARLYNE: Out of memory for your mother...

SALLY: *(To Ruthie. he knows he's beaten.)* Will you talk to her?

RUTHIE: Just say you're sorry. What's the big deal?

SALLY: *(Angrily.)* For the love of Christ, Ruthie, I...*Okay!* All right! Fine!

(Sweetly, head down; like a four year old boy.) Arlyne, I'm sorry I swore so much. Okay?

ARLYNE: I understand there's terrible problem, but, does foul language help anything...

SALLY: No, but it helps *me!* It makes me feel a little better.

ARLYNE: Do you work alone?

SALLY: *(Still a boy.)* No...*(Raises his head and attitude, slightly.)* Come *onn*, Arlyne, we are in trouble here!

ARLYNE: *Salvatore!*

SALLY: *(Head down again.)* Okay, okay. I said I was sorry.

(To Ruthie.) Tell her! Didn't you hear me tell her I was sorry? Didn't I?

ARLYNE: I accept.

(Arlyne offers her cheek for Sal to kiss. He does, head still down. Arlyne kisses Sal's cheek. All is forgiven.)

SALLY: *(Regains the old manly control.)* Get set up...all'a'ya's!

JOSIE: Good for you, Arlyne.

RUTHIE: My motha' is *tough!*

ARLYNE: You have to stand your ground. You have to stand up to them. You can't let them get an edge.

RUTHIE: She's known him since the crib.

(Sally is humiliated. he storms into Locker area, where Florence stands, smoking a cigarette.)

SALLY: Get out here and pull your part of the load! What da'ya' think you are: *special?* I told ya' ta' lay off'a me today, didn't I? I told you I had enough pressure on my head without your bullshit, didn't I? But, could you back off? Nooooo! Could you give me a break for even *one measley day? Noooooooo.* And I'm s'pose'ta'take you serious when you ask me ta' think about what you're askin' me ta' think about? What are you: off yo'r gourd?

(Sally storms into freezer, screaming for Porker.)

SALLY: Yo, Martino! You partying in there? What's up?

(Sally enters freezer, slamming door closed behind him. All eyes on Florence, who exits locker-area and moves to "line." Suddenly, Florence starts flinging frozen fish-sticks about the room, furiously, in a rage. Some of the fish-sticks clunk against the kitchen-office window, causing Shimma to stand and look down, frightened.)

FLORENCE: I've had it! I have fucking *had it!!!*

JOSIE: Hey, Floey...

(She dumps breading onto the floor, making a horrendous, disgusting mess.)

FLORENCE: Fucking men!

MAUREEN: Hey, Flo, come onnn...

ARLYNE: Florence...

RUTHIE: Floey, heyyy...

(She knocks one of the tables over. Porker and Sally enter, pushing hand trucks with crates of already-wrapped/labeled frozen fish. They see Florence and stop in their tracks.)

SALLY: You'd better do something...

PORKER: Me? Shitt...

(Porker runs to Florence and she beans him with a breaded frozen fish-brick.)

PORKER: Heyy, you tryin' ta' kill me, or what?

FLORENCE: *LEAVE...ME...ALONE!*

(Florence paces, trapped, caged.)

SALLY: What the hell gives here? Did you do this, Rizzo?

FLORENCE: *(To Porker, about Sally.)* Just keep him the fuck away from me!

PORKER: Just let her calm down a little, Sal...

(Sally cannot believe his eyes; rages at Florence.)

SALLY: What are you? *Warped?* With a new inspector around? You make
this mess? What are you? Flipped out? You need a straight jacket, or
what? You want me ta' call down ta' Danvers...have 'em bring the
nut-wagon over? Or what?

*(Florence charges at Sally, slapping him, punching him, scratching him,
kicking him. Sally does nothing offensively. He ducks her punches, absorbs
her slaps; twists out from under her scratches, dances away from her kicks.
For him, it is all accomplished quite easily. He giggles and guffaws, childishly, cruelly.)*

FLORENCE: I'll kill you...I'll kill you...

SALLY: Look at her! Look at this one! What? You wanna' kick me? You
wanna' scratch my eyes out? C'mon, c'monnn...what's yo'r trouble,
huh? Come onnn, dooo ittt...

ALL OTHERS: *(Call to them.)*
—Hey, Floey...
—Knock it off, you two...
—Grab Florence...
—Poor kid...
—Do somethin', Porker!
—Grab her, Porker!

FLORENCE: *(Screams, suddenly.)* Fuckin' coward...hitting women...beatin'
women...murderer...Everybody knows...everybody knows....mur-
derer!

*(During the fight, Shimma has quietly exited the kitchen and entered the
main work area, standing upstage, watching. Sally stops his giggling on
Florence's final "Murderer!" and grabs the now-hysterical Florence by the
throat with his left hand, and he raises his right hand, poised to strike
Florence. Porker screams at Sally.)*

PORKER: *Hold it, Sal! HOLD IT!*

SALLY: What, Martino, what? You don't want me ta' hit your girlfriend?
You don't think I should make over her face? What?

PORKER: You're bein' observed...*(He nods towards Shimma.)*

SALLY: What? *(Looks, sees Shimma; snarls at her.)*

What are *you* starin' at? This is a private matter. This is company business...

(Shimma stares at him, silently. Sally releases Florence, shoving her away from him.)

SALLY: You're free, you...

(Florence circles the plant floor, still in a rage. Animal-like moans issuing from her: deep-throated, primal. Sally goes to Porker and "sucker-punches" him in the stomach; hurting him, humiliating him.)

SALLY: That's for your girlfriend, you...

(Porker skids and falls in a crumpled, humiliated heap.)

Get back to work! Get set up for re-wraps! *Hustle!* You're all gettin' paid, *yes?*

(The women restart their labor in near-robot fashion, mechanically, automatically. their eyes meet, one by one. Sally is deeply ashamed and embarrassed, but unable to apologize. He cleans some of the mess. Suddenly, Sally screams at Shimma.)

SALLY: You won't close us down, sister! No matter how much you shove, North Shore Fish is stayin' on it's feet...

(To the women) I'll bring the product out...

(To Porker.) Get up and gimme a hand, you!

(Porker stands, silently. He starts toward Sally after flashing a look at Florence, who stands facing Sally, her body heaving a silent sob every tenth count, as does a child after a tantrum. Sally yells at Florence, through clenched teeth, pointing his finger.)

SALLY: If you ever, *ever*, come at me again, I'll... *(He doesn't complete his sentence. He moves to the freezer.)* I'm getting the product. Get set up...

SALLY: *(To Porker.)* You comin', or what?

(Porker moves to Sally, wordlessly. He is embarrassed, beaten into humiliation, hangdog. Sally and Porker exit into the freezer.

There is silence, but for Florence's sharp sobbing intakes of breath: her post-tantrum gasps for oxygen. Shimma is shaken. She holds back her tears; makes pronouncement, to women on the "Line.")

SHIMMA: You tell that blow'ah I ain't passin' no fuckin' inferior product for *noooooobody*. You tell him I got people lookin' over my shoulder...and I'm coverin' my own ass, no matter what. Even if I have ta' close this plant down. If I hav'ta, I hav'ta! I'm just doin' a job. You get my point here?

(All nod understanding.)

SHIMMA: You tell that blow'ah what I just spoke...

(Shimma turns, exits into kitchen, slamming door closed behind her.

After the doorslam, there is a small silence. We see Shimma, through the window. She sits in chair, bows her head, extremely upset. The women watch her a moment, then look at one another, gravely concerned. Arlyne cocks her head. She is worried. The lights fade to black.)

END OF ACT ONE

ACT TWO
Scene One

Lights out in the auditorium. In darkness, we hear the sound of a radio playing: Willie Nelson singing "All Right Woman, All Right Man." Lights up in plant. Five hours later. The women are squashed together on either side of the end of the processing "line," at the wrapping table. They are all involved in the unwrapping and rewrapping of frozen fish dinners: boxed. At the moment, they are stripping the boxes of their "A&P" labels, and rewrapping the boxes with "Good Deal Market" labels. Neither Porker nor Sally is on stage. Shimma is in her kitchen, at the typewriter, writing reports. The women sing along with the Willie Nelson song.

(Porker and Sally enter, wheeling hand trucks loaded with fish product in crates. The women are all singing full-voiced, wholeheartedly. Porker and Sally stop, astonished, as Willie and women head toward a big finish.)

WILLIE AND WOMEN: "You gotta' be a doooooo right all niiiiights mannnnn."

(Shimma hears Sally, looks up and out, as Sally switches radio "off.")

SALLY: What's up? What gives here? We workin' or we partyin', huh? We got a plant fallin' apart here and what are you all doin'? Singin'? This is very bright, very *swift!*

JOSIE: C'mon, Sally, we've been singin' all afternoon and we still wrapped sixty crates of Stop & Shop.

SALLY: I just walked in here and half of you wasn't doing a single stick of work.

RUTHIE: We're almost finished, Sal.

PORKER: Maybe if they just played it and didn't sing along?

SALLY: *(Turns on Porker cruelly.)* What is this I'm hearin' now?

PORKER: *(Shows Sally his palms.)* Just an idea…

SALLY: You wanna come in to Markie with me and maybe take it up with him? *(Pretends to be Porker talking to the boss.)* "Markie, I know we're goin' out'ta business and all, and I know we got a new inspector turnin' down every piece 'a product we process and you're probably gonna' hav'ta' sell the building and the land and all, but, couldn't the girls just have some music ta' listen to, instead of doin' their last couple'a days of paid work? *Hmmmmmmmm?*"

PORKER: *(Interjected into above speech.)* Right, okay…Okay, Sal…Okay, we'll drop the playin'-music idea…

SALLY: What have you got? Some private income?

PORKER: Okay, okay, you made your point…

SALLY: I don't hear an answer to my question, Martino!

PORKER: C'mon, Sal, enough, huh?

SALLY: I would like to hear an answer to my question, Martino!

PORKER: C'mon, Sal, will you?

SALLY: I would like to hear an answer to my question, Martino…

PORKER: Come onn, Sal, a joke's a joke, huh!

SALLY: I said that I would like an answer to my question. Did you not hear me?

PORKER: Okay, fine. What's your question?

(The women all stand silently watching.)

SALLY: Do you have a private income?

PORKER: No, Sally, I don't. I don't have a private income.

(Porker is humiliated; head down. Florence walks to radio, switches it back on. James Taylor, "Fire and Rain," blares out. Sally turns and faces Florence.)

SALLY: What's this?

(There is an enormous tension now in the plant. Sally moves to Florence, who stands her ground, defiantly, singing along with James. And then, Florence stops singing, allowing James to continue on alone. She stands her ground, staring at Sal coldly, silently. There is a long "hold." Sally talks to Porker, without ever breaking his stare at Florence.)

SALLY: Turn it off. Martino, turn off the radio.

PORKER: Hey, Sally, will ya'…

SALLY: You workin' for North Shore Fish or what?

PORKER: I'm workin'…

SALLY: Turn it off.

(After a long, tense pause, Porker heads toward the radio. As he passes Florence, they share a moment. he cannot find the strength she wants him to find: he goes to the radio; switches it "off." Whilst looking at his shoes, Porker speaks.)

PORKER: I'll be right back. I gotta' go to the bathroom…

(Porker exits upstage, out of sight-lines. There is another moment's pause. Sally feels he has won; Florence absorbs Porker's small defeat.)

SALLY: I called the broker, myself. We can move now on the re-wrap job for A&P…eighty thousand units. Everything's in house. I got the labels, I got the product…

(Porker speaks up. He hasn't, of course, been to the bathroom. He has simply stepped out of sight.)

PORKER: What product?

SALLY: We're gonna' re-wrap everything we got. Tommy Fusco's brought me labels from Mass Coastal. We're in business here, yes?

ARLYNE: *You* did this, Salvatore?

SALLY: I did, yuh, I made the call myself...I made the sale.

JOSIE: Does Markie know this?

SALLY: I told Markie I could move the stock, yes...

FLORENCE: We're selling off all the stock we've got?

SALLY: I'm making work. I'm covering overhead...

ARLYNE: Are we makin' a profit?

SALLY: What is this? I have to make reports to the wrappers?
> *(False laugh. After a pause, Sally continues; answers Arlyne.)*

SALLY: We're breakin' even. We're payin' ourselves. We're makin' our own work...
> *(There is another small pause. Then Sally screams his orders, officiously.)*
> I want everybody on unwrappin'. I want all the labels pulled and then we'll all go on to wrapping...Could we please *start*?
> *(Everybody starts unwrapping boxes of frozen fish.)*
> Porker, go get the rest of the stock...*(Nods to Porker.)* Let's go.
> *(Porker and Sally exit, with hand trucks, after leaving crates at end of wrapping table.)*

ARLYNE: I don't like the sound of this...

JOSIE: It doesn't sound great...

FLORENCE: Looks like the end of the road.

RUTHIE: How so, Floey?

FLORENCE: You can't sell fish if you got no fish to sell!

MAUREEN: Sally must know what he's doing...

FLORENCE: How come you say *that*, Maureen?

MAUREEN: I dunno'.

MARLENA: He's good looking...

FLORENCE: Right. You got it...*(Smiles, nods to Maureen.)* Your cousin catches on fast.

MARLENA: Something wrong?

FLORENCE: Nope.
> *(Porker re-enters with handtruck loaded with cartons of frozen product.)*

PORKER: This don't look good...

RUTHIE: It's work, like Sally said...

PORKER: If we sell off all our stock, under-priced, then we ain't got nothin' ta' play with...to broker. I mean, where's the future?
> *(Florence laughs. Sally re-enters, unloads his truckload of frozen product.)*

SALLY: If ya's all are smart, you'll work hard now, and save yo'rselves a job for tomorrow…if you get my message.

(Sally exits again. The women unwrap product, diligently.)

ARLYNE: No harm in workin' hard…

JOSIE: When have we ever done anything but?

MARLENA: Hard work's the best thing in the world, really…

MAUREEN: The Japanese give their first loyalty to their work, second to their families. That's why their country's making so much money…

FLORENCE: Same thing here, ain't it? Who do yo know who's giving' their first loyalty to their family?

(Florence moves to breading machine. After a moment's work, Arlyne sings, alone, not conscious of anyone listening, or caring.)

ARLYNE: "If you want a dooo-right-all-night's womannn…" *(Thinks; speaks.)* If John Wayne had been a singer, he would have sounded just like Willie Nelson…

JOSIE: I think that's true…

FLORENCE: After Willie Nelson's dead, he'll sound just like John Wayne.

PORKER: I don't get it.

FLORENCE: *(Explains.)* John Wayne's dead now. After Willie Nelson's dead, they'll sound alike. Get it?

PORKER: *(Disgusted.)* What's *with* you?

RUTHIE: *(To Marlena.)* My mother's hung up on John Wayne…

ARLYNE: I'm not "hung up." I *like* John Wayne. I enjoyed his acting. He was excellent!

JOSIE: They say he had a tiny organ. Miniscule.

PORKER: I'm in the room, ya' know.

JOSIE: So what?

PORKER: I hear what you're sayin.

JOSIE: "Miniscule" isn't dirty, Porker. It means the same as "tiny"…

MAUREEN:…like your Toyota…

RUTHIE:…like your Christmas bonus…

FLORENCE:…like your *mind*…

JOSIE:…like John Wayne's wee-wee!

PORKER: What is *with* this one?

RUTHIE: John Wayne's real name was Marion Morrison…

ARLYNE: She does this to annoy me.

RUTHIE: It was *so!*

FLORENCE: Marion?

RUTHIE: It's in my "What To Name The Baby" book. Marion Something Morrison. They have this whole long list of famous name-changes.

PORKER: John Wayne was a fag?

FLORENCE: What's this?

PORKER: Isn't that what Ruthie just said? John Wayne had a girl's name...
(*Sally re-enters with another hand truck load.*)

SALLY: Now, what's the chatter?

PORKER: John Wayne was a fag!

SALLY: What's this?

PORKER: Ruthie found it in a book. He was a fag. He had a girl's name.

SALLY: What are you saying, Martino?

PORKER: John Wayne's real name was a goddam *girl's name*...The Duke,
huh? The *Duchess*, that's what!

SALLY: If you ain't the fuckin' limit!
(*Sally dumps the contents of his hand truck and exits, angrily.*)

PORKER: What's with Sally? Everything I say pisses him off.

FLORENCE: Maybe 'cause Sally's a girl's name, huh?

PORKER: What the hell are you *tellin'* me here? You *know* somethin'?
What's with this insinuendo, huh?
(*The women roar with laughter. Shimma walks down stair-case, from
kitchen, above. End of laughter.*)

SHIMMA: I called into Boston. I can't allow the rewraps to go out of here.
I don't care if you've been doin' it before. I can't allow it to go out of
here, now. (*Pauses.*) It's not my decision...

PORKER: What are you saying here?

SHIMMA: Once product is wrapped, it's wrapped and it's gotta' be shipped.

PORKER: But, we didn't wrap it! It's bought already wrapped. It's our stock.
That which we don't process and pack ourselves we buy, already
wrapped. It's our stock. That's the business...Oh, shit! (*Porker runs
off-stage, to get Sally. There is a pause.*)

SHIMMA: It's not my decision...

FLORENCE: So, if you get this plant closed down, then what?

SHIMMA: I'm not lookin' to get this plant closed down. I'm just doing my
job. If I don't, somebody else will come in and do the very same
thing...(*Shrugs.*) I'm not lookin' to get any plant closed down...
(*Sally enters on the run; skids to a stop.*)

SALLY: What's this?

SHIMMA: I can't approve the rewraps. There's no way.

SALLY: There's nothin' you can do about it. There's a government pass on
every package...It all passed.

SHIMMA: Not after you unwrap the package there isn't...

SALLY: The government doesn't pass the label. It's the *product* that's been passed...

SHIMMA: You've never heard of "shelf-life"? This stuff's double-dated...

SALLY: What shelf-life? These are frozen goods! What the hell are you talking about?

SHIMMA: It's not my decision. I called Boston...I gotta red-tag.

SALLY: Now, wait a minute. Wait a fucking minute, here...You ain't gonna' red-tag none of this product...*(Sally starts to move in toward Shimma.)*

PORKER: Hey, Sally, come on...

SALLY: You ain't closin' us down, sist'ah!

SHIMMA: I'm only doing my job!

(Sally arrives at Shimma, grabs her, backs her against wall. he raises his fist.)

FLORENCE: *Don't, Sal!*

PORKER: *Sal!*

(Sally is about to hit Shimma, when, suddenly, Ruthie screams out.)

RUTHIE: *Oh, God, Mama, it's coming! The baby! Oh, God!*

(Everybody turns and looks.)

RUTHIE: *Oh, God, Mama, it's coming NOW! It's coming FAST!*

(There is a moment's pause. Blackout.)

END OF SCENE ONE

Scene Two

Fade in music: Otis Redding sings on tape: "Oh, she may be weary... Young girls do get weary...wearing that same shaggy dress...but, when she gets weary...try a little tenderness..." Music fades out.

Lights up in plant, fifteen minutes later. Maureen, Florence and Marlena are sitting, center, smoking cigarettes. N.B. The 1st glow from their cigarettes is the cue for the stage-lighting. Ruthie and Arlyne are off-stage, in the lounge. Ruthie is about to deliver her baby. Josie and Sally are with them. Shimma is in her kitchen, on the telephone. Porker enters from off-stage.

FLORENCE: How's she doin'?

PORKER: Any second now…Any word from the doctor?

FLORENCE: She's callin' his office. He should'a been here by now…

PORKER: He can't be here if he doesn't know about it…

MARLENA: I was born on my father's boat… *(Pauses.)* My mother was overdue, so my father took her out for a ride on the boat, to shake her
up…It worked…Of course, I was a third baby for my mother.
(Pauses.)
I guess I came too fast…

PORKER: You *what* too fast?

FLORENCE: Jesus, Porker, you are *disgusting!*
(To Marlena.) One thing on his mind! Honest ta' God!

PORKER: What's with you? I was just interested in what she was sayin'…

FLORENCE: Oh, yuh, sure…

PORKER: *(To Marlena.)* I was born on my father's lobster boat. Same thing,
kinda'. My mother was frightened she'd have me while my father was
out on the boat…So, she came along…I was her fourth baby.
(Smiles.) They say they figured if she went into labor, they'd have time
to get up to Addison-Gilbert, 'counta' they weren't too far out, just
lobsterin' off of Bass Rocks… *(Shrugs.)* I guess they figured it wrong…

FLORENCE: A long line of great thinkers…

MAUREEN: My Uncle Kevin got born in the old Central Grammar School.
My grandmother used to clean there. Then he went to school there
himself…

FLORENCE: Didn't he teach there, too?

MAUREEN: That's my point. After he finished college up to Salem Teachers, he taught there…all his life 'til they retired him at sixty-
five…Now, it's city-subsidized housing and he's movin' in there.
Imagine: born in the same buildin', school in the same buildin'…and
now he'll be livin' there!

FLORENCE: The Central Grammar School?

MAUREEN: Practically the same room he taught in…Same floor. It's amazing, huh?

FLORENCE: I got two aunts livin' up there. Nice place…

MAUREEN: A whole life, in one building…

FLORENCE: Arlyne's like that with this place. She started here, same as my
Mum, when she was about fifteen. She must be, what?, sixty, now?

MAUREEN: Close to it…she's been shop stewardess here, probably thirty-
five years…

FLORENCE: That's why my Mum was so happy ta' get laid off. It was like a ticket *out'ta* this place… *(Pauses; then bitterly.)* Bloodless fuckin' people, layin' her off after so many years, huh?

PORKER: Puts the food on the table…

FLORENCE: What the hell are you *sayin'*, Porker?

PORKER: I'm just sayin' that workin' here puts food on the table. That's not too complex an idea, is it? What's with your attitude?

(We hear: Siren, off-stage, to indicate arrival of police car. We might also see the glow of a flashing red light reflected on a wall. Shimma enters from kitchen, then goes off-stage to back room, to Ruthie, etc. Josie pokes her head in from back room, calls to Florence and Porker.)

JOSIE: He's here.

(Josie disappears back into back room. There is a moment's pause. The sound of the siren stops. The car has arrived. Arlyne appears, poking head into room, then re-exits, into back room. There is another moment's pause. Sally appears from back room, for a brief statement.)

SALLY: The doctor's here! *(Nervous laugh.)* I sent him around back to the loading door. *(Sally re-exits into back room.)*

FLORENCE: Gives me the creeps, havin' the police come here like that again…so soon…

MAUREEN: Me, too…

FLORENCE: Seein' the son-of-a-bitch comin' in, same look on his face…*(She imitates Sally.)* The doctor's here…

(Adds in Sally's nervous laugh. Florence punches her fist into her hand.) Gives me total willies, that's what. Saddest thing there is. Saddest goddam thing there is, I swear to God!

(Florence turns away. Maureen explains to Marlena.)

MAUREEN: When Dot died—She's the one we was tellin' ya' about— the doctor showed up in the Gloucester police cruiser, same exact way.

MARLENA: She died *here?*

MAUREEN: We found her in the freezer, when we opened up.

PORKER: *I* found her.

MARLENA: Oh, Jees. That must'a be'n *weird!*

MAUREEN: Same exact sound: police cruiser with the sireen goin' soft-like, then the brakes screechin', stoppin'…

FLORENCE: Mist'ah Macho comin' in with that same look on his face: half puppy-dog, half shit-eating grin…*(Imitates Sally again, words and laugh.)* "The doctor's here…" *(Pauses.)* Saddest goddam thing there is…

PORKER: *(Softly.)* Floey? Hey, Floey, c'mon, huh…

(Florence looks at Porker, half-smiles, bravely. The two old friends share a private moment of grief.)

MARLENA: *(After a pause.)* What...happened?

PORKER: I opened up, same as usual...hit the daytime generators, mopped up, set out the waste cartons, the usual. Then I went into the freezer to load a pallet with blocks. We were doin' Grade "A" orders for McDonald's then...before we lost the account...The freezer was full of exhaust fumes...*(Without pause.)* Dotty was on her back on top of a stack of #6 blocks. She was wearin' her dress, street shoes, lab coat on top, open...

MAUREEN: She killed herself...

MARLENA: No kidding?

MAUREEN: Length of garden-hose tapped into the freezer-engine...

PORKER: The fumes were wicked...*(Pauses.)* To tell you the God's honest truth, I still didn't think she was dead. Her eyes were open and she was starin' straight at me...

MARLENA: That musta' be'n creepy!

PORKER: She was kinda' half-smilin'...her eyes all sad...

MAUREEN: The doctor caught a ride up in the police cruiser. They were all in Dunkin' Donuts when the call came in...

PORKER: Co-incidence...

MAUREEN: Same exact sound: police cruiser with the siren goin', soft-like, then the brakes screechin', stoppin'...

PORKER: She was in the family way. The G.D. Times said she was "despondent"...

MAUREEN: She was havin' Sal's baby...

FLORENCE: No, she wasn't. She killed it, two days before, over Beverly. She went to Sal and he told her to kill it...set it up for her...

MAUREEN: Dot's a super devout Catholic, too. Her whole family. Her brother's a priest, down Revere...

FLORENCE: It drove her nuts, killin' off the baby...

PORKER: Made her despondent...

FLORENCE: Sal made her kill it...

(Sally enters, looks about, smiles.)

SALLY: Any second now...*(Laughs.)* Too much for meee...*(Smiles.)* It's an amazing thing. Absolutely amazing...

JOSIE: *(Pokes her head into room; excitedly.)* It's the baby! The head's come out!

PORKER: Boy or girl?

JOSIE: Just a *head's* out! Jesus, Porker!

(Josie exits again into back room. Sally looks up at Florence, not smiling.)

FLORENCE: Are you gonna' shoot this one with a gun? Or are you gonna' let this one live?

SALLY: *(Shows his palms to Florence.)* Right. Great. Fine.

PORKER: What's this?

FLORENCE: You're quite a fella', Sal…

SALLY: That's what they tell me.

FLORENCE: I hope you die.

PORKER: Hey, Floey, what gives here?

SALLY: I probably will…fifty-sixty-seventy years after you do, I hope…

PORKER: Hey, Sally, what gives?

(We hear: The sound of a baby crying, softly, off-stage. Maureen crosses herself, as does Marlena and Sally.)

PORKER: Goddd…

(Josie runs in.)

JOSIE: It's a girl!

(Everyone cheers enthusiastically. Josie runs off, returning to Ruthie, off stage.)

MARLENA: I love girls.

SHIMMA: *(Enters, smiling.)* It's a girl! *(Shimma goes up stairs, to her kitchen; closes door. Arlyne enters, smiling.)*

ARLYNE: Girl!

(Everyone cheers, again. They gather around Arlyne, hugging and kissing her: children around a triumphant mother.)

MAUREEN: How's Ruthie?

ARLYNE: Hardly a peep. We deliver easy.

(She looks around at Porker and the others, smiling at them, happily.)

ARLYNE: Wonderful thing, isn't it, bein' born right here, right in the middle of it…*Gawdd! (Sobs.)* I wish my mother coulda' been alive ta' see it. Gawdd! *(Smiles; instant recomposure.)* It's a girl! Ruthie's fine. You wanna' come see?

MAUREEN: Great!

(To Marlena.) Wanna'?

MARLENA: Great!

(Maureen and Marlena exit into back room. Josie re-enters, momentarily)

JOSIE: *(To Arlyne.)* She's askin' for ya'…

(Josie and Arlyne re-exit. Sally, Porker and Florence are alone on stage. Sally nods to Porker.)

SALLY: Give us two minutes to ourselves here, okay?

PORKER: I'm not listening. *(Shows his palms.)* I'm not listening!

(Sally goes to Florence.)

SALLY: Can I try to explain something here?

(Florence looks at Sal, wordlessly; shrugs.)

SALLY: I was seventeen, Carmella was sixteen. All'a fuckin' *Gloucester* knew what was happening! I mean, come onnn...two kids leave high school and get married 'cause they're *so in love*? Seventeen years old, standing up in Our Lady Of The Good Voyage Church, looking out the door to Destino's while Father Gambriana's sayin' "Do you, Salvatore, take this woman...?" And you know what I'm really doin'? I'm lookin' out the door and across the street and I'm seein' Porker's girlfriend, Jumbo-jet Josie Evangelista, hoppin' up the steps to Destino's for her second cold-cut sub of that particular morning, and I'm thinkin' about what it would be like to be bouncing up and down on her moons-over-Miami!

(Porker quickly runs to top of stairs to basement/changing room; checks to be certain that Josie can't hear.)

PORKER: Josie's nothin' *like* my girlfriend!

SALLY: Yuh. Sure. And you're not in love with Florence here, neither, right?

PORKER: What's this?

SALLY: I thought you wasn't listening!

PORKER: I'm not!

FLORENCE: Did you?

SALLY: Did I what?

FLORENCE: Bounce on Josie?

SALLY: I did...about two weeks after the wedding. *(Pauses, looks away: a private moment.)* I'm seventeen and Carmella's *six*teen, and nobody's got the sense ta' get it taken care of! I mean, come *onnn*. Carmella was probably second or third best grades in the whole Junior class...already accepted down to Salem Teacher's, right? Futures? Forget about it! "The family *Pride*," my father's tellin' me. Her old man...you remember looney Yo-Yo Shimmataro, before he fell out of his brother's dragger?

PORKER: I remember Yo-Yo...No great brain *there*...

SALLY: Yuh, well, Yo-Yo corners me, over back of the old Rockaway. I was drinkin' beers all night with Bootsy McMahon, and I'm off havin' myself a piss...my thing is out, and all's'a sudden there's Carmella's old man, right beside my doo-dad. I'm thinkin' "Swell! He's gonna' cut it off!" and I hear Yo-Yo sayin' in this sincere fuckin' voice: "I knocked her mother up, same way, and we've been together thirty-something years, already, and we're *pretty happy*, sometimes. I'm glad

Carmella's marrying a *man!*" What'd he think Carmella was marrying: a fucking *toad? (Pause.)* Seventeen years old: they fix us up with a two-day honeymoon in some summah cottage Carmella's mother cleans, over Riverdale. She's got the key so we use it for two days...the place stinks of mold and mustiness. Then we both start workin' here, at North Shore Fish: Carmella stays on the line, wrappin', til she's big like Ruthie...Me: I start right out in the office, coverin' Markie Santuro's ass, which I will never stop doin' til I fucking *die!* And Carmella goes home to mind the baby. She closes the door behind her and she never gets to see daylight again!

(Confidentially, to Florence, trying to exclude Porker.)

Let me ask you a question, Florence, straight and simple: Knowin' how I wrecked Carmella's life as I did...not to mention knowin' how I've probably been the worst husb'in in the history of the whole North Shore, tell me something: How am I s'pose'ta walk out on this person, Florence? How?

PORKER: Walk out on who, Sal? Walk out on who?

(To Florence) What's he sayin', huh? What's he talkin' about? Come on, you guys? What gives?

(Josie re-enters. She is upset, holding back tears. She makes eye-contact with Florence and Sally; smiles, bravely.)

JOSIE: Nice little girl...

(Then, without warning, Josie goes directly to Porker and folds herself into his arms, weeping.)

Makes me so sad... *(Sobs.)* Oh, God, it makes me so sad...

PORKER: What does, Jose?

JOSIE: Babies bein' born...

(Sobs.) If I weren't so fat, he'd come home, wouldn't he?

PORKER: You're not fat!

(To Florence and Sally.) Is she fat?

(Florence shrugs. Sally shrugs. Porker makes a fist at both of them. He grabs a coffee mug, fills it from Maureen's thermos; hands mug to Josie.)

PORKER: Drink some of my sister Rose's coffee. It'll make your troubles seem miniscule.

(She takes mug; sits on steps. She tries not to cry. She sips the coffee. She makes a face. Porker sits beside Josie on steps.)

PORKER: I think she adds Oregano.

(Josie smiles; briefly. And then she speaks, sadly.)

JOSIE: He used to touch me all the time. I don't just mean high school: I mean years and years afta'... *(Sobs.)* I don't know why I eat so much,

Porker. I get so *frustrated*…doin' the same things day in and day out…havin' no money…seein' the same bunch'a'ya's, day in, day out…sayin' the same dumb things…*(Sobs.)* Don't take this personal. It's not personal. It's not against any of ya's, honest ta' God, but, I really hate my life…*(Pauses.)* I'm sick of the neglect. Being his wife is like being a dog in a dead man's house.

(Josie is now a sobbing jelly-mass in Porker's arms. Porker looks around helplessly at Florence. Florence starts to cry. She holds her stomach and she wails with grief. Sally goes to her; speaks softly.)

SALLY: Floey?

FLORENCE: What?

SALLY: I'm tryin' to say something to you, Florence. Something about *life* I think I'm finally learnin'…something that's, I dunno', *appropriate* right now about, well, *us*.

FLORENCE: Yuh, swell, let's hear it.

SALLY: People like us are like pieces of wood floating on the water. We float in—sometimes we touch—sometimes, we even *bang together*…but, then, we float off. We're not really in control of these things, Florence. There's like some *big tide* moving us here and there…We an't really be *blamed*.

(Florence hits Sally. It is a startling backhand blow.)

JOSIE: Hey! Florence!

PORKER: Ah, shit, you guys, c'mon, will ya's…

(Sally holds his hand to his cheek.)

FLORENCE: Tell Carmella to set a couple of extra places at the table for next Christmas dinner. Tell Carmella I'll be comin' over for next Christmas…me and the baby.

SALLY: I'm s'pose'ta walk out on her 'cause you and I are *so much in love*, right? What a joke, huh? I oughta' send it in to CBS-TV. They can use it on the television!

(He starts away from Florence; stops; turns to her again.)

You wanna' tell Carmella and Little Sal and Michael and Angela about everything, this is fine with me, you do that! You do that…and a'course, then I get to tell Bradley and Emily about their mother bein' the Town Pump, right?

(Florence points her finger at Sally and seems to want to yell something accusatory, but, cannot form the words. She sobs, instead, pointing her finger inscrutably. Sally moves towards Florence, just as Maureen and Marlena re-enter. They are both smiling brightly.)

MAUREEN: She's beautiful…

MARLENA: She's *sooo* nice!

MAUREEN: You should go in and see her, Josie. It'll make you feel good.

MARLENA: She's really such a nice little baby…

(Maureen and Marlena feel the pain in the air.)

SALLY: I'm gonna' go tell Markie. I gotta' tell him about the baby and about the red-taggin'. I gotta' report in to Markie. *(Sally turns on his heel and exits into back office.)*

JOSIE: It's all big loud thunder and very little rain. You know what I mean? *(Sighs.)* Cookie's giving me about half what he used'ta'…and that's with me houndin' him day and night. My fatha' keeps tellin' me to take nothin'…to let him pick up the bills and just throw Cookie out altogether…*(Pauses; weeps.)* I'm thirty years old. I don't want my fatha' payin' my bills…*(Sobs.)* My fatha' wants to kill him, ya' know. My fatha's knows that Cookie's be'n beating me. *(Sobs.)* Before you beat a dog, you better make sure whose dog it is. That's the way I see it.

FLORENCE: A dog is a dog [is a dog]. That's the way *I* see it.

JOSIE: I don't like that mouth of yours, sistah! You got something shitty between you and Salvatore, this is fine, this is great, but this is between the rotten two of ya's, so, don't be draggin' us all inta the middle! Nobody's got the guts ta' bring it up, but we all remember the price certain people paid for gettin' caught between the pair of ya's sluggin' it out, okay?

PORKER: Maybe you oughta' just leave it be, Josie, huh?

FLORENCE: What are you gettin' at?

PORKER: Me?

FLORENCE: Her!

JOSIE: What I'm sayin' here is maybe if you never started in with Sal, things might'a' be'n a little different for Dot, huh? You ever think of that?

PORKER: Hey, Josie, Jesus! Is *that* what you were sayin'?

FLORENCE: Yo'r mouth is as big as your ass, ain't it?

PORKER: Hey, come *on*, will ya's!

FLORENCE: *(Circling towards Josie.)* I seen Cookie down the Rigger, ya' know…

JOSIE: Yuh, so?

FLORENCE: So, am I sayin' things out loud?

JOSIE: What am I sayin' out loud?

FLORENCE: What are you? *Simple?* Your ears can't hear what your mouth is speakin'?

JOSIE: I didn't say nothin'! Did I say anything bad, Porker? You're right here. You heard! Did I?

PORKER: What do I know? People say things. It's intense around here right now. No big deal...

FLORENCE: Not to you, maybe, shit-for-brains, but, if I'm carryin', that's my personal stuff and havin' it talked about in front of everybody is no little deal to *meee!*

JOSIE: Who the hell said you was carrying?

PORKER: Now, you lost me there, Flo...I gotta' tell you: You lost me there...

JOSIE: *(To Porker.)* Did you hear me say she was carrying?

PORKER: Carrying what?

JOSIE: A baby, you dodo!

PORKER: A baby? You're having a baby, Florence?

FLORENCE: Come off the shit, Porker! Sal told you. He wouldn't keep something like that to himself...

PORKER: Cross my heart!

FLORENCE: *Porker!*

PORKER: Okay, so he said something, but, honest'-ta'-God, I didn't believe him for a second. Sal's always braggin' about this and that, right?...How far along are you?

JOSIE: Jesus, Porker, what's *with* you?

FLORENCE: I'm havin' it taken care of during lunch-break, tomorrow. I made the appointment...over Beverly. That's where lady-killer sends his ladies, right?

JOSIE: Don't let Arlyne hear...

FLORENCE: What do I care? You think the Pope's gonna' be any happier if there's one more pathetic kid runnin' around Gloucester, wonderin' where the hell his fatha' is...wonderin' why the hell he was put on Earth? For *this?* For cutting and packin' TV-fucking-dinners? Taste-O-The-Fucking-Sea-Fish-Fingers??? What are you all? *Crazy???*

JOSIE: You know what Arlyne will say to that: "We're in the fish business. We're fish people. We're doin' what we were born to do...

FLORENCE: Can you believe this one? This is not the fish business, Josephine! This is the non-union, bottom-of-the-barrel, end-of-the-road, frozen, breaded *dung* business! I know what fish is. Fish is alive until you kill it. Fish is something that bleeds when you cut it open. You see this already-wrapped-and-unwrapped-twenty-seven-times-frozen-*dung?* (She breaks apart a frozen fish-brick into its component parts.) One little fish-neck, two little fish-backs, piece of a tail, piece of another tail…Answer me a question: Did you ever in your entire life see anybody actually *eat this shit?*

(Sally walks out of the back office; re-enters; stands facing Porker, Florence, Maureen, and Marlena. He is ashen; whitefaced.)

PORKER: Sally.

FLORENCE: *What?*

PORKER: Sally's back…

FLORENCE: So what?

SALLY: I think one of you should stop me…

PORKER: What?

SALLY: Me: I should be stopped.

PORKER: From what, Sal?

SALLY: You'll see "from what?" when I get to her goddam door…

(Sally climbs stairs to kitchen. He screams at Shimma.)

SALLY: Get out here, you Commie KGB pig!

(Shimma presses her nose against the window, frightened. She locks door. Satisfied that door is locked, Sally goes to door, bangs on same.)

SALLY: *GET…OUT…HERE!!! GET* (BANG) *OUT* (BANG) *HERE!!!* (BANG BANG BANG)

(Shimma stares out from behind the glass, trapped, but safe from Sally's rage. Sally kicks the door, three sharp kicks. He then climbs on structure, screaming in through window at a terrified Shimma.)

PORKER: Hey, Sally, what's *with* you?

SALLY: You better stop me, Martino, or else I'm gonna' break this door down and murder this one…

PORKER: Why now? What's she done now? She couldn't have red-tagged nothin' more 'cause we haven't mastered nothin' more. Nothin's gone into the master pack for more'n an hour and a half.

SALLY: Markie's sold the plant.

PORKER: What?

SALLY: You have waxey ears or what? Markie's sold the goddam plant out from under us…

FLORENCE: What are you sayin', you?

SALLY: Am I not speaking the King's fucking English? Markie Santuro has sold the plant. North Shore Fish is sold.

FLORENCE: To who?

JOSIE: To who?

MAUREEN: To whom?

MARLENA: What's happening?

MAUREEN: He's saying the plant's been sold…

MARLENA: Will you still get your paid vacation?

MAUREEN: Jesus, Marlena, I'm just hearin' this same as you…

MARLENA: I don't wanna' be a pain in the ass, but, I've got to schedule out my time…

MAUREEN: Shut up! *(Maureen moves to Sally.)* Who'd Markie sell the plant to, Sal?

(Sally doesn't answer.) Sal?

SALLY: It's gonna be a fitness center…

FLORENCE: What?

SALLY: Nautilus, aerobics classes, that shit…

JOSIE: I'll join up! My prayers are answered!

PORKER: Are you shittin' me, Morella? This plant is *sold?*

SALLY: Sold. The equipment goes on the dump. The new people move in as soon as possible…

PORKER: Like when?

SALLY: I dunno'…Tuesday, Wednesday…We hav'ta' clear our personal stuff out'ta here, today…

PORKER: Wait a minute, wait a minute. North Shore Fish is sold and it's gonna' have weight-lifting and dancing classes startin' *Tuesday* or *Wednesday?* *(Laughs.)* This is a fact of life?

SALLY: *(Smiling.)* This is a definite fact of life. There is no changing this. Markie's had these fitness people on "hold" for about six weeks, 'til he saw whether or not the business turned around. He's pretty torn up about it, himself, I can tell you that. This plant's been in the Santuro family more'n a hundred years…

PORKER: *(Laughing and snorting.)* Wait a minute, wait a minute, wait a minute! This plant is definitely sold and weight-lifting and Nautilus are definitely comin' in here as soon as possible, maybe Tuesday or Wednesday of this coming *week?*

SALLY: *(Starts laughing, infected by Porker's laugh.)* Definite, definite, definite…

(Florence and the others giggle as well, also infected by Porker's laugh.)

PORKER: You're not my boss, anymore, Morella? You're not over me? I'm not under you? This here set-up between us is over and done?

SALLY: *(Laughing.)* Over and done.

(Without warning, with total purpose and precision, Porker goes to Sally and punches him in the stomach.)

PORKER: You miserable prick! You greaseball, fuck-your-own-children, miserable brown-nose prick!

(Porker pummels Sally with slaps, swats and punches. This is the fight

that Porker has stored away for some twenty years: since 5th grade. The fight is, thus, like that: formless; childlike…a school-yard brawl.)

MAUREEN, FLORENCE AND MARLENA:

—Hey, Porker, off him…

—Hey, Porker, stop…

—Grabs his arms…

—Porker, knock it off…

—He's killin' Sal!

—Stop it, Alfred!

—Stop punching, Porker!

—You split his lip!

—Porker, you'll kill him!

(Instant chaos: Porker and Sally are in a heap. The women pile on and try to pull Porker off of Sally.)

PORKER: *(A tad hysterical.)* I'LL KILL HIM! I'LL RIP HIS HEART OUT! I'LL BREAK HIS ARMS OFF! GIMME HIS MISERABLE TONGUE AND LEMME PULL IT OUT"TA HIS MISERABLE MOUTH! LEMME KILL HIM! I WAITED MY WHOLE FUCKIN' LIFE FOR THIS! GIVE HIM TO MEEEE!

FLORENCE: *(Sees Ruthie coming up stairs, from below.)* The baby! Stop! The baby!

(Ruthie enters, supported by Arlyne. Ruthie's hair is matted, stringy. She is sweaty, exhausted, but joyously aglow. She wears Shimma's white lab-coat; carries her baby, swaddled in white towels. [N.B. A note on the "baby": not a baby-doll, but, instead, a couple of towels swaddled in a couple of towels.] Porker stops his rant when he sees Ruthie. All others look up as well, amazed. The women pull Porker off of Sally, who rises from the floor, slowly. His lip is split, bloodied. Sally holds his jaw; Ruthie holds her baby. A unique class-reunion photo could be shot now.)

RUTHIE: I'm totally fine. Don't' any of you worry. They're takin' me up Addison-Gilbert, but, it's only for the rules. I could go straight home if I had to. I'm totally fine…

ARLYNE: I'm gonna' run up to the hospital with Ruthie while they check her and the baby out…if that's okay with you, Sal…

FLORENCE: *(To Sally; sternly)* Don't you tell her!

SALLY: It's fine, Arlyne, fine. No problem. Have a good weekend.

ARLYNE: What happened, Sal?

SALLY: Why? What's the matter?

ARLYNE: Your lip's all bloody.

SALLY: I fell down.

ARLYNE: The doctor's still out in the cruiser, if you hustle out there…
FLORENCE: He's okay.
MAUREEN: He's fine, Arlyne. It's superficial.
ARLYNE: It's on your coat, too. It looks like you've been cleaning live fish.
FLORENCE: Dead fish.
ARLYNE: Hmmm?
FLORENCE: He's fine, Arlyne. Go with Ruthie…
RUTHIE: I'm naming her "Roxanne"…
   (There is an embarrassed pause: un ange qui passe.)
FLORENCE: Don't do that, Ruthie. "Roxanne" is a shitty name…
RUTHIE: You think so?
FLORENCE: It's *horrible*. She'll hate being "Roxanne"…
RUTHIE: You all think so?
   (*Simultaneously.*)
        MAUREEN: I don't like it…
        PORKER: I wouldn't…
   (*Simultaneously.*)
        JOSIE: It sounds kinda' *cheap*, don't'cha think?…
        SALLY: I wouldn't, Ruthie. Roxanne's not really too great.
RUTHIE: *(To Marlena.)* How about you? I know you're temporary, but, I'm kinda' interested…
MARLENA: I dunno'…Roxanne's okay, I guess…
ARLYNE: I thought "Roxanne" was elegant.
FLORENCE: It's shitty, Ruthie. Trust me.
RUTHIE: How about "Florinda"?
FLORENCE: *(Rolls her eyes to heaven.)* Jesus, Ruthie!
RUTHIE: Well, how about "Joyce?"
FLORENCE: Yuh, well, maybe…
JOSIE: Maybe…
PORKER: Nothin' wrong with "Joyce!"
FLORENCE: I would go with "Joyce," Ruthie.
RUTHIE: Maybe I'll wait and go through the what-to-name-the-baby-book, again, tonight… *(To the baby.)* You don't mind not havin' a name one more day, huh? *(To all, with a giggle.)* She's cute, isn't she?
FLORENCE: I haven't seen her…*(Walks to baby; looks.)* She's beautiful, Ruthie. She looks just like…you and your mother. Same eyes.
RUTHIE: Yuh…*(Ruthie crosses slowly, painfully, to the door; stops at threshold. To baby.)* Say "bye-bye"…
ARLYNE: She'll be back…
RUTHIE: No, she *won't*, Ma! *(Embarrassed by the suddenness of her response;*

to all.) Just joshin'… *(To Arlyne.)* I'm feeling just slightly weak. We'd better go… *(To all.)* I'm really fine. Don't any of ya's worry.

MAUREEN: 'Bye, Ruthie. Congratulations…congratulations to Earl, too!

MARLENA: Nice to meet'cha'.

RUTHIE: I'll probably be back in a week from Monday, Sal, if that's okay?

SALLY: Whatever you want, Ruthie, that's fine.

RUTHIE: *(Affectionately; admiringly.)* You're the greatest, Sal!
    (Simultaneously.)
        PORKER: *(Disgusted.)* Oh, *yuh!* "You're the greatest, Sal!"
        SALLY: *(Touched.) Nawww!* Congratulations, Ruthie, huh?…and
            say congratulations for me to Earl, too…

RUTHIE: I will. Come visit, everybody… *(Giggles.)* I guess you've seen the baby, already, but, come visit, anyhow…
    (Simultaneously.)
        FLORENCE: We will, Ruthie!
        JOSIE: I'll come by, Sunday!
        PORKER: 'Bye, Ruthie!
    (Simlutaneously.)
        SALLY: 'Bye, Ruthie!
        MARLENA: Nice to meet you both!

ARLYNE: Good weekend, everybody. Don't do anything I wouldn't do!
    (Ruthie and Arlyne exit the play. There is a moment's pause. Suddenly, as though by some force of elision, Porker attacks Sally with precisely the same schoolboy intensity as before.)

PORKER: Miserable prick! Lemme kill you! Lemme put you out'ta' yo'r misery!
    (Once again, Porker muckles Sally and once again the women pile on top, pulling Porker from Sally before he does mortal damage.)

FLORENCE, MAUREEN AND MARLENA:
    —Porker, come onnn…
    —Grab his arms…
    —You'll kill him…
    —He's a lunatic!
    —Get off, Porker…
    —Stop hitting…Porker…
    —Jesus, Porker, STOP!

PORKER: I'LL RIP HIS HEART OUT! I'LL TEAR HIS MISERABLE TONGUE OUT'TA HIS HEAD! *LET ME!!!*
    (The two men are once again separated. Sally's lip is again cut and bleed-

ing. Porker rages out of control, moaning and ranting. The three women try to hold him back.)

FLORENCE: You gotta' calm down, Porker. You'll bust a blood vessel!

PORKER: Let me go, Florence! Let me at him!

FLORENCE: I can't do that, Pork!

PORKER: *(Breaks loose; charges at Sally, swatting him with terry-cloth towel.)* You blew it, Morella! My grandfather worked in fish, my father worked in fish, and I am gonna work in fish. You can sink and submerge this plant but you can't pull real people like us down with you! I will bury you before I'll sink with you, and that is a fucking fact of life, you *faggot!*

SALLY: You split my lip, you *dick!*

PORKER: I'll split your dick, you *derr...*you *peckerhead...*you *pussy...* *(Sally finds a wet rag, and swats back at Porker.)*

SALLY: I didn't put this plant under, you *dink...*you *donk...*you *diddlyshit.* I kept this plant goin'! I kept this plant alive! I breathed precious life inta' this operation. I put the food on your goddam table, Martino! *(To all.) All of ya's!* I kept you workin'...kept you earnin' money. I put the food in your babies mouths, if you wanna' know the goddam truth of it! And this is the thanks I get!

FLORENCE: What are you? *Demented?*

SALLY: Yuh, right, I'm demented. Takes one to know one, Florence...

PORKER: *(Screaming.)* Don't dignify the dork, Floey! Honest ta' Christ, just treat him like somethin' dead. Just treat him like a bad smell. Just act as though he ain't happenin', 'cause you *ain't*, Morella, you really *ain't!*

MAUREEN: *(Out of nowhere.)* Is my vacation paid, or what, Sal?

SALLY: What's that s'posed'ta' mean?

MAUREEN: What's that? Too *complex?* Is my vacation a paid vacation or a vacation that is not a paid vacation? Which?

SALLY: The plant is closin', Maureen. Closing. C-l-o-s...

MAUREEN: *(Picks up Josie's half-filled mug of Rose's old, cold coffee.)* Don't you fuckin' spell at me, you! *(Maureen pours coffee on Sally's head.)*

SALLY: Nice. Thanks, Maureen, very nice...

MAUREEN: You're lucky it wasn't boiling, 'cause that's what you deserve! You're lucky it wasn't a knife in your heart, 'cause that's what you *really* deserve! *(Maureen goes to Sally and spits at him.)* Scumbag! *(To Marlena.)* He's playin' up ta' all of us, all this time. He even comes on ta' old Arlyne, this one...

SALLY: Come on, Maureen, huh?

MAUREEN: Sweet talkin' shit, keepin' all the girls scared they're gonna' get laid off if they don't come across...

JOSIE: We all know the opposite to "laid off" workin' a line under you, don't we, Sally-boy?

SALLY: I never touched you once, Josephine, and you know it!

JOSIE: What are you? *Brain-damaged?*

SALLY: When? Name a single touch!

JOSIE: I'm s'pose'ta' spiel off when you touched me, in front of Floey and Reenie and Hotlips Martino?

SALLY: One touch: come on...let's hear!

JOSIE: Greasy-Pole Contest, Stage Fort Park, under the old bandstand floor!

SALLY: That was years ago!

PORKER: What's this?

JOSIE: How'd you lose your memory? Horse step on your head?

PORKER: Is she makin' this up, or *what?*

SALLY: That was years and years ago!

JOSIE: Not so many...

SALLY: Eight!

JOSIE: Five!

SAL: *(Shrugs.)* Five.

JOSIE: You were married to Carmella, already...I was workin' under you, already...

FLORENCE: Hard to find anybody who hasn't been workin' under this one...if ya' catch my drift.

PORKER: What am I hearin' here?

FLORENCE: Kinda' hard ta' grasp, ain't it, Pork?

SALLY: I never thought I'd see the day you'd be blurtin' it out in front'a everybody...

JOSIE: Every dog has her day, Sal...

SALLY: You were goin' with Cookie, already, ya' know...

JOSIE: "Goin' with" is hardly "married to," you cheatin' bast'id!

PORKER: See? That's why I never did it...

FLORENCE: You never *did it*, Porker?!

PORKER: Ho, ho, that's rich. That's why I never got *married*...

JOSIE: What's why?

PORKER: On accounta' there's no point to it if nobody's ever gonna' be *faithful.*

FLORENCE: Also, on accounta' the fact that every goddam one of us said "no" when you asked us...

PORKER: *(After a beat.)* Now, that was a miserable cruel thing ta' say out loud.

(Simultaneously.)

> MAUREEN: It was, Flo.
>
> JOSIE: It was pretty low, Flo...
>
> SALLY: It was, Flo.

FLORENCE: I guess...

MARLENA: *(After a pause.)* Is it true? Did he ask all'a ya's?

PORKER: Will you come on?

FLORENCE: All of us, all of Rockport, Manchester, Ipswich, Essex, even Woburn!* (Pronounced woo-bin)

PORKER: Nice.

MARLENA: *(To Sally.)* Does this mean my workin' here next week is off, or what? Hey, I'm askin' you a question!

SALLY: What?

MARLENA: Does it?

SALLY: The plant is closed. Closed. What do you think it means? We clear out our stuff, we go home, we never come back unless we're takin' aerobics. Is that clear enough for you?

MARLENA: *(After a pause, to all: screams.)* He grabbed me in the freezer, you know...

SALLY *(in unison with)* PORKER: Come onnn...

MARLENA: Both of 'em! First him, then him! The greaseball pretty-boy jumped me and started pawin' all over! The little one snuck up and started in kissin' me. In the freezer!

FLORENCE: Teamed up?

MARLENA: Uh uh. One at a time. That one asked me to give him a hand with fish-fingers, then he jumped me on this huge frozen grey lump of something. I whacked my leg wick'id!

PORKER: When was this?

MARLENA: About 11, maybe 11:30, this morning...

PORKER: *(Disgusted.)* Jesus, Sal...

SALLY: What's with the "Jesus, Sal"? When did *he* come at you?

MARLENA: At least he said something nice! You just grabbed like I was, I dunno'...*product!*

SALLY: I got no time for this. Come on, Martino. We got a freezer to inventory...

PORKER: Do it yourself.

SALLY: What's this?

PORKER: Fuck you.

SALLY: This is exactly the gratitude I expect…

PORKER: Fuck you and fuck your grandmother!

SALLY: This I won't be forgetting… *(Sally makes a sign of the curse [Italian variety] at Porker; exits, swaggering, into the freezer. Porker is smiling.)*

FLORENCE: What'd he say?

MARLENA: Hmmm?

FLORENCE: This one: Porker: what "nice thing" did he say?

PORKER: What is the matter with you?

FLORENCE: Just curious, Pork… *(She smiles at Marlena; pauses.)*

MARLENA: I don't remember… *(Pauses.)* Something about me being "special"…

FLORENCE: Special?

MARLENA: I dunno'… *(Pauses.)* Something about me bein' "different from the hometown pigs"…

JOSIE: Nice, Porker. Tasteful, too…

FLORENCE: What? Like your bein' an out-a-town pig kinda' thing?

MAUREEN: Come on, you two!

MARLENA: I ought'a warn you that once I start swingin', I don't stop. I mean, I gotta' *be* stopped. You follow my point?

FLORENCE: No, I can't follow your point. I got dropped on my head and I'm a stupid fool… *(Talks to herself.)* Show her. How many fingers am I holding up? *(Holds up three fingers; answers her own question.)* Dahhh, I dunno', Flo, *six?*
(To Marlena, menacingly.) You wanna' swing, Suzie, you swing! If I ain't afraid of him or him, I certainly got no fuckin' fear of a bimbo like you!

PORKER: Hey, come onnn, will ya's, no rough stuff!
(Without warning, both Florence and Marlena slap Porker, at precisely the same time. Porker reels backwards, holding his face. He is totally humiliated. He confronts the women, Marlena first.)

PORKER: I ain't gonna' hold you responsible for this, so, don't worry…
(To Florence.) You neither… *(To Maureen.)* Your bein' her cousin doesn't phase me against you, neither… *(Nods in direction of freezer, where Sally exited.)* It's the asshole in the freezer I'm gonna' kill!
(Porker charges off into the freezer, screaming at Sally.) Dukes up, Morella! You're gonna be dead meat!
(All pause. We hear: The sound of the freezer door slam shut click closed. Marlena looks at Florence.)

MARLENA: I apologize for losing it. I was a little wiped out to hear the news that I was workin' for no money…

FLORENCE: It's no sweat. I'm a little wiped out, myself.

(*Shimma enters from office. She walks to Florence.*)

SHIMMA: This wasn't my doing. I asked the owner straight out. He'd had this offer on the table for two months, maybe more. This wasn't my doing...

FLORENCE: What's the diff?

SHIMMA: I just wanted to say that...I mean, this puts me out of work, too, you know...

FLORENCE: No problem...

SHIMMA: I've been waiting for this job to clear for me for weeks and weeks. I'm out now, too...

FLORENCE: Nobody's pointing fingers. Don't sweat it...

(*Porker enters on the run, worried.*)

PORKER: Sally's knocked out...

JOSIE: Hey, good goin', Porker...

PORKER: It wasn't my fault. He slipped...

JOSIE: Don't be modest, Porker...

PORKER: He hit his head and cut it...

FLORENCE: What are you sayin'?

MAUREEN: Is he critical?

JOSIE: Is he dead?

PORKER: No, but he's hurt. He knocked himself out. We were rollin' around it the freezer and he whacked his head on this big chunk of tuna Markie keeps in there for personal use...Maybe I should get the doctor back...

MAUREEN: Is he still out cold?

PORKER: He came to, but he's groggy and his head's hurt bad...

FLORENCE: Gushing?

PORKER: No, but cut...and banged.

SHIMMA: Put some ice on it.

PORKER: You think so?

SHIMMA: I took First Aid in school...

PORKER: Where'll I get ice?

FLORENCE: I thought you said you were in the freezer.

PORKER: Oh, yuh, right...

FLORENCE: Jesus, Porker...

(*Porker exits off, again, on the run. There is a moment's pause. The women begin to pack their belongings, ready to leave.*)

SHIMMA: This is the first work I've had in four months...At least I've got no stuff to pack up...

FLORENCE: *(Emptying her locker.)* Makes no difference to me...*(Pauses.)* I'm just about breaking even, anyhow...*(Pauses.)* Babysitters make just about the same as me, after I pay tax and dues...*(Pauses.)* My mother ain't gonna' live forever...*(Pauses.)* Makes no difference to me...Anybody got an extra shopping bag?

MAUREEN: *(Tosses bag to Florence.)* Here...

FLORENCE: No sweat. I should chuck all'a this...

MAUREEN: *(Packing.)* Me, too...

MAUREEN: Anthony and I have been plannin' this trip for about two years now...*(Pauses; smiles.)* He'll probably be happy to call it off now. I don't think he ever wanted to go, really...he was just being nice...He's got no real interest in seein' Connecticut...just me.

FLORENCE: Connecticut? Is that where you were goin'? Connecticut?

MAUREEN: Connecticut has great natural beauty.

FLORENCE: You've never been to Connecticut?

MAUREEN: Yuh, well, so what?

FLORENCE: Don't miss Bridgeport. *Full* of natural beauty...

MAUREEN: I'm not goin' anywhere. Anthony's gonna' be scared about makin' our mortgage payments, with me out'ta work again...

JOSIE: At least you own a house...

MAUREEN: Yuh, I guess...

JOSIE: You could sell it. Arlyne said her cousin just sold her house over East Main Street for two-hundred-thousand...They moved to Vermont—got a gorgeous place.

MAUREEN: I don't wanna' move to Vermont.

SHIMMA: We tried to buy something in town here...Couldn't even come close...

JOSIE: How come you wanted to buy here?

SHIMMA: My husband's from here...

FLORENCE: From Gloucester?

SHIMMA: Yuh. Years back...

JOSIE: What's his name?

SHIMMA: Billy Shimma...

FLORENCE: He about thirty-eight?

SHIMMA: Thirty-seven...

FLORENCE: There you go...

JOSIE: Where'd he live?

FLORENCE: Lane's Cove, over by the sauna...

SHIMMA: That's right.

JOSIE: *That* Billy Shimma? With the pink Buick?

SHIMMA: I never saw the Buick. I only heard about it...

JOSIE: Small goddam world, huh?

(*Porker leads Sally on. Sally holds a packette of frozen fish product against his head wound.*)

PORKER: I think he needs some stitches...

JOSIE: Is he gushing?

PORKER: No, but it's open...Somebody ought to run him up to the hospital...

MARLENA: I'll do it. I've got a car...

(*Everybody looks at Marlena; surprised.*)

FLORENCE: The new girl.

MARLENA: I'm heading home anyhow. No point in paying a sitter for *this*. My kids are home from school already. No point in paying a sitter if the plant's closin' down...

(*Goes to Sally, looks at his head wound.*) I'll take you...You know the way?

SALLY: I'm gonna' be okay...

(*To all.*) Don't any of ya's worry. I looked at my reflection in the chrome cover on the freezer pump and I've seen worse, so, don't any of ya's worry...(*Pauses.*) Listen, I've got feelers out already and I've already gotten nibbles from a couple of places...Maybe something's gonna' open up at Gorton's, for example. There's also something I don't wanna' mention, yet, but I want ya's all ta' know, definitely, when I'm settled, you're settled, and that is a promise...

JOSIE: We know, Sal...

SALLY: To tell you the God's honest truth, I'm glad Markie sold. He's been threatening for so long now...

PORKER: Sally's be'n keepin' it from ya's...

SALLY: I didn't want none of ya's ta' worry...but I've seen this fitness clown hangin' around Markie for a couple'a weeks now...

PORKER: The weightlifter type of musclebound Mafioso jamoca Earl kept seein' when he picked up our garbage. I kinda' suspected som'pin, myself, personally...

SALLY: I kept it under my hat. I saw no point in every one of ya's bein' under the gun, too...

PORKER: ...feelin' the pressure kind of thing...

SALLY: To tell you the truth, I'm glad it's finally over. this way, I can set up something solid for all of us...

JOSIE: We know you will, Sal...

SALLY: You guys all...mean something to me...

JOSIE: You mean something to us, too, Sal…

SALLY: I swear this to ya's all: I'll set up something new for all of us inside of three months, four at the very max…

MAUREEN: We know you will, Sal. You've got my number, right?

SALLY: 'Course, I do. I got everybody's…

FLORENCE: Yuh.

SALLY: *(Pauses; touches head.)* I'd better head up there…

MARLENA: It was nice meeting you all…

FLORENCE: Oh, yuh. It's gotta' have been one of the absolute high-points of my life…

SHIMMA: I'm sorry it didn't work out. My husbin'll never believe this one, really…*(Goes to Sally; offers hand.)* No hard feelin's, I hope…

SALLY: Naw. I know you were just doin' a job…

SHIMMA: Well…

(Looks at all; shrugs.) Good luck, everybody. I loved meeting ya's…*(Exits.)*

JOSIE: Me, too…

MAUREEN: Me, too…

MARLENA: We'd better, huh?

SALLY: Yuh, sure…

(Sally moves to Florence.) I'm gonna' be sayin' "goodbye", now…

(Florence turns away from Sally. He starts to move to door; stops; turns again to face everyone. Suddenly, without warning, Sally begins to cry. He sobs and moans, openly, like a hurt child.)

SALLY: It ain't fair, it ain't fuckin' fair! It ain't my fault. I did my job. I got out the product…I got out the product!

(To all, embarrassed.) It's the loss of blood, that's gettin' ta' me, probably. *(Pauses, clears his head; makes a pronouncement.)* I loved every woman who ever worked for me. I did. I'm not ashamed of it, neither. I'm a natural leader…you watch me: before Labor Day. You watch me. I'll have ya's all workin' back under me in some local fish situation, before Easter. *(Exits the play.)*

MARLENA: 'Bye, everybody…*(Exits the play.)*

(Maureen moves from her locker, carrying a huge stack of papers, books, stuff.)

MAUREEN: I need a Sherpa…

JOSIE: What's a Sherpa?

MAUREEN: They live in Nepal. They carry stuff up Mount Everest for explorers…

FLORENCE: You know everything, don't you, Maureen?

MAUREEN: *(Blushes.)* I like to read about things…*(Shrugs.)* Things interest me…*(Drops some books.)* Dammit! *(Picks them up.)* Lookit all this
stuff. I never thought I'd be leavin' here. Got my own little Sawyer
Free Library goin'…*(Picks up top-most book; looks at it.)* A book on
fish. I don't know anything about fish, really…

FLORENCE: Who knows anything about fish? I mean, fish don't tell you
anything much, do they? You ask 'em a question, they flop around…
(Ruefully, suddenly.) What's the secret of life, Reenie?

MAUREEN: For fish, it goes like this. The female gets pregnant because she
drops eggs and the male swims around and shoots his sperm at 'em…at
the eggs. The eggs pop open and about a million little fish swim around
together. The females drop their eggs, the males shoot their sperm on
'em, and about ten million more fish pop out, swim around…

FLORENCE: I'm sorry I asked…

MAUREEN: The schools…the fish that swim around together…they're all
the same age. They never see their fathers again, after the sperm gets
shot, never. They just swim around with fish their same age, and have
their own little fish…*(Smiles.)* Wanna' borrow the book?

FLORENCE: It sounds too depressing. I'll stick to *Cosmopolitan.*

MAUREEN: If Anthony and I bag Connecticut, maybe you and I can spend
a morning down Salem?…In the historic houses?

FLORENCE: Again?

MAUREEN: I was just thinkin'…

FLORENCE: Sure. I'd like that, Reenie…as long as we can skip the House
of Seven Gables…looks just like what I grew up in…hit your head
every time you move…
(Maureen suddenly cries.)

MAUREEN: I never thought we'd actually close up…

PORKER: Don't cry, Reenie…

MAUREEN: I better go…*(Suddenly.)* Do you mind puttin' this stuff in the
dumpster, Porker? There's nothin' here I need…

PORKER: No problem…You sure?

MAUREEN: I'll call you guys. 'Bye, Josie!
*(Josie moves from locker, carrying plastic bags filled with her belongings,
to Maureen. The women look at each other for a moment, silently, sadly.
Suddenly, they hug.)*

JOSIE: I'll call you later, Reenie!

MAUREEN: *(Sadly.)* I'd better go.
(Turns; exits. Josie moves forward, carrying her belongings, ready to leave.)

JOSIE: What a miserable "effin'" day, huh? Call me, Porker, huh?

PORKER: Uh, yuh, sure, Jose, sure…

JOSIE: See ya', Flo…

(Josie starts to exit; Florence stops her.)

FLORENCE: Who's gonna' take Arlyne and Ruthie's stuff to them?

JOSIE: Want me to?

FLORENCE: Uh uh. It's okay. I'll take it. I just didn't want you stickin' me with the errand. Long as you offered no matter…I'll take it to them…

JOSIE: That reminds me. I left a whole bunch'a ice cream and stuff in the freezer…*(Josie exits into freezer. Florence looks at Porker.)*

FLORENCE: You and Josie are doin' it, huh?

PORKER: What's with you?

FLORENCE: *(Imitates Josie.)* Call me, Porker, will ya?

PORKER: Don't talk stupid…*(Pauses.)* It's none of your business…*(Smiles.)*

FLORENCE: I knew it!

(Josie exits refrigerator; crosses to Porker, winks at him, exits, carrying bag of ice cream containers.)

JOSIE: See you guys…How's about I call you after supper, Floey? About 6:30?

FLORENCE: 6:30's fine…

(Josie, by habit, pulls her time-card from the rack and "punches out." The clock's bell rings, sharply. Florence and Porker turn around, startled. They smile. Josie shrugs, smiles, exits the play. There is a pause. Florence turns to Porker, who looks down.)

FLORENCE: I s'pose with Jose you get more for your money…

PORKER: I won't dignify that smart remark…

FLORENCE: You wanna' go out with me, Porker?

PORKER: Tonight like?

FLORENCE: Tonight, tomorrow night…

PORKER: You know I do.

FLORENCE: Okay. We'll go out.

PORKER: That is *great!*

FLORENCE: What's gonna' become of us, Porker?

PORKER: In what way?

FLORENCE: Life is so full of shit…*(She looks about the room; sadly.)* My motha' was thirty years here…breading, wrapping. For what, huh?

PORKER: Come onnn. She *loved* it!

FLORENCE: *(Smiles.)* She did, yuh…*(Pauses.)* She's really lookin' awful, lately, Porker. Thirty years, not once bein' out sick, not once bein' late, not once leavin' at the bell, neither, and they lay her off like she did somethin' wrong. I mean, that's what she's thinkin'. That's what she's tryin' ta' figure out: what wrong thing did she do that she got punished for? She's got nothin'...Nobody's got nothin'...None of us: none of the old people...I mean the real people: the *Gloucester* people...I'm gonna' end up just like my motha', Porker; wicked miserable lonely, cookin' too much food when somebody finally breaks down and visits, chewin' stuff over and over again that happened years and years ago, makin' out that it was good, makin' out that somethin' that happened to her mattered...goin' over and over the past. No plans for nothin'...

PORKER: Come onn, Floey. Sally'll hook up to something, soon. He's workin' on four five possibilities...*(Shrugs; smiles.)* We can collect...The weather's good...

FLORENCE: I guess...What're we s'pose ta' do now, Porker?

PORKER: Us? I dunno'...we'll clean up. We'll put out the lights, we'll go home, wash ourselves up, you'll cook somethin' up for Bradley and Emily, I'll eat some of my sistah' Rose's horrendous cooking, we'll go ta' sleep, get up in the mornin' and face the fact we got no jobs, kill the day, maybe meet up and go down ta' the Capri in Beverly, get sick on pizza, catch a movie, get married...I dunno. Why don't you go home, start pickin' out somethin' to wear?

(Florence turns and sees that Porker has mopped and tidied the work-area: it sparkles.)

FLORENCE: What's with you? The plant's closed...

PORKER: No reason to leave it filthy...

FLORENCE: You're okay, Porker...*(She starts to weep; doesn't.)*

PORKER: Yuh, well...

FLORENCE: *(Tries not to weep; turns; starts to exit.)* See you around, huh?

PORKER: *(Stops her; sings, with Sinatra voice.)* "Love was just a glance away...a warm, romantic chance away..."

(Florence stops, laughs; turns and faces Porker; sings.)

FLORENCE: "If you want a dooo riiiight allll niiiight's womannn..."

PORKER: You wanna' get married, Florence?

FLORENCE: What's this?

PORKER: If you're carrying and all, you oughta' be married...

FLORENCE: What about Carmella and their kids?

PORKER: To *me*, Florence. I mean to me.

(There is a long, long pause.)

FLORENCE: I think your mind's snapped, Porker, 'counta' the plant closin' down and all...

PORKER: A baby oughta' have a fatha'…

(Florence stares at Porker, suddenly cries.)

You don't have to answer right away. We'll be goin' out and all…

(Porker moves to Florence, wants to embrace her, thinks better of it.)

I'll ask you again, maybe Tuesday night, say…

(Pauses. Florence is really in trouble: she is sobbing.)

Are you cryin' 'cause I asked you to marry me?

FLORENCE: That isn't it…

PORKER: I can understand and all…getting stuck, just 'cause of yo'r situation and all…

FLORENCE: (Looks around at empty plant.) This is all I know how ta' do, Porker. Me, my mother, my grandmother, all of us…We know the fish business. (Pauses.) I've got nothing left to teach my children, Porker. They're gonna' look at me and that's what I'm gonna think… (She sobs, chokes back her tears, continues.) I got nothin' left to teach my children…

(Porker looks sadly at Florence; tries to cheer her.)

PORKER: Don't cry, Flo, huh? (Motions to boxes on assembly line.) It's only work…(Shrugs.) It ain't life!

(Florence sobs. Porker goes to her; they embrace.

Music in: repeat of lyric that started scene: Otis Redding, singing "She may be weary…young girls do get weary .. wearing that same shaggy dress…" The light begins to fade. Florence sobs in Porker's arms. They stand under one of the industrial lights over assembly line: in their own "natural" spotlight. The stage lights are now out. Otis Redding completes lyric: "…try a little tenderness…" And the industrial light—their spotlight—fades to black.)

END OF PLAY.

Strong-Man's
Weak Child

For Rachael, Matthew,
Adam, Hannah, and Oliver,
with love, Pop.

PRODUCTION HISTORY

Strong-Man's Weak Child had its world premiere at the Los Angeles Theatre Center, in a collaboration production with Gloucester Stage on May 19, 1990. The play was directed by Mr. Horovitz; sets and lights by D. Martyn Brookwalter; costumes by Ann Bruice; sound by Jon Gottlieb; stage managers Danny Lewin and Cheri Catherine Cary.

Francis Farina . . . . Nick Mancuso
August Amoré . . . . Peter Iacangelo
Fast Eddie Ryan. . . . . Don Yesso
Dede Farina . . . . Sally Levi alternating with
Sheridan Gayr

Strong-Man's Weak Child subsequently played at the Gloucester Stage Company. The play was directed by Mr. Horovitz. The assistant director was Jayme N. Koszyn and the production manager was Madison Stewart. Lighting Design by John Ambrosone, Scenic Design by Jay McLauchlan, Sound Design by Jon Gottlieb, and Costume Design by Janet Irving.

Francis Farina . . . . John Fiore
August Amoré . . . . Nicolas Mize
Fast Eddie Ryan. . . . . Don Yesso
Dede Farina . . . . Jessamine Dana, alternating with
Sprague Grayden, Jennifer Pearce, and Katie Rabbit
Evvie Farina. . . . . Elizabeth Dann

CHARACTERS

Francis Farina, a former body-builder, late thirties, medium height, powerful.

August Amoré, significantly fatter than Farina, less muscular; same age, same height.

Fast Eddie Ryan, a body-builder, ~ame age as Farina and Amoré, but shorter than others, and with much more significantly defined musculature.

Dede Farina, nine years old, small, sickly, in a wheelchair.

PLACE

A reasonably well-equipped weight-lifting gym housed in Franny Farina's garage, Gloucester, Massachusetts.

TIME

A succession of early mornings, just after dawn, spanning four weeks in Fall, the Present.

ACCENT

The same North Shore Massachusetts "Pa'hk Yo'r Ca'h In Hav'id Yah'd" accent required in earlier plays of mine, such as "The Widow's Blind Date," "North Shore Fish," "Henry Lumper," "Year Of The Duck," "Park Your Car In Harvard Yard," etc. etc.

NOTE TO THE DIRECTOR

I recently directed the world premiere of "Strong-Man's Weak Child" at the Los Angeles Theatre Center, and, wearing the hat of Director, observed that it is advisable to cast this play with male actors who are hobbyist bodybuilders, rather than with bodybuilders who are hobbyist actors.

While the three male actors should be "big," only Fast Eddie need have the appearance of a professional-level bodybuilder. Franny's musculature can be far less defined than Fast Eddie's [musculature]. Auggie's musculature can be buried deep in a history of overeating. The powerlifting contest should be acted, not real. Barbells and dumbells are props: under-weight. I have insinuated into the stage directions in this text some tips about the handling of the weights within the contest.

We rehearsed our L.A. production for four weeks. We trained together, daily, at Gold's Gym in Venice Beach. Further, we were able to rehearse with the props and weight-lifting equipment that would be on our set…so our work-outs continued, non-stop. It is not at all important—or wise—for the actors to attempt to lift heavy weights. Instead, proper weight-lifting form and familarity with weight-lifting equipment should take precedence.

No costume change is worth a wait.

All scene changes should be executed in transition lighting. Music is used to indicate scene changes. I chose music that that people of this play would have listened to—and loved—whilst together in high school.

The play should be performed without an intermission. The running time for our LATC production was 1 hour and 31 minutes.

I.H., Los Angeles, June, 1990.

POST SCRIPT

During the Gloucester Stage production, I determined that the play was better contained with Evvie, Franny's wife, cut from the text, thus, centering the action on Dede and her essential (three) strong-men.

I.H., London, January, 1991.

STRONG-MAN'S
WEAK CHILD

We hear: a Boston radio station playing "easy listenin'" music over a real radio on the set. Local weather and chat interrupt the songs. The time is 4 a.m. The setting for the play is a converted garage filled with weight-lifting equipment, assorted related junk. There is one mirrored wall, upstage, in front of the dumbbell rack. The "4th wall" facing the audience is to be used as if it is mirrored, as well. The center-piece of the room is a combination squat rack/bench press rack. There is a lat pull-down machine, and a leg extension machine. There is a dip-bar/chinning bar, upper left. The floor is covered with black rubber mats. Lots and lots of weight-lighting magazines are strew about the set. There is a doorway into the house visible. The 3-step staircase to the door has been ramped. The ramp has a faulty board in evidence. A tool box, a fresh board and a saw are in evidence, nearby. The ramp is about to be repaired. Blow-ups [photographs] of Auggie, Franny, Fast Eddie, Evvie and Dede hang in front of the set as the audience enters the auditorium. When the lights fade out for the play to begin, the photographs will be flown out of the audience's sight. [Note: If photos cannot be flown, possible to attach them to set and spotlight them or project slides.] In darkness, we hear three sharp raps: someone is knocking on garage door.

AUGGIE: *(off)* Yo, Franola! Hurry it up! I'm burning my fingers here!
(Lights up on Franny Farina, a large, powerful man in his thirties. He is doing pullups: lifting his own weight. He calls out.)

FRANNY: It's open.
(Auggie Amoré enters. He is the same age as Franny, as strongly built, but fatter and rounder than Franny. Auggie wears over-sized oddly-rimmed eye-glasses; probably has a moustache.)

AUGGIE: I got two pipin' hot coffees goin' with faulty sip-lids!
(Daintily, his arm outstretched, Auggie carries paper bag emblazoned with Dunkin' Donuts logo. Coffee drips from bottom of bag on to floor. Evidence of earlier drips on Auggie's pant-legs. Both men wear sweat-pants and cut down sweat-shirts, leather weight-lifting belts, hi-top leather sneakers. Auggie wears a Boston Red Sox baseball cap, and an old tweed overcoat pulled over his shoulders like an opera impresserio.)

AUGGIE: Yo.

FRANNY: Yo.

AUGGIE: *(Slips out of overcoat.)* They got this new Henna'd redhead workin' takeout down Dunkin' Donuts. She's like so *into my forearm definition*, she slips our two regulars into the bag, up-side down. They got these killer sip-lids…invented by the same Nazi who came up with the idea for hot-air dryers for hands! The same bastard probably invented sliding screen doors, also, and them little dark-brown plastic to-go cups with the half-and-half. *(Auggie licks his hands. He sees the large coffee stain on his pant-leg.)* Didn't notice nothin' drippin' til just now when I was walkin' from my Cherokee to your door. *(Sets bag down, kneels beside it, strips away soggy bag-parts.)* How's Dede doin'?

FRANNY: Not great.

AUGGIE: She sleep?

FRANNY: She was awake most of the night, again, cryin'…

AUGGIE: Til late?

FRANNY: Three…she finally fell asleep, no more than an hour ago.

AUGGIE: You must feel pretty rough, huh? How's Evvie?

FRANNY: Not great.
(Franny goes to radio, turns it off.)

AUGGIE: *(Inspecting remains of miniature doughnuts.)* Your Munchkins are mush. You got a spoon?

FRANNY: I'm not hungry.

AUGGIE: It's only quarter pah'st four. You eat breakfast *already?*

FRANNY: I'm not hungry.

AUGGIE: You gotta' eat, Fran! You don't wanna' get small, do ya'?

FRANNY: I'm just not hungry, okay?

AUGGIE: Suit yo'rself. *(Scoops up some mushy Munchkins, eats same; swigs some coffee.)* Poor man's steroids. They say the powdery white Munchkin-sugar's loaded with testosterone. It'll grow a beard on your mother, if she eats enough of it.

FRANNY: I'll call up my mother and tell her, soon as we finish our work-cut. She's always wanted a beard.

AUGGIE: She's got a beard!

FRANNY: *Riiiiight!*

(Auggie strips off his sweatshirt, revealing a cut-down tank-top, upon which is emblazoned the word "BARBARIAN" above a garish illustration of a muscle-man/ape combination. Auggie catches glimpse of himself in the imagined "mirror," out front, and strikes a body-building pose. He holds it for a moment and then strikes another pose.)

AUGGIE: *(A TV announcer's voice.)* Is August Amoré cut like a fine diamond, or *what?* Is August Amoré not ripped wicked nicer than you ever thought a good lookin' guinea could ever be? *(Yells.)* August Amoré, ladies and gentlemen. This is not a blurred picture of Frank Zane: this is *August Amoré*...in the flesh! So, let's hear those mother-fucking *cheers! (He imitates a crowd cheering.) Rrrrrrrahhhhh!*

FRANNY: Yuh, right, Amoré. Like when the moon hits your eye like a big pizza pie.

AUGGIE: *(Heavily ironic.)* Oh, I get it! A joke on my name: Amoré...big pizza pie...like the *song!* Jeeeezzzz, I never would'a thought of that one! *(Vaguely embarrassed; changes subject.)* What are we doin' today?

FRANNY: Legs.

AUGGIE: We did legs, yesterday.

FRANNY: No, we didn't. We did chests.

AUGGIE: You're nuts. We did legs.

FRANNY: Chests.

AUGGIE: What are you? Off your goard? My quads are still burning from my five sets of squats.

FRANNY: Touch your pecs.

AUGGIE: My pecs are fine. It's my legs that're smokin'...

FRANNY: Touch your pecs.

AUGGIE: My pecs are fine!

(Franny swats Auggie's chest; Auggie winces with pain.)

AUGGIE: Ah, shit. I think you're right. *(Taps his leg.)* I'm wasted all over! Christ!

FRANNY: *(Smiling.)* That's the price of perfection… *(Pats Auggie's stomach.)* You're *almost* perfect, Auggie…but, if you want to get off this old plateau and soar to new heights…

AUGGIE:…I gotta' hurt myself?

FRANNY:…Exact. You gotta' hurt yourself.

AUGGIE: Oh, God…

(Auggie starts to move into workout position, sees himself in "mirror," again, goes to it; studies his chins.)

AUGGIE: My water level's off. Fast Eddie Ryan says muscle is 80% water. You drink too much, you get bloated. You drink too little, you lose muscle-mass.

FRANNY: *(Instantly angry at mere mention of Ryan's name.)* Eddie Ryan don't know dick.

AUGGIE: The man's big.

FRANNY: The man's a known juicer.

AUGGIE: No more. He's as clean as us! He hasn't touched any juice in years!

FRANNY: You read his bullshit article in the paper, last night?

AUGGIE: I did.

FRANNY: So, it's simple! Fast Eddie Ryan's nothin' but store-bought health-club fancy bullshit technique from California muscle magazines and Joe Weider send-away books. *(Disgusted.)* The man's not a real *lifter*, Auggie. The man's got no strength, any more. The man's got nothin' but a fashion-model-body-builder's mentality! If it ever came down to real strength — to a *power-lift contest* between us, even in the shape I'm in these days, I would whip his ass, easy! No doubt about it!

AUGGIE: What are you? Shittin' me? Fast Eddie Ryan won Mr. North Shore, three years runnin', before his trouble, and now he's back, he's totally clean, and he's a definite contender for Mr. Massachusetts…

FRANNY: That's not *lifting,* that's *posing…body-building…*5-foot-5-and-under category…He's got no competition! We're talkin' midget class here!

AUGGIE: Come on, Fran, will ya'?…The man can't change his height. Gettin' big and gettin' tall are like two very different things. I mean, you're not just pissed off at Eddie 'count'a old scores, are ya'?

FRANNY: What "old scores"?

AUGGIE: You know…with Evvie kind of thing. Or maybe you're still pissed 'cause he won Mr. North Shore and you never did kind of thing.

FRANNY: *(Rage; loses it.)* What are you? Nuts or something with that stuff? That is the stupidest stuff I ever heard of!

AUGGIE: Yuh, well, okay. Eddie Ryan may not be your greatest brain, or even your basic not-a-bad-guy-I-like-him kind of person, but, even you gotta' give the man credit: he's taken a shitty little sawed-off runt twerp kind of body and blown the doors right the fuck off. Do you agree with me on this?

(Franny goes to the squat bar; loads weights on the bar. Franny tries to ignore what Auggie is saying.)

FRANNY: Are we doin' legs or what?

AUGGIE: All's I'm sayin' is the man has had some wicked awful obstacles to overcome…

FRANNY: And all's I'm sayin' is "Are we doin' legs or what?"…

AUGGIE: Fine. *(Auggie hits another pose.)* Eat your heart out in Venice, California, Arnold…You are looking at the Testosterone Terminator: August Amoré! *(Another pose.)* That is Amoré, motherfucker: as in Italiano for *Love!* *(Auggie yells a beast-like yell.)* Arggggh!

FRANNY: *Will you come onnn!* Evvie and Dede are sleepin'!

AUGGIE: Oh, shit, sorry, sorry.

FRANNY: C'mon! You're up!

(Auggie steps in to the squat rack, lifts the bar-bell on to his shoulders, steps backwards, does squats, Franny spots.)

FRANNY: You hear what your pal Asshole Eddie Ryan did over Glen Asaro's gym, yesterday?

(Auggie continues to do squats, grunts a "no.")

FRANNY: He was spottin' Glen's last set of bench presses. Glen is about to pop his normal final set: five reps of 385's, or somethin' wicked in-human like that…

AUGGIE: The man's an animal…

FRANNY: Go all the way down.

AUGGIE: If I go all the way down, I ain't comin' all the way up!

FRANNY: Do it! I'll help you!

(Auggie does.)

FRANNY: Asshole Eddie Ryan swaggers up to Glen…speakin' with this bullshit phoney Southern accent he picked up in prison, right?…He bets Glen fifty bucks Glen can't burn out with twelve reps with 315…

AUGGIE: You are shitting me! You bet Glen Asaro he can't make twelve reps with 315, he'll make *twenty* reps with 315!

FRANNY: Exact. So Glen says "You're on"…does his first ten presses, easy, right? Asshole Eddie's on the spotter's stand behind him, watchin' close…knows he's losin' fifty bucks, if he doesn't think of something, fast, right?…So…all's'a'sudden dickhead Ryan plucks the bar out of Glen's hands, before Glen can get to twelve, says "I told you you'd never finish!," and walks out the door.

AUGGIE: You are makin' this up!

FRANNY: I'm tellin' ya! Dickhead Ryan goes out the door, throws the bar into his pick-up, drives off God knows where! If he ever sets his foot in Gold's Gym, again, Glen's gonna' rip his pecker off! Fast Eddie Ryan: your pal.

AUGGIE: The man's a comic *genius!*

FRANNY: The man's a comic *asshole!* Eddie Ryan's got himself banned from every gym, ten towns around. Jack Meany, the new guy that runs the "Y" —nicest guy you'd ever wanna' meet, yes?…

AUGGIE: *(Gestures showing he's not entirely certain that Jack Meany is in fact the "nicest guy you'd ever wanna' meet.")*

FRANNY:…He rescinded Ryan's "Y" card! Tore it up. Null, void, cancelled, revoked, history!

AUGGIE: Eddie Ryan's never made friends, easy, or kept friends, too long, it's true.

FRANNY: "Asshole" is the word that springs to mind. We're staring at the 21st-Century, yes? And is he not still into singin' old Bo Diddley tunes? Yes or no? Yes or no?

AUGGIE: Yes.

FRANNY: Yes! He was annoying doing this when he was seven, he was annoying doing this when he was seventeen, and he is annoying doing this when he is thirty-seven, yes? *[Note: Use correct age of actor, here.]* Yes or no? *Am I right on this?*

AUGGIE: It's just the music he likes.

FRANNY: Starts with "A," ends with "hole."

(Auggie weakens, his set loses form.)

FRANNY: You never finished your set. Go for three more reps.

AUGGIE: I'm dead…

FRANNY: What do you mean you're dead? Alls you've lifted so far this mornin' is one coffee and three Munchkins! Come on! Two more! Do it! *(Ad libs in Italian**)* **Come on, you're lazy! Make an effort!

AUGGIE: *(Answers in Italian**)* **Okay, but only two and then I'm finished!

(Auggie does one more squat; starts to fold. Franny eases the weight by lifting the bar with his fingers. Auggie finishes his final squat.)

FRANNY: Uno…duei! You got it.

AUGGIE: Mug up?

FRANNY: Okay, mug up.

(Auggie goes quickly to mirror, poses: highlighting his quads.)

AUGGIE: I'm just gonna' tell you one thing: a lot of local hearts are gonna' break when they see this leg-development. *(Hits a pose.)* You just get better and better, Amoré.

(Auggie goes upstage to bench, picks up magazine. Franny goes to downstage bench and length of lumper. Starts to measure out board to saw, as Auggie chats.)

I was readin' this article here where Mario Martinez bends his bars every time he works out. Every day, he's gotta' straighten 'em out with a hammer before he can start his morning routine. When he was a kid, maybe 15 or 16, he could already clean and jerk 400 pounds! Mario Martinez. M.M. Maximum Mass.

FRANNY: If that "I've got'ta' be bigger than everybody" power-lifter kind of mentality is what you're lookin' for, I say "fine," I say "great." But, my goal's never just "Get bigger"…it's…

AUGGIE: *(Completes Franny's thought.)*…"Bigger and Better"…

FRANNY:…"Bigger and Better"…You better believe it! You look at Martinez, he may be able ta' lift his house off the ground, but, the man is *smooth*. And, as you well know, as far as I myself am personally concerned, "smooth" is a dirty word. Shreaded: that's the ticket!

(Franny begins to saw board.)

AUGGIE: I'm with you on that, but, you don't have to play the priest in the pulpet here or nothin'. I'm just sayin' that Martinez bends his bars, that's all.

FRANNY: *(Unwarranted rage; throws saw down, madly.)* Martinez couldn't striate his wallet!

AUGGIE: *(Stunned.)* Jesus, okayyyy! What is *with* you, today, anyway? I can't open my goddam mouth without you bitin' my head off!

FRANNY: I'm a little edgey, that's all. I guess things are just kinda' *getting to me*. I apologize.

(Franny offers his hand to Auggie, who stands, fakes accord, but pulls his hand back, points at Franny.)

AUGGIE: Fuck you...

FRANNY AND AUGGIE: *(In unison; both smiling.)*...and fuck your Grandmother!

(They both laugh. Franny moves to bench. He is quite upset, still. Auggie moves across stage to start another set of squats. Franny breaks the silence; quietly.)

FRANNY: *(Without any warning.)* She's dying, Auggie. Dede. It's a definite fact: Dede is dying. Dr. Goldbaum says we've got to accept it.

(Auggie sets barbell back on squat rack. He walks around rack and faces Franny, across stage.)

AUGGIE: Jesus, Franny. He's gotta' have that wrong. I mean...Jesus! He's just one Jew doctor, right? Out of how many? I mean, there are a million of them out there, right?

FRANNY: We had her in to Childrens Hospital for treatments maybe fifty times, now. She's throwin' up all the time. Her hair's fallin' out. She ain't gettin' no better, I can tell you that. I'm pullin' the plug, Aug. I'm not putting her through any of that no more. I can't see the point no more. It's gotta' be in God's hands now. I'm pullin' the plug.

(Franny sits down and sobs. Auggie stands by, watching his friend. He thinks of various things he might do to help, but does nothing. Finally, Franny looks up.)

FRANNY: You say nothin' on this to nobody. I'll hav'ta' kill you if you so much as breathe a word of this! You get me?

AUGGIE: I swear on my father's grave.

FRANNY: Good.

END OF SCENE ONE

Scene Two
THE REUNION

Music In: Bo Diddley tune. Note: At first, music source is cassette, played over auditorium loudspeaker. Lights crossfade to Fast Eddie Ryan, same age as Franny, but much, much shorter, much, much stronger. Fast Eddie wears California weight-lifting togs: flowery, baggy pants, tank top on cut-down sweat-shirt, Gold's gym high-tops. He is extremely colorful, extremely out of place. Fast Eddie bursts into spotlight; yells.

FAST EDDIE: Argggghhhh!

(Fast Eddie holds a pose, center stage. Note: Music fades under. Fast Eddie is now source of Bo Diddley tune. He is prancing about, practicing a rather energetic dance/posing routine in the imagined "mirror," downstage center: out front. Franny stands sawing wood, opposite side of stage. He is repairing the ramp. Fast Eddie dances and sings as he snaps from pose to pose, flexing his biceps, popping his glutes. Finally, he looks over and smiles at an astonished Franny.)

FAST EDDIE: It feels good to be back, Fran…

FRANNY: Back in shape, or back in town?

FAST EDDIE: Town. I never got out of shape.

(Hits new pose, bends over, drops trousers, exposes red bikini briefs…and glutes.)

See these glutes pop? That's 'cause I cut out all egg proteins. Egg proteins'll smooth out your glutes faster than chocolate fucking pudding. You look at your real super-stars…Flex Wheeler, Lee Haney, Dorian Yates, Aaron Baker, Lee Priest, Paul Dillet…these guys have striated glutes that make you think their asses are packed full of walnuts. You think any of them touch egg proteins? I say "hell, no!" No egg proteins, and triple sets of squats, three days a week: that's the ticket.

(Sings, again; then, smiles at Franny.)

FAST EDDIE: How's the family?

FRANNY: Family's good..

FAST EDDIE: Evvie's good?

FRANNY: Evvie's good, yuh.

FAST EDDIE: Dede: she's good, too?

FRANNY: *(Drives nail into ramp.)* Yuh, Dede's good, too.

FAST EDDIE: You makin' enough money doin' this?

FRANNY: I do okay.

FAST EDDIE: You still lumpin' for extra money, now and then?

FRANNY: *(Drives nail into ramp.)* Now and then, yuh.

FAST EDDIE: I seen Auggie drivin' away.

FRANNY: *(Drives nail into ramp.)* Yuh, he works out here regular. He enjoys his workouts.

FAST EDDIE: The man's wastin' his time. He's lookin' fatter than ever.

FRANNY: *(Drives nail into ramp.)* He likes to eat, yuh.

FAST EDDIE: It's *what* he eats: I seen him eatin' two-three-four helpings of fried dough down at Fiesta…

FRANNY: He's got his own unique nutrition program, yuh.

FAST EDDIE: What are you, crazy? "Unique nutrition program"? The man eats like a toilet!

(Walks across stage toward Franny who looks up from completing his work on ramp.)

FRANNY: What?

FAST EDDIE: You still hate me, don't'cha'?

(Fast Eddie sits on bench, wraps knees with ace bandages. Franny tosses hammer into toolbox; stands, faces Fast Eddie.)

FRANNY: I don't still hate you, Eddie. I wouldn't honor you with still hating you. I don't even *think* about you. You don't even *happen* for me! You wanna' pay me five bucks a session to work out here, I say "fine." I say "I'm open to the public." I say "business is business." I say "I'll take *anybody's* five bucks." That's the whole deal here. No hate in it. Far as I'm concerned, if you fell in the ocean and sunk straight down, I wouldn't lift a finger, either way. Somebody walks in here and says "Fast Eddie Ryan's out there drowning!", I say "Oh, yuh? What are we doin' today? Legs, arms or abs?"

(There is a long pause. Fast Eddie stares at Franny, eyeball to eyeball. Fast Eddie smiles.)

FAST EDDIE: Abs.

(Suddenly, Fast Eddie turns away from Franny, faces imagined "mirror", lifts shirt, displays his chiseled abdominal muscles.)

FAST EDDIE: Check out these gut ruts.

(Rolls his stomach displaying abs.)

There's only one way to chisel abs: work the lower chamber first with V-ups til your inside lowers collapse; then, a hundred quick upper-ab crunches, non-stop.

(Fast Eddie sits on bench, upstage right, begins a series of leg raises and V-ups.)

FAST EDDIE: You got yourself four basic gut-muscles you've gotta' shread: obliquus externus, obliquus internus, transversalis and rectus abdominis.

(Pauses.)

You still competing, or you give up?

FRANNY: *(Sweeping up saw-dust, putting tool box away beside stairs.)* What's this?

FAST EDDIE: I was thinkin' of maybe throwin' Mr. North Shore into my schedule, for old times' sake…while I'm workin' up to Mr. Massachusetts kind of thing. You ever tryin' Mr. North Shore, again, or what?

FRANNY: Don't know why you're worryin' about me, Eddie. We ain't in the same category, unless one of your Joe Weider send-away books shows you how to grow a couple of inches.

FAST EDDIE: Height, delts, or dick?

FRANNY: Height.

FAST EDDIE: Okay, fine, I'm a short guy. I know it. It don't bother me none. You know what Paul Simon says: "God bless the goods we were given, and God bless the U.S. of A.…I'm havin' a good time."

FRANNY: Who's Paul Simon?

FAST EDDIE: What are you? Shittin' me? Who's Paul Simon? "Bridge Over Troubled Water"? "You Can Call Me Al"? "Born at the Right Time"?

FRANNY: Oh, yuh. He's short, too, right?

FAST EDDIE: Yuh, right, Francis. You got it. The man's had seven or eight or nine platinum records and you call him short. You got it.
(Fast Eddie moves to squat bench.)

FAST EDDIE: Spot me. I'm doin' full squats.
(Franny spots Fast Eddie watching his form, carefully, competitively.)

FAST EDDIE: You hit 200 or 300 of these, three days a week, your ass'll be ripped so wicked nice you'll be able to pop the caps off your Bud bottles by backin' up to 'em!

FRANNY: That's not one of my personal goals.

FAST EDDIE: *(As he completes set of squats.)* I gotta' tell you something, Francis. I'll admit it: I've been in hospitals and I've been in jails and I've had beers with the devil, himself, that's what. But now I'm out and I'm back and I'm totally clean and I've learned my lesson. And now there's nothin' can scare me, not now, not any more…nothin' and nobody. No fuckin' body. And there's nothin' or nobody's gonna' stop me, neither. I'm goin' for the limit, man. I'm goin' the gold…I'm goin' for Mr. Olympia: Mr. O.

FRANNY: *(Laughs.)* What?

FAST EDDIE: Something funny?

FRANNY: Nope. Nothin's funny, Eddie.

FAST EDDIE: Confidence is my main ticket. I got myself into one jam after another because I lacked confidence. *(Strikes a pose.)* I got confidence comin' out'ta both my ears now. *(Strikes another pose.)* You wouldn't personally know what it feels like, 'cause you've never been there...sold-out auditorium, national TV hookup, top-level judges who've sat lookin' at the Gods, man, the fucking Gods... and who are they starin' at now? I'm gonna' tell ya' who: Eddie Ryan, Prospect Street, Gloucester, Massachusetts, U. S. of fucking A.

FRANNY: Where'd all this happen?

FAST EDDIE: California, Francis. California...where everything happens.

FRANNY: What contest are we talkin' here?

FAST EDDIE: Last year's Mr. USA, Francis. Didn't you hear?

FRANNY: You did last year's Mr. USA?

FAST EDDIE: I didn't *do* it. I *saw* it. Front row of the 2nd balcony. I invested major bucks in my own personal future and I flew out to California...three nights in a 1st class motel...my own Hertz Rent-a-Car car...a semi-private tour of the TV stars' homes...plus workin' out *triples,* every day: morning workouts at Gold's Gym in Venice, afternoon workouts at Muscle Beach, and light late-night workouts at World Gym. Fast Eddie Ryan has spent his money and he has seen the Gods of Body-building! And he will *do* Mr. USA after he *wins* Mr. Massachusetts.

FRANNY: *(Softly.)* Yuh. Me, too.

FAST EDDIE: What's that? You say something?

FRANNY: Yuh. I said "Me, too"...I'll do Mr USA after I win Mr. Massachusetts, too.

FAST EDDIE: What's that: some kind of joke?

FRANNY: Yuh, you got it, Eddie. That's some kind of a joke.

(Fast Eddie crosses to water thermos, upstage right, drinks cup of water. Franny lies back on bench, center, does light warm-up presses.)

FAST EDDIE: I'll tell you the difference between the Goods and the Gods, m'boy: that one extra fat little "O." That's all it takes to hold you back. How do you break out'ta' that "Goods" plateau? The Two "D"s: Dream and Desire. D-R-E-A-M and D-E-S-I-R-E. If you don't Dream it and you don't Desire it, you get the third "D": Dick! I Dream it and I Desire it, Francis, but I lack one thing...

FRANNY: *(Interjecting.)* The dick?

FAST EDDIE: Right. You got it. I got up at 3:30 this mornin' and drove all the way up here to tell you I got no dick! I'm talkin' about the "J.E.," Farina: the Judge's Eye. That's why I'm here. That's why I'm takin' shit from the one guy in Gloucester who's lookin' to sign my name on my tombstone: you: Francis Farina: a nowhere "Portegee" with a two-bit gym in his garage…a local-yocal who looks way out'ta shape, but he knows more about shreddin' muscle than any Joe Weider or Joe Gold or Arnold, and that's the God's honest. I got the Dream and I got the Desire, but you got the Judge's Eye. That's why I paid my five bucks, and that's why I set foot in your house. Period…

(Fast Eddie returns to squat rack for second set.)

FAST EDDIE:…So, check out my squats.

(Fast Eddie executes a squat. Franny answers without even looking, his back to Eddie.)

FRANNY: They're not full enough.

FAST EDDIE: That's stupid. My ass is hitting your floor, already. Any fuller, I'll be under your garage!

FRANNY: *(Moves into spotter's position behind Fast Eddie.)* Your legs are too spread. You wanna' work your glutes better, spread 'em less. Change the torq…

(Fast Eddie changes his foot-positioning.)

FAST EDDIE: How's this?

FRANNY: Try it.

(Fast Eddie squats, winces.)

FAST EDDIE: I pulled something.

FRANNY: That's your full glute workin'. Probably the first time you ever worked it right.

FAST EDDIE: Good. I like this. Maybe I'll pay you six bucks.

FRANNY: Five's my price. Five's what you'll pay me.

FAST EDDIE: Maybe I'll come regular…

FRANNY: I keep lumpers' hours: training sessions start at 4 a.m. I close up at noon-time.

FAST EDDIE: When do you do your own workout?

FRANNY: Right off, when I open.

FAST EDDIE: You got a training partner?

FRANNY: Nothing official. Auggie usually trains with me…

FAST EDDIE: Maybe I'll join ya's…

FRANNY: Suit yourself. It's a free country, 's'long as you pay your five bucks a workout, cash, no credit, no checks, no plastic. Oh, yuh…there's one other thing.

FAST EDDIE: What's that?

FRANNY: No singin' no Bo Diddley tunes.

FAST EDDIE: Ever?

FRANNY: "Ever" is your own business. In here: I mean no singin' 'em in here...during your workouts.

FAST EDDIE: Deal.

FRANNY: *(Nods; speaks quietly.)* Deal.

(The lights narrow to spotlights on Fast Eddie and Franny.)

END OF SCENE TWO

Scene Three
"DADDY! DADDY!"

Music In: Final lyrics of Paul Simon's "Havin' A Good Time"..."So God bless the goods I was given/God bless the US of A/ and God bless our standard of livin'...I'm, having a good time..." etc, etc...through sax riff. Franny and Fast Eddie do a mini-workout for two minutes, wordlessly, in spotlights to rhythm of Paul Simon's music until its completion...a sort of body-builder's ballet. Fast Eddie super-sets bi-cep curls and tri-ceps raises. Franny alternates between lat pull-downs and bi-cep curls. At the end of the music, the lights brighten and widen into new scene.

FAST EDDIE: Does Evvie know I'm back?

FRANNY: In town?

FAST EDDIE: Yes, in town.

FRANNY: You're feedin' stories about your doin' this and that and shit to the *Gloucester Times,* right? "Former Mr. North Shore Returns Home" kinda' crap. I mean, I open last night's paper, nothin' but you plastered all over the goddam thing. Evvie'd hav'ta' be *illiterate* not ta' know you're back.

FAST EDDIE: Does she know I'm workin' out with you in her house?

FRANNY: You ain't in the house. You're in the *garage.* You ain't in Evvie's house and you ain't ever gonna' be in Evvie's house, again, in your lifetime, unless you're lookin' for sudden death and no overtime! You get me on this?

(There is an embarrassed pause.)

FAST EDDIE: Evvie come in here much?

FRANNY: No women are allowed in the gym here, 'less they pay five bucks to train.

FAST EDDIE: You get many women training here?

FRANNY: Not too many, yet, no.

FAST EDDIE: How many?

FRANNY: So far? None.

FAST EDDIE: None is definitely "not too many."

FRANNY: I've only been open a month or so. I haven't taken out no ads or nothin'…just word of mouth, ya' know, from the guys I used'ta' train up the "Y" or down Cody's Gym, years back…

FAST EDDIE: Cody's was the best.

FRANNY: Yuh, it was good.

FAST EDDIE: Mike ran a straightforward gym.

FRANNY: This is true.

FAST EDDIE: No chrome bullshit. Nobody wearing Spandex. No scrawny 10K runners or boney lettuce-eating aerobic bunnies that look like they're all ready to be cremated. Mike Cody's gym was nothin' but real men and cold steel.

(Does dumb-bell curls as he gets lost in a memory.)

FAST EDDIE: We didn't know shit, then — nothin' *scientific.* Just liftin', liftin', liftin'…

(Pauses; continues his squats.)

You, me, Glen, Mike, Mick, John and Austin Connors…

FRANNY: Petey, Porker, Guido…

FAST EDDIE: Poor fuckin' Guido…

FRANNY: Least he died on the water.

FAST EDDIE: Those were the days, huh, Franny?

FRANNY: Those were the days, Eddie, yuh.

(Suddenly, we hear Dede calling from off-stage.)

DEDE: *(Offstage.)* Daddy…

(The two men stiffen — freeze — at the sound of the girl's voice.)

DEDE: *(Offstage.)* Daddy?

(Both men turn to door; startled. They share a moment. Franny calls out.)

FRANNY: Don't come in here! Stay there til I come get ya'!

(Franny looks at Fast Eddie.)

FRANNY: Out! *(Goes to door; holds same open.)* Now! Out!

(Fast Eddie nods. He picks up his towel, sweat-shirt, gym bag.)

FRANNY: *Move it!*

FAST EDDIE: *(Not happy.)* Okay, fine, I'm goin'…*(Exits.)*
(Franny sets long wooden "bar" into place locking garage doors, wordlessly. Franny looks out of glass pane in door to where Fast Eddie exited, to make sure that Fast Eddie is really gone. Satisfied that he's alone in the gym, Franny moves to door to house: to Dede.)
FRANNY: I'm coming, Honey…*(He opens the door. We see Dede, sitting in a wheelchair, her bald head covered by a hat. She is adorable, but, obviously very, very ill.)* You ready to count boats, or what?
DEDE: I'm ready, Daddy.
FRANNY: Let's do it.

(Franny wheels Dede to double-doors. They exit. We hear: Joe Cocker singing final verse of "You Are So Beautiful." The lights fade to transition light.)

END OF SCENE THREE

Scene Four
AUGGIE IS AMAZED

Video switches on: TV monitor set on shelf over refrigerator. We see: A Gold's Gym work-out video playing without sound. At the same instant, Music in: Randy Newman's "Short People." Lights up on Auggie, and Fast Eddie, entering. Fast Eddie moves into spot-light, yells "Arggghhh!" Auggie moves into spot-light, yells "Arggghhh!" They then face each other, yell "Oooogh Oooogh Oooogh Oooogh!" Leap into air and execute a "high 5." They begin training together. Fast Eddie sits on Auggie legs on bench, as Auggie lies on back on floor doing sit-ups. Franny joins them, entering from house. He has a bandage on his leg, moves with a slight limp, as he re-sets weights on bench-press bar, readying bar for Fast Eddie's set. Fast Eddie sits on Auggie's legs, rudely criticising Auggie's workout.

FAST EDDIE: What you're doin' wrong is repeating the same workout, over and over.
AUGGIE: I guess…
FAST EDDIE: I *know*. You get bored and your muscles get bored. What

you've got'ta do is vary the exercise. You know when your muscle's pumpin' up good.

AUGGIE: I s'pose…

FAST EDDIE: Stands to fuckin' reason, yes? You do the exact same routine, over and over, you ain't getting the pump. It just ain't happening.

(Auggie finishes his set of sit-ups, nearly collapses.)

FAST EDDIE: You're out of shape.

AUGGIE: I ate way too much eggplant at my mother's, last night…

FAST EDDIE: You're way out of shape…

(Franny moves to downstage side of bar-bell and adds final weight to long bar, looks over at Fast Eddie ragging Auggie.)

FAST EDDIE: I could eat eggplant til it was comin' out of my ears, and I would never show fatigue like you're showin'. You're way out of shape…Come on! Six more, Amoré! Come on! One, two, three…

(Fast Eddie notices Franny's limp and the bandage on his leg.)

FAST EDDIE: What's with your leg?

FRANNY: I hurt it.

FAST EDDIE: Yuh? How?

FRANNY: Doin' stuff.

(Auggie and Franny exchange a glance.)

FAST EDDIE: *(Continues riding Auggie.)* You got muscles in there, Amoré, ya' know that? I mean, everybody's got muscles in there…even *nuns.* You just gotta' uncover 'em…get the fat off…let yo'r muscles see the light of day!

(Auggie smiles sickly, holding his temper, as Fast Eddie laughs at each of his own [alleged] jokes, whilst continuing his cruel diatribe.)

FAST EDDIE:…I mean, you're probably ripped wicked nice under all that linguisa and all them jelly donuts, August, but who the hell's gonna' know what's buried under the six inches of disgusting blubber, right? Unless, a'course, they do surgery? C'mon, six more sit-up. Let's go! One…two…three…

(Fast Eddie guffaws. Auggie does six more sit-ups. Franny yells across to stop Fast Eddie's insults.)

FRANNY: You're set up, Ryan!

FAST EDDIE: Four…five…six…

(Franny yells to Fast Eddie, again.)

FRANNY: I said "You're set up, Ryan"!

FAST EDDIE: I'm doing my presses. Who's spottin' me?

AUGGIE: I'm spottin'.

(Auggie gets out from under Eddie, moves into spotting position. Fast Eddie moves to bench, stopping downstage left at imagined "mirror" to roll his pecs. He then lies back on the bench, readies himself for his set, whilst continuing his remarks to Auggie, who hovers above Fast Eddie, spotting. Franny stands off to one side, watching, thinking)

FAST EDDIE: I'm workin' my outer pecs. What are your flabby tits up to now, Amoré? Double "E" cup, or what?

(Fast Eddie chortles; executes his first bench press. Franny discreetly touches one end of the barbell, causing the weight to go out of balance.) *(Screams up to Auggie.)* Hey! You touch the bar?

AUGGIE: *(Smiling.)* Uh uh. I'm standing here, spottin'. I didn't touch nothin'…

(To Franny.) Did I?

FRANNY: *(Smiling.)* Uh uh.

FAST EDDIE: Jesus, the end dropped.

(Fast Eddie starts another rep. Franny touches end of bar, again. Bar tips again, frightening Fast Eddie.)

FAST EDDIE: Heyyy! You're touchin' the fuckin' bar!

AUGGIE: I'm not touchin' any bar…

FRANNY: *(Smiling.)* He's not touchin' any bar, Ed.

AUGGIE: *(Smiling.)* Wonder what's causin' this?…Looks ta' me like your right arm's developin' bigger than your left arm?

FAST EDDIE: What are you givin' me here?

AUGGIE: *(Overacting.)* Check this out, Fran…

(Franny pretends to compare Fast Eddie's arms, seriously.)

FRANNY: *(Smiling.)* By God, I think you're right, Aug. You been usin' protein powder, Ed?

FAST EDDIE: What's this? Some kind of joke? 'a'course I been using protein powder.

FRANNY: How much of it?

FAST EDDIE: Three 16-ounce glasses a day, mixed in skimmed milk.

AUGGIE: Which hand you been using to drink from?

FAST EDDIE: What kinda' question's that? My left hand. Why?

AUGGIE: *(Overacting.)* There you go…

FRANNY: *(Overacting.)* There's your answer…

AUGGIE: *(Overacting.)* It's a hell of a shame…

FRANNY: *(Overacting.)* *Damn* shame!

FAST EDDIE: I never heard such ridiculous horse-shit!

(Fast Eddie rests the bar on his chest. He tries to raise the bar again, to

return the bar-bell to the rest-slots, but can not move it off of his chest. He is pinned under the bar-bell. He yells at Auggie.)

FAST EDDIE: Hey! Are you spottin' me here, Amoré?

(Fast Eddie is literally pinned under the weight. He screams for help.)

FAST EDDIE: Hey! Get me the fuck out'ta' here! I am pinned under this fuckin' bar!

(Franny and Auggie pretend not to hear Fast Eddie's screams.)

AUGGIE: Check out my arms: they're symmetrical, right?

(They move in front of the mirror. They pretend to compare arm-symmetry. They both pose and playact intense concentration.)

FRANNY: You look a little bigger on the left. Check me out.

AUGGIE: You look bigger on the right.

FAST EDDIE: *(Screams.)* Hey! Stop screwin' around! I'm pinned under this fuckin' bar! Hey! Hey! *HEY!*

AUGGIE: You've probably been lifting your beers with your right hand, Fran.

FRANNY: Damn, that's it, Aug! I hav'ta' try ta' remember ta' drink two beers at once…

AUGGIE: One in each hand…

FRANNY:…One in each hand. Exact.

FAST EDDIE: *(Screams.)* Farina! Get me the fuck out'ta' here!

FRANNY: Somebody callin'? *(Playacts realization.)* You want something, Eddie?

FAST EDDIE: Get me out'ta' here! My fuckin' chest is cavin' in! I'm pinned under 315 here, goddammit!

FRANNY: *(Playacts being upset.)* Oh, God, sorrrrrrrryyyyy, Eddie…

AUGGIE: *(Moves in slow motion, as if under water.)* Oh, Jeez, sorrrrry, Eddie…I'm hurrying right over there…

(Auggie and Franny help Fast Eddie lift the ends of the bar-bell, find the rest-slots. Fast Eddie crawls off bench. He rubs his chest, shakes out his arms and pecs. He is humiliated; enraged.)

FAST EDDIE: Very fucking funny.

AUGGIE: We were so totally into checkin' our arm symmetry…

FRANNY: The balance of bigness…

AUGGIE:…We didn't hear you…

FRANNY:…We didn't hear you.

FAST EDDIE: Very fuckin' funny, you two. Fucking hilarious…

(Fast Eddie goes to mirror. With discernable panic, He compares the size of his right arm to the size of his left arm.)

FAST EDDIE: What's with you two blow'ahs, anyway? My arms are exactly the same size.

(Auggie and Franny are frantically trying not to laugh. Franny turns upstage, away from Fast Eddie. Auggie's laugh cannot be contained. It explodes.)

AUGGIE: *Harrrrgggghhh!*

(Auggie's laughter infects Franny, whose laugh now explodes out of him, too. Franny and Auggie now sputter, giggle and guffaw, openly. They are crippled with laughter. They cannot stop. Fast Eddie is outraged.)

FAST EDDIE: This's your idea of a joke? This's your idea of something funny? Some of us are serious about bodybuilding, ya' know? Some of us are lookin' ta' improve, ta' be something? Fast Eddie Ryan ain't lookin' ta' be held back from body perfection, ta' be dragged down to the likes of you two local-nowhere-wick'id-fuckin'-out'ta'-shape-yokels. Fast Eddie Ryan is big-time! Fast Eddie Ryan is somewhere neither of you never fuckin' dreamed of bein'...Fast Eddie Ryan is fuckin' beautiful ta' look at! Fast Eddie Ryan is a winner! *(Nods triumphantly, as though he's won the contest, the insult-bout.)* Fast Eddie Ryan is out of here. Fast Eddie Ryan is history.

(He exits the garage. He stops just outside door, returns; spits his words at Auggie and Franny.)

FAST EDDIE: I didn't get out'ta my bed at 3:30 in the fuckin' mornin', drive all the way up here to your miserable fuckin' garage in the fuckin' dark, ta' not do my workout. I paid my five bucks and I'm workin' out! Just stay the fuck away from me, both a'ya's!

(Fast Eddie drops his gym bag back down on to the floor. He goes to the bench; strips weights down to 135-lbs: two Olympic plates.)

FAST EDDIE: I'll do this myself! I need no fuckin' spotter.

(He begins a fresh set of presses, counting out loud, loudly.)

FAST EDDIE: That's one, that's two, that's three, that's four, that's five, that's six, that's seven, that's eight, that's nine, that's ten...eleven... that is IT!

(Franny and Auggie are hysterical with laughter. Fast Eddie returns the bar-bell to the rest-slots on the bench. He stands quickly, poses in mirror, tightening his pumped-up muscles. He screams a primal scream.)

FAST EDDIE: *Arggggghhhh! (He glares at Franny and Auggie.)* You assholes gonna' work out, or are you gonna' sit there laughin' like hyenas?

FRANNY: Come on, start your presses, I'll spot you.

(Franny and Auggie go to bench. Auggie lies on his back, ready to start his bench presses. Fast Eddie poses in front of "mirror.")

FAST EDDIE: I'm practicing my new posing routine for Mr. O!

(Fast Eddie sings, dances, poses. Auggie falls off of bench, laughing, again. Fast Eddie is furious, again. Suddenly, we hear: Evvie's voice, offstage, calling to Franny.)

EVVIE: *(Offstage.)* Francis?…*(Evvie knocks on the door.)* Francis?

(The three men freeze. There is an emotional shock felt among them. Franny calls out.)

FRANNY: Don't come in here!

EVVIE: *(Offstage.)* I need you to come in the house, right away, Francis.

FRANNY: Okay. I'm comin' in.

(Franny looks at Fast Eddie. He then exchanges a glance with Auggie. He moves quickly to the door. He speaks to Evvie through the door, before exiting.)

FRANNY: Move back from the door, so's I can open it. I'm comin' in.

(He exits the garage into house, sneaking out of the door and quickly closing same behind him. Note: When door is open, we are able to see glimpse of Evvie. She is dressed in old plaid bathrobe, hair up, exhausted. There is a moment's silence. Fast Eddie breaks it.)

FAST EDDIE: She calls him "Francis"?

AUGGIE: I guess.

FAST EDDIE: Stupid fuckin' name.

AUGGIE: No worse than Edward, is it?

FAST EDDIE: Yuh, but who ever calls me "Edward"? Evvie never called me "Edward"…

AUGGIE: *(Shrugs.)*

FAST EDDIE: They gettin' along?

AUGGIE: Is who getting along?

FAST EDDIE: You know…Evvie and Francis. They gettin' along good?

AUGGIE: Evvie and Franny? Sure. The best. Why would you ever think different?

FAST EDDIE: I dunno'…my mother never called my father "James" unless she was pissed off at him. She called him "Jim" when they were getting along…and "Jimmy" when they were in their bedroom kinda' thing.

AUGGIE: She must'a called him "Jimmy" a lot!, right?…Thirteen kids! *(Laughs.)*

FAST EDDIE: Wicked humorous, Amoré…You ought'ta be on the stage. There's one leavin' in five minutes.

AUGGIE: Evvie and Franny are getting along fine, Eddie. Don't worry about them?

FAST EDDIE: I don't. *(Fast Eddie powders his hands again, readies himself for another set. Auggie fixes weights on the barbell for his presses.)* How come she's not allowed in here?

AUGGIE: Who's not allowed in here?

FAST EDDIE: Evvie.

AUGGIE: Who says she's not?

FAST EDDIE: You could see that for yourself. She just called in from behind the door.

AUGGIE: Maybe you're reading things into things?

FAST EDDIE: I dunno'…She always used'ta like to watch me work out…

AUGGIE: Yuh, well, it's only ha'pahst four in the mornin', still. Maybe she comes in here to watch Franny work out, later in the day.

FAST EDDIE: He ain't workin' out later in no day! He's workin' out now — mornings — when he opens up!

AUGGIE: Jesus, Eddie! What do I know? I'm just tryin' ta' do my workout, same as you, okay?

(Both men attend to their exercises for a few moments. Auggie goes to fridge, finds sandwich, starts to eat it.)

FAST EDDIE: What's up with Farina, anyhow? He's way out of shape.

AUGGIE: He's coming back.

FAST EDDIE: Yuh, so's Halloween! He looks like he hasn't lifted anything in years!

AUGGIE: Maybe he's been busy.

(Long pause. Fast Eddie goes down-stage and super-sets tri-cep raises with light barbell. Auggie sits on bench, upstage, eats four quick bites of his tuna salad sandwich.)

FAST EDDIE: You lumpin' much?

AUGGIE: I'm back ta' lumpin', part-time, yuh. *(Puts sandwich down on bench between his legs, starts his set of bench presses.)* I was workin' over North Shore Fish for a couple'a years, but they closed down, sold the property. Got turned into a fitness center. Some Boston yuppie-Mafioso-shake-your-rump type of person started it up. Nautilus, aerobics, white Reeboks, that shit. Five-six hundred a year, nobody joined, place folded after maybe six months. Building's still for sale, all boarded up. I did some fishin' and lobsterin' for a while, but, you know, that's pretty dead…

(Finishes set. Eats rest of sandwich. Fast Eddie moves to bench, lies back. Auggie moves behind bench, into spotter's position.)

FAST EDDIE: Gloucester's changin' wick'id… *(Executes a press.)* Hard ta' believe, really… *(Executes a press.)* I went down ta' mornin' shape-up at State Wharf, yesterday, lookin' for work. I thought I might do some lumpin'. Not for the money: for the fitness-benefit… *(Executes a press.)*

AUGGIE: There's no work…

FAST EDDIE: *(Executes a press.)* Nothin'. Must'a be'n fifty men waitin' for work, and Philly Shimma calls out only maybe nine jobs, max…

AUGGIE: It's pathetic!

FAST EDDIE: *(Executes a press.)* Eight-nine-ten years ago, there must'a be'n two hundred lumpers workin' regular!

FAST EDDIE: I heard he quit his regular job over Gorton's to do this. That so?

AUGGIE: Who?

(Fast Eddie sets bar-bell back on rack, rises, crosses to thermos, drinks cup of water.)

FAST EDDIE: Don't wiseass me, okay, Amoré? We ain't been talkin' about the Pope, have we? We're talkin' Farina here, okay? I saw Porker Martino down to his sister Rose's used clothing boutique. We go the usual "Hi"—"Hi"—"How'ya' been?"—"Good. How's yourself?"—"Good." Then I tell Rose she's lookin' good. This and that. Then I happen ta' mention to Porker I'm workin' out here, mornin's, he tells me Farina walked away from a big job—Head of Maintenance—over Gorton's. Profit sharing, sick leave, paid vacation, pension, the works, and this idiot quits it all to open a miserable gym in his miserable goddam garage, trainin' people like you for five bucks a session. Now this, ta' me, is fuckin' *unbelievable.*

AUGGIE: Maybe he's got his reasons, Eddie, huh? Maybe it ain't your business.

(Fast Eddie stares at Auggie.)

FAST EDDIE: You think what Farina's earning ain't my business? Think about what you're sayin'…

(Fast Eddie nods an inscrutable nod.)

AUGGIE: *(Astonished.)* You think about what *you're* sayin', huh?

FAST EDDIE: I'm doin' my fourth set. You spottin' me, or what?

(Fast Eddie lies on his back on the bench, starts a final set of presses. Auggie moves into spotting position.)

FAST EDDIE: *(Executes a press.)* Eight-nine-ten years ago, there must'a be'n two hundred lumpers workin' regular! *(Executes a press.)* If my father came back ta' earth, he wouldn't believe it! *(Executes a press.)* I personally never *left* earth, and I can't fuckin' believe it, myself! *(Fast Eddie executes eight more presses; finishes his set.)*

AUGGIE: You've been gone, Eddie. Gloucester's had it. Real estate's gone dead. Fishin's dead, too. So's lobsterin'. Lumpin' and fish-cuttin' are history! Hotels and tourist-restaurants are closin' left and right. I even hear the drug-dealers are leaving town, business is so far off.
(Fast Eddie slams bar into rack; jumps up, faces Auggie. Fast Eddie seems to have hurt feelings.)

FAST EDDIE: What's that s'pose'ta be? Some kind of *smart personal remark?*

AUGGIE: I didn't mean nothin' personal there, Ed.

FAST EDDIE: I hope ya' didn't, Amoré…unless you wanna' find your arm up your ass in the mornin'…

AUGGIE: Hey, come on, huh, Eddie? There's no need ta' for you to start squaring off with me here or nothin'! I said there was no smart personal remarks comin' at you from me, and I meant it, okay? But, I gotta' tell you something straight in your face, man to man: I've been takin' unrelentless vicious shit from you, all mornin', and frankly, I'm beginning to think enough's enough! You get me on this?

FAST EDDIE: You wanna' come at me, Amoré, huh? Come on! Come at me! Let's see what you got!
(Auggie rushes out from behind squat rack and heads toward Fast Eddie, bristling with anger.)

AUGGIE: Dont push me, Eddie! I'm warning you! I'm three times your size! If I hit you, you won't be playin' dead: you'll BE dead!

FAST EDDIE: I'm fucking shakin' in my shoes!
(The door opens. Franny enters, just as Auggie reaches the point at which he will have to hit Fast Eddie or back down.

AUGGIE: *(To Franny.)* What?
(Franny is ashen. He has changed into better, cleaner clothes. Franny's voice is soft. He is shaken. He rummages through his desk, looking for his Blue Cross card.)

FRANNY: I, uh, gotta' go off somewhere. Can you stick and cover me, Aug?
(Auggie and Fast Eddie whirl around to face Franny.)

AUGGIE: What's up?

FRANNY: Nothin's up. I just got'ta go off. Can you cover for me? I'm expectin' maybe fifteen workouts in between now and 10:30...

AUGGIE: You won't be back til 10:30?

FRANNY: I, uh, I dunno'. Why? You got something you gotta' do?

AUGGIE: Me? No. Nothin' special.

FRANNY: If I'm not back by 11, and you gotta' go off, just pull the door down and put a note on it. Tell people I'll be back when I get here.

AUGGIE: I'm okay. I'll cover for you...

FRANNY: I know Mick and Matza are comin' in at ha'pah'st seven...probably Mick's bringing Nicholas, too. Artie What'sis comes in at nine, never misses...

AUGGIE: It's okay. Don't sweat it. I'm on the case.

(Franny pauses at the door.)

FRANNY: Thanks, Aug.

AUGGIE: Hey, don't sweat it. I'm only doin' it for the money, okay?

(Franny smiles at his friend; exits. There is a small silence. Auggie turns and faces Fast Eddie.)

FAST EDDIE: What the fuck was that about?

AUGGIE: *(Shrugs.)*

FAST EDDIE: You think they're fightin' or something? Evvie and Farina: you think that's what's goin' on there?

AUGGIE: *(Shrugs.)*

FAST EDDIE: So, what do you think?

AUGGIE: *(Shrugs; takes cup of water from thermos on top of desk, near TV. His back is to Fast Eddie; he stares at video on TV.)*

FAST EDDIE: What is *with* you? I am asking you a question, Amoré. Are you deaf, or what?

(Auggie switches TV set off; turns, faces Fast Eddie.)

AUGGIE: Naw, I ain't deaf. I'm just fuckin' paralyzed from amazement from what I know about you, and from what you fuckin' know I know about you, huh?. I'm gonna' ask you a question, pal: How can you live with it, Eddie? Huh? How can you fuckin' live with it?

(Fast Eddie and Auggie continue to stare at one another, but, now, wordlessly. Lights fade down to single spotlight on Fast Eddie for a 3-count.)

END OF SCENE FOUR

Scene Five
AUGGIE HITS EDDIE

Note on transition:
1. Spotlight on Eddie. He turns away from Auggie, head down.
2. Music in: Jimmy Cliff "Many Rivers To Cross."
3. Spotlight now crossfades to Auggie, seated on bench, head down, 3-count. Fast Eddie exits in dark.
4. Spotlight now crossfades to Franny at door to house, head down. We see: Franny now has bandage on upper arm.
5. Light widen to full stage lighting.
6. Music crosses into on-stage radio: Jimmy Cliff "Many Rivers To Cross."

AUGGIE: *(He watches Franny a while.)* I heard.
　　(Auggie eats cruller from a take-out bag of food at his feet.)
FRANNY: How'd you hear?
AUGGIE: I dunno'…I hear things.
FRANNY: Yuh. So?
　　(Franny moves to bench, lies back, does light dumb-bell over-head raises. Music is now heard clearly on radio on set.)
AUGGIE: It's bad, huh?
FRANNY: I dunno. Yuh, it's bad.
AUGGIE: Does it hurt?
FRANNY: Me? I dunno'…Not too much.
AUGGIE: How's Dede?
FRANNY: Sleepin'…
AUGGIE: So?
FRANNY: So, we wait and see if it takes.
AUGGIE: Jesus, Franny. It ain't fair.
FRANNY: What ain't fair?
AUGGIE: Dede. All of it. The whole thing.
FRANNY: *(Explodes angrily.)* What is with you? I just got myself calmed down. I don't need you ta' get me goin', again, okay? *(Franny goes to radio, turns it off.)*
AUGGIE: You're right. Don't mind me, okay? I'll keep my dumb trap shut. *(Sets down his gym bag; takes coffees out of take-out bag; offers same to Franny.)*

AUGGIE: Coffee and sugarless whole wheat crullers from Mac Bell's new health food super-market, over Washington Street.

FRANNY: What's this?

AUGGIE: I'm watchin' what I eat.

(Goes to "mirror." Tries to fasten weight-lifting belt, nearly can't: it's grown too small for his girth. Note: A 2nd belt, smaller than other, is used here.)

Eddie's been riding my ass about, you know...my ass.

FRANNY: Eddie's been riding your ass about your ass?

AUGGIE: *(Poses; checks his stomach in reflection in "mirror.")* Yuh, that, too...Look at me! I musta' gained 25 pounds! *(Pats his belly.)* I don't understand it! I'm here every day. I never miss a work-out. *(He eats his whole wheat cruller; studies himself in "mirror.")* I got'ta' make the effort.

FRANNY: Why? You like to eat. Why not eat?

AUGGIE: What are you *sayin'*?

FRANNY: Hey, look, Aug, *really*...You ain't bein' scouted for the Olympics or nothin', right?

AUGGIE: That's no reason not to look your best! *(Shrugs.)* What am I tellin' *you* this for?

(Auggie crosses to bench. Franny finishes his set; looks at his watch. He stands, crosses to door, looks out of window-pane.)

FRANNY: He's late.

AUGGIE: Yuh, so what?

FRANNY: I...I dunno'...No big deal. Don't go makin' nothin' out'ta' that. He's late, that's all.

AUGGIE: He'll be here. He hasn't missed yet.

FRANNY: Fine. Good. Fine.

(There is a small awkward pause.)

AUGGIE: What are we doin' today? Arms?

FRANNY: How long've you been training with me?

AUGGIE: Here, or everywhere?

FRANNY: Everywhere.

AUGGIE: Let's see? Five years down to Cody's...maybe what? Ten years at the "Y"...couple'a years at Glen's place...maybe 18 years, total...

FRANNY: You ever once remembered what we were doin'?

AUGGIE: You mean arms-legs-abs-delts-traps kind of thing? *(Pauses.)* Sometimes I do, don't I?

FRANNY: When? Name one day in the last nineteen years!

AUGGIE: You kiddin' me?

FRANNY: Uh uh.

AUGGIE: Jesus, *really?* (*Pauses.*) It's amazing what you can still learn about yourself, even at our age. (*Pauses.*) I'm gonna' hav'ta' write things down. (*Gets pencil and note-book from gym bag, under bench, at his feet.*) So, what are we doin' today?

FRANNY: Arms: bi's, tri's, delts, maybe pecs.

AUGGIE: What are we doin' tomorrow?

FRANNY: Legs: quads, calves, ads, abs.

> (*Fast Eddie enters. Franny sees him; Auggie doesn't.*)

AUGGIE: What are we doin' Saturday?

FRANNY: *(Refers to Fast Eddie.)* Drugs.

AUGGIE: *(Confused.)* Huh?

FAST EDDIE: What's this? Some kind of personal slanderous-type remark?

AUGGIE: *(Laughs.)* Yo, Eddie? What's up?

FAST EDDIE: Usual. How about you?

AUGGIE: Usual. *(They slap hands.)* Check it out… (*Proudly offers daily coffee and cruller from brown paper bag.*) Whole wheat sugarless crullers from Mac Bell's.

FAST EDDIE: Good boy. *(Sees Franny's bandaged arm.)* What's with your arm?

FRANNY: What's the matter with my arm?

FAST EDDIE: You got it bandaged.

FRANNY: Oh, that.

FAST EDDIE: What's with it?

FRANNY: Nothin'.

FAST EDDIE: How'd you hurt it?

FRANNY: I dunno. Doin' stuff.

FAST EDDIE: What are we doin' today?

FRANNY: Tell him.

AUGGIE: *(Looks at list.)* Arms: bi's, tri's, delts, maybe pecs.

FAST EDDIE: *(Laughs.)* How the hell would you know?

AUGGIE: *(Smiles.)* I write these things down.

FAST EDDIE: *(To Franny.)* Yuh, so, what are we doin'?

FRANNY: Arms: bi's, tri's, delts, maybe pecs. He told you, didn't he? You hard of hearin', or what?

> (*Fast Eddie stares at Franny's arm.*)

FRANNY: What are you lookin' at?

FAST EDDIE: Nothin'. *(Smiles; shrugs.)* So, what are we doin?

FRANNY: Cross-face tricep extentions…*(Picks up dummbbell from rack.)* We'll work the outer tri's…Clear the bench.

(Auggie moves, Franny lies back on bench, lifts dumb-bell over head, one-handed.)

You point the elbow out this way .. *(He screams in pain.)* Shit! *(He wheels around, drops dumbbell, falls to floor, holding arm.)*
(Simultaneously.)

AUGGIE: You okay?

FAST EDDIE: What's the matter?

FRANNY: I'm okay.

AUGGIE: You sure you're okay?

FRANNY: *(Yells.) I said I'm okay, okay?*
(There is a small silence.)

FAST EDDIE: *(Crosses to bench.)* Check me out on these. *(Picks up 35-lb. dumbbell. Positions himself; points elbows.)* This what you mean?

FRANNY: *(Absently as he passes by Fast Eddie.)* Yuh. Good.

FAST EDDIE: *(Starts the set.)* I got faulted on outer tri's, once…first time I ever tried for Mr. Massachusetts. *(Continues set.)* Fuckin' cattle call. Musta' been a hundred of us in the pre-judgin'. I was just a kid…eighteen, maybe…facin' these bloodless steely-eyed judges. I got pre-judged out. The first one ta' go…*(Pumps out two more reps.)* I hit my tension poses, my heart poundin' out of my chest. I see 'em check out my outer tri's. Thumbs down. Heartbreak City. Over, history, out the fuckin' door. *(Finishes set, places dumbbell on to floor; clears bench for Auggie.)* The Judge's Eye. They know. They don't hav't'a' waste any time. One look: they know where the weaknesses are.

AUGGIE: *(Takes 20-lb. dumbbell; lies back on bench, prepares to start his set: same exercise.)* The average eye can't tell.

FAST EDDIE: The average eye sees dick!

(Auggie places dumb-bell across his neck, elbow pointed correctly. he struggles under the weight of the dumbbell unable to move it from his neck. He screams out; choking.)

AUGGIE: *Jesus!* I musta' grabbed the wrong one. *(Sees that weight is in fact what he'd wanted.)* It's the same twenty I've been liftin' all month! I ate too much fish chowder down my mother's last night. I'm feelin' weak!

(Fast Eddie laughs cruelly. Auggie looks up, angrily. Franny sits across stage, on bench, deeply depressed, totally lost in thought: depressed. Fast Eddie laughs, again.)

AUGGIE: Who the hell are *you* laughin' at?

FAST EDDIE: The both'a' ya's! *(Motions to Franny.)* Him, sittin' there, head down, mopin'...You, sittin' there like a beached whale! *(Moves downstage, back to Auggie; laughing still, even more cruelly.)* You're pathetic, Amoré! You're fuckin' *hopeless!*

AUGGIE: I'll show you who's hopeless! *(Without warning, Auggie charges at Fast Eddie, punches Fast Eddie's left arm.)*

FRANNY: Hey! Auggie! Yo! Hey! Back off!
(Fast Eddie is amazed. He glares at Auggie, then runs to "mirror," rips off outer shirt, stares at struck arm.)

AUGGIE: I ought'a kill you, you prickless juicehead!
(Franny leaps in to break up the fight. Franny pushes Auggie back.)

AUGGIE: Lemme' kill the dork, Franny! Lemme' put him out'ta his misery!

FRANNY: *Knock-it off, dammit!*

AUGGIE: *(Paces up and down stage, right.)* Maybe you don't wanna', but I wanna'! I'll do it for both of us! Lemme' kill him, Franny!

FAST EDDIE: *(Shocked; paces up and down stage, left, in parallel line to Auggie.)* You hit my fucking arm, you idiot! You dink, you donk, you *dodo!* *(Runs to Franny, center, as if to daddy, rubbing his arm.)* I put my fucking application in the mail for fucking Mr. Massachusetts, this very day, you brainless asshole! If you raised a bruise on this arm — if there is any visible discoloration, whatsoever — I will hunt you down and I will tear you to fucking pieces and I will feed you to the fucking lobsters. *Do you understand me?*

FRANNY: *(Trapped between them.)* Both of ya's...stop it!

AUGGIE: *(Charging forward, using Franny as protection.)* *You* wanna' come at me, douche-bag, huh? Huh? Come at me! Come at me!

FAST EDDIE: You see this one? You see the brains in this one's head? I am competing for Mr. fucking Massachusetts and he fucking thinks I'm gonna' risk fucking bruising and fucking losing just to fucking kill him? He's not just fucking *stupid:* he's fucking *crazy!* *(To Auggie.)* Did you hear what I just said, you? You're not just fucking *stupid:* you're fucking *crazy!*

AUGGIE: That's it! You die, you homo drug-dealing fucking jail-bird! You fucking die! That is *it!* You fucking *die!*

FRANNY: Stop it!

FAST EDDIE: What did you call me, you dodo? You pathetic, out-of-shape, pathetic *dodo!*

(Franny tosses a 5-lb weight at Fast Eddie's feet, and another 5-lb weight at Auggie's feet. Each weight hits the floor between Fast Eddie and Auggie, scaring them, both.)

FRANNY: Stop it!

(There is a small astonished silence.)

AUGGIE: Jesus, Fran, you could'a really hurt us, if we got hit with them things…

FAST EDDIE: Smart. Brilliant. Great. If any of that had hit me, goodbye, Mr. North Shore, goodbye, Mr. Massachusetts, hello, every fuckin' lawyer on Cape Ann…*(Rubs arm; checking it in "mirror.")* I got a chemical instant ice-pack out in my truck. I'm gonna' ice my arm down. One tinge of discolor, and you're name ain't Amoré: it's *Morté…*

(Fast Eddie storms out of garage. There is a pause. Franny looks at Auggie, who moves past him to leg-extension machinee.)

AUGGIE: Don't talk to me. I'm doin' my work-out!

(Starts doing exercise.)

FRANNY: Why?

AUGGIE: I said "Don't talk to me!"…

FRANNY: Why?

AUGGIE: Because, I can't stand lookin' at the miserable bast'id, knowin' what I know.

FRANNY: There's nothin' we can do, Auggie. No you, not me. Nothin'.

AUGGIE: Can I ask you something?

FRANNY: What?

AUGGIE: Can I donate stuff to Dede?

FRANNY: What?

AUGGIE: I'd like to donate marrow to Dede, Fran. I wanna' do that. I could go into the hospital with you and…ya' know…donate stuff from my leg and all…Like you and Evelyn have been doin'. Maybe my stuff'll take. I mean, who knows, right?

FRANNY: You'll wreck your leg, Auggie…They go right into your bone with these thick double-needles, to suck the stuff out. Once you're missing bone-marrow, every bit of fitness you got in that leg goes. No blood gets made right for weeks. The muscle starves, atrophies. You lose all your conditioning…Look at me: my leg, my arm…

AUGGIE: What the hell, huh? Like you said: I ain't exactly bein' scouted for the Olympics, right?

FRANNY: Jesus, Aug, huh? I couldn't ask anybody to…Jesus, Auggie, huh?...*(Laughs bravely.)* You're okay, Auggie. I don't care what your mother's always tellin' everybody about you...You're okay, Aug. *(Sobs; then laughs at his own display of emotion.)* Jesus, look at me, huh...*(Smiles at Auggie.)* Thanks for offering, Aug, but, it won't work from you, either, same as it ain't workin' from me. *(Pauses.)* You ain't her natural father, either. No matter how much they take from me or you and inject into her, it's only gonna' work for a couple of days, it's only like temporary, 'cause we're not Dede's blood relatives. It don't "take" properly. Evvie's donations worked for a good long time, two years, almost...but she's got nothin' more to give. Evvie's in pretty bad shape herself from doin' this, Auggie. Saddest goddam thing to see...*(Pauses.)* Dede's gonna' die, Aug...

AUGGIE: Don't give me that! We're gonna' get marrow from her natural father?

FRANNY: Don't talk dumb!

AUGGIE: It's the only real chance she's got left, right? Isn't this what you're sayin' here, or what?

(Franny looks up at Auggie, doesn't speak.)

AUGGIE: Yuh, so, we'll ask him.

FRANNY: Don't talk stupid, okay? It ain't gonna' happen. Put it out of your mind.

AUGGIE: We'll make the pecker do it. We'll give the dork no choice on this. You gotta' take your pride and shove it, man! This is Dede's life we're talkin' here!

FRANNY: How are we gonna' make him do this, Auggie?

AUGGIE: I dunno...What I'm thinking here is that we're gonna' hav'ta' have a contest.

FRANNY: Why are you sayin' here?

AUGGIE: Who's the most competitive son of a bitch on the face of the earth?

FRANNY: Besides me?...

(Fast Eddie re-enters. He clutches an ice-pack to his arm. Auggie and Franny stare at him. Fast Eddie senses the fierce intensity of their staring. He stops, frozen in place.)

FAST EDDIE: What? What are you lookin' at me for? What? What? What?

AUGGIE: We were just thinking...talkin' to each other...sayin' "Eddie Ryan's always bullshitting about being competitive on big-time super-star levels and all, but he's gonna' hav'ta' win on a local level kind of thing, first, yes?" What do you personally think on this, Eddie?

FAST EDDIE: What the fuck are you givin' me here, Amoré?
   (*Auggie and Franny exchange a glance.*)
FRANNY: There's only one other lifter in Gloucester you have to worry
   about, Eddie. Only one lifter you got'ta beat…
FAST EDDIE: What the fuck is this?
FRANNY: What we're sayin', Ryan, is that there's somebody in Gloucester
   who can out-lift you…
FAST EDDIE: Oh, yuh? Who?…Who?
FRANNY: You're lookin' at him, Eddie.
   (*Fast Eddie laughs.*)
FAST EDDIE: What are you, shittin' me, Francis? I can outlift you with one
   hand tied behind my back.
FRANNY: Talk's cheap, Ryan. You wanna' try to outlift me?
FAST EDDIE: Any time, any place, any stakes you want, Farina.
FRANNY: How's about here and now?
FAST EDDIE: I'm ready. What are the stakes?
FRANNY: If you beat me, you get every piece of equipment in this gym.
   I hand it over…yours. You own everything you see. And I train you,
   for nothing.
AUGGIE: And I'm adding a thousand bucks…cash…to sweeten the bet.
FAST EDDIE: What if I don't win?
   (*Franny and Auggie exchange a worried glance.*)
AUGGIE: You gotta' give something to a friend of ours. Nothing expen-
   sive. It's more like *physical*…what you've gotta' do.
FAST EDDIE: What the fuck are you talking about, Amoré?
FRANNY: If you lose, you're gonna' have to give bone marrow donations
   to Dede…all she needs.
FAST EDDIE: What?
FRANNY: You're not worryin' about losing, are you Ed?
   (*Fast Eddie laughs.*)
FAST EDDIE: Let's do it.
   (*Music crashes in: The Band's "The Weight."*)

                    END OF SCENE FIVE

(*Lights shift suddenly to…*)

Scene Six

THE COMPETITION

Transition into new scene: in low-level, brightly-colored light:

1. Music in: Over loudspeaker, we hear: The Band's "The Weight," on tape, near completion.
2. Actors quickly load/prepare weights for Power-Lift Contest.
3. Auggie wheels castored black-board, on rolling stand, into position, center/stage.
4. Spotlight on Fast Eddie, who lies back on bench, prepares for bench press. Auggie and Franny, spot him.
5. Fast Eddie succeeds in making press. As metal bar-bell hits rack, music ends and lights widen to full stage.

Auggie, Franny and Fast Eddie are in the midst of a power-lift contest. Franny is competing with Fast Eddie. Auggie is acting as referee. The black-board features the following chart:

	World Top	Cape Ann Top	Franny	Fast Eddie
1. Bench:	465	410	400	385
2. Dead: lift	650	600		
3. Squat:	660	550		

As lights widen, full-stage, Fast Eddie lies on back on bench, presses the full weight, 405 lbs., cleanly, triumphantly. note: The contest is already in progress. Thus, this is Bench Press, #4. Auggie and Franny assist Fast Eddie in getting the bar settled back on to the rack.

AUGGIE: Jesus, Eddie…beautiful!

FRANNY: Good goin', Ed.

(Fast Eddie rises from the bench. He is silent, expressionless. Suddenly, he explodes in self-congratulatory cheer.)

FAST EDDIE: Allll riiiight! Eddie Ryan presses four-oh-fuckin'-five, folks! Let's hear it! *(Screams.)* Hhhhaahhhhhhhhhhh!

FRANNY: Up ten.

FAST EDDIE: *(Sings.)*

"Bo Diddley, Bo Diddley, where you been?

Up your house, and gone again…

Bo Diddley, Bo Diddley, have you heard?

My pretty baby she flew like a bird."

(Wordlessly, Franny stands, walks to corner of room, as far away from Fast Eddie as possible.)

All your life, you take shit from people 'cause you're short. Not in this event. The short man rules here, don't he?

(Fast Eddie poses in front of mirror: three quick poses; then looks over at Franny, in mirror's reflection.)

I'm glad we're doin' this, Francis. Honest ta' Christ, I'm really glad. *(Looks directly at Franny.)* Years and years and years of makin' me feel guilty. There was no need ta' make me feel like that, ya' know. As far as I was concerned, I was doin' the generous thing! What the fuck did you want? Me, comin' around Dede, sayin' "I'm your real father, ya' know?" I was leaving the three of you alone, stayin' out of your hair. You shoulda' been kissing my fuckin' hands, that's what! Instead, you fuckin' snub me, make me feel like shit, like some kind of foreigner! *(Fast Eddie suddenly yells at Franny.)* Are we havin' a contest here or what?

FRANNY: *(Stands, faces Fast Eddie.)* Yuh, Eddie, that's what we're doin' here: havin' a contest.

(Note: This is Bench Press, #5. Franny walks to the bench, lies back, prepares.)

AUGGIE: You can press this, Franny. Just take your time. Concentrate, man…Push it through the roof!

(Auggie and Fast Eddie stand close-by, as spotters. Franny readies himself. He screams.)

FRANNY: Arrrrgggghhhhh!

(He presses the bar upward, but fails to be able to straighten his arms. The bar falls back down on top of Franny.)

FRANNY: Take it! *Take it! Get it off me!*

(Auggie and Fast Eddie quickly lift the bar from him, and replace barbell on the rack. Franny has lost the Bench Press event. Fast Eddie leaps up in the air, triumphantly.)

FAST EDDIE: Allll riiiiight! *(Chants sing-song, childlike poem.)* Fast Eddie Ryan…Pumps awesome iron!

(He hits three quick poses in mirror. Auggie records score on blackboard. The score, at the moment, is Fast Eddie=405 and Franny=400.)

AUGGIE: *(To Fast Eddie)* Are you takin' your last lift here, or what?

FAST EDDIE: No need to!

(Auggie goes to Franny, who sits on bench, rubbing his shoulder.)

AUGGIE: You okay?

FRANNY: *(Nods.)* Yuh. Fine.

AUGGIE: You almost had it.

FRANNY: Almost don't count.

AUGGIE: 400's great goin'…

FRANNY: Not bad, yuh. I'll get him dead-liftin'.

AUGGIE: You ready?

FRANNY: Yuh.

AUGGIE: *(To Fast Eddie.)* You ready?

FAST EDDIE: Does the Pope fart in the woods?

AUGGIE: You got yourself a nice way with words, Eddie…

(Fast Eddie hits a fresh pose; glares at his own reflection in mirror.)

FAST EDDIE: Let's do this.

AUGGIE: This here's the dead-lift part of it. Same rules: three lifts. Eddie won the Bench Press, so it's Eddie's call: who goes first?

FAST EDDIE: *(Fast Eddie sits eating a banana; looks across to Franny.)* Go.

FRANNY: *(To Auggie)* Five plates…four-ninety-five.

AUGGIE: You sure?

FRANNY: *(Nods.)*

AUGGIE: *(Whistles.)* You got it. *(Auggie loads five Olympic plates on each side of the bar.)*

I remember back in high school when we were havin' a power-lift contest, the three of against Gus and the Connor brothers. We ran out of real weights and hadda add an old tire rim my father had layin' around out back…

FAST EDDIE: That was Gus's father's rim.

AUGGIE: I think you're right.

(Auggie starts to move bar-bell into position for dead-lift contest; cannot budge it.)

(To Fast Eddie.) Grab a middle, will ya', Eddie?…

FAST EDDIE: You got it.

(Fast Eddie hops up behind bar. He, Franny and Auggie move bar-bell together: teamed. They set bar down, center-stage, front, facing audience. Dead Lift, #1. Franny approaches the bar-bell, twists one hand facing

front, the other facing back; stoops, grips bar; lifts. The bar comes up clean. Franny stands straight. Franny: 495+400=895.)

AUGGIE: (Calls out.) Good.

(Franny drops bar-bell to floor. It crashed down, making a most impressive noise. Note on weights: All 45-lb Olympic plates are wooden: fake...except for the two end plates, which are metal: real. The fake plates should be manufactured so that they are fractionally smaller than the real plates, thus, the real plate hits the floor. There should be a rubber mat under the lifters...and a metal plate under the rubber mat.)

FRANNY: *(Smiles at Fast Eddie.)* Just warmin' up.

(Franny turns and faces mirror. For the first time in the scene, Franny's depression lifts. Auggie laughs. Auggie and Franny hit "high fives.")

AUGGIE: That was beautiful, Franny! Beautiful!

(Fast Eddie chalks his hands. Wordlessly, Fast Eddie goes to bar, adjusts his hands, appropriately, grips the bar, lifts. Dead Lift, #2. The bar-bell leaves the ground. Fast Eddie's legs stiffen. He stands straight. Fast Eddie: 495+405=900.)

Good.

(Fast Eddie drops the bar; screams.)

FAST EDDIE: *ARRRRGGGGHHHH!*

(Fast Eddie hits a pose in mirror; smiles at Auggie in reflection. Franny looks across.)

FRANNY: Add two plates.

AUGGIE: Jesus, Franny, that's five-eighty-five!

FRANNY: Let's go.

(Auggie adds a 45-lb. weight to each end of the bar-bell. Fast Eddie watches. He is deeply impressed...and worried. Dead Lift, #3. Franny approaches bar-bell, adjusts his grip, pauses, readies himself. He jerks the bar-bell upward, stiffens his legs. He succeeds. He drops bar, immediately. Franny:400+585=985.)

AUGGIE: Holy shit! You did it, Franny! You did it!

FRANNY: I did, yuh.

(Franny turns to mirror; poses. He is very, very happy.)

FAST EDDIE: Up five.

AUGGIE: You got it, Eddie. Five-ninety...*(Auggie adds 2-1/2-lb. weights to each end of the bar-bell.)*

FAST EDDIE: It ain't over til it's over. *(Fast Eddie walks well off to one side, concentrating.)*

Franny's leading, at the moment, by, uh…eighty-five pounds…

(Franny and Auggie share a small smile.)

AUGGIE: Any time you're ready, Eddie.

(Fast Eddie glares at Auggie.)

FAST EDDIE: Don't, Amoré, okay? I know what's at stake here. I ain't fuckin' up my legs by lettin' doctors stick no double fuckin' needles in 'em…throwing away my fitness, throwing away Mr. North Shore, throwing away Mr. Massachusetts, throwing away any chance for Mr. O, throwing away my fuckin' *dreams*…on account'a some half-wit nowhere Guinea asshole's *raggin'* me…so get the fuck off my case, and keep your fuckin' trap *shut*, Amoré, okay?

(Fast Eddie moves to Franny; confronts Franny.)

FAST EDDIE: You can beat me by liftin' more: that's one thing. Or you can beat me by havin' your stooge here drive me fuckin' bananas: that's another kind'a thing altogether, yes? You agree?

(Franny doesn't reply.)

FAST EDDIE: You agree?

FRANNY: *(Softly.)* Yuh, I see your point…

FAST EDDIE: What? I can't hear what you're sayin'!

FRANNY: *(Yells.)* I said "I see your point," Ryan! We're havin' a contest, are we not? I dead-lifted five-eighty-five, did I not? You have one more try, do you not? Are you tryin', again, or are you givin' up?

(After a substantial pause, Fast Eddie goes to bar-bell, readies himself, wordlessly; lifts. Dead Lift, #4. The bar comes up. He straightens his legs. He has succeeded. He drops the bar; screams. Fast Eddie: 405+ 590=995.)

FAST EDDIE: I'm leading by ten now, am I not? *(Faces mirror; poses; screams.)* Arrrggggghhhh!

FRANNY: Up thirty. Six twenty…

AUGGIE: I…

FRANNY: Do it!

(Auggie adds the necessary weight to the bar, chatting nervously as He does.)

AUGGIE: 620 is like so incredibly unbelievable, I gotta' pinch myself here. Jesus, imagine how great we coulda' be'n if we never stopped training together?

FAST EDDIE: What are you…soft in the head, Amoré?

AUGGIE: I'm just thinkin' out loud, that's all…

FAST EDDIE: Yuh, well, don't, okay?

AUGGIE: Okay, okay. I'm just excited, that's all!

(Dead Lift, #5. Franny walks to the bar, without preparation dead-lifts the weight, successfully; drops bar down to floor.)

AUGGIE: *Holy shit, Franny! Great!*

FRANNY: I'm up twenty-five.

FAST EDDIE: You never lifted anything like six-twenty before in your whole life, Farina, and you know it!

FRANNY: I have now, though, haven't I?

(Fast Eddie flashes a look at Auggie.)

AUGGIE: I ain't laughin'. I'm sayin' nothin' here.

(Auggie fails to contain his laughter. He chokes, chortles, moves away from Fast Eddie and Franny, until his laughter is under his control, again. Fast Eddie moves to barbell.)

FAST EDDIE: I gotta' match ya' ta' be up five.

FRANNY: Looks like it, yuh.

FAST EDDIE: *(Goes to punching bag, punches, talks to himself trying to psych himself for the lift.)* Just do it, Eddie…just step up and do it. You're boss, you're champ, you're the best here. Do it, Eddie, just do it.

(Dead Lift, #6. Fast Eddie walks to bar-bell, readies himself. He fails to lift the weight. He has lost the Dead Lift event. The bar-bell crashes back down to the floor. Auggie looks over at Franny.)

AUGGIE: Franny leads by twenty-five…We're on to squats.

(They all move to the squat rack.)

FRANNY: I'll follow.

FAST EDDIE: Let's load five-fifty.

FRANNY: What's this?

FAST EDDIE: You got some kind of hearin' problem? Five-fifty. *(Playacted enunciation.)* I am starting at five hundred and fifty pounds, Francis. *(Auggie and Fast Eddie load appropriate weights on to bar-bell on squat rack.)*
If you ever once had come ta' me and said "She's *your* Daughter, Eddie, really…take her for a while," I would've taken her in a fuckin' shot. Instead, what did I get? Opposite, right? "Nobody wants or needs you comin' around here, Eddie? Stay fuckin' clear of here!" Now everybody figures I'm s'pose'ta' wreck my arms and legs tryin' ta' save her?
(Fast Eddie crosses to Franny; stares at Franny, directly.)
I may not be what you'd call particularly *well read*, but I'm not dumb, Farina. I know people, and I pick up on signals a lot faster than the

average guy, and that's no shit. And I got plenty of negative fuckin' signals from you, every fuckin' time I showed my face in Gloucester. A lesser man would've never come back into this fuckin' town...

(Auggie completes the loading of weights; steps back from squat rack. Fast Eddie puts on knee-wraps.)

FAST EDDIE: What'd this town ever give Eddie Ryan, huh? I took shit for bein' short, I took shit for bein' poor, I took shit for bein' lousy in school, I took shit 'cause my father was what he was...I took shit for every fuckin' thing that ever was...No more, huh, Francis. No fuckin' more. Eddie Ryan's short but he's big...he's strong...he can lift...he's a fucking *champion*...He is *world class!*

(Suddenly, Fast Eddie makes his move. He walks directly into squat rack, shoulders bar, staggers backwards away from rack. Auggie and Franny spot him. Squat Lift, #1. He squats until his thighs are parallel with the floor. Auggie calls out.)

AUGGIE: Good.

(Fast Eddie rises up. He succeeds in making his lift. Fast Eddie: 550+995=1545. Franny and Auggie take some of the weight of the bar from his shoulders as Fast Eddie staggers forward, re-placing the bar-bell on squat rack. Fast Eddie turns and faces Franny.)

FAST EDDIE: It ain't over til it's over.

FRANNY: *(Without hesitation.)* Mine!

(Franny approaches squat rack, shoulders bar, staggers backwards into squatting position. Fast Eddie watches carefully, as Franny shoulders the bar. Squat Lift #2. Franny squats until his thighs are parallel to the floor.)

AUGGIE: Good!

(Franny strains upwards. He succeeds in making his lift. He lunges forward, as do Auggie and Fast Eddie, replacing the bar-bell on to the squat rack.)

FRANNY: You're right, Eddie. It ain't over til it's over.

FAST EDDIE: Five ninety.

AUGGIE: Five-ninety comin' up.

(Auggie adds the necessary lbs. to the bar-bell. Fast Eddie goes off into the corner by himself, back turned toward the others. Suddenly, he strides across the gym to the squat rack. He shoulders the bar. Squat Lift #3. Fast Eddie dips toward the floor until his thighs find the proper parallel position.)

AUGGIE: Good.

(Fast Eddie rises up, slowly, powerfully. He has succeeded. Fast Eddie:1545+40=1585. He leans forward. Franny and Auggie assist: spot. The bar-bell is returned to the rack.)

FRANNY: Mine!

(Without hesitation, Franny moves in to bar, quickly, decisively. He shoulders the bar, staggers backwards into position, squats. Squat Lift #4. Franny's thighs hit the parallel. He rises. He screams.)
Arrrgggghhhhhh!

(He succeeds in making his lift. Franny:1020+590=1610. Auggie and Fast Eddie assist in getting the bar-bell back on to the rack. Franny again leads by 20 lbs. Auggie is beside himself with joy.)

AUGGIE: *Jesus, Franny, Jesus! Five-ninety! Five-ninety! Five-fucking-ninety!*
(Fast Eddie glares at Auggie, who instantly contains his enthusiasm. Franny walks away from others to the steps by door to house. He sits, silently, rubbing his shoulder. After a long pause, Fast Eddie speaks; quietly, respectfully.)

FAST EDDIE: Good lift, Francis. That was a good one.

FRANNY: Yuh. Thanks, Eddie.

FAST EDDIE: I gotta' lift six fifteen just to match?

FRANNY: Seems like it, yuh.

FAST EDDIE: Six-twenty.

AUGGIE: I can't believe my fuckin' ears, that's what: I'm loading six-twenty…Right here, Evvie and Franny's garage, East Main Street, East Gloucester, Massachusetts, U.S. of A.
(Auggie opens garage door, pokes head outside; looks up to Heaven; screams to God.)

AUGGIE: Is God paying attention? We are loading six-twenty!
(Auggie loads the additional weight on to the ends of the bar-bell.)
Last person in Gloucester to lift at this level was Alvie Chincilla's mother when she lifted the front end of their Dodge off Alvie's little brother. She broke her back doin' it, but she saved the kid's life, didn't she? *(Pauses.)* It's an amazing goddam thing what people can do when they know they have to!

FAST EDDIE: *(Fast Eddie has been silently praying. He turns, faces squat rack.)*
Let's go.
(Franny moves to spotter's position, opposite end of the bar from Auggie. Fast Eddie approaches the bar. He "crosses" himself. Squat Lift #5. Fast Eddie shoulders the bar. He dips. He reaches the needed parallel position.)

AUGGIE: Good.
  (Fast Eddie strains to rise, but falters and fails.)
FAST EDDIE: Take it! *Take it!*
  (Auggie and Franny grab the bar, walk it back into the rack with Fast Eddie.)
  (Walks through rack.) You win it, Francis.
  (Auggie leaps up in the air; screams out.)
AUGGIE: You did it! *You beat him!* Sixteen-ten, Franny! Sixteen-fucking-ten! That is like top top *top* level, man! That is *fan-fucking-tastic!* You beat him!
FAST EDDIE: You beat me, Francis.
FRANNY: Yuh, I did, Eddie. I had to.
FAST EDDIE: You tear something?
FRANNY: I think so, yuh, on my last bench-press. It went out'ta' joint right away, and I never got it back in right.
FAST EDDIE: Want me to try to set it?
FRANNY: Uh uh. I think I'll hop up to Addison Gilbert, have a doctor look at it, maybe get an x-ray…It's pretty bad. *(Smiles.)* We're about a hundred pounds off of what top class power-lifters can do, but we ain't so bad for a couple'a Gloucester assholes, huh?
FAST EDDIE: What was your best squat before now?
FRANNY: Five-fifty.
AUGGIE: Want me ta' run you up?
FRANNY: I wanna' go by myself. I need you ta' cover the place, Aug…I'm gonna' have early mornin' workouts comin' through the door, any time now.
AUGGIE: No sweat. I ain't done my own workout yet! I'm psyched! You two blow'ahs are *inspirational!*
  (Auggie completes scoring on black board.)
FRANNY: *(Looks at Fast Eddie; speaks quietly.)* Eddie?
FAST EDDIE: Yuh, I know.
FRANNY: We got a deal here, yes?
FAST EDDIE: I said "I know," didn't I?
FRANNY: I'll pick you up at your Sis'tah's house in an hour. We'll drive into Boston together, in my car, okay?
FAST EDDIE: Who's goin'? *(Pauses.)*…In the car, with you and me?
FRANNY: Nobody. Just you and me. Evvie's in at Mass General, waitin' for us, already…with Dede. It's all set up. *(Rubs arm.)* My shoulder's throbbin' wicked. I'll see you up your Sis'tah's…in an hour.

(Franny exits the garage. There is a moment's pause.)

FAST EDDIE: Spot me.

AUGGIE: What the hell are you doin', Eddie?

FAST EDDIE: I'm gonna' show you what a six-twenty squat looks like, Amoré.

AUGGIE: Jesus, Eddie! Be careful, huh! I dunno if I can spot this kind of weight on my own!

(Fast Eddie then shoulders the bar; staggers backward.)

You okay? You got it?

(Fast Eddie dips until his thighs are parallel to the ground.)

FAST EDDIE: *Say* something, asshole!

AUGGIE: Good!

(Fast Eddie rises, slowly. He sreams.)

FAST EDDIE: *Arrrrgggggghhhhh!*

(He succeeds in lifting the weight.)

AUGGIE: Nice lift, Eddie. Nice goin'…Jesus! Beautiful!

(Fast Eddie staggers forward, re-placing the bar on to the rack. Auggie stares at Fast Eddie, wordlessly, astonished.)

That is amazing, Eddie! Fucking *amazing!*

(Fast Eddie turns from the squat rack, faces Auggie. The two old friends hold eye-contact for a moment.)

FAST EDDIE: Promise me something…Nobody's ever ta' know I just did six-oh-five just now! Just you and me, right?

AUGGIE: If that's what you want, I promise I'll shut up.

FAST EDDIE: You swear to God?

AUGGIE: I swear to God.

FAST EDDIE: I better get myself home and cleaned up.

(Fast Eddie stops at squat rack, touches weights; thoughtfully,)

I ain't goin' be squatting nothing for a while, am I?

(There is a pause.)

AUGGIE: When did you decide to throw it, Eddie?

(Fast Eddie packs his gear into his gym-bag, preparing to leave. He picks up the banana peel he left on the bench, earlier in the scene.)

FAST EDDIE: I know people around Gloucester say savage, putrid vicious, generally shitty things about me and I need you to combat this. I want you to say nice things to people about me. That's what I want. "Fast Eddie Ryan's okay" kind of thing. Is this a deal?

AUGGIE: Deal. *(Auggie reaches out to grab Fast Eddie's hand.)*

FAST EDDIE: I'm gonna' hold you to it, Amoré.

AUGGIE: Absolutely. I swear to God.

(Fast Eddie puts the banana peel in Auggie's hand instead of shaking Auggie's hand.)

AUGGIE: Nice.

(Auggie crosses to waste basket, tosses banana peel. Fast Eddie starts to door; stops, looks at Auggie.)

FAST EDDIE: Yuh, so, well…?

AUGGIE: *(Auggie keeps his word with overdone sincerety; big voice.)* You're okay, Eddie.

FAST EDDIE: *(As if surprised and delighted.)* Why, thank you!

(Fast Eddie bows; Exits. Auggie goes to the dead-lift bar; looks across [out front] to his reflection in "mirror"; talks to it.)

AUGGIE: You're gonna' lift this, Amoré. You got no excuses.

(He leans forward, grips the bar, straightens his back. He has succeeded in lifting the weight.)

(Screams.) Arrrrggggghhhh! (Pauses at the top of his lift; yells at his reflection in "mirror.") Good!

The lights black out.

END OF SCENE SIX

Scene Seven
THE WAKING

Music in: Final lines of The Band's "The Weight" play to completion. Thunder and lightning. Seagulls, groaners, and sounds of a significant storm.

Slides of Franny, Dede and Evvie are projected on to the set. Images are of a happy family…Dede is 4 years old, healthy, happy. Gloucester, summer and sunny, visible in background.

New music in: Joe Cocker singing The Beatles' "With A Little Help From My Friends"…

Spot-light now fades up on Franny, who sits on bench, center of gym.

Another spotlight fades up on Fast Eddie, standing in doorway from house to garage/gym, having just exited the house. Both men wear ill-fitting black suits, white shirts, black neckties, black arm-bands.

Thunder and lighting and rain continue, outside. There is a metal pail set, center-stage, into which falls a constant drop of water…a leak…a tear-drop from Heaven. Thunder and lighting wanted throughtout scene, as well as sound of rain, seagulls, and distant groaners. Lights now widen to full stage and music fades out.

FAST EDDIE: Thanks for letting me sit alone with her.

FRANNY: It's okay.

FAST EDDIE: I thanked Evvie, too. She's back in with her, now.

(Fast Eddie crosses to dumb-bell rack, chooses a dumb-bell, does a few curls.)

She's got my Father's mouth…*(Pauses.)* She's got my Mother's eyes.

(Fast Eddie suddenly turns away from Franny.)

Oh, God…Christ, Franny…*(He punches the air, ten punches.)* Why? Why? Why? Why? Why? Why? Why? Why? Why? Why? *(Faces Franny.)* I'm sorry I didn't help out sooner. I really am…

FRANNY: I know you are, Eddie. It wouldn't'a mattered, anyhow. It wouldn't'a changed nothin'…

(Fast Eddie goes to padded curl-rack, upstage right, punches it, knocking same over. He then faces Franny, slightly calmed.)

FAST EDDIE: At least, I did the right thing, finally? I mean, I did a good thing, finally, yes?

FRANNY: Yuh, you did, Eddie. You did a good thing, yuh.

(He lifts curl-rack from floor, sets it upright, again. Faces Franny.)

FAST EDDIE: So, you don't hate me so much, any more?

FRANNY: Not so much. No.

FAST EDDIE: *(Sudden rage.) I come from the wrong people! (He grabs a dumb-bell from the floor, does curls, again, roughly.)* That's what they told me when they had me in the hospital, up Walpole: "I come from the wrong people." That was like my *bad break*. What I hav'ta' try to do is try to get past it…to forgive my father and move on. So I don't end up bein' an old man, still fightin' with him in my dreams every night, still imitating him…or, worse, bein' him altogether: druggin', drinkin', mean ta' women and kids, no friends…always hearin' people say shitty things when I walked near 'em…*(Fast Eddie suddenly sobs.)* Who would'a guessed, when we were kids, Franny, huh? Who woulda' guessed that our lives coulda' turned out ta' be so full of shit?

FRANNY: When Dede first got sick, I did nothin' but feel sorry for myself. I stopped trainin'…Everything pissed me off…everybody, too… Evvie…even Dede. I kept thinkin' to myself "How come *I'm* struck with this?" *(Pauses.)* The worst was tryin' to believe it was really happening. We kept changing doctors. Every time a doctor would tell us anything like the truth, on to a new one. We were looking for lies.

FAST EDDIE: That's gotta' be normal…I mean, who can face sickness…especially a kid's?

FRANNY: *(Crosses upstage right to thermos, drinks cup of water.)* My mother died. She had a stroke. Did you know this?

FAST EDDIE: *(Crosses downstage right to lat machine, sits, faces Franny.)* I heard, yuh. I'm sorry about that.

FRANNY: Yuh, well, thanks…When my Mother died…it'll be three years, June 10th…We had to tell Dede what was goin' on. I mean, my Mother was here every day, helpin' Evvie out, readin' Dede stories, doin' pictures with her and all…I mean, I was still workin' up Gorton's…with Evvie's folks both gone, my mother was like the only help we had, right? Dede was (what?) six, almost. She knew my Mother didn't like go home to her house at night and then just forget to come back here, again, ever. She knew I didn't just quit my job for the fun of it, neither! I mean, Dede knew something was really *wrong.* I wouldn't let Evvie tell her nothin'. I myself kept tryin' ta keep up a lie with Dede. I was in the middle of tellin' her this bullshit story about "Grandma went to her cousin Tony Gentile's mother's house in Florida, for a visit kind of thing, and out of nowhere Dede goes "Grandma died, didn't she, Daddy?" I go "Yuh, she did, Dede" and Dede goes "Don't be scared, Daddy. It's okay, really. Grandma knew she was dying, like me, and she wasn't scared… and I'm not scared…and you shouldn't be scared, neither." *(Franny turns upstage, away from Fast Eddie, sobs, and then laughs.)* Can you imagine, Eddie? Not even six, and she's sayin' these things…tellin' *me* "Don't be scared."! *(Franny takes a cup of water, drinks.)* We're all down Rockport, watchin' the 4th of July Parade…Dede's in her wheelchair full-time, Evvie and me are sittin' on both sides of her in these ugly fuckin day-glo pink beach-chairs Evvie got down K-Mart. Dede's real happy, laughin', holdin' our hands…I look at all the people marchin' in the parade, and they're all laughin'…actin' like life's a piece a' fuckin' cake, and it hits me, like fuckin' lightning: We're all dying, Eddie. The only difference between Dede and me and you and Evvie and Auggie is that the doctors named what Dede got. And for some crazy goddam reason, once it gets named, once there's this definite time-limit, everybody's like *shocked*…everybody's like pissin' and moaning kind of thing. Everybody's treating her nice. Grownups, kids…every-fuckin'-body! *(Pauses.)* Before the doctors named what Dede got — before there was this definite time-limit — it was all the normal shit: "Clean your room! Pick up your toys! Don't talk back to your parents!" kind of hoss'shit…But once we all knew the name, then it's all this *love,* all this *gentleness,* all this *kindness, thoughtfulness,* all this phoney *caring…(Pauses.)* We're all terminal cases, Eddie. Everybody's who's breathin' has got to be treated with good medicine. Everybody who's on their feet, movin', needs that kind of carin', that kind of understanding…(Pauses.) That's what I learned from your Daughter, Eddie.

(Fast Eddie turns away, breaks down; sobs. Franny goes to him, tries facing Fast Eddie, directly; cannot.)

FRANNY: I'm sorry I've been so shitty to you over the years, Eddie… *(Pauses.)* I guess I was always afraid Dede would choose you over me…because you're her real father and all…*(Faces Fast Eddie now.)* I guess I was frightened I'd lose her back to you…that she was just something I kinda' *borrowed* from you, and that you'd change your mind and take her back. Anyway, I'll always be grateful for what you done. It was brave and it was generous, and I offer you my handshake in friendship.

(Franny holds out his hand. Fast Eddie shakes Franny's hand in their ritualistic handshake.)

FAST EDDIE: Fuck you…

FAST EDDIE AND FRANNY: *(In unison.)*…and fuck your Grandmother!

(Auggie enters from house wearing brown suit, white shirt, black necktie, black arm-bands.

AUGGIE: I figured I'd find you guys in here. *(Pauses.)* Biggest wake I ever been to. Everybody turned out.

FRANNY: They do that for kids, yuh.

AUGGIE: Remember the kid's wake when we were in first grade, the kid from Traverse Street?…Oh, God…

FRANNY: Charlie What'sis's cousin…Billy something…

AUGGIE: *(Remembers.)* Shimma!

FRANNY: Billy Shimma. He could spit farther than any of us!

FAST EDDIE: We got the day off from school, didn't we?

FRANNY: Uh uh. We went to his funeral first, up Mt Pleasant Street Cemetary, then we all went from there to school and told stories about him…

(Franny sobs, suddenly. Auggie watches him a moment and then Auggie, too, starts to sob. They both now begin to laugh.)

AUGGIE: *(Half laughing, half sobbing.)* I was doin' great til just now...

(Auggie blows his nose into a Kleenex paper tissue. The three men laugh.)

FAST EDDIE: I was cryin', non-stop, all this week. It was fuckin' ridiculous! When I wasn't cryin', I was laughin' at myself. I couldn't be near any mirrors, 'cause I kept catchin' a glimpse of what I looked like cryin', and then I'd start laughin'. *(Suddenly, without warning.)* I got no friends. You and Amoré are the best friends I got! Can you fuckin' believe it?

(Fast Eddie does some stretching exercises; fades upstage.)

AUGGIE: What's the matter with me, Franny? Sometimes I think that I'm in your family.

FRANNY: Well, you are, sort of...

AUGGIE: *(Sobs.)* That ain't it.

FRANNY: What's it, Aug?

AUGGIE: It's that you and Evvie are the Mother and Father, and Dede and I are the kids.

(Thunder and lighting continues, off.)

FRANNY: You're my training partner, Auggie. That's what you are, and that's a life-deal, isn't it?

AUGGIE: I guess.

FRANNY: I know. I got no plan to stop liftin'...Why? Do you?

AUGGIE: Plan ta' stop liftin'? Uh uh? It's just that I'm not much good at it. When I watch you and Eddie lift at your levels, I start feeling like I...I dunno'...don't belong in the sport.

FRANNY: You belong. *(Franny goes to Auggie, hugs him.)* Asshole!

AUGGIE: Asshole!

FAST EDDIE: *(Playacts disgust.)* I always knew there was something funny goin' on between the two of ya's.

(Fast Eddie is at the punching bag. He, suddenly, throws five punches, desperately trying to relieve his anger, his depression. After a moment's embarrassed pause, Fast Eddie faces Franny and Auggie, again. His mood is calmer, more rational.)

FAST EDDIE: When they had me in up to Walpole, I was in this lifters' group. We trained together, and we met with counselors together. We like talked things out. They used to make us tell what we thought of each other, out loud. Most of the guys used'ta say these real positive things...how great everything and everybody was...bullshit, mostly, just to suck up to the counselors…make 'em think they were getting healthy…you know…rehabilitated…so they might get points towards early parole or somesuch. *(Pauses.)* I used to be on everybody's case. Didn't bother me. Right to their faces. "You're an asshole! You're a dork! You're a dipshit! You're a wimp!" I mean, I was *ridiculous!* These guys are all *lifters* like me! I mean I'm like *training with these guys every day!* I'm locked up in a prison with 'em for three years, and for an hour, three times a week, I'm tellin' them to their faces they're assholes, dorks and dipshits…and then I'm always wondering why they don't seem to like me too much! I am just like my fucking *father!*

(Fast Eddie crosses himself; shrugs; stands, takes off jacket.)

FAST EDDIE: I'm movin' out to California.

AUGGIE: When?

FAST EDDIE: Right away…tomorrow.

AUGGIE: Jesus…*really?*

FAST EDDIE: Yuh, well, why not?

AUGGIE: I dunno'…You're *from here.*

FAST EDDIE: What's that got to do with anything?

AUGGIE: I dunno'…California, huh? What part? L.A.? The fitness magazines all say L.A.'s "The Heart of California"…

FAST EDDIE: I'm movin' to Venice Beach: California's Bicep.

FRANNY: That's great, Eddie. Maybe we'll all come out and visit you.

FAST EDDIE: You think you would?

AUGGIE: What are you? Shittin' us? Of *course* we will! Havin' a place ta' stay in Venice Beach, California, is like havin' a room waitin' in Heaven.

FAST EDDIE: I know this guy who's livin' out there. Monster big. Unlimited Class. Dead-lifts in the high sixes almost every day… We are talking pull-out-the-door-frame-so-this-guy-can-stoop-down-and-fit-into- the-room kinda' big!

(Franny lifts wheelchair ramp from stairs.)

FAST EDDIE:…Jumbo Montel. He was in Walpole with me, all three years. Classmates! We were the two everybody hated the most. He's from out there, and he told me if I ever wanted ta' move to California, he'd put me up…til I found my own place kind of thing.

FRANNY: You know his address?

FAST EDDIE: Oh, yuh, it's totally real. I called him just now from my Sis'-

tah's house. Woke him up. It's earlier out there. I forgot. He's says it's cool for me to come out, any time. He's got plenty of room…
(Franny carries wheelchair ramp out-side, through garage door.)
…I told him I was sorry I said all the shitty things about him I said in front of everybody…in the mandatory Psychological Group, up Walpole. He goes "What's'a *matter* with you, Ryan? You goin' soft?" *(Smiles.)* I can't stick here. Too much heavy crap for me ta' remember. I love Gloss'tah. I do. Most beautiful place on Earth. But I can't stick here…
(Franny re-enters.)

FAST EDDIE: That'd take more guts, more strength, than I got. I could lift til my neck dissappears, altogether, and I ain't never gonna' have *that* kind of strength. That's you, Franny. That's Evvie and Dede. That ain't me.
(Fast Eddie pulls off his sweat-shirt, pulls a $5 bill from his pocket, tosses it in cash-box of Franny's desk.)

FAST EDDIE: I got time for one more training session on this Coast, before I head West to start my build-up for Mr. O. You girls workin' out, today, or you just gonna' watch?
(Franny pulls off his jacket, unbuttons his shirt. He holds the black arm-band in his hand for a moment, tosses it into wastebasket.)

FRANNY: What you gave us when you gave us Dede was a great thing, Eddie. We had nine years of happy times. I got'ta thank you for that.

FAST EDDIE: Thank you for lookin' after her so good, Franny. She was the luckiest kid ever lived to have a parent like you. I wasn't her parent. You were. I just get an assist for bein' her father. No big deal in it. It's parents that count. Parents are the ones that stick around and take care of kids. That's the way I see it. *(Embarrassed by his emotion.)* We doin' a work-out or what?

AUGGIE: *(Crosses to scale.)* I'm gonna' miss you wick'id, Eddie. The only good thing about your goin' is that I'm definitely definitely…(At scale, pleased he's lost some weight.)…*definitely* comin' out ta' visit! *(Auggie pulls off his jacket. He moves to the "mirror," down-stage center.)* Cover your eyes, Middle America. August Amoré is about to take off his shirt!
(Auggie removes his shirt, hits a pose. Fast Eddie and Franny laugh, share a moment of enjoying their old friend.)

AUGGIE: Is that Larry Scott, first to win the Big Three: Mr. America, Mr. Universe, and Mr. O?

FAST EDDIE, FRANNY and AUGGIE: *(In unison.)* NOOOOooooooo!

AUGGIE: Nooooo, that is not Larry Scott! That is August Amoré… ripped wicked nice…cut like a crystal fuckin' vase!

FAST EDDIE, FRANNY and AUGGIE: *(In unison; they imitate a crowd cheering.)* Hhhhahhhhhhhhhhhh!

(Franny pats Auggie's shoulder, then moves to rack, picks up a dumb-bell, starts to warm up. Fast Eddie takes a light bar-bell, starts his warm-up.)

FAST EDDIE: *(To Franny.)* You goin' back to your job, or what?

FRANNY: I dunno'…I hav'ta talk it through with Evvie, but, I kinda' like doin' this. Not just *this,* not just doin' this kinda' gym here in the garage…I mean, havin' a gym. Auggie and I always kid around about maybe buying the old North Shore Fish building…goin' in partners. *(Fast Eddie loads 425 lbs on bar-bell for bench press.)*

AUGGIE: It's got the showers and everything all set up, from when they did the Nautilus and shit…

FAST EDDIE: Somebody tried opening a gym?

AUGGIE: It was all chrome and colored lights. A thousand bucks a year. Nobody joined.

FRANNY: I hav'ta' talk it through with Evvie, but, I dunno'…I think I might like to take a stab at it. Goin' back to a job doesn't interest me much right now. Evvie talkin' about goin' back to school, herself. I dunno'…I think it's time to maybe reach for something…try stuff. *(Fast Eddie finishes loading weights on bar-bell: 425 lbs.)*

FAST EDDIE: Spot me.

FRANNY: *(Looks at bar-bell, laughs.)* What're you doin'? You got four-twenty-five on there! *(Fast Eddie lies back on the bench, shirt off, bare-cheasted; readies himself to press weight.)*

FAST EDDIE: If I make this lift, it'll be the best lift I've ever made in my life. *(Fast Eddie grips the bar. His arms tense.)* This one's for Dede… and for everybody else I ever loved in Gloss'tah, Massachusetts, U.S. of A….and for all the other sons'a'bitches, too… *(Auggie and Franny stand by, spotting him. Fast Eddie screams.)* Ar-rrrgggghhhh! *(Fast Eddie's arms stiffen, fully. The weight has been lifted. It crashes into the rack. The sound of the metal hitting metal is miked, amplified. Franny and Auggie cheer.)*

END OF PLAY

Unexpected Tenderness

Mary Mary,
Quite contrary,
How does your garden grow?

With brittle shells,
And broken bells,
And one magnificent Fame Lily.

For my mother.

PRODUCTION HISTORY

Unexpected Tenderness had its world premiere at the Gloucester Stage Company, Gloucester, Massachusetts on August 19, 1994. It was directed by Grey Johnson (Israel Horovitz, Artistic Director, Ian McColl, Managing Director). The set was designed by Charles F. Morgan, the lighting by John Ambrosone, the costumes by Jane Stein. The stage manager was James Conway. The cast was as follows:

Roddy Stern (the Elder)/Archie Stern. . . . . Will LeBow
Roddy Stern (the Younger) . . . . Ben Webster, David Rich
Molly Stern. . . . . Paula Plum
Sylvie Stern . . . . Jessica Semeraro
Haddie Stern . . . . Patricia Pellows
Jacob Stern . . . . Barry Zaslove
Willie . . . . Mick Verga

Subsequently, the play had its New York City premiere on October 16, 1994 at the WPA Theatre. It was directed by Steve Zuckerman (Kyle Renick, Artistic Director). The set was designed by Edward T. Gianfrancesco, the lighting by Richard Winkler, the costumes by Mimi Maxmen and the sound by Aural Fixation. The production stage manager was Mark Cole. The cast was as follows:

Roddy Stern (the Elder)/Archie Stern . . . . Steve Ryan
Roddy Stern (the Younger) . . . . Jonathan Marc Sherman
Molly Stern . . . . Caitlin Clarke
Sylvie Stern . . . . Karen Goberman
Haddie Stern . . . . Scotty Bloch
Jacob Stern . . . . Sol Frieder
Willie. . . . . Paul O'Brien

CHARACTERS

Archie Stern, late 30s, handsome, strong, sad-eyed, suspicious. Note: same actor plays Roddy (The Elder) throughout play.

Molly Stern, Archie's wife; slightly younger than Archie; small, full-breasted, strikingly beautiful.

Sylvie Stern, Archie and Molly's daughter, 15, skinny, sad-eyed, pretty.

Roddy (the Younger) Stern, Archie and Molly's son; 14, small, skinny, an easy smile. Note: Could be played by slightly older actor, age 20-25.)

Haddie Stern, Archie's mother; nearly 70; small, strong-backed, plump.

Jacob Stern, Archie's father; same age as Haddie; has severe Parkinson's Disease; slurred speech; cannot walk unassisted.

Willie, Archie's helper, 40; vaguely dapper.

PLACE

Kitchen of Stern family home, small town New England.

TIME

Early 1950s; Eisenhower is in.

ACCENT

If possible, a North Shore Massachusetts accent ("Pahk Yo'r Cah In Hav'id Yahd") should be used by all, but for Haddie and Jacob, who should speak with an accent that is a blend of Eastern Europe and Western Massachusetts.

UNEXPECTED TENDERNESS

ACT ONE
Scene One

Music In: Chopin, on piano, lightly, sweetly. Soft white light fades up on Roddy the Elder Stern, center stage. He is in his late thirties; wears clothing of a truck-driver...matching grey "chino" pants and shirt, work boots, etc. He is handsome, sturdy, strong. A second spotlight fades up on Roddy the Younger, standing on staircase, facing audience.

RODDY (THE ELDER): For the past few months, I wake during the night, two or three times, every night, and I hear voices in the kitchen. It's my mother and my father. I hear them bickering, mostly...But, sometimes, they laugh, and when their laughter stops, I know that they're kissing.

RODDY (THE YOUNGER): *(Smiles at audience speaks.)* Each time, just before their voices go silent, they take turns yelling up the stairs for me to get ready for school.

MOLLY'S VOICE: *(Off.)* Roddy! You'll be late for school!

(Roddy the Elder turns, yells. Note: he is now playing Archie.)

ARCHIE: Do you hear what your mother's saying, you? *(He switches back to playing Roddy the Elder, without hestitation…or explanation to audience.)*

RODDY (THE ELDER): When I give in to my curiousity and go downstairs, the kitchen's empty, of course, and I'm filled with despair.

MOLLY'S VOICE: *(Off.)* Roddy! You'll be late for school!

(Roddy the Elder yells upstairs. He is, again, playing Archie.)

ARCHIE: It's six-thirty, you! Are you quitting school?!

(No reply.)

Do you hear me? I am asking you a question: Are you quitting school?!

(Archie turns, faces audience, again; smiles. He is, now, once again, playing Roddy the Elder.)

RODDY (THE ELDER): Oh, there's something I should warn you about. I'll be playing Archie, my father—like I just did, there, when I yelled. The boy who's playing Roddy (me, young) will sometimes talk to you, directly, when I'm too busy playing Archie to stop and explain things.

RODDY (THE YOUNGER): *(Smiles at audience; speaks.)* This confusion of father and son might be a bit disquieting, at first, just like the confusion of father and son is in life. *(Nods to Roddy the Elder.)* Okay?

RODDY (THE ELDER): *(Nods "okay"; smiles at audience.)* You're clever. You'll get used to it.

(Suddenly, Roddy the Younger runs upstairs, and Roddy the Elder moves to bottom of staircase, yells upstairs. He is, once again, playing Archie.)

ARCHIE: Excuse me! Am I talking to myself here?

(Lightrs widen to reveal kitchen, Archie and Molly Stern's modest apartment. The dining table is set for breakfast. Sylvie, the daughter, 15, sits at upright piano, practicing Chopin étude. Sylvie is dark-haired, sad-eyed, skinny, pretty. She wears a Girl Scout uniform; many merit badges. Archie, standing at bottom of staircase, yells upstairs, again.)

ARCHIE: Do you not hear me? I have to be back on the road in one half hour, precisely!…Willie's waiting in the truck! Do I not deserve to have breakfast with my family? Do you think I'm a stupid person, or what?

(Roddy the Younger, Archie's 14-year-old son, yells down stairs.)

RODDY (THE YOUNGER): *(Off.)* I'm up! I'm up!

ARCHIE: Yuh, right! So's Mrs. Woolf!

RODDY (THE YOUNGER): *(Off.)* Who's Mrs. Woolf?

ARCHIE: Your teacher's not Mrs. Woolf?

RODDY (THE YOUNGER): *(Off.)* My teacher's Mrs. Foxx!

SYLVIE: His teacher's Mrs. Foxx.

MOLLY: *(Off.)* His teacher's Mrs. Foxx.

(Molly enters, from bedroom, upstairs. She is slightly younger than Archie, small, large-breasted, strikingly beautiful; wears robe belted tightly at waist. She takes command.)

MOLLY: The toaster popped! Sylvie! The toaster popped!…Are you a deaf person?

SYLVIE: *(Stops playing piano.)* Okay, fine, I'm getting it!

(Sylvie goes to toaster, places toast on plate; goes to stove, begins scrambling eggs. Molly busily prepares family breakfast; sets table, pours coffee, etc.)

MOLLY: *(To Archie.)* Why isn't he up?

ARCHIE: He's up.

MOLLY: How do you know?

ARCHIE: Because, he's talking. He said the words "I'm up," twice. I heard him. If he weren't talking and I didn't hear him, it would be a different story. *(Eyes Molly's robe.)* Close your robe tighter.

MOLLY: *(Tightens belt on robe; yells up stairs to Roddy.)* Are you really up, you?

(No reply.)

Roddy!

RODDY (THE YOUNGER): *(Off.)* I'm really up! I'm really up! I'm practicing my speech for the Red Feather Oratory Contest!

ARCHIE: Now, we both heard him. He's really up. He said he's practicing his Red Feather speech.

MOLLY: Friday, he said he was practicing his speech for the Red Feather Oratory Contest, and, forty-five minutes later, I went upstairs…still in bed…

ARCHIE: You told me…

MOLLY: …Sound asleep.

ARCHIE: You told me this.

MOLLY: *(Screams up staircase.)* If you're not downstairs by the time I count twenty-five, there will be no Red Feather Oratory Contest, no bicycle, no skating, no YMCA, and, definitely, no Buzzy Levine!… One!…Two!…*(Brings coffee to Archie.)*…Three!… Four!…Five!… *(They kiss. Molly breaks from kiss; yells upstairs to Roddy.* Ten! *(Lights crossfade with Archie, as he steps forward into spotlight; talks to audience.)*

RODDY (THE ELDER): Oh, I know what you're thinking…"Sweet, nice little family…ethnic comedy…New Englandy…" …If I could rewrite it, and make it sweet and nice, I would have done just that…many years ago!

(Suddenly, Roddy the Elder turns upstage, screams at Sylvie, who has prepared a breakfast tray. He is now, again, playing Archie. Molly resumes meal-preparation.)

ARCHIE: What do you think you're doing with that?

SYLVIE: Bringing Willie's breakfast out to him.

ARCHIE: *(Enraged. He moves upstage, to kitchen.)* Jesus! Stop, you!…Stop!

SYLVIE: Why? I did it, yesterday!.

ARCHIE: That was yesterday! I…said…"Stop"!

SYLVIE: *(Skids to a stop.)* Okay! I stopped!

ARCHIE: *(To Molly.)* Did you see her? Did you see your daughter? Did you see where she was going?

(To Sylvie.) If I ever—EVER—see you near that one, alone, you'll pack your bags.

SYLVIE: I won't ever, daddy.

ARCHIE: You're goddam right you won't ever! Gimme that!

(Sylvie hands breakfast tray to Archie.)

SYLVIE: Here, daddy.

ARCHIE: Where's his coffee?

SYLVIE: In the thermos bottle. I'll get it.

(Sylvie finds thermos, hands it to Archie, who tucks it under his arm, carries tray to door.)

ARCHIE: I'll be right back. *(Archie goes to door, stops, turns to Sylvie.)* It's a good thing I asked you, isn't it? *(Exits.)*

SYLVIE: *(After a pause; to the world.)* I never get anything right for him!

MOLLY: Did you finish your Chopin?

SYLVIE: I finished my Chopin.

MOLLY: *(Looks at table.)* No napkins? Are we eating like Irish people?

SYLVIE: I thought I put napkins on the table. *(Sylvie gets napkins from counter; puts them on table.)*

MOLLY: Did you brush your hair?

SYLVIE: I think I did.

MOLLY: Brush it, again.

SYLVIE: But, I really think I brushed it, already!

MOLLY: Either put a sign on your head that says "I think I brushed it, already," or, go brush it!

SYLVIE: Both of you hate me!

(Sylvie runs up stairs. Molly completes the counting.)

MOLLY: Twenty-two!…Twenty-three!…Twenty-four!…

(Roddy the Younger runs down stairs and into room. He is 14-years old; dark-eyed, small, skinny.)

RODDY (THE YOUNGER): *(Radio-announcer's voice.)* And, once again, ladies and gentlemen, Rodney Stern is saved by the click of his Shick!

(Molly slaps Roddy's hand, twice.)

MOLLY: This is for your being late, and this is for your Mr. Wiseguy mouth!

RODDY (THE YOUNGER): Thank you.

(Jacob enters with Haddie. He is nearly seventy; has severe Parkinson's Disease. He walks backwards, she walks forward. It is almost as if they are dancing. When Jacob talks, his words blur.)

HADDIE: Doesn't he look better?

MOLLY: Much better.

JACOB: I…d-d-d-don't!

HADDIE: You do!

MOLLY: Say "Hello" to your grandmother.

RODDY (THE YOUNGER): Hullo, Grandma.

HADDIE: Hello, Roddy. Did you sleep?

RODDY (THE YOUNGER): I slept.

MOLLY: And not your grandfather?

RODDY (THE YOUNGER): Hullo, Grandpa.

HADDIE: Doesn't Grandpa look much better?

RODDY (THE YOUNGER): I guess.

HADDIE: Look at his color.

RODDY (THE YOUNGER): That's nice, Grandpa.

(Haddie and Jacob have negotiated a crossing of the kitchen and now attempt to negotiate a seating.)

HADDIE: Chair!

MOLLY: Chair!

(Roddy grabs chair, pulls it back from the table. Haddie seems to be dumping Jacob on to the floor. At the last possible second, Roddy the Younger places the chair under Jacob's bottom, and he is seated. This is a well-rehearsed, often-performed Stern Family acrobatic act.)

HADDIE: You're comfortable?

JACOB: N-n-no.

HADDIE: Why not? What's to be uncomfortable about? It's your chair! It's your family!

RODDY (THE YOUNGER): Do you want your cushion, Grandpa?

MOLLY: *(Passing by enroute to pantry.)* Hasn't he got his cushion?

HADDIE: He's got his cushion…He wants his newspaper…I'll get your newspaper.

(Haddie exits into back room; out back door. Jacob looks at Roddy the Younger, furtively.)

JACOB: T-t-take…

RODDY (THE YOUNGER): Take your cushion away?

JACOB: Y-y-yes.

(Roddy the Younger tries to extricate cushion from under Jacob's bottom, but cannot manage the move.)

RODDY (THE YOUNGER): Can you kinda' hop up a little, grandpa?

(Jacob tries, but, his hops get him nowhere.)

MOLLY: *(Re-enters from pantry; enroute to table.)* What are you doing to your grandfather, you?

RODDY (THE YOUNGER): His cushion's bothering him.

MOLLY: Take it out from under him.

RODDY (THE YOUNGER): I'm trying to.

(Archie appears at window, peeking inside at his family, discreetly, mysteriously. Roddy the Younger sees him. After a moment's pause, Archie disappears from window.)

RODDY (THE YOUNGER): He's coming back inside!

MOLLY: He's coming back inside!

JACOB: He's c-c-c-c…

MOLLY: Shhhhh!

(Archie re-enters from outside.)

ARCHIE: Willie's sick…I'll have to take him to the doctor.

MOLLY: What's the matter?

ARCHIE: He's sick. He's got a sickness.

MOLLY: Should he be out there in a cold truck?

ARCHIE: He's not coming in here!

MOLLY: I'm not suggesting anything!

ARCHIE: I won't be able to eat.

(Archie goes to Molly, kisses her, lightly. He pats her bottom; lets his hand linger and rub.)

ARCHIE: I'll call you. *(Looks at her robe.)* Aren't you getting dressed, today?

MOLLY: As soon as they leave for school.

ARCHIE: I don't want to leave you not dressed.

MOLLY: So, wait.

ARCHIE: I can't wait. I've got to go.

MOLLY: As soon as they go to school, I'll get dressed.

ARCHIE: I don't like you trapsing around in front of everybody in a bathrobe.

MOLLY: What everybody? There's you, me, your mother, your father, our children! I'll get dressed as soon as they go to school.

ARCHIE: Fine.

JACOB: T-t-t-take…

RODDY (THE YOUNGER): You're gonna' hav'ta hop, Grandpa!

(Roddy the Younger tries, again, to extricate the cushion from under Jacob. Archie sees.)

ARCHIE: What are you doing to your grandfather?

RODDY (THE YOUNGER): I'm trying to get his cushion out.

ARCHIE: Leave it! He needs his cushion for comfort!

RODDY (THE YOUNGER): But, it's making him uncomfortable!

ARCHIE: Who says?

RODDY (THE YOUNGER): He says!

ARCHIE: He said that?

RODDY (THE YOUNGER): He did!

JACOB: I d-d-d…

ARCHIE: So, take it out from under him.

RODDY (THE YOUNGER): I'm trying to!

ARCHIE: I'm leaving, now.

MOLLY: Kiss your father.

(Archie offers his cheek to Roddy the Younger to kiss. Roddy the Younger kisses cheek.)

RODDY (THE YOUNGER): Aren't you eating breakfast with us?

ARCHIE: Willie's sick.

JACOB: *(Manages to shift his position in chair; smiles with relief.)* Ahhhh! B-b-b-better! Th-th-th…

RODDY (THE YOUNGER): You're welcome, Grandpa…

(To Archie.) Are you leaving right now?

ARCHIE: Right now. Why?

RODDY (THE YOUNGER): I was kind of hoping I could try out my speech on you.

ARCHIE: Now?

RODDY (THE YOUNGER): I was kind of hoping so.

ARCHIE: I can't, now. Willie's sick.

(Haddie re-enters from back door, carrying newspaper.)

HADDIE: Here. Your paper. I froze getting it.

(Without pause, she goes to Jacob, lifts him by his collar, scoots cushion out from under him; puts newspaper in his hands.)

JACOB: D-d-d-don't m-m-move m-m-me!…Dammit!

HADDIE: What are you complaining about, you?

RODDY (THE YOUNGER): I think he was comfortable with the cushion under him.

HADDIE: What does he know? *(To Archie, as she crosses to pantry.)* Why is your coat on?

ARCHIE: I have to leave early.

HADDIE: Why are you leaving early?

ARCHIE: Willie's sick.

HADDIE: I'm not surprised. *(Exits into pantry.)*

RODDY (THE YOUNGER): Do you think you could help me with my Red Feather speech, Grandpa?

JACOB: N-n-now?

RODDY (THE YOUNGER): Well...soon.

JACOB: A-a-ask your g-g-grandm-m-mother.

RODDY (THE YOUNGER): Grandma, can Grandpa help me with my Red Feather speech?

HADDIE: *(Re-enters from pantry.)* Aren't you making yourself late for school?

RODDY (THE YOUNGER): Why? What time is it?

HADDIE: Nearly seven-thirty. You shouldn't be speaking, now. You should be eating, now.

(Suddenly, Molly screams at Roddy the Younger.)

MOLLY: Nearly seven-thirty, you, and still no socks on?

RODDY (THE YOUNGER): I couldn't find any socks.

MOLLY: So, instead of looking and finding them, you're going to school with no socks?

RODDY (THE YOUNGER): You were screaming at me to come downstairs!

MOLLY: No socks, like an Italian? *(Screams up staircase to Sylvie.)* Sylvie!

SYLVIE: What? What is it? What?

MOLLY: Come downstairs, you, and kiss your father goodbye!

SYLVIE: *(Off.)* Did you already eat without me?

MOLLY: Nobody ate anything! Your father's leaving early! Come downstairs and kiss him goodbye! *(To Roddy.)* There are clean socks in the airing cupboard! Put them on.

RODDY (THE YOUNGER): What color?

MOLLY: Blue or brown, either color.

(Roddy exits, loping up staircase; Molly screams up to Sylvie.)
Your father is waiting to be kissed!

RODDY (THE YOUNGER): *(Off.)* You just sent me up for socks!

MOLLY: I am talking to your sister!

ARCHIE: She doesn't have to, if she doesn't want to.

MOLLY: What are you saying, you? *(Molly moves to bottom of staircase; screams upstairs.)* What is taking you?

RODDY (THE YOUNGER): *(Off.)* Me or her?

MOLLY: Her!

SYLVIE: *(From staircase.)* I was on the toilet! *(Enters room; goes to Archie; kisses Archie's cheek.)* Why are you leaving before we eat breakfast?

ARCHIE: I've got to do something.

SYLVIE: In my whole life, you never missed eating breakfast with me, before, not once, not ever!...

ARCHIE: I never eat with you on weekends...

SYLVIE: Schooldays, I mean schooldays...

ARCHIE: I have to do something.

SYLVIE: What?

MOLLY: Don't pester your father!

(Roddy the Younger enters carrying two pairs of socks: one red pair and one green pair.)

RODDY (THE YOUNGER): There's no brown or blue, only red and green, and they smell bad.

MOLLY: Did you get those from the airing cupboard or the hamper?

RODDY (THE YOUNGER): The hamper.

MOLLY: I said the airing cupboard!

RODDY (THE YOUNGER): I wasn't listening.

ARCHIE: Give me a kiss. I'm going.

SYLVIE: I just kissed you!

ARCHIE: Him. I'm talking to him.

(To Roddy the Younger.) Will you hurry, please?

RODDY (THE YOUNGER): *(Goes to Archie; kisses Archie's cheek, again.)* Bye, daddy. I hope you don't hit traffic.

ARCHIE: What smells bad?

RODDY (THE YOUNGER): It's my socks. I got the wrong color.

MOLLY: Your son took dirty socks from the hamper.

RODDY (THE YOUNGER): Dirty!? Oh, God! I thought they smelled funny! I'll put them back.

(Roddy the Younger runs upstairs, as Archie goes to Haddie; kisses her cheek.)

ARCHIE: Bye, Ma...I'm goin'.

HADDIE: Goodbye, Arthur. I hope you don't hit traffic.

(Archie goes to Jacob; touches his bald head, affectionately. Jacob looks at Archie, disapprovingly. Archie withdraws his hand; kisses his father's cheek.)

ARCHIE: Bye, Pop.

JACOB: B-b-bye...I h-h-h-hope...

ARCHIE: The traffic will be fine, Pop...*(To everyone.)* Well...

> *(Suddenly, there is a knocking on the door. We can see the figure of a man, other side of curtains on door's window-pane. Everyone turns, stares; seems startled. No one moves or speaks.)*

WILLIE: *(Off.)* Arch?

> *(Archie breaks the in-house silence.)*

ARCHIE: I'm coming right out, Willie!...

WILLIE: *(Off.)* I'm really feeling wick'id sick, Arch.

ARCHIE: Go back to the truck! I'll come right out!

WILLIE: It must be the Virus-X! I'm feeling really punk.

ARCHIE: Go back to the truck!

WILLIE: *(Off.)* Can you make it snappy, Arch? I'm really feeling terrible!

ARCHIE: I said I'm coming, didn't I? Go back to the truck!

WILLIE: *(Off.)* Okay, Arch, sorry...I hate ta' bother you when you're with your family and all...

ARCHIE: *(Yells.)* When you're back in the truck, I'll come out! Not before!

> *(There is a pause.)*

WILLIE: *(Off.)* Okay, Arch...I'm goin'.

> *(After a moment's pause, Archie speaks to his silent family.)*

ARCHIE: I'd better start out.

RODDY (THE YOUNGER): *(Re-entering, from stairs.)* Who was that at the door?

SYLVIE: *(Whispers.)* Willie.

RODDY (THE YOUNGER): Oh.

ARCHIE: I'm starting out.

MOLLY: Kiss your father.

RODDY (THE YOUNGER): I did, already!

MOLLY: Kiss him, again!

> *(Roddy kisses Archie's cheek; no hug.)*

RODDY (THE YOUNGER): Bye, Daddy.

> *(Sylvie kisses Archie's cheek; no hug.)*

SYLVIE: Bye, Daddy.

ARCHIE: *(To Molly.)* So?

> *(Molly kisses Archie full on the lips; big hug, moderate groping.)*

ARCHIE: Are you going out, today?

MOLLY: Nothing special.

ARCHIE: You're sure on this?

MOLLY: I'm sure.

ARCHIE: Expecting any visitors?

MOLLY: Will you please?

ARCHIE: Yes or no.

MOLLY: Arthur…

ARCHIE: Yes or no!?

MOLLY: Arthur!

ARCHIE: Yes or no?!

MOLLY: No!

(There is a pause.)

ARCHIE: It's Monday.

MOLLY: So, it's Monday.

ARCHIE: Your Mah Jong group isn't playing here?

MOLLY: My Mah Jong group isn't Mondays.

ARCHIE: So, when is it, then?

MOLLY: Tuesdays.

ARCHIE: Fine. I'm starting out. *(Looks at Molly; threateningly.)* I'll call you in an hour.

(We hear: truck's horn being tooted—three toots.)

Bastard! *(Awkwardly.)* Well…I'm off. *(Archie goes to door, opens it, disappears outside. Five count. Archie re-enters room.)* It's raining. I need my slicker. *(He grabs his raincoat from coat-tree; goes to door; pauses.)* Well…I'm off, again.

(Archie exits. There is a small silence…five count…and then Molly takes full command.)

MOLLY: *(To Roddy the Younger.)* You! Tie your shoes!

(To Sylvie.) You! Pull up your knee-socks!

(To both.) Both of you! Eat your breakfast! You are not being late for school, again! Sit! Eat! *(Flashes looks at Haddie and Jacob.)*

HADDIE: We're eating!

JACOB: W-w-w-we're ee-ee-ee…

MOLLY: Not you! Them!

(Archie re-appears at downstairs window, peering in from outside.)

SYLVIE: Daddy, Mama.

(Molly sneaks a peak at Archie…sees him, looks away, quickly.)

MOLLY: Oh, God! Smile, please!

(Molly looks at her children and smiles her happiest smile. The children join in, as do the grandparents. The entire family is now smiling and eating breakfast, happily…like a picture-book family. It's all for the benefit of Archie, who spies on them.)

MOLLY: *(To Haddie.)* Your son will put me in my grave!

HADDIE: I hate to say it, but...

MOLLY: Don't say it, then!

HADDIE: I have to say it!

MOLLY: So, say it.

HADDIE: My son is crazy.

JACOB: *(Tries to yell at Archie, in window.)* G-g-g-get awa-awa-awa...

MOLLY AND HADDIE: Don't let him see you looking!

JACOB: F-f-f-fine.

> *(We hear: truck's horn being tooted, again—three toots. Archie scowls, turns, exits from window.)*

RODDY (THE YOUNGER): He's gone.

MOLLY: Don't let him see you looking!

RODDY (THE YOUNGER): He's gone!

MOLLY: Come, sit, you! Eat your breakfast!

> *(Roddy the Younger sits; joins family meal. Molly smiles at all.)*

MOLLY: Now, please, may we have ten consecutive seconds of sitting and eating in peace?

> *(Archie re-appears in downstairs den window, peering into his own house, discreetly spying on his family. He is framed in window as if on a giant TV screen. Sylvie is the first to notice Archie.)*

SYLVIE: Daddy!...*(Whispers.)* He's back, Mama.

MOLLY: *(Whispered.)* I see him.

RODDY (THE YOUNGER): *(Whispered.)* He's back!

MOLLY: *(Whispered.)* I see him.

SYLVIE: *(Whispered.)* She sees him.

JACOB: *(Full voice.)* Ar-ar-ar...

ALL EXCEPT JACOB: She sees him!

> *(All begin eating, animatedly, enthusiastially, as though Archie is not in the window. After a moment, Molly covers her eyes, bows her head. Light's dim in kitchen. Roddy the Younger stands, moves from table into spotlight, downstage. Roddy the Younger talks to audience.)*

RODDY (THE YOUNGER): My father never left for work, easily. He was always certain that what he called "visitors" would be sneaking into our house, as soon as he was gone. Because he drove his own truck, he was able to drive by the house several times a day and pop in...just to check on things. We never knew exactly what kind of "visitors" he expected to find in our house...earthlings or aliens. Only he knew for sure. And we never knew exactly what purpose the visitors would have in our particular house. What we did know, however, was not to be frightened when a man almost always appeared, peeking in through one of the ground floor windows, shortly after our father left for work…or, shortly before our father got home from work. The fact is, it was kind of a shock the first time I had a sleep-over at Sal Cataldo's house, and his father, Mr. Cataldo, went straight to work and never once showed up in any of the downstairs windows. I also noticed that Sal and his father, Mr. Cataldo, both Italians, wore socks. And Mrs. Cataldo (who told me she was Irish before she got married) used a napkin!

(Music in: A romantic 1940's tune, sung by Sinatra or Crosby. Lights fade up in kitchen behind Roddy the Younger. We see: Molly and Archie slow-dancing, cheek to cheek, sensually, romantically. Roddy the Younger looks into kitchen, watches his parents dance, for a moment. Then, he smiles at audience.)

RODDY (THE YOUNGER): Things weren't always totally crazy between my mother and father. Sometimes, their romance was delicious. They loved to dance, cheek to cheek. Most of all, they loved to dance cheek to cheek at home…in the kitchen…after Grandma and Grandpa and Sylvie and I had gone to sleep. Sylvie and I would lie in our beds and hear Sinatra or Crosby, crooning…and my mother and father, giggling.

(Archie and Molly giggle…kiss, passionately. Light fades out in kitchen. Roddy talks to audience.)

RODDY (THE YOUNGER): I'd better get to school. I'm going to practice my Red Feather speech in front of Mrs. Foxx, today. I'm competing in the Red Feather Oratory Contest at school. "We have nothing to fear but fear itself."…That's the name of my speech. I didn't pick it. It was given to me by Mrs. Foxx. It's a quote from Franklin Delano Roosevelt. *(Simply.)* Franklin Delano Roosevelt was a crippled president who hated Jews.

(Lights fade to black.)

END OF SCENE ONE

Scene Two

Music in: A simple Chopin piano piece, simply played. Light's fade up in kitchen, an hour later. Molly, still wearing robe, sits at piano, playing. Haddie shuttles between table to sink, bringing dishes from table. Jacob sits in his chair, newspaper on lap, asleep.

HADDIE: If your husband catches you playing the piano, he'll be furious!

MOLLY: He won't catch me. *(She plays.)* It's a waste of good money to pay for lessons for one child, when, for the same money, the mother, if she's clever and she pays attention, can learn to play the piano, also. *(She plays.)*

HADDIE: If he comes back and catches you playing the piano, there will be hell to pay.

MOLLY: He won't catch me. *(She plays.)*

HADDIE: I won't protect you.

MOLLY: Fine. *(Stops playing.)* Are you happier?

HADDIE: I'm ecstatic.

MOLLY: Good. I'm glad. *(Molly goes to sink; dries dishes.)* Don't forget we're going out in a while.

HADDIE: When?

MOLLY: In a while.

HADDIE: Where?

MOLLY: Hmm?

HADDIE: Where are you going?

MOLLY: Where am I going?

HADDIE: That's what I asked: where are you going?

MOLLY: Out.

HADDIE: Alone?

MOLLY: Excuse me?

HADDIE: Are you going out alone?

   (Molly turns, looks at Haddie, annoyed. Haddie explains herself.)
   If your husband comes home and you're out and I don't know exactly where or with who…

MOLLY: *(Slips in correction.)*…with whom…

HADDIE:…with whom, there will be trouble. And I, personally, couldn't give a fig where you're going or with whom, but, you can understand my demanding an answer, yes?

MOLLY: Did you wash this cup?

HADDIE: You certainly didn't.

MOLLY: It's filthy.

HADDIE: I think it's fine. If you think it's filthy, wash it again.

(Molly places cup in waste basket.)

You threw the cup away?

MOLLY: It was filthy. If you don't want me to throw it away, take it out of the wastebasket and wash it.

HADDIE: It's a perfectly good cup.

MOLLY: The decision is yours to make.

(Haddie goes to waste basket, retrieves cup.)

HADDIE: It's not filthy.

MOLLY: Filthy.

HADDIE: It's a little soiled.

MOLLY: Drink from it, you'll be a little diseased.

HADDIE: Fine. *(Washes cup.)* You're not going to tell me?

MOLLY: I'm going swimming.

HADDIE: In this weather?

MOLLY: Yes, in this weather.

HADDIE: You want me to tell your husband you went swimming in this weather?

MOLLY: You wanna tell him I went swimming in different weather?

HADDIE: And with who?

MOLLY: With whom.

HADDIE: I hate that.

MOLLY: It's the object of a preposition.

HADDIE: I just hate that.

MOLLY: How do you expect the children in this house to speak English correctly, if the adults in this house don't speak English correctly?

HADDIE: They're your children. You want them to spend their lives worrying about propositions [sic.], this is your business. I'm just the grandmother.

MOLLY: Fine.

HADDIE: You didn't tell me with who.

MOLLY: With whom.

HADDIE: *(Annoyed.)* Fine. You didn't tell me with whom.

MOLLY: With you.

HADDIE: What are you giving me?

MOLLY: This is Monday. This is the day you and I are using the free trial passes they sent us for the new "Y" pool.

HADDIE: I forgot.

MOLLY: I only told you ten times.

HADDIE: I forgot. Next time, tell me twelve times! I'm an old lady. Shoot me.

MOLLY: You found your bathing suit?

HADDIE: I don't know.

MOLLY: You don't know if you found your bathing suit?

HADDIE: That is not it.

MOLLY: What is it?

HADDIE: *(After a thoughtful pause.)* I don't know.

MOLLY: What don't you know?

HADDIE: *(Discreetly; so that Jacob doesn't overhear.)* I don't know if I can parade around in a bathing suit at a YMCA, you know, in front of people.

MOLLY: *(Discreetly; a harsh whisper.)* Stay in the water. Don't parade. It's not a parading pool, it's a swimming pool.

HADDIE: Where am I supposed to put him while I'm swimming?

MOLLY: They have a creche with a full-time babysitter.

HADDIE: I'm supposed to leave him with children?

MOLLY: For a half hour! He can read his paper.

HADDIE: I don't know.

MOLLY: What don't you know, now?

HADDIE: *(Nods to Jacob.)* I've never undressed in front of him.

MOLLY: In front of who?...Whom?

HADDIE: Your father-in-law. You see what I'm saying? If I've never undressed in front of your father-in-law, how can I undress in front of the world?

MOLLY: *(Shocked; faces Haddie, directly.)* Wait a minute, wait a minute, wait a minute! You've never undressed in front of your husband?

HADDIE: I change in the closet.

MOLLY: Wait a minute, wait a minute, wait a minute! You change in the closet?

HADDIE: None of this is anybody's business!

MOLLY: You change in the closet?

HADDIE: I think men and women should do things privately.

MOLLY: Does he change in the closet, too?

HADDIE: Not any more. The man can't even walk by himself. If I put him in the closet, I couldn't leave him in there, alone!...He'd suffocate!

MOLLY: So, you change him, and then you go into the closet and change yourself?

HADDIE: Approximately.

MOLLY: My Goddd!

HADDIE: This is nobody's business.

MOLLY: Did your mother change in the closet?

HADDIE: With me?

MOLLY: That never occured to me. Did she?

HADDIE: Of course not! Why would my mother change in the closet with me?

MOLLY: I don't know. Why would you change in the closet by yourself?

HADDIE: Because it's private!

MOLLY: Couldn't you change in the bathroom?

HADDIE: I'm done talking on this subject.

MOLLY: Wait a minute, wait a minute, wait a minute, wait a minute! If your husband can't move on his own, why can't you just leave him somewhere where he can't see you, and then change? Why do you have to go into the closet?

HADDIE: This is really none of your business. *(Pauses.)* For one thing, I have to go in the closet, anyway, to get my night-gown. And in the morning...

MOLLY: Your clothes are in the closet.

HADDIE: Exactly.

MOLLY: *(Smiles.)* So, he's never seen you naked?

HADDIE: This is nobody's business.

MOLLY: Not even once?

HADDIE: Once or twice.

MOLLY: On purpose or by accident?

HADDIE: I won't dignify a question like that?

MOLLY: Fine.

(The women continue their housework, wordlessly, for a few moments.)

MOLLY: "Once or twice"?...That's all?

HADDIE: I suppose you just change in the open?

MOLLY: He's your son. What do you think?

HADDIE: I couldn't begin to guess.

(Molly considers what she's just learned about Haddie. She begins to laugh, aloud, quite joyously.)

MOLLY: This is really something!

(Haddie looks at Molly, deeply annoyed. Molly, with some difficulty, stops laughing.)

MOLLY: How many years have you and Pa been living with us, now? Ten? Twelve?

HADDIE: Five.

MOLLY: That's all?

HADDIE: Five.

MOLLY: It seems like more.

HADDIE: Five.

MOLLY: It's seems like ten.

(Haddie suddenly screams at Jacob.)

HADDIE: Have you been listening to everything? Have you been faking sleep and listening?

(Jacob laughs.)

HADDIE: You are disgusting!

JACOB: *(Enraged.)* M-m-m-m-meee? I-I-I-I'm dis-g-g-g...?

(Archie appears outside kitchen window, peering in, spying on Molly, discreetly, mysteriously.)

MOLLY: *(Sees Archie.)* Oh, God! He's back! Don't turn around!

HADDIE: *(Sneaks a discreet peek.)* He must have forgotten something.

MOLLY: He's driving me crazy!

HADDIE: For you, crazy is not a long drive.

(Archie disappears from window.)

MOLLY: He's coming in!

HADDIE: *(To Jacob.)* Don't you tell him anything that we said, you!

JACOB: W-w-w-w-would I-I-I t-t-t...?

HADDIE: Shush, you!

(Archie enters kitchen. He playacts not seeing anybody downstairs; yells upstairs.)

ARCHIE: I'm hooooommmme!

MOLLY: What are you yelling upstairs for? We're all right here.

ARCHIE: Oh. I didn't see you in here.

MOLLY: Something wrong?

ARCHIE: Uh uh. Why?

MOLLY: Truck troubles?

ARCHIE: Truck's fine.

HADDIE: Your wife's probably wondering why you're not working.

ARCHIE: Stay out of this, Ma!

HADDIE: Don't start in, Arthur!

ARCHIE: *(White-faced anger.)* Stay out of this!

JACOB: D-d-d-d-on't s-s-s-s...

ARCHIE: I want you in your bedroom!

JACOB: Ar-ar-ar-ar...

ARCHIE: I want to talk to my wife...alone!

(Haddie shoots a look at Molly.)

MOLLY: It's okay, ma.

HADDIE: Sometimes, I feel like I don't know my own son.

ARCHIE: Fine.

(Haddie goes to Jacob.)

HADDIE: Your son is banishing us from the room.

JACOB: I-I-I d-d-don't…

HADDIE: Shah, you! Grab ahold.

(Haddie lifts Jacob, "dances" him backwards into bedroom.
There is a moment's silence after they leave the room. Molly looks at
Archie…bravely.)

MOLLY: Let's have it.

ARCHIE: Is that a fresh mouth?

MOLLY: *(After a pause.)* No.

ARCHIE: I was riding with Willie up near the Stoneham line. He's sitting,
dead quiet. I ask him "What's up with the quiet?"…He goes "Ah, you
know, Arch…I'm feeling really sick with this virus-X and all." I say
nothing on this. Then, no prompting from me, he goes "Molly's looking wicked good, these days, Arch." I am stunned. *(Pauses, as if he's
dropped a bombshell.)* "Molly's looking wicked good, these days,
Arch." Hmmmm? *(Pauses.)* I think this through for about a minute,
and then I put the pieces together. *(Archie walks around Molly, in a
circle, wordlessly, staring at her…looking her over.)*
Who are you meeting?

MOLLY: Excuse me?

ARCHIE: Who are you meeting means "Who are you meeting?"…That's
English I'm speaking, yes?

MOLLY: Meeting, where, Arthur?

ARCHIE: That's another thing I don't know. I don't know "Who" and I
don't know "Where."

MOLLY: I'm not going anywhere and I'm not meeting anybody.

ARCHIE: Excuse me?

MOLLY: I'm not going anywhere and I'm not meeting anybody.

ARCHIE: *(Screams.)* I will not put up with this in my own house! I am working like a trojan, for what? So, I can go off with a derilect maniac in
a truck and you can have meetings? Meetings? Do you think I'm
stupid?

(No reply.)
Answer me! I asked you a question…Answer me!

MOLLY: *(Quietly; holding back tears.)* What's your question, Arthur?

ARCHIE: Do you think I'm stupid?

MOLLY: *(Tears betray her courage.)* No, Arthur, I don't think you're stupid.

ARCHIE: *(Suddenly; to bedroom door.)* Get in here!

 (No reply.)

 I said "Get in here!"

 (Haddie enters from bedroom, head down, alone.)

HADDIE: What?

ARCHIE: Where was she planning to go?

HADDIE: What are you asking me, you?

ARCHIE: Nobody speaks English in this house? Where was she planning to go?

HADDIE: Where was who planning to go, Arthur?

ARCHIE: My wife: where did my wife tell you she's planning to go?

HADDIE: She didn't tell me she was planning to go, anywhere, Arthur.

ARCHIE: Oh, but, she did…mother.

HADDIE: Swimming.

ARCHIE: Excuse me?

HADDIE: Swimming. Your wife is planning to go swimming.

 (Archie turns and faces Molly.)

ARCHIE: Swimming? You're going swimming? How interesting. *(Pauses.)* In the lake?

MOLLY: In the new pool, at the YMCA…with your mother.

HADDIE: *(To Archie.)* I hadn't definitely agreed to go!

 (To Molly.) I didn't say "yes, definitely"!

MOLLY: Fine.

ARCHIE: I don't think so.

MOLLY: Fine.

ARCHIE: Fine, in what sense?

MOLLY: I won't go. I'll stay home.

ARCHIE: All day?

MOLLY: All day.

ARCHIE: You promise me this?

MOLLY: Yes.

 (There is a substantial pause in which Molly looks down at her shoes, silently, seething, on the brink of tears. Archie stares at her a moment; then, he stares at Haddie, who loses her courage; looks down. Archie laughs. He now goes to the piano, checks it over.)

ARCHIE: Was anybody playing the piano in here?

 (No reply.)

 I asked a simple question.

MOLLY: No.

ARCHIE: No, what?

MOLLY: Nobody was playing the piano in here.

ARCHIE: *(To Haddie.)* You agree?

HADDIE: *(After a small hesitation.)* No.

ARCHIE: No, what?

HADDIE: No, nobody was playing the piano in here.

ARCHIE: Really?

(We hear: Jacob screaming from downstairs bedroom, off.)

JACOB: *(Off.)* She's l-l-lying!

(Molly and Haddie wince; exchange a conspiratorial glance.)

ARCHIE: *(Smiles.)* How interesting.

(We now hear: the sound of the truck's horn, off. Three beeps.)

ARCHIE: Willie. The sex-fiend's got ants in his pants. *(Looks at watch.)* I have to go. We're already an hour late with this load. If the mill closes for lunch, before I get there, I'll be stuck in the truck with him for two extra hours. *(Goes to door; turns to Molly.)* We'll talk more about this piano-playing, later. *(Stares a moment, silently.)* I hope you're planning to put some clothes on, today. *(Archie turns to the door, again, then, turns, again, looks at both women, then, turns to door a final time; exits. There is a pause. Then, Archie appears at window, staring inside at his mother and his wife.)*

MOLLY: Did God create men to curse women?

(The women exchange another glance; then, exit together, straight upstage, arm in arm.)

END OF SCENE TWO

(The lights crossfade to…)

Scene Three

Spotlight on Sylvie, sitting at piano. Music in: Chopin piece, played by Sylvie, under. Roddy the Younger practices his speech, more or less for Sylvie's benefit.

RODDY (THE YOUNGER): "We have nothing to fear, but fear itself." That famous quotation from President Franklin Delano Roosevelt may not make a lot of sense, now, but, it made great sense to over a hundred million Americans, just a decade ago, when this great Nation was plunged into War with Hitler and many many other maniacs...

(Sylvie turns, faces Roddy with a look that says she is somewhat disgusted by his attempt. Roddy turns from Sylvie, upset. He sees his own reflection in the wall-mirror; goes to it; starts over.)

"We have nothing to fear, but fear itself." Just a decade ago, when this great Nation was plunged into War with Hitler and many many other maniacs, Franklin Delano Roosevelt spoke that famous quotation as he led America into a war to save the Jews, even though President Roosevelt personally hated the very Jews he was saving! *(He pauses, himself disgusted by this attempt. He moves to mirror, nose to nose with his own reflection; starts over.)* "We have nothing to fear, but fear itself." That famous quotation was spoken by President Franklin Delano Roosevelt as he and many many other Jew-hating maniacs plunged this great Nation into War!... *(He pauses, totally disgusted by this fresh attempt; kicks chair, rolls eyes to Heaven.)* Shit!

(Sylvie stops playing piano, turns to Roddy, picking up conversation from sometime earlier, middle of a private thought.)

SYLVIE: And you're really, honestly not frightened of him?

RODDY (THE YOUNGER): *(Turns upstage.)* Of Daddy? Am I not frightened of Daddy?

SYLVIE: No, of President Eisenhower!

RODDY (THE YOUNGER): Why should I be frightened of President Eisenhower?

SYLVIE: That was a joke, you derr!

RODDY (THE YOUNGER): Did you have the dream, again?

SYLVIE: Last night and the night before.

(Light shifts to spot on Roddy. He speaks directly to audience.)

RODDY (THE YOUNGER): Sylvie has this dream, all the time, in which my father wears a Nazi uniform around the house, and keeps asking if anybody's seen any Jewish girls hiding in the attic.

(Lights restore.)

SYLVIE: Last night, I killed him.

RODDY (THE YOUNGER): You killed Daddy?!

SYLVIE: *(Stops playing piano.)* Shhhhh!

RODDY (THE YOUNGER): *(Whispers.)* You killed Daddy?

SYLVIE: Not really!

RODDY (THE YOUNGER): I know that.

SYLVIE: I mean in my dream!

RODDY (THE YOUNGER): I know that!

SYLVIE: I had a machine gun and troops.

RODDY (THE YOUNGER): What kind of troops?

SYLVIE: Troops. Men…soldiers…working for me. He came upstairs looking for young Jewish girls, and he spotted me, ya' know, reading, in my bed…and he started goose-stepping and yelling really scary things in German…

RODDY (THE YOUNGER): And you killed him?

SYLVIE: I gave the order and the troops killed him.

RODDY (THE YOUNGER): What about your machine gun?

SYLVIE: *(Looks up; weeping.)* After he was dead, I shot him, again.

RODDY (THE YOUNGER): How many times?

SYLVIE: …A lot.

RODDY (THE YOUNGER): A lot? *(Whistles.)* Jesus, Sylvie. Jesus. *(Pauses.)* You really think you ever would?

SYLVIE: *(Weeping.)* Don't ask me that!

RODDY (THE YOUNGER): Well, you know, I'm really curious, that's all. I mean, if he came at me in a Nazi uniform and all, goose-stepping…speaking scary things in German… *(Pauses.)* Jesus, Sylvie, I'm glad it's you having the dream, instead'a me. *(Pauses.)* You wanna' take a walk downtown with me?

SYLVIE: Uh uh. I wanna' practice for a while, before they come home.
    (Sylvie turns to piano; plays.)

END OF SCENE THREE

(Lights crossfade to…)

Scene Four

Spotlight on Roddy the Elder, on stair-case. He speaks to audience, directly.

RODDY (THE ELDER): When I look back over my childhood, there are many, many highpoints to remember…Humming "God Bless America," in my bathtub, under soapy water, for 47 seconds and not dying!…Getting Pesky and Williams to autograph mint-condition rookie cards in the same season!…Homering against Lincoln School with two men on!…The Red Feather Oratory Contest…"We have nothing to fear, but fear itself."...But, most of all, I remember the day when my father and I rode in his green '51 Chevy flat-bed truck, together, down to the Congo Church, where he pulled my sister Sylvie out of her Girl Scout meeting by her hair in front of the whole troop, plus, a bunch of visiting Boy Scouts.

(Lights shift to Roddy the Younger, down-stage. He takes over narration; speaks to audience, directly.)

RODDY (THE YOUNGER): Sylvie was thirteen, and my father thought she had done something really bad with her friend, Robert Dutton, who Sylvie had promised my father she'd never talk to, again, a week after my father had caught Sylvie and Robert kissing on the sun-porch.

(Lights switch, suddenly, to Roddy the Elder, now playing Archie. Archie faces Sylvie, who sits on piano stool, center, sobbing. Archie paces in circles, around the girl, railing at her. Haddie stands behind Jacob, in his chair, up-stage left. Molly stands at sink. All watch, silently, sadly.)

ARCHIE: *(Enraged.)* Marcus Rosenman's daughter went to Girl Scout camp for two months...FOR TWO MONTHS!...Do you know what happened to her? Do you know what happened to her? *(No reply..)*
I asked you a question, young lady, and I am not hearing an answer!

SYLVIE: *(Sobs.)* What's your question, daddy?

ARCHIE: Do you know what happened to Esther Rosenman?

SYLVIE: I don't know, daddy.

ARCHIE: I'm sure you don't. Do you know what "prostitute" means?
(Simultaneously.)

> HADDIE: Arthur!
> JACOB: D-d-d-d...
> MOLLY: Stop, you!

SYLVIE: I don't know what that means.

ARCHIE: Oh, please, will you? Do you think I'm stupid?
(Sylvie sobs.)

ARCHIE: I asked you a question!

SYLVIE: *(Sobbing.)* I don't know what "prostitute" means, daddy! I don't! I really don't! I just know it's a really bad thing!

RODDY (THE YOUNGER): *(To audience.)* At this point, my mother has usually had enough. She will step between my father and my sister and take control. After a moment, when it looks like my mother and father will finally kill each other, I will step in, get myself clobbered... But, I will defuse the bomb.

ARCHIE: The thing I hate more than a young girl's looseness is a young girl's lying!...And you are lying to me!

SYLVIE: I'm not!

(Archie pulls Sylvie, roughly, down-stage; slams her down in kitchen chair; screaming...)

ARCHIE: You are lying to me!

SYLVIE: I'm not lying to you, Daddy! I'm not!

ARCHIE: Don't talk back to me, you!

(Archie raises his hand, threatening to slap Sylvie, who winces and sobs. Suddenly, Molly approaches Archie with an extremely impressive bread knife in her right hand.)

MOLLY: That's enough, you! You shut that mouth, now, you!

(Simultaneously.)

> HADDIE: Molly!
>
> JACOB: D-d-d-d...
>
> SYLVIE: Mama, nooo!

ARCHIE: What's this, you?

MOLLY: You stay back from her! You're a crazy person!

ARCHIE: I'm a crazy person?

MOLLY: You heard me!

ARCHIE: I'm not the one with a bread-knife in my hand!

MOLLY: You've got a bread-knife for a tongue, you! Humiliating your daughter in front of her friends! Hurting her! Calling her names like I've never heard in my life!

ARCHIE: You want a daughter like Marcus and Ruth Rosenman's daughter, fine, that's you, but, that's not me, sister! I would rather be dead, than live to see such a thing! Believe me, I know where your daughter learns to make secret meetings.

MOLLY: What "secret meetings"?

ARCHIE: Hah!

MOLLY: She was at a Girl Scout meeting...with girls!

ARCHIE: Those were not boys, there, too? Those were girls dressed up like boys?

MOLLY: They were Boy Scouts!

SYLVIE: They were Boy Scouts, daddy!

MOLLY: It was a co-ed meeting...to make bird-houses!

SYLVIE: We were making bird-houses, daddy.

ARCHIE: That wasn't Robert Dutton, there, next to you, who you promised me—PROMISED ME!—you would never talk to again as long as you live?!

SYLVIE: *(Sobbing.)* I didn't know he was going to be there, daddy! I didn't know any of the Boy Scouts were going to be there!

ARCHIE: He was next to you! You and he were laughing!

SYLVIE: He told me a joke!

ARCHIE: I'll bet he did! *(His anger is building, quickly.)* I'll bet he did! *(Archie is now violent; hand in the air, threatening Sylvie.)*

ARCHIE: I'LL BET HE DID!

MOLLY: *(Moves in between Archie and Sylvie, bread-knife firmly clenched in her hand.)* Back, you! Get back!

(Simultaneously.)

> HADDIE: Molly!
>
> JACOB: D-d-d-d...
>
> SYLVIE: Mama, nooo!

ARCHIE: Come on...Come ONNNN! *(Archie now raises his fist toward Molly, threateningly. Roddy the Younger looks at audience, shrugs, then, suddenly, runs straight at his father.)*

RODDY (THE YOUNGER): Get away from her! Get away from her! Get away from her! *(Roddy the Younger shoves Archie backwards, against the table.)*

(Simultaneously.)

> HADDIE: Roddy!
>
> JACOB: D-d-d-d...
>
> MOLLY: Roddy, noo!

ARCHIE: Are you out of your mind, you?

(Roddy the Younger shoves Archie again.
Archie slaps the boy, violently. Roddy the Younger flies backwards, squeals; then, rushes at Archie again.)

RODDY (THE YOUNGER): God damn you! God damn you! God damn you! *(Archie laughs; then, suddenly, violently, backhands the boy, who flies backwards.)*

SYLVIE: Daddy, don't!

(Simultaneously.)

> HADDIE: Roddy!
>
> JACOB: Roddy!...
>
> MOLLY: Roddy!

(There is a moment of stunned silence.)

ARCHIE: *(Goes to Haddie.)* He hit me, first. I just had a physical reaction...He hit me, and I hit him back. It was a physical reaction! *(To Molly.)* I didn't want to hit him, but, he hit me, first, and I just hit him back. *(Goes to Roddy, tries to help him up. Roddy pulls away; moves downstage.)* Get up. Roddy, get up. I'm sorry. I said it: I'm sorry. Now, come on, get up. Get up!

RODDY (THE YOUNGER): *(To audience.)* At this point, my father will break down and sob, uncontrollably, begging everybody's forgiveness.
(Suddenly, Archie starts to sob. His sobbing is enormous. His body heaves, racked with sorrow.)

ARCHIE: I'm sorry I get so mad. It's just that…Oh, God, what is wrong with me?! I'm sorry. I apologize to everybody. I can't stop myself. I'm sorry. I am…

RODDY (THE YOUNGER): *(To audience.)* And Sylvie, instead of ordering her troops to fire…
(Suddenly, Sylvie runs into Archie's arms, hugs him.)

SYLVIE: Don't cry, daddy! It's okay, daddy! It's okay, daddy! Don't cry, daddy! Don't cry, daddy! It's really okay.

ARCHIE: *(To Haddie.)* I'm sorry, mama…I get so mad all the time. I get so mad. I'm sorry, mama…I'm sorry, mama…I am.

HADDIE: *(Consoling Archie.)* It's fine, Arthur. No harm done. It's fine. It's fine, Arthur. It's fine. It's fine.

ARCHIE: *(To Jacob.)* What's the matter with me, Pa? Am I a crazy person who can't control his temper? I'm so sorry, Pa.

JACOB: *(Reaches out; takes Archie's hand.)* It's o-k-k-k-k…

ARCHIE: Don't stop loving me, please, Molly, please. I'm so sorry. I'm so sorry. Don't stop loving me, please, Molly, please. I'm so sorry. I'm so sorry.
(Archie is really sobbing, now. Molly is somehow deeply moved. She puts down bread-knife, opens her arms, moves to Archie.)

MOLLY: Oh, God…Come on. Come here.

ARCHIE: I get so mad all the time, Molly. I can't stop myself. I can't stop myself.

MOLLY: *(Cradles Archie's head in her arms. He weeps.)* I know. I know. Shh-hhh. Shhhhh. It's okay.

SYLVIE: *(Hugs Archie, as well.)* It's okay, Daddy. Don't cry. Don't cry, Daddy. I love you so much, Daddy. Don't cry, Daddy. Please? Please?
(The entire family, with the single exception of Roddy the Younger, gathers tightly around Archie, consoling him, comforting him.)

RODDY (THE YOUNGER): *(To audience.)* The entire room is now filled with an unexpected tenderness from which I am totally and utterly…excluded. *(Roddy the Younger moves slowly across kitchen floor to the staircase, past his family, unnoticed. As he climbs the stairs, the lights fade out.)*

END OF ACT ONE

ACT TWO
Scene One

Music in. Lights up on Roddy the Elder, downstage, carrying chair and steering wheel, which he sets into position, downstage-stage center.

RODDY (THE ELDER): As my father never worked weekends, I rarely had a chance to ride in the truck with him…except when school was closed for the odd, indigenous Boston holiday like Patriots Day, or, say, Cardinal Cushing's birthday. I also used to ride to the mills with him on major Jewish holidays like Rosh Hashona and Yom Kippur. *(Pauses.)* Sylvie, never. In her entire life, not once. *(Pauses.)* Sylvie and I weren't allowed to go to school on Jewish holidays…because we were Jewish. Of course, we didn't ever actually go to synagogue, because my father thought the local rabbi, who was a dentist, full-time, and a rabbi, part-time, was only in the rabbinical game to have secret meetings with many many married Jewish women who were active in the Temple Sisterhood. But, that's another story.
(Roddy the Elder begins to "drive" his truck…acts shifting gears and turning steering wheel.

RODDY (THE ELDER):…Because my father was himself raised as a synagogue-going Jew, he felt that he had to somehow observe the Holiday, even though he was in a truck, on a highway, far from makeshift temples and fornicating rabbis. So, he said his High Holiday prayers in his Chevy flat-bed, on the way to the Felulah Mill in Fitchburg, Massachusetts.
(Roddy the Younger enters carrying another chair, sets it down beside Archie, sits; takes over the narration.)

RODDY (THE YOUNGER): And I got to ride along with him…and Willie.
(Willie enters, carrying a chair, which he places, sideways, next to Roddy's chair. Willie sits with arm on chair-back, as if resting on truck window-ledge. Roddy the Younger is sandwiched between the two grownups in a truck-cabin designed for two. The truck lurches left…and then, right. The three men sway, side to side, appropriately. Suddenly, Willie spots something. He leans his head out of truck window, like a large dog. He begins whistling and cat-calling to an imagined female passerby. Note: The actor who has been playing Roddy the Elder is is now, again, playing Archie.)

WILLIE: *(Five shrill whistles, first; then, screams.)* Hey, hey, hey, heyyyy,

Hedy Lamar! Where'd you get those gambinos! Wanna' wrap 'em around my coconuts?! *(Shrill whistles, again.)*

ARCHIE: Not in front of the boy, Willie!

WILLIE: *(Leans out of imagined window. Shrill whistles, again; screams to imagined female passerby again.)* Stuck-up, conceited bitch! Stick your nose up in the air any higher and I'll hav'ta climb a tree to dick ya'!

ARCHIE: Did'ya hear me say "Not in front of the boy," Willie?

WILLIE: *(Leaning out, still glaring at imagined passerby.)* Oh, look'it that, Arch! I get it! She's with somebody, Arch! This is why we're not gettin' the time of day!...There you go! This is the reason we're getting nothin' off'a her, Arch! Jesus, she's kissin' the lucky bast'id! *(Calls out to imagined man.)* Hey, you lucky bast'id! Bring your mother and father around, and I'll marry them! OOoooo, Gawd bless us! She's tonguin' him, Arch! *(Calls out to imagined couple.)* Parlez-vous Frenchie kiss-kiss! Oui oui oui!

ARCHIE: Not in front of the boy, Willie, will ya'?!

WILLIE: Roddy probably knows twice as much as us both, put together, Arch, huh? *(Willie squeezes Roddy the Younger's leg.)* Don't'cha', Rod, huh? *(Toussles Roddy the Younger's hair.)* I'll bet they don't call ya' "Rod" for nothin', right?

ARCHIE: What are you? Demented?

WILLIE: Let the kid answer for himself. *(Toussles Roddy the Younger's hair, again.)* I'll bet they don't call ya' "Rod" for nothin', huh?

RODDY (THE YOUNGER): I guess not.

ARCHIE: *(To Roddy the Younger.)* What are you saying, you?

WILLIE: *(Illustrates his point, graphically.)* I'm just sayin' I'll bet they don't call yo'r boy "Rod" for nothin'.

ARCHIE: I'm talkin' to him. Why do you think we named you Roddy?

RODDY (THE YOUNGER): Because you had an Uncle Rodney who died, and you loved him, and you named me for him.

ARCHIE: *(To Roddy the Younger.)* Exactly.
(To Willie.) This is the way it's done in the Jewish faith, Willie.

WILLIE: Hey, listen, no problem, Arch. *(Suddenly, Willie leans out of window; screams to new, imaginary, female passserby.)* Is that your ass, or are you stealing basketballs?
(Roddy giggles.)

ARCHIE: Not in front of the boy!

WILLIE: Hey, whoa, slow down, Arch, slow down, slow down, slow down! Look, look, look, look, look!
(Archie acts downshifting gears, slows and stops truck....The three men

playact watching imagined female passerby walk across street in front of truck. Their eyes follow her, slowly, from right to left.)

ARCHIE: *(Laughs.)* You're right. She's stealing basketballs.

(Roddy sees his father laugh; laughs loudly.)

WILLIE: You're boy's laughin', Arch! He gets it! Little Rod gets the joke, Arch!

ARCHIE: What's so funny, you?

RODDY (THE YOUNGER): I think she's stealing watermelons.

WILLIE: *(Roars with laughter; toussles Roddy the Younger's hair.)* Watermelons, Archie! Did you hear your kid? Watermelons!

ARCHIE: *(Unable to hide his pride.)* I heard him.

(Willie looks out of window at other imagined passersby; giggles, out of context; toussles Roddy the Younger's hair.)

WILLIE: *(Philosophically.)* I'm gonna' tell ya' what's really great about getting up at 4 o'clock in the mornin' and riding a truck the way we do, Little Rod: What's really great about getting up at 4 o'clock in the mornin' and riding a truck the way we do is you get an opportunity to see many, many 1st-shift female factory workers in many, many neighborhoods. In Wakefield, Stoneham, Woburn, you get your many laundry-girls and dry-cleaning plant workers…clean, starched uniforms. Oh, yummy yummy yum yum! You can just taste what's underneath!

ARCHIE: What is with you? Are you brain-damaged, or what?

WILLIE: Lynn, Beverly, Salem, Swampscott, Marblehead, Gloucester give you your many female fish-plant workers…your female fish-stick packers and your female cutters. This is the other end of the globe from a point of view of clean hands kinda' thing. Your female fish-plant workers are bloody and thinkin' about death all the time. They're also thinkin' "Life's tough, so, why not?"…This makes them readily available to the passing stranger, especially, if he's a sharp dresser with a good sense of humor and a long stiff tongue such as moi!

(Archie begins to rock forward and back, slowly, mumbling a Hebrew prayer, under his breath. Willie stops talking, looks at Archie.)

WILLIE: What's gives, Arch? You feelin' car-sick, again?

ARCHIE: I'm praying. It's a Jewish High Holiday!

WILLIE: No problem, Arch.

RODDY (THE YOUNGER): *(Looks up at Archie.)* Me, too?

ARCHIE: Did you convert? Are you an Episcopalian, now?

(Roddy the Younger clasps his hands together, closes his eyes…imitates Archie by rocking back and forth, slowly…prays. Willie stares at both of

them for a few moments, silently. He, then, looks up at Heaven, "crosses" himself…and he, too, begins to pray. They all pray for a few moments, as Archie continues to "drive" the truck, millward.)

ARCHIE: Red light. *(Archie acts pulling truck to a stop at imagined red light. They all continue to pray for a moment, until, suddenly, Willie notices an imagined beauty in car stopped next to them at red light. He smiles to Heaven, gratefully.)*

WILLIE: *(To God.)* My prayers have been answered!

(Leans out of window, speaks to imagined beauty.) Hullo, Baby-Doll-face! Whose little girl are you? Wanna' suck a lollipop?

(Archie and Roddy the Younger are astonished. Both stop praying. Both roll their eyes to Heaven. Lights switch to black. After two count, lights restore. Willie is gone, his chair is empty.)

RODDY (THE YOUNGER): From time to time, Willie would go off on what my father would call "a sex fiend's errands," and my father and I would be left alone to talk about life, together. We were not what you might call naturally comfortable with each other.

ARCHIE: So, well, uh, Rod…How's school?

RODDY (THE YOUNGER): School's good, dad.

ARCHIE: School's good, huh?

RODDY (THE YOUNGER): Oh, yuh, school's good.

ARCHIE: That's good.

(There is a substantial pause.)

ARCHIE: How's your sister?

RODDY (THE YOUNGER): Sylvie?

ARCHIE: Well, Sylvie's your sister, yes?

RODDY (THE YOUNGER): Well, you see her as much as I do.

ARCHIE: Not as much. You see her after I go off to work and, you know, before I come home. And if I go to bed, early, you sometimes stay up talking to her and all.

(There is a small pause.)

RODDY (THE YOUNGER): I think she's fine.

ARCHIE: You think so?

RODDY (THE YOUNGER): I do. I mean she's never said she's not fine…not to me, privately.

ARCHIE: I'm glad to hear this.

RODDY (THE YOUNGER): *(To audience.)* After a minute or so of silence, while he tried to find a subtle way to ask me what he really wanted to ask me, he'd, well, give up, and just ask me…straight out.

ARCHIE: Does your sister ever talk to you about her doing weird things with boys?

RODDY (THE YOUNGER): Oh, God, never! I don't think she even knows any boys...except, ya' know, you, me and grandpa. Uncle Arnold.

ARCHIE: If she ever talks to you about doing weird things with boys, you'll say something to me, right?

RODDY (THE YOUNGER): *(To Archie; quietly.)* Sure, I will.

ARCHIE: It's for her own good. You know this, yes?

RODDY (THE YOUNGER): Sure.

ARCHIE: You promise me on this?

RODDY (THE YOUNGER): Sure. I promise. *(Glances to Heaven, privately; grimaces.)*

ARCHIE: Your mother never says anything oddball to you, does she?

RODDY (THE YOUNGER): Mama? Uh uh.

ARCHIE: Never?

RODDY (THE YOUNGER): Mama? Never. *(Pauses.)* Grandma, neither. If either of them ever do, though, I'll tell you, right away.

ARCHIE: Good.

RODDY (THE YOUNGER): *(To audience.)* We played endless variations on this particular theme of Sylvie, Mama and/or Grandma's saying and/or doing weird and/or oddballs things to and/or with men. And each time, when the interrogation was done, my father and I would ride through a thousand embarrassed pauses as pregnant as the harlot Sylvie of my father's wildest dreams. We shared these silences as though the passing landscape were somehow suddenly intriguing, as though we weren't suffering the pain of such shared awkwardness.

(Archie and Roddy the Younger now stare straight ahead, sadly, each avoiding visual or spiritual contact with the other. For this brief moment, each is undeniably alone, each is undeniably in pain. Over the scene, we have been hearing a small musical refrain, probably Chopin. When music ends, Roddy the Younger talks to audience, directly.)

RODDY (THE YOUNGER): It happened on an October morning. School was cancelled for a teachers' convention, and Willie was off Godknowswhere doing Godknows what to Godknowswhom. My father and I had done the morning mill-run to Fitchburg, without saying a single word. On the trip back home, on a back road, somewhere near Leominister, Massachusetts, my father broke the silence.

(Archie looks at Roddy the Younger. The boy returns the look. They share a silent stare for a moment. Then, Archie speaks.)

ARCHIE: Rod?

RODDY (THE YOUNGER): Yes, sir?

ARCHIE: You like to play baseball, don't you?

RODDY (THE YOUNGER): I do, yuh.

ARCHIE: Are you any good?

RODDY (THE YOUNGER): I could be better, I guess.

ARCHIE: Can you hit?

RODDY (THE YOUNGER): I can hit okay. I'm a great fielder…Not ground balls, so much as fly balls. I can catch 'em.

ARCHIE: That's great. *(Pauses.)* It's a pain in the neck I don't get much of a chance to play ball with you.

RODDY (THE YOUNGER): That's okay. Mama plays with me a lot. She can't really hit 'em hard, but, it's still practice.

ARCHIE: We don't do much, together, I mean.

RODDY (THE YOUNGER): It's okay. *(Brightly.)* We get to ride in the truck, together.

ARCHIE: You like doin' this?

RODDY (THE YOUNGER): Are you kidding me? I love this!

ARCHIE: *(Happily.)* Me, too.

(Both stare straight ahead. Both are smiling.)

ARCHIE: How's your Red Feather speech coming?

RODDY (THE YOUNGER): Oh, well, it's okay.

ARCHIE: It's getting close, huh?

RODDY (THE YOUNGER): Four weeks, three days…*(Looks at Archie's wristwatch.)*…sixteen hours. *(Pauses.)* If I win my school, I get to go on to the sub-regionals, and maybe, you know, the New England Finals and all.

ARCHIE: *(Whistles, appreciatively.)* Big stuff, huh?

RODDY (THE YOUNGER): Oh, yuh. The national winner gets a $2000 college scholarship. I could pay my own way kind of thing.

ARCHIE: Scared?

RODDY (THE YOUNGER): Me? About the contest? Not too much. I just wish it was, you know, better.

ARCHIE: What was better?

RODDY (THE YOUNGER): My speech.

ARCHIE: Wanna' try it on me?

RODDY (THE YOUNGER): You kidding?

ARCHIE: Naw. What the heck…It's just us, riding, together…two guys… father and son kinda' thing. We won't hit home-plate for at least an hour. How long is it?

RODDY (THE YOUNGER): My speech? Three minutes.

ARCHIE: That's all?

RODDY (THE YOUNGER): Oh, yuh. There's a time limit.

ARCHIE: That's all the whole speech is?

RODDY (THE YOUNGER): Well, yuh…yes. We also get an extemperaneous part to do.

ARCHIE: Oh, yuh, right.

RODDY (THE YOUNGER): *(Senses Archie's confusion; explains, gently.)* That means they give you a subject, right then and there, and you have to make up a speech on that subject with no preparation…

ARCHIE: Just sort of make it up on the spot kind of thing?

RODDY (THE YOUNGER): Exactly.

ARCHIE: You're probably good at that.

RODDY (THE YOUNGER): Oh, yuh. I'm better at that part than the prepared part…you know…"We have nothing to fear, but, fear itself" kind of thing.

ARCHIE: What's this?

RODDY (THE YOUNGER): That's my prepared part. I could do some of it for you. I wouldn't have to do the whole three minutes. I could just do the start of it.

ARCHIE: No, no, no. Do the whole thing.

RODDY (THE YOUNGER): Really?

ARCHIE: Sure. Why not? I mean, as long as we're doing things, together, we might as well do whole things, together, right?

RODDY (THE YOUNGER): Well, yuh, sure! The thing is, I'm not really finished.

ARCHIE: Do whatever you've got.

RODDY (THE YOUNGER): Well, okay… *(Clears his throat.)* Are you sure you wanna' hear this, Daddy? You don't have to!…I mean, I've got plenty of other people who don't mind…

ARCHIE: Come on! Let me hear it!

RODDY (THE YOUNGER): Well…okay…sure. *(Clears his throat.)* "We have nothing to fear, but fear itself." That famous quotation was spoken by President Franklin Delano Roosevelt…

ARCHIE: Roosevelt said this?

RODDY (THE YOUNGER): He did, yuh.

ARCHIE: Roosevelt was a Jew-hating bastard!

RODDY (THE YOUNGER): I know. I talk about this in my speech.

ARCHIE: You don't say "bastard" in front of your teacher, do you?

RODDY (THE YOUNGER): No, no. I use a different word.

ARCHIE: Let me hear.

RODDY (THE YOUNGER): "We have nothing to fear, but fear itself." That famous quotation was spoken by President Franklin Delano Roosevelt as he and many many other Jew-hating maniacs plunged this great Nation into War!...

ARCHIE: "Maniacs"...good...I like "maniacs."

RODDY (THE YOUNGER): I tried it different ways, but, I liked "maniacs" best of all. Maybe I should wait till I get it finished more.

ARCHIE: No, no, no. I like hearing your speech. I like doing this...just us kinda' thing.

RODDY (THE YOUNGER): *(Does the first part, again, rapidly, skipping over the lines to get to the yet-unspoken lines.)* "We have nothing to fear, but fear itself." That famous quotation was spoken by President Franklin Delano Roosevelt as he and many many other Jew-hating maniacs plunged this great Nation into War!... *(Having re-capitulated the start of the speech, Roddy now slows his delivery down to a proper pace.)* What did President Roosevelt mean, exactly, when he uttered that famous quote? Did he mean that the things that scare us most aren't real? That they're imagined things...like ghosts and boogey-men, which we, after all know aren't real?...

ARCHIE: Ghosts may be real.

RODDY (THE YOUNGER): You think so?

ARCHIE: I dunno. I have this really weird kinda' sense of my Uncle Herman all the time...He was a Rabinowitz, on my mother's side. Uncle Herman Rabinowitz was kind of, you know, crazy. He was actually very crazy. He used to whistle in public...patriotic marches...from Poland. I think they were from Poland. He was arrested for exposing himself. You know what that means?

RODDY (THE YOUNGER): Not exactly...kind of. Like showing your private parts to people kind of thing?

ARCHIE: Sort of...it means, more like showing your private parts to people who don't really want to see your private parts kind of thing.

RODDY (THE YOUNGER): Oh, sure, right...I get you.

ARCHIE: Uncle Herman Rabinowitz did this a lot.

RODDY (THE YOUNGER): Gosh.

ARCHIE: He was arrested. Uncle Herman said he was peeing, but, the lady who turned him in said he was doing more than that. *(Pauses.)* Don't ever tell your grandmother I told you any of this stuff, okay?

RODDY (THE YOUNGER): I won't!...

ARCHIE: You've gotta' promise!

RODDY (THE YOUNGER): I promise!

ARCHIE: Good.

RODDY (THE YOUNGER): Would you mind if I waited to show you the rest of my speech til I've done a little more work on it?

ARCHIE: Hey, you're the boss! It's your speech.

RODDY (THE YOUNGER): Really?

ARCHIE: Sure!

(There is a moment's pause, during which both men are smiling. Then, Roddy pops The Big Question.)

RODDY (THE YOUNGER): When do you think you could teach me to steer?

ARCHIE: You're not s'posed'ta touch a wheel til you're sixteen!...You're not allowed! This is Massachusetts! I could go to jail for letting you steer! Sixteen's the law!...

RODDY (THE YOUNGER): You told me grandpa taught you to steer when you were my age.

ARCHIE: That was different! We had no money!...*(Archie acts pulling truck over to side of road; stops truck.)* Come on, over here.

(Roddy the Younger squeezes into Archie's "embrace," as Roddy clutches steering wheel and Archie guides him...Roddy pretends to steer truck. Both men are, for the moment, very, very happy.)

RODDY: *(To audience.)* We rode together that way, me, steering...He, with his arms around me, guiding me, sharing an against-the-law risk with me for at least four minutes.

ARCHIE: That's enough.

(Archie stops the truck; Roddy the Younger relinquishes the steering wheel, slides away from Archie; looks out to audience, directly.)

RODDY (THE YOUNGER): In my entire childhood, I only remember my father hugging me that one time.

END OF SCENE ONE

(The lights crossfade to...)

Scene Two

Haddie shuffles on, calls out to Roddy the Younger.

HADDIE: Okay, Roddy, I'm ready to listen to your speech, now.

Haddie moves to stove, makes cup of tea for herself, as Roddy the Younger, moves to her, practicing his speech.

RODDY (THE YOUNGER): Okay, Grandma…Here goes…What President Roosevelt was teaching us was to get over our fears, before they cripple us…the way polio crippled him—Roosevelt—who was a cripple. So, when Roosevelt says "We have nothing to fear, but fear itself", he's telling us to find the courage to confront the thing itself instead of our fear of the thing itself, before we, ourselves, become crippled like Roosevelt, who, of course, got crippled by polio, not fear. *(Pauses, confused; disgusted by still another lamentable failure. He mouthes an appropriate word, behind his Grandmother's back.)* [Shit!]

HADDIE: Maybe you'd better not type it up, just yet.

(Haddie takes teabag from teacup, tosses tea-bag into wastebasket, crosses upstage to kitchen table; sits, waits for Roddy to join her.

The lights crossfade with Roddy the Younger, who moves quickly into spotlight down-stage right; speaks to audience, directly.

RODDY (THE YOUNGER): Just before my Grandma Haddie died, she told me the most amazing thing about my family, Grandpa Jacob included.

(Lights fade up on Haddie.)

HADDIE: The men in our family are crazy people, all of them!

(Roddy crosses to table, sits in chair beside Haddie.)

They think every woman is loose! My own father, may his soul rest in peace, used to make my mother wear an overcoat, all through the summer, so, no man could see that she had big breasts. In the meantime, my father's own uncle, Duddy, on the Zuckerman side, may his soul never rest a minute, used to touch me in private places, when I was a very little girl. His wife said he used to light fires in front of pictures of naked ladies. Your own grandfather is no picnic, himself. In all the years we've been married, which is forty-seven, he has never once let me shop, alone. He was not only convinced the butcher was after me, he was also convinced that I was after the butcher! Once, he kicked a hole in the dining room wall, because I let the butcher sell me an extra-lean rib-roast. *(Shrugs.)* Go figure!…I used to tell him "You're just like your father!" and this would always drive your grandfather crazy, because he really hated his father, your great-grandfather, who used to yell things at women on the street that you should never know about! God forbid!…I'm going to tell you something, Roddy. No matter how crazy your grandfather got when I told him he was like just his father, I'm telling you he was just like his father! Maybe worse. Your own father (my son), I don't have to tell you much about, because you're living in the story, yourself, yes? But, I have to tell you one story…from the zoo in Stoneham, when he was little. Your grandfather and I took him there on a very sunny Sunday morning. There was a crowd in front of the lion's cage and we were way at the back…So, Arthur, your father, squeezed in through the people, up to the front, all by himself. When he got there—to the front—for some reason, the lion roared. It was really quite a roar. Long, loud, really enormous. Everybody—all of us, kids and grownups, got scared. And then we all laughed. But, I knew your father would have gotten very scared, so, I pushed my way up front. When I got to him, he was off to one side, roaring like a lion. There were tears all over his face and his sailor-shirt, but, he was roaring, really loud, just like the lion. The sound coming out of him was enormous. I let him roar for a while, until he got himself calmed down. *(Pauses.)* Sometimes people do this, Roddy…Sometimes, people have to imitate the things that scare them the most. *(Haddie pauses; moves to Roddy; speaks to him, confidentially.)* I'm only telling you any of this, because, between us, I don't like these shooting pains in my head I'm getting, and somebody's got to talk straight to you, before you, yourself, start, you know, roaring.

RODDY (THE YOUNGER): I'm never going to do any roaring, Grandma.

HADDIE: Fine. I'm glad to hear this, but, maybe you should try to remember my story, just in case you ever hear yourself roar a little.

RODDY (THE YOUNGER): I will.

HADDIE: Good.

RODDY (THE YOUNGER): You have pains in your head, Grandma?

HADDIE: This is between us. Promise me.

RODDY (THE YOUNGER): I promise you. *(Pauses.)* I'm sure you're going to be fine, Grandma!

HADDIE: Maybe I don't want to be fine? Maybe enough is enough? *(Pauses; smiles.)* Let me say what I'm trying to say to you, simply and clearly, Rodney…All of the men in this family are crazy people. Wait. You'll see.

(Haddie's light fades out.)

END OF SCENE TWO

Scene Three

Roddy the Younger moves into spotlight, down-stage, right; speaks to audience, directly.

RODDY (THE YOUNGER): We always thought Grandpa would die before Grandma. I guess we hoped he would. So, when Grandma died, like she did, before Grandpa, we didn't know what we were going to do with him.

(Lights crossfade with Roddy the Younger as he moves to Jacob. Offstage, we hear: the sound of "Kaddish," the Hebrew prayer for the dead.)

RODDY (THE YOUNGER): We should go back into the front room, now, Grandpa. They're saying "Kaddish," again.

JACOB: They've got their ten men. They've got twenty men! *(Leans in, discreetly.)* Your grandmother had a lot of men-friends, Roddy.

RODDY (THE YOUNGER): You think so?

JACOB: I know so. *(Looks at Roddy, smugly.)* That's all I'm going to say on this subject.

RODDY (THE YOUNGER): *(To audience.)* Grandpa Jacob's Parkinsonian stutter cleared up the minute Grandma Haddie was in her grave.

JACOB: It was hell being married forty-seven years to a beauty like your grandmother, Roddy. If I can give you one piece of advice, straight from my heart, when you're ready to get married, find the ugliest woman you can find...somebody so horrible other men will avert their eyes when she passes. This woman, if she has any brains at all, will know how unappealing she is to the male multitude, and she will love you for marrying her...And she will serve you, without any of the pain I had with a beauty like your grandmother. This is advice from my heart, Roddy. I gave this advice to your father and he didn't take it, and now look at him!

(Jacob motions to window. Archie is outside, peering into the house, suspiciously. After a moment, Archie disappears from the window.)

RODDY (THE YOUNGER): Do you think all of the men in our family are crazy. Grandpa?

JACOB: Did your grandmother suggest this to you?

RODDY (THE YOUNGER): She did, yes.

JACOB: Your grandmother knew a lot about people, Rodney...especially, men!

(We hear the sound of male voices singing "Kaddish." Molly enters. She is in mourning, wears a black dress; calls out to Jacob.)

MOLLY: Get in here, Pa! They're saying "Kaddish!"

JACOB: *(Screams, suddenly.)* For her, not for me! I'm not dead!

MOLLY: Who said you were dead? *(To Roddy the Younger.)* Did I say such a thing?

RODDY (THE YOUNGER): It's the prayer for Grandma, Grandpa. Come on, I'll go inside with you.

JACOB: No! You're just a young boy! I don't want you in there! Young boys shouldn't have to see such things. *(Motions to Molly.)* She'll take me in.

MOLLY: Come on, Pa. Grab ahold.

(Molly leans in, places Jacob's hands on her shoulders, starts to lift him from his chair. Jacob begins to cry; yells at Molly, directly.)

JACOB: How could she leave me alone by myself with people like you? How could she? How?

(We hear again, male voices singing "Kaddish," under the scene, as Jacob continues to sob, openly, now, calling Haddie's name, in German/Yiddish.)

JACOB: Haddelah...mein Haddelah...Haddelah...liebling...

MOLLY: *(Quietly.)* Come on, Pa...I'll take you in. *(Molly leads Jacob into room. He walks backwards, she walks forward...as if in a waltz.)*

RODDY (THE YOUNGER): *(To audience.)* Grandpa Jacob died that night. We all heard it...his scream. It would have been too corny, even for Grandpa Jacob's favorite radio show, "Portia Faces Life."

JACOB: *(Screams, from off, from the darkness.)* I don't want to live without her! Arrrrhhhh!

RODDY (THE YOUNGER): We knew he would be dead when we went in there.

(Lights up in kitchen, suddenly, on switch, as Roddy the Younger, Sylvie and Molly run to door of back bedroom; stop before entering.)

MOLLY: Pa?

RODDY (THE YOUNGER): Grandpa!

SYLVIE: Grandpa!

ARCHIE: *(Off.)* Paaa? *(Archie runs down stairs, crosses kitchen to Jacob's bedroom, runs inside. Beat. He screams.)* Paaaaaaaaaaaa!

(Music in. We hear, again, male voices singing "Kaddish," offstage. Roddy the Younger, Sylvie, Archie and Molly stand framed in doorway to Jacob's bedroom. They bow their heads and weep, as music concludes.)

END OF SCENE THREE

Scene Four

Lights crossfade to spotlight downstage center on Roddy the Younger, who faces audience. Music in: Chopin étude, played on piano, lightly.

RODDY (THE YOUNGER): The night after Grandpa Jacob died, I was laying awake, thinking about things, and it crossed my mind that when Roosevelt said "We have nothing to fear, but fear itself," he could have been completely full of shit! We have plenty to fear!...We have old age to fear. We have loneliness and disease to fear. We have some very crazy people around us all the time to fear! We also have things like Red Feather Oratory Contests to fear! And we also have The Worst to fear. *(Pauses.)* The Worst happened to me and my family on the morning of the Red Feather Regionals. If I live to be sixty, I will always wonder if either Grandpa Jacob or Grandma Haddie had lived just a little longer and had been alive that day...if either of them had been, you know, home in the house with Mama, whether it would've changed anything...Or whether all bad things are meant to happen and they just do: they just happen, no matter what.

(Lights widen, lighting kitchen and Molly at piano, playing Chopin. She is wearing her bathrobe and bedroom slippers. A man is peering through the upstage-right window into the house from outside. Note: audience should assume the man is Archie. The man disappears from window, as suddenly as he had appeared. Roddy the Younger continues speaking to the audience, directly.)

RODDY (THE YOUNGER): He must have come into the house around around ten-thirty in the morning. Sylvie and I were both in school. What I remember most of all about the day was that I learned about Congressional Franking Privileges. Sylvie says she has no memory of the day, whatsoever. Daddy was supposed to be with Willie in Fitchburg, unloading the truck. But, Willie had called in sick with the Virus-X.

(The man, suddenly, reappears at other window, peers in at Molly. We now see that it is Willie in window, not Archie. Molly continues to play, oblivious to Willie in window. Willie disappears from window, suddenly; then, reappears at door. He knocks on door, three times. Molly, intent on her piano-playing, doesn't hear him.)

RODDY (THE YOUNGER): There are moments that re-define an afternoon, and there are moments that re-define a life. This was, alas, a moment to re-define my entire family.

(Roddy the Younger exits up staircase, as Willie enters house, stops and watches Molly play. Molly senses Willie's presence in room and, certain it is Archie who has entered, she whirls around, away from piano.)

MOLLY: I was only seeing if the piano was out of tune!…*(Sees it's Willie, not Archie.)* Willie.

WILLIE: I didn't know you played piano. You play wicked good, don't'cha'?

MOLLY: *(Re-belting her robe, tightly.)* You shouldn't be in the house, Willie.

WILLIE: I was feelin' a lot better after my nap, so, I hopped on over here to see if I could catch Arch before his second mill-run.

MOLLY: Archie's not here. He left over an hour ago.

WILLIE: *(Appreciating her body.)* Archie never talks about you playing the piano, Moll. Never mentions it, ever. You play Classical, too. So-phisticated. *(Looks around room; smiles.)* It's nice bein' in the house with you, just us, like this. It's a shame about Archie's folks and all. Still and all, they lived life, didn't they. I mean, that's what life's for, ain't it…livin'. Ain't it, Moll? *(Looks Molly over.)* You're lookin' good, Molly. I was just sayin' this very thing ta' Arch, not all that long ago: Molly's lookin' wick'id good. *(Laughs; looks Molly over, again.)* You really are lookin' wick'id good, Moll. You're puttin' on weight in all the right places. Not that you're lookin' heavy. I ain't sayin' that. You're lookin', I dunno, what's the word?…Comfortable. Some women are built for speed, but, you're very definitely built for comfort.

MOLLY: You shouldn't be in the house, Willie. You're not allowed. You know this.

WILLIE: Allowed? I'm not allowed? *(He laughs.)* That's a funny thing you just said, Moll. *(Moves to door of back bedroom; peeks inside.)* This is where they slept, huh? The old ones. *(Smiles at Molly.)* Must be lonely in the house for you, now, huh, Moll?…Kids at school…Arch off somewhere in the truck as he is…Just a good-lookin' girl like you, alone, in a big house like this. *(Moves to staircase; looks upstairs.)* I never be'n upstairs. Weird, huh? All these years workin' for Arch and all, and I never be'n upstairs in his house. I mean, he's be'n upstairs in my house, plenty, right?

MOLLY: You can't be in the house, Willie. You're going to have to leave, now.

WILLIE: I don't think so.

MOLLY: Willie, please! I must insist you leave the house.

WILLIE: *(Stares at Molly; smiles.)* Uh uh.

MOLLY: Willie, please? I'm asking you, nicely. *(She opens door for Willie to leave.)*

WILLIE: Oh, well, if you put it that way…*(Willie starts to door, as if he's leaving…but, then he slams door closed, confronts Molly.)* Not a chance. *(Sees Molly looking about, furtively.)*

WILLIE: How come you're talking like somebody else is listening? Nobody's listening! It's just us.

(Willie caresses Molly's cheek, pushing her hair out of her eyes. Molly is stunned. She cannot possibly misinterpret Willie's intentions. She steps backwards from him, stiffly.)

MOLLY: Willie, get out of this house!

WILLIE: *(Moving toward her, again.)* You like me, don't you, Moll?

MOLLY: If you don't leave, I'll leave.

(Molly starts to door. Willie blocks her path. At same moment, Archie appears in window, peering inside house; sees Willie, pulls back; disappears from window.)

MOLLY: Willie, get out of my way!…I want to go outside.

WILLIE: In your bathrobe? You wanna' go outside in your bathrobe, Molly?

(Willie starts to move slowly toward Molly, laughing. Molly backs up, terrified.)

MOLLY: Willie!

WILLIE: I seen you lookin' at me, for years and years, now, four mornin's a week, never changin' out'ta your bath-robe til after I'm gone and all, right?…Flashing this and that at me…Smilin' at me, makin' my lunches and all…Askin' all the time if my coughs and colds are gettin' better kind'a thing! I seen and felt all this attraction coming from you, Moll.

(Molly looks inside kitchen drawer for breadknife. It's not there. Willie steps forward, tried to embrace Molly. She slaps his face. It is a stunning blow. Willie staggers backward, shakes his head clear; laughs.)

WILLIE: I knew you'd fight me!

(Willie steps in, grabs Molly, firmly, tries to kiss her. She wriggles and screams, trying to get loose from him. Suddenly, the door opens; Archie enters the kitchen. He is ashen.)

WILLIE: Jesus, Arch! You look wick'id pissed!…Take it easy, Arch, huh? I can explain myself, here!…She invited me in, Arch. I would'a gladly waited outside, like you said, but, she…

(Archie moves past Willie, wordlessly; goes directly to Molly; slaps Molly. She screams; falls backwards against table. Archie slaps her, again. Willie stares at Archie, amazed.)

WILLIE: Jesus, Arch! What are you doin'? What are you hittin' *her* for?
  (Archie never looks at Willie. Instead, he slaps Molly, again.)
ARCHIE: Your boyfriend's askin' what I'm doing. You hear him?
  (Molly doesn't reply.)
ARCHIE: You're not answering me?
  (No reply. Archie slaps Molly, again.)
WILLIE: *(Horrified.)* Jesus! Nothin' happened between us, Arch! Honest ta'
  God! You gotta' calm yourself down, Arch, before you do damage!
ARCHIE: Whoaaa! You hear this?
  (No reply. Archie slaps Molly, again.)
ARCHIE: Your boyfriend's protecting you. Do you not hear him?
  *(Archie raises his hand to hit Molly, again. Willie reaches in to stop him;
  barely touches Archie, who recoils from his touch, violently.)*
ARCHIE: No touches, you! No touches! *(Archie slaps Molly, again.)* Every
  time your boyfriend protects you, you're getting hit! You get me! You
  get me?
WILLIE: Jesus, Arch!…Jesus! *(Willie turns, runs out of door; exits play.)*
ARCHIE: *(In a murderous rage; stands ready to hit Molly, again.)* I seen this
  coming, lady, believe-you-me! You couldn't even wait til my mother
  and father were cold in the grave, could you? Could you? Could you?
  *(Archie raises his hand; moves to hit Molly…the lights black out, on
  switch.)*

END OF SCENE FOUR

Scene Five

  *In the darkness, we hear; microphone "feedback" and then…announcer's
  voice over public address system, heavy Boston accent.*

ANNOUNCER'S VOICE: Ladies and Gentlemen, our next competitor in The
  Red Feather Oratory Contest New England Finals is our youngest
  competitor. He is a 15-year-old high school student from Wakefield,
  Massachusetts. Welcome, please, Rodney Stern!
  *(We hear applause. Spotlight fades up on Roddy the Younger, upstage,
  near piano. He delivers his Red Feather Oratory Contest speech…with
  poise, confidence…and an abundance of appropriate hand-gestures.)*
RODDY (THE YOUNGER): Fellow Red Feather Oratory Contest competi-

tors, Judges, Ladies and Gentlemen…"We have nothing to fear but fear itself." When President Franklin Delano Roosevelt spoke those words, he was trying to trick the citizens of the United States of America into finally going to War against Hitler. FDR knew America should have gotten into the War, years and years before, but, Roosevelt was waiting as long as he could, hoping that Hitler would kill all the Jews, first, because Franklin Delano Roosevelt, like Adolph Hitler, hated the Jews. Finally, after the Japanese bombed Pearl Harbor and killed some non-Jewish Americans, Roosevelt knew he couldn't wait any longer. He declared War on Japan…and on Japan's teammate: Hitler. *(Pauses.)* The only thing that's kept a lot of people from saying all this stuff about Roosevelt out loud is fear. I myself felt a lot of fear thinking about saying this out loud in my Red Feather Oratory Contest speech, but, it's the truth, and nobody should ever be frightened to speak the truth, should they? *(Roddy the Younger pauses, allowing his question to hang on the air. The lights fade up in the kitchen. Molly enters, carrying two suitcases, which she sets down on floor near back door. She is badly bruised; battered. She busies herself, preparing to close up the house. She checks to see that the gas is off, water faucets are tightly shut, windows are closed and locked, etc. Roddy the Younger continues…)*

RODDY (THE YOUNGER): To be heroic, you first have to be unlucky enough to find yourself in a terrible situation…and then, you have to be lucky enough to find your dignity…and that will lead you to do what you have to do.

(We hear: a car horn, off-stage.)

RODDY (THE YOUNGER): *(Calls out to his mother.)* The taxi's here!

(Molly opens back door; calls outside to imagined taxi-driver.)

MOLLY: We'll be right out!…*(She moves to base of staircase; calls upstairs.)* The taxi's here! Are you ready?

(Sylvie calls down from upstairs.)

SYLVIE: *(Off.)* I'm ready!…

RODDY (THE YOUNGER): *(To audience.)* Sylvie went downstairs, first. I hung back in my room and hid a copy of my Red Feather Oratory Contest Speech under a loose floorboard in my closet. I started down the stairs, but, then, I ran back to my room and tossed my signed Williams and Pesky rookie cards under the floorboard with my speech!…I don't know why I did that. It's one of my life's few major regrets.

(Sylvie enters from upstairs. She, too, wears a Winter overcoat. She, too, carries suitcase. She, too, has been crying.)

SYLVIE: I'm ready.

MOLLY: We have to do this.

SYLVIE: I said I'm ready.

MOLLY: It's only a house. It's not a life.

SYLVIE: Fine.

MOLLY: Are you mad at me, Sylvie?

SYLVIE: No. I dunno. Maybe. Maybe I'm just sad.

MOLLY: It's just a house. It's not enough reason to stay.

SYLVIE: Were you and daddy ever happy?

MOLLY: I can't remember.

SYLVIE: You were never happy?

MOLLY: I can't remember.

SYLVIE: Why did you have children?

MOLLY: We thought it would make us happy.

SYLVIE: Are you sorry you had us?

MOLLY: What are you saying, you? You and Roddy are the best things that
ever happened in my life!

SYLVIE: *(Sobbing.)* Roddy, maybe. But, aren't you a little sorry you had me?

MOLLY: *(Moans.)* Oh, God, nooo, Sylvie! Don't ever think like that! I love
you. I'm so glad that you're my daughter. *(Molly hugs Sylvie, both
weeping.)* Us girls have got to stick together. *(Taxi horn honks, again,
off. Molly looks up.)* Where is he?...Rodney!
*(Roddy the Younger enters down staircase, carrying jacket and suitcase,
ready to leave.)*

RODDY (THE YOUNGER): Here I am.

MOLLY: Are you ready?

RODDY (THE YOUNGER): I'm ready.

MOLLY: Did you clean your room?

RODDY (THE YOUNGER): I cleaned my room.

MOLLY: You made your bed?

RODDY (THE YOUNGER): I made my bed.

MOLLY: *(To Sylvie.)* You made your bed?

SYLVIE: I made my bed.

MOLLY: Listen to me, children...I don't know much, but, I know something. Here's the thing: you can never be what you just were, two seconds ago. Things have got to keep changing. This is Life. And me, I
say "Thank God for this!"
*(Molly and Sylvie exit the house. Roddy pauses at door, sets down his suit-
case, turns, speaks to audience. Lights dim in kitchen to spotlight on
Roddy.)*

RODDY (THE YOUNGER): I went to visit my father, a couple of days later. He was staying at his cousin's house in Woburn.

(A spotlight fades up on Roddy the Elder, now playing Archie, alone, downstage, sitting on chair, looking out of imagined window. Roddy the Younger goes to him.)

RODDY (THE YOUNGER): Hi, daddy.

ARCHIE: You're alone?

RODDY (THE YOUNGER): Yes, sir.

ARCHIE: You know where your mother is?

RODDY (THE YOUNGER): *(After a pause.)* Yes, sir. I do.

ARCHIE: You're not going to tell me?

RODDY (THE YOUNGER): No, sir.

ARCHIE: You scared of me, Roddy?

RODDY (THE YOUNGER): Yes, sir. A little.

ARCHIE: Don't be. I used'ta be scared of my father, too. You saw what my father was like, when he got old, yes? In the end, there's nothing to be scared of, believe me.

RODDY (THE YOUNGER): I'm going to stay on living with mama.

ARCHIE: You're what?

RODDY (THE YOUNGER): I'm, uh, staying on living in with mama.

ARCHIE: Why?

RODDY (THE YOUNGER): Because I want to.

ARCHIE: Why?

RODDY (THE YOUNGER): Because it's what I want to do.

ARCHIE: Did she poison you against me?

RODDY (THE YOUNGER): No, sir. She didn't say anything, either way. I decided this myself.

ARCHIE: It's probably better. If you stick with me, the way I stuck with my father, you'll end up...

(Archie stops, mid-sentence. sobs. Roddy speaks to audience.)

RODDY (THE YOUNGER): My father never finished his thought. He never told me how, exactly, I might have ended up, if he hadn't done what he was about to do...if he hadn't reached out and cured me of the family disease, once and for all. *(Beat.)* I'll never know if my father planned it, or whether it was an accidental gift, but, in one split second of unexpected tenderness, my father changed my life and the lives of generations to follow...He set us free.

(Suddenly, Archie moans, in deep despair.)

ARCHIE: Somebody's got to stop me, Roddy! I'm a crazy person! I can't help myself!

(Archie continues to sob. Roddy watches his father, awhile. sadly. Then, the boy moves to his father, touches Archie's shoulder. Without warning, Archie backhands his son, violently. The sound of the slap is amplified in the auditorium. It echoes, reverberates. Roddy flies backwards, stunned; hurt. Archie sobs, again. There is a substantial pause in which the boy will realize that he is free.)

RODDY (THE YOUNGER): Thank you, sir. I…I'm going.

(Roddy returns to staircase; faces audience, completes his contest speech. His voice is amplified.)

I want to close by telling you the story of a friend of mine who had to conquer a lot of fear. My friend lived in a little town with his mother and his father and his sister. He wasn't very happy, but, he wasn't too unhappy, either. Most of the men in my friend's family were a little crazy. They didn't trust women very much. They always thought women were doing bad things. One day my friend's father hit my friend's mother…really beat her up. My friend's mother and father got divorced and my friend had to go to court and decide whether he wanted to live with his mother and his sister, which meant he'd have to move away from his little town, or stay and live with his father. My friend was frightened to leave his town, and his school, and his friends…He really wanted everything to just stay the way it always was, but, that wasn't possible. So, my friend thought about everything for a long, long time, and, finally, he thought about what Roosevelt said "We have nothing to fear but fear itself," and my friend thought that Roosevelt was really right, after all: Fear itself was probably the thing we have to be frightened of the most!…Even though Roosevelt wasn't the great man everybody thought he was, he had figured something out about Life, and people could, regardless of his faults, learn a lot from him. My friend found his courage. He chose to live with his mother and move away. I'm telling you this story, because, I, too, have learned a lot from Franklin Delano Roosevelt, and I also learned a lot from working on this speech. I learned how to think about things…I learned how to stand up in front of people…and speak my thoughts. For this opportunity, I want to thank the Red Feather Oratory Contest organizers, and I want to thank you: the audience. Thank you.

(Lights crossfade to Roddy the Elder, standing downstage. He speaks directly to audience.)

RODDY (THE ELDER): My mother found her dignity and she was heroic! She and my sister and I moved in with my mother's cousins. After a couple of months, we moved into our own apartment. It wasn't a beautiful place, but, it was partly furnished...with a piano.

(Light fades up on Molly at piano, playing Chopin nocturne.)

RODDY (THE ELDER): My mother learned to play Chopin and Bach and Brahms. We woke every morning to her playing, and fell asleep every night, same way. Our house was full of music. My mother never married again. She said "One marriage was enough." Sylvie never married, either. She moved to New York City, where she does something important in publishing. *(Pauses)* My father stayed alone for the rest of his life. He always blamed my mother for his profound unhappiness. I called him just about once a month, on the phone, but, I never saw him, again, not face to face, until he died. *(Pauses; smiles.)* Me? I got married, had a bunch of kids...one boy, three girls...all of them lovely. My wife is brilliant and strong and beautiful, and I'm almost always proud of her, even though I'm also almost always jealous of other men staring at her beauty as they do. *(Smiles.)* I don't know much about people, really, but, I do know this, about myself: When the pressure's on me, my first thought is always to roar like a lion. But, I try to stop myself. Mostly, I do.

(Light fades up on Roddy the Younger, outside house, staring in through upstage window, coldly, grimly, suspiciously...exactly as Archie did, in earlier scenes. But, then, the boy smiles at Roddy the Elder...waves to him, happily. Roddy the Elder smiles, waves back. Light fades out.)

RODDY (THE ELDER): *(To Audience.)* My son's a lot like me, only nicer. He never roars at all.

(Now, Roddy the Younger enters house, goes to Molly, takes Molly's hand. Molly stops playing piano, rises from piano bench. Note: Music continues without interruption, on tape, over sound system in auditorium. Roddy the Younger and his mother dance to the music. Roddy the Elder watches them dance for a few moments, happily, before speaking the play's final words.)

RODDY (THE ELDER): *(To audience, directly.)* Like my mother used to say: "Things have got to keep changing! This is Life."... And me, I say "Thank God for this!"

(All lights fade out, but for light on Molly and her son, dancing. And then, after a moment, that light fades out as well.)

END OF PLAY

BIOGRAPHY

ISRAEL HOROVITZ is the author of nearly fifty plays that have been translated and performed in as many as twenty-five languages, worldwide. Among Horovitz's best-known plays are *The Indian Wants the Bronx, Line* (now in its 20th year, off-Broadway, at the 13th St Repertory Theatre), *Rats, It's Called The Sugar Plum, Morning, The Primary English Class, The Wakefield Plays* (a 7-play cycle, including *Hopscotch, The 75th Stage Directions, Spare, Alfred the Great, Our Father's Failing, and Alfred Dies), The Good Parts, Mackerel, Sunday Runners in the Rain,* and the *Growing Up Jewish* trilogy, *Today, I am a Fountain Pen, A Rosen By Any Other Name,* and The *Chopin Playoffs.* Other recent Horovitz work includes a cycle of Massachusetts-based plays, including *North Shore Fish, Henry Lumper, Firebird at Dogtown, Strong-Man's Weak Child, The Widow's Blind Date, Park Your Car in Harvard Yard, Year of the Duck, Fighting Over Beverley,* and his most recent plays, *Unexpected Tenderness* and *The Barking Sharks.* Mr. Horovitz's screenplays include *The Strawberry Statement, Author! Author!, A Man in Love* (written with Diane Kurys), *Believe in Me,* and, recently, screenplays for two upcoming Warner Bros films: *James Dean,* based on the life of the actor; and a new version of *A Star is Born.* He is currently completing screenplays for film-adaptations of his stage-plays *North Shore Fish* and *The Widow's Blind Date.* (He will direct the film of *The Widow's Blind Date* for NBC, in the USA, and for theatrical release in Europe.) Horovitz has won numerous awards, including the OBIE (twice), the EMMY, the Prix de Plaisir du Théâtre, The Prix du Jury of the Cannes Film Festival, The Drama Desk Award, an Award in Literature of the American Academy of Arts and Letters, The Elliot Norton Prize, a Lifetime Achievement Award from B'Nai Brith, and many others. Mr. Horovitz is founder and Artistic Director of the Gloucester Stage Company, and of the New York Playwrights Lab. Horovitz is the father of five children: film producer Rachael Horovitz, novelist Matthew Horovitz, Beastie Boy Adam Horovitz, and unemployed 9-year-old twins, Hannah and Oliver Horovitz. He is married to Gillian Adams-Horovitz, former British National Marathon Champion. The Horovitz family divides its time between homes in NYC's Greenwich Village, London's Dulwich Village, and the seaport city of Gloucester, Massachusetts. Mr. Horovitz works frequently, in France, where he often directs his plays in French language.

(July, 1995.)